Creating Blogs
with Jekyll

Vikram Dhillon

Apress®

Creating Blogs with Jekyll

Vikram Dhillon
Orlando, Florida, USA

ISBN-13 (pbk): 978-1-4842-1465-7   ISBN-13 (electronic): 978-1-4842-1464-0
DOI 10.1007/978-1-4842-1464-0

Library of Congress Control Number: 2016943682

Managing Director: Welmoed Spahr
Acquisitions Editor: Ben-Renow Clarke
Development Editor: Matthew Moodie
Technical Reviewer: Massimo Nardone
Editorial Board: Steve Anglin, Pramila Balen, Louise Corrigan, James DeWolf, Jonathan Gennick, Robert Hutchinson, Celestin Suresh John, Nikhil Karkal, James Markham, Susan McDermott, Matthew Moodie, Ben Renow-Clarke, Gwenan Spearing
Coordinating Editor: Nancy Chen
Copy Editor: Teresa Horton
Compositor: SPi Global
Indexer: SPi Global

Distributed to the book trade worldwide by Springer Science+Business Media New York, 233 Spring Street, 6th Floor, New York, NY 10013. Phone 1-800-SPRINGER, fax (201) 348-4505, e-mail orders-ny@springer-sbm.com, or visit www.springer.com. Apress Media, LLC is a California LLC and the sole member (owner) is Springer Science + Business Media Finance Inc (SSBM Finance Inc). SSBM Finance Inc is a Delaware corporation.

For information on translations, please e-mail rights@apress.com, or visit www.apress.com.

Apress and friends of ED books may be purchased in bulk for academic, corporate, or promotional use. eBook versions and licenses are also available for most titles. For more information, reference our Special Bulk Sales–eBook Licensing web page at www.apress.com/bulk-sales.

Any source code or other supplementary materials referenced by the author in this text is available to readers at www.apress.com. For detailed information about how to locate your book's source code, go to www.apress.com/source-code/.

Printed on acid-free paper

To the pioneers of the Internet: I wrote this book as requiem to you. Hear it sing, for your work has brought freedom to the world.

To Clara, for the tremendous mental support which kept me doing. It should be noted that she helped me rethink about a lot of the topics in the book, please direct complaints accordingly.

But most of all, I dedicate this book to you, the reader, because without you, my work would have no meaning.

Contents at a Glance

Contents

About the Author

Vikram Dhillon is currently a research fellow in the Institute of Simulation and Training at University of Central Florida. He holds a Bachelor of Science degree in Molecular Biology from the University of Central Florida, where his main focus was bioinformatics. He has published a few scientific papers on computational genomics. He has worked as a software and business development coach at the Blackstone Launchpad to mentor young entrepreneurs and startups through the process of building technology products. He was previously funded by the National Science Foundation through the Innovation Corps program to study customer discovery and apply it to commercialize high-risk startup ideas. He is a member of the Linux Foundation and has been very involved in open source projects and initiatives for the past several years.

He often speaks at local conferences and meetups about programming, design, security, and entrepreneurship. He currently lives in Orlando and writes a technology-focused blog at opsbug.com.

About the Technical Reviewer

Massimo Nardone holds a Master of Science degree in Computing Science from the University of Salerno, Italy. He has worked as a Project Manager, Software Engineer, Research Engineer, Chief Security Architect, Information Security Manager, PCI/SCADA Auditor, and Senior Lead IT Security/Cloud/SCADA Architect for many years. He currently works as Chief Information Security Office for Cargotec Oyj. He has more than 22 years of work experience in IT including security, SCADA, cloud computing, IT infrastructure, mobile, security, and Web technology areas for both national and international projects. He worked as visiting lecturer and supervisor for exercises at the Networking Laboratory of the Helsinki University of Technology (Aalto University). He has been programming and teaching how to program with Android, Perl, PHP, Java, VB, Python, C/C++, and MySQL for more than 20 years. He holds four international patents (PKI, SIP, SAML, and Proxy areas). He is also the co-author of *Pro Android Games* (Apress, 2015).

Acknowledgments

I want to acknowledge my editors, Ben, Mark, and Nancy, who guided me through every stage of this book. Their patience and advice helped tremendously in shaping this book.

I want to thank Zachary Loparo for helpful discussions about the projects included in this book and the overall direction.

I would like to thank Anthony Nguyen for opuning up to me and showing me the the world of puns.

Finally, I want to thank Katelyn Rae MacKenzie for organizing those Ruby Meetups at Cloudspace. Without that first meetup, this book might never have happened. Thank you for all the hard work that you do!

Introduction

This book is more than just a standard text on Jekyll. Anyone who tries to learn about Jekyll is faced with instructions on how to set up a blog in 10 minutes and confounded with commands to type on the terminal. What has been missing is a thorough introduction to the landscape surrounding Jekyll as a static site generator: Where did the idea for Jekyll come from? Why did it become relevant? How can Jekyll integrate new web technologies and tools to create functional and stylish web sites?

This book answers those questions in a practical manner, and provides a theoritical framework to transfer that "Jekyll thinking" to your own personal projects. A tool like Jekyll is very versatile, but you have to think creatively to apply it toward a problem that you are trying to solve. Most problems don't lend themselves to easy solutions, but we will apply Jekyll features toward creating custom blogs. Sometimes, just reformulating the problem leads to better solutions.

This book is organized as follows. The content material has been divided into three distinct sections, with each one focusing on a specific theme or set of questions. The first section is about the development of static generators like Jekyll and how the Internet got started. It was a much different time then, and the economic factors shaped what the Internet was capable of doing. The dot-com bust was one of the most important financial crises, and it had a lasting impact on society. For the Internet to survive and make it through, many changes were required, and a complete technical overhaul enabled exactly that. This section answers the question of how Jekyll came about.

The second section of this book dives into the fundamental tools required to use Jekyll appropriately. You can think of Jekyll essentially as a collection of technologies that work together to create a static site. To begin working with Jekyll regularly, you'll have to learn how to use these prerequisite tools. After covering these fundamentals, we are ready to start creating projects with Jekyll. This section answers the question of what makes Jekyll work.

The last section covers a variety of projects in which Jekyll is applied to create a static web site for solving problems. These project ideas include casual or hobby web sites as well as more serious ones that have a particular social inclination. The story behind a project mostly serves as a way to demonstrate the application of Jekyll and related web technologies to an existing problem. The chapters actually build up and slowly increase in complexity and application, leading up to the boss-level last chapter. This section answers the question of how Jekyll can incorporate new web technologies as exciting features into a new personal blog. As you go through this section, I hope that you obtain practical advice as well as potential inspiration for your own projects.

Stay Hungry. Stay Foolish. Keep doing more, and write about it using Jekyll. Good luck!

PART I

History and Development

The first section focuses on the story of the Internet and blogging as a whole. Here, we start by looking at how the Internet began as nothing more than a tool to connect physicists. Eventually, it turned into more than just a toy, and today we cannot imagine life without it. We also spend some time reviewing the economic and financial environments around the time when the Internet had just taken off. The dot-com bust and the revival of belief in Internet startups launched the Web 2.0 movement, and improvements to the infrastructure allowed for new services and social media to take over the Internet. We then discuss how the evolution of the Internet supercharged blogging and how the tools that people used to blog changed with time, gradually ending up at static generators. Finally, we end this section by talking specifically about static site generators and other options available besides Jekyll.

■ ■■ ■

## CHAPTER 1

Static Web

The journey of a thousand miles begins with a single step

—Lao Tzu

The world was a very different place before the Internet was around. Most of the social media and microservices we use today would not have made sense in the past, and for very good and valid reasons. In the past, they would have been a waste of time. Why would you use a toy like the Internet to talk to people when you could simply meet them in person? Spending an entire Saturday looking at cat pictures would have been considered madness! Times have changed, though. The story of blogging is perhaps the greatest story told using the Web. It is a story of change; not just how society changed, but how the mindset of a generation changed with time. The times have changed to such an extent that the Internet is now perceived as a common tool, available to everyone. How did such a paradigm shift happen? Moreover, how did the beginning of Internet become associated with blogging? What applications was the Internet supposed to provide in the early days? These are some of the questions we explore in this chapter.

Here Be Dragons

CERN is often hailed as the birthplace of the Internet, but the developments leading to the foundations of the Internet can be traced back further. The first description of connecting multiple machines in some sort of interacting network was proposed in 1962 by J. C. R. Licklider, a scientist at MIT. He had worked on a new aspect of networking that he called *packet-based networking* and wrote a series of letters explaining his ideas in August 1962. This early concept was one of the first proposals for a connected network and this idea eventually matured into a concept known as the galactic Network. Licklider envisioned a globally interconnected set of computers through which everyone could quickly access data and programs from any site. Philosophically, this concept was very much like the Internet that exists today, but the infrastructure to make it possible did not exist at the time. The story of Internet is also a testament to heavy investments made by the government in research that would one day connect the world.

■ **Note** The Internet essentially started as a tool to allow scientists to communicate with each other. That's why a historical account of developments is provided here. It is truly phenomenal to see how investments in curiosity-based research more than 50 years ago have completely changed the world today.

Electronic supplementary material The online version of this chapter (doi:10.1007/978-1-4842-1464-0_1) contains supplementary material, which is available to authorized users.

Licklider was the first head of the computer research program at the Defense Advanced Research Projects Agency (DARPA), a military research organization that was finding practical uses for the computer. While Licklider was at DARPA, he convinced a few MIT researchers, including Lawrence G. Roberts, of the importance of his networking ideas. Leonard Kleinrock, also at MIT, had just published the first paper on packet switching theory in July 1961, probably the first person in the world talking about this new idea. Eventually he would publish a full book on the topics initially explored in that paper and the broader subject in 1964. Kleinrock talked to Roberts about this new idea, as he really wanted to explore it further and see what kind of information could be passed through packets. Kleinrock convinced Roberts of the theoretical feasibility of communications using packets rather than circuits, which was a major step along the path toward computer networking.

Roberts joined DARPA in 1966 and continued to work on developing his computer networking ideas further into the future. He later proposed an idea for the first "galactic supernetwork" that would link up research scientists in labs. He quickly put together his plan for the network, which he called ARPANET, in 1967. He presented the work and his paper at an international conference. Surprisingly, at the same conference, another paper by Donald Davies from National Physical Laboratory (NPL) in the United Kingdom talked about a similar packet networking concept. This new group had worked on a prototype for transmission of voice securely through a network of connected machines for the military since 1964. Coincidentally, this work at MIT and NPL proceeded in parallel without either group knowing about the work being done by their fellow researchers. Their subsequent collaboration would progress over time to the point when ARPANET became NSFNET, which was an effort to connect all publicly funded supercomputers. Even more developments would come to these networks before file transfer and sharing protocols became stable. On the other hand, primitive versions of Transmission Control Protocol/Internet Protocol (TCP/IP) were being developed and packet-based transfer was beginning to be well understood in the 1980s. At this time, the Internet was still only usable in research labs, and the general public didn't have access to it or any application for it. Eventually, in the mid-1990s, ARPANET and NSFNET would be decommissioned and the Internet would be opened to the public through the introduction of web browsers.

A very interesting transition happened around the late 1980s. There were various ideas about what the future of the Internet would look like but no one took it seriously. Most big technology companies and the general public were thinking about a new idea called the information superhighway (Figure 1-1). This highway was going to connect the world and make information available at super high speeds. It would be much better than the toy that was the Internet.

Figure 1-1. *Depiction of the information superhighway that would connect the world.* Photo credit to Popular Mechanics magazine.

Commercial Internet: CERN

Thankfully, all the talk about an information superhighway turned out to be just hype and it never turned into anything practical. The information superhighway was closed source and the intention was that only big companies would be adding content and bringing information to the general public. The world would be such a different place if the Internet was not as open as it is today. To understand how the Internet got into the hands of pragmatic folks and how this transition happened, we need to spend some time exploring the motivations behind the transition. More often than not, world-changing technologies comes to light after years of research and development. It was expected that the Internet would achieve mass adoption, but to accomplish that it had to be trendy and appealing. This can be done very well in existing capital markets and this was one entry point for startups to get involved and make the Internet easily accessible. After a certain point, a tool or a project can reach a large enough user base that a revenue model can be developed and attached to it. The primary motivation in commercializing a research outcome and mass adoption is having well-defined distribution and revenue models. This is the crucial evolutionary step where the tool or a product becomes a company and the company can put more wood behind the fire, because the returns will be that much greater. There was still more work to be done before private companies could become interested. The first major development was a standardization of protocols that can be used to connect machines with each other.

It was March 1989 and a researcher at the European Nuclear Research Organization (CERN) had just finished writing a proposal that he sent to his boss, Mike Sendall. Sendall read the proposal and wrote three famous words: "Vague, but exciting." That historical comment was written on a proposal called *Information Management: A Proposal*, shown in Figure 1-2. The writer was none other than Sir Tim Berners-Lee. The proposal dealt with the complexities of information management at CERN, and ways to easily transfer data among physicists at a faster rate. This could be applied to a much broader context, though, and Berners-Lee recognized that. This proposal, which really was intended to result in a more effective CERN communication network, was the birth of the World Wide Web (WWW). For a long time, it would remain just a toy that only physicists used. We explore here how the Internet become more than just a toy and what was needed to make it widely available.

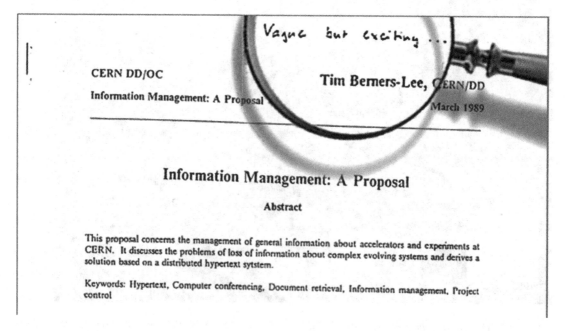

Figure 1-2. Information Management: A Proposal

Eventually, in efforts to make the Internet more practical, the idea of web sites came into existence. The first web site is shown in Figure 1-3.

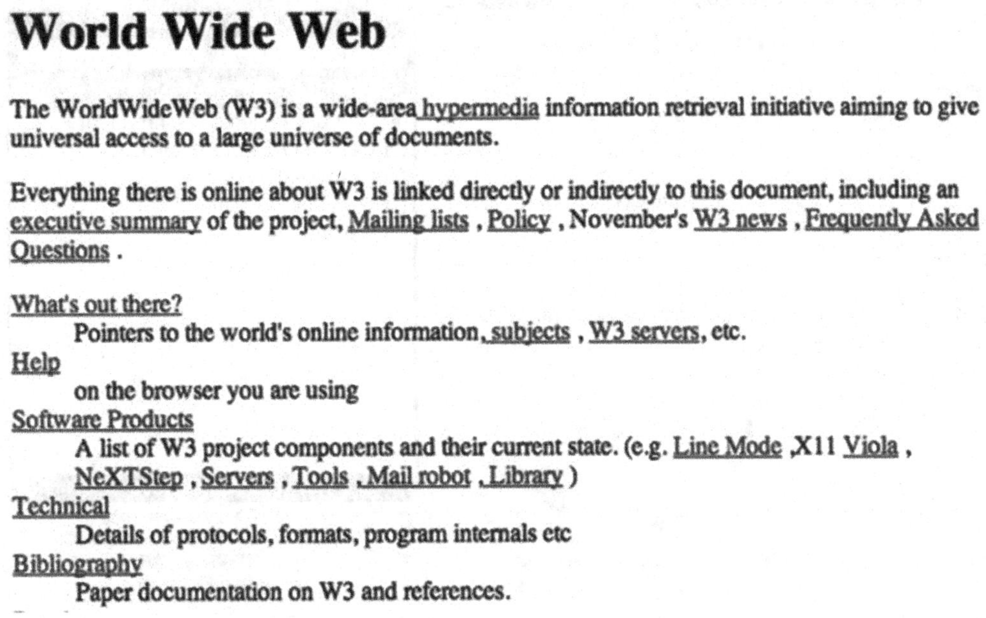

World Wide Web

The WorldWideWeb (W3) is a wide-area hypermedia information retrieval initiative aiming to give universal access to a large universe of documents.

Everything there is online about W3 is linked directly or indirectly to this document, including an executive summary of the project, Mailing lists , Policy , November's W3 news , Frequently Asked Questions .

What's out there?
      Pointers to the world's online information, subjects , W3 servers, etc.
Help
      on the browser you are using
Software Products
      A list of W3 project components and their current state. (e.g. Line Mode ,X11 Viola ,
      NeXTStep , Servers , Tools , Mail robot , Library)
Technical
      Details of protocols, formats, program internals etc
Bibliography
      Paper documentation on W3 and references.

Figure 1-3. *A screenshot of the first web site*

The way fundamental research works is that some researchers spend time at the frontier of what they study. They work very hard trying to push the boundaries of what we know, and as they continue moving toward the future, they leave behind a trail of routine tasks. These routine tasks can be performed much more efficiently by a different entity that specializes in repeating just one particular task. This is where private enterprise takes over and capital markets show their power. The Internet also benefited from a very similar phase: After the foundations had been fleshed out through government-funded research, private companies such as Netscape took over to provide a commercially viable infrastructure for the Internet.

It must be noted that the evolution of the Internet surprised everybody; no one can look at this history and say that they expected things like JavaScript and Secure Sockets Layer (SSL) to come out as private companies started to stabilize the Internet and make it profitable. It was eventually inevitable that the Internet would become stable enough to allow the e-commerce economy to bloom and superstores like Amazon would allow people to buy things from across the world. These were some of the promises that startups were making in the early 1990s, but it would still be some time before that goal could be accomplished and brought to fruition. Nonetheless, the beginning of privatization allowed anyone to have access to this open protocol that connected thousands of computers and promised to connect the entire world. This would allow incredible virtual economies to form around web sites. One example of an early marketplace is shown in Figure 1-4. Many other monetization ideas would spring up, like advertisements that profoundly influence what it would mean to be an entity of this brave new world.

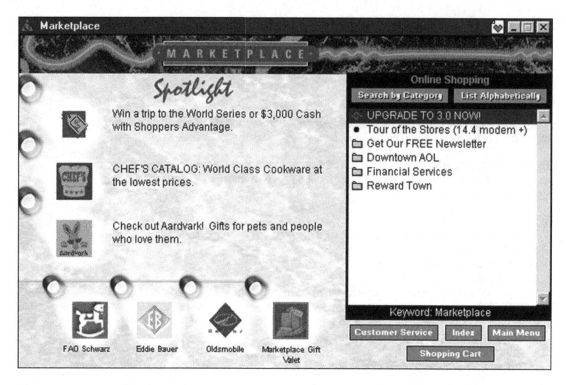

Figure 1-4. *A screenshot of an early marketplace on the Internet, powered by America Online (AOL)*

Summary

This chapter reviewed the beginnings of the Internet. A historical account was presented to help the reader understand how world-changing technologies get their start, and more important, how fundamental research has an impact felt only 30 to 40 years after it got started. The fact that the Internet was an open platform for anyone meant that everyone could develop Internet-based *things*. No one had any idea what those would be, but in hindsight, we can see the applications developing. Taking the Internet from just a toy that physicists used to something that every person on the planet could use was a drastic paradigm shift. The world was becoming connected and the Internet was really a very big deal. Even though the Internet had gotten off to a great start, we are still talking about the old Internet, the static net. There were more drastic changes to come, and the new Internet is different. How did iconic companies like Netscape completely change how the Internet worked? How did they change what it meant to be an Internet company? We explore these issues in the following chapters.

Further Reading

1. *Information Management: A Proposal.* Tim Berners-Lee, CERN.
   http://www.w3.org/History/1989/proposal.html

2. *19 Key Essays on How the Internet Is Changing Our Lives.* Open Mind.
   https://www.bbvaopenmind.com/en/book/19-key-essays-on-how-internet-is-changing-our-lives/

REVIEW

In this review, let us compare the old Web that was just beginning to come about to some of the latest state-of-art technologies that will one day change what it means to connect to the Internet.

1. **Search Task:** A new super-glue of sorts is emerging to connect all our devices in a seamless manner called the Internet of Things. What is this new idea?

2. **Search Task:** Google recently announced Brillo, a home automation toolkit that would make it easier to connection home-automation devices. What are the ideas behind Brillo?

3. **Search Task:** The idea of Internet-based tasks is very intriguing. Some services allow you to put the Internet to work for you and automate simple tasks. One such service is IFTTT (If This, Then That). What does IFTTT allow one to do? We revisit this service in detail later in the book.

We end our story of the old Web and talk about how the new changes created a revolution called Web 2.0 in the upcoming chapter.

CHAPTER 2

■ ■ ■

Web 2.0

It's never the changes we want that change everything.

—Junot Díaz

The static world that we looked at in the last chapter was just the beginning. Once web sites became the norm on the Internet, capturing people's attention with interactivity and speed became necessary. A landslide of technical updates over the next decade helped the Web mature into a stable platform for serious development and web applications. The need for speed has changed the Internet and the people using it. The tools and technologies that we have today enable us to communicate at such incredible speeds that our view of the world has become instantaneous. We send a text and expect a reply back within a few minutes, we tweet and receive tweets from the most recent events as they are happening, and live streaming has become very popular on most social media platforms. This instantaneous environment has been enabled by the Internet, but how did it get transformed from being slow, clunky, and static into fast, dynamic, and responsive? These are some of the questions that we explore in this chapter.

Early Web Browsers

We left off the story previously at the Internet just becoming something more than a toy. The major developments that came to the Internet were a result of commercialization, but what does commercialization even mean? Essentially, commercialization is a process by which a tool or technology ends up in the hands of the general public and other developers that can stretch it further into future. This is a very lengthy process involving complicated market economics and network effects that have been the subject of entire books themselves! Those topics are beyond the scope of our discussion, but it is worth spending a little bit of time to discuss the economic and financial environment in which the World Wide Web got started.

It was the early 1990s, and a group of students at the University of Illinois Urbana-Champaign had created the first browser called Mosaic. It was a revolutionary piece of technology for its time, funded by the National Science Foundation. This was done on a very small scale and Marc Andreessen was one of the core developers behind that browser effort. Another key player in this story is Jim Clark, a legendary serial entrepreneur who had just left Silicon Graphics, which he had helped create. On his last day at work, he was looking for new avenues to explore after leaving this job when a colleague asked him to write an e-mail to Andreessen to talk about potential ideas for a second company. The browser was actually not the first idea they started working on together. The first project they took on was creating interactive television: The technology needed to make it happen was nonexistent at the time and very soon the duo learned that the interactive TV idea would not work. The next idea was to work on what would be modern-day equivalent of the playStation or Xbox network but with the Nintendo 64 consoles. They started to crunch some numbers to determine the type of Internet infrastructure they would need in place to accomplish their goal and the numbers were just not feasible.

They were really not sure about which direction to take, but an unexpected clue led them to the best possible outcome. After Andreessen left the Mosaic group, the development of the browser continued and he kept himself on the internal mailing lists. Their group had released Mosaic under a split license: It was free for personal use but required a license and payment for commercial use. They left this statement blank, not particularly sure about what to charge. Eventually, the commercial inquiries mailing list hit more than 1,000 messages when Andreessen and Clark realized that the browser could become an interesting and viable startup. Following this lead, the duo started working on polishing the browser and creating a larger suite of add-ons to complement the browser. This was the second wave of developments after the Mosaic browser, the release of Netscape Navigator and the server-product line.

■ **Note** Netscape released its version of a browser, Netscape Navigator, first; eventually, it was made available for free. The next line of products generated their main share of revenue and included the Netscape Enterprise Server (web server), Netsite Communications Web server (mail, news and calendar, with SSL included), Netsite Commerce Web Server, and Netsite Proxy Server. These products eventually were either open source or became the foundation for future web technology. One such example is the Firefox browser. Shortly before Netscape was acquired by AOL, it released the source code for its browser and created the Mozilla Organization to coordinate future development. The Mozilla developers completely rewrote the Netscape browser with the Gecko engine and provided us with the modern browser that we now use.

Netscape completely redefined what it meant to be an Internet company, and the technology at the core of the company would become foundational in making the Internet available to developers. It laid the groundwork for much of the early security infrastructure, and more important, the first versions of the JavaScript engine came out of Netscape by Brendan Eich. These were the early days of the Internet, but one of the toughest tasks had already been accomplished: bringing the Internet to the general public. There was still much work to be done: More people would have to be brought online to the Internet and software was not directly available on the Internet. It seems obvious to us now that the easiest way to get a new tool or play a new game is to download the tool or game from the Internet, but this was not at all obvious 20 years ago. The services portion of the Internet was far from prime time, but in the past decade years or so, the software as a service model has become much more ubiquitous. Additionally, it seems that the year 2012 has been the tipping point for Software as a Service (SaaS), as even the largest companies in the world are switching over to SaaS models. Interestingly, this method of recurring revenue seems to be beneficial to the companies: As opposed to a single point of sale, they can now charge for any arbitrary time for which they want to offer their licenses. This model has become the new standard for a host of new Internet companies in a remarkable period of Internet history called Web 2.0.

Defining Web 2.0

The term Web 2.0 was popularized by Tim O'Reilly and Dale Dougherty at the O'Reilly Media Web 2.0 Conference with a great focus on user-generated content being the new web. As a result, the web sites of the old Internet became the interactive apps that we now use. This has largely turned out to be true, as user-generated content on the Internet has increased massively. Some examples of Web 2.0 include blogs, forums, social media platforms, wikis, video sharing web sites, photo hosting services, and so on. The criteria mostly remains that nearly any user-content-generating platform comes under the Web 2.0 banner. The key difference to notice is that in Web 1.0, there were only a few content creators. This made the vast majority of users consumers of content. The limited number of content creators limited the scale of the old Web. Web 2.0 is based on the principles of the Web as platform and giving independence and freedom to the users. The technological standards were also updated. Initially the Web was a scattered sea of different technologies, but Web 2.0 became more universal. A "standards-based" Web was what we were after, a place where we could unify these wild and different ideas into one commonly usable protocol that can be used by developers to bring more people to the Internet. We envisioned a world where integration between these separated ideas would happen smoothly.

One way to measure the impact this had is to just look around today to see how much content gets created through blogs, social media, and videos. Just those three forms of media end increase the volume of new content by large amounts. If the main objective of Web 2.0 was to make content creation widely available, the results are overwhelmingly obvious and this goal has been accomplished. We are only fleshing out the details and making it easier, but for the most part, we have made it incredibly easy to share pictures, videos, and written media. The smartphones we carry have powerful enough cameras to take high-quality pictures, and apps like Instagram now make it incredibly easy to share those pictures. Almost every big social media outlet is now trying to approach video and make that native to the Internet. Finally, we have ever more powerful blogging engines that power the Web like WordPress, to create and share written content very easily. The plug-in system built around it makes life even easier.

A better way to describe Web 2.0 is some new features that were introduced to it, although some of those have been superseded by new technologies. Many regard syndication of web site content as a Web 2.0 feature. This is generally done through Extensible Markup Language (XML) and Really Simple Syndication (RSS), which are both fairly new, although recently their use has become a little more niche. Syndication uses standardized protocols to allow end users to repurpose a site's data in another context such as another Web site or a browser plug-in. There are several protocols that permit for syndication, but the most popular one is RSS, shown in Figure 2-1, and Atom, all of which are XML-based formats. Web 2.0 also allows for very interesting machine-based interactions through features such as representational state transfer (REST) and Simple Object Access Protocol (SOAP). Many web platforms expose the data contained and generated within them through application programming interfaces (APIs). These APIs come in many shapes and forms, but all of them share one commonality: The APIs make the data stored in a platform available to developers for processing and interesting applications. Most communication channels through APIs involve the use of XML or JavaScript Object Notation (JSON) payloads. Different APIs exist for different use cases, but standard APIs have also emerged to take care of common tasks, for instance posting to a blog or notifying subscribed readers about a blog update and so on.

The Power of RSS Feeds

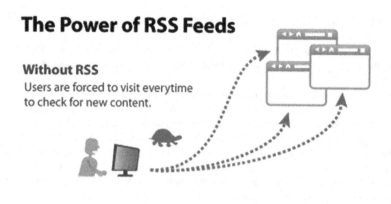

Without RSS
Users are forced to visit everytime to check for new content.

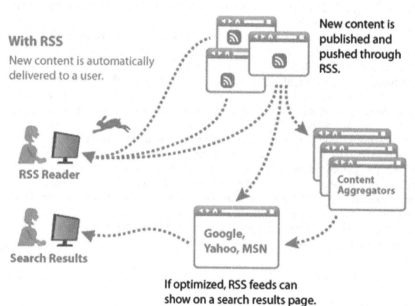

With RSS
New content is automatically delivered to a user.

New content is published and pushed through RSS.

RSS Reader

Content Aggregators

Search Results

Google, Yahoo, MSN

If optimized, RSS feeds can show on a search results page.

©2007 Elliance, Inc. | www.elliance.com

Figure 2-1. *An overview of the RSS protocol and feeds.* Photo credit to Elliance for the RSS protocol.

Many of these technologies have since become standards for the Web: JSON, REST, and SOAP are just a few examples where the underlying technology has become the foundation for entire new industries. Medical informatics is one such example where the data being shared uses JSON and REST protocols very frequently and in innovative ways that allow sharing of that data between hospitals at large scales. These are all momentous achievements of the Web 2.0 and it continues to change the world in unexpected ways. In the summary for the last chapter, we talked about this idea of the Internet of Things, which seems to be one of the hottest trends driving the Internet forward. This is the idea of creating another network that can be used just by our devices to connect with each other and seamlessly transmit data among each other. This is the new cutting-edge application of networking today, the new horizons that might eventually become Web 3.0. What set of changes will power Web 3.0? Search with context, more video-based content, secure private networks, automation, and intelligent applications are ripe for innovation. Even though the future will be much different from today, the technologies that power Web 3.0 will operate on principles derived from current ideas.

It must be noted that Web 2.0 did not arise in a vacuum. Just like most modern inventions, it was a response to the events taking place at the time. There was a period in early Internet history when for the first time, Internet companies clashed with the economy in a very real and potentially dangerous way. This was the dot-com bust, which taught us many important lessons, some of which are worth discussing here. Let's spend a little bit of time talking about that time period and how it shaped Web 2.0.

Boom and Bust

The dot-com bubble is an important stop in our story, as much of what happened after was a direct response to the bubble and the story of blogging is incomplete without a discussion of that time period. Let's begin with a rough sketch of the timeline:

- **1995–1997:** Large investments in the Web and Internet companies.

- **1998:** A financial crisis: Avian flu spreading, Russia defaulted, and eBay goes public.

- **1999:** People are planning initial public offerings (IPOs) of their startups before the companies are even incorporated.

- **2000:** All the IPO madness comes to a screeching halt and the financial market crashes.

This timeline roughly shows the environment before the dot-com bust when NASDAQ crashed and the stock market lost most of its value. This left investors in a really troublesome situation, as they lost a lot of money and did not believe in Internet-based companies anymore. Their disbelief was justified because there were some deep problems in the investment landscape around 1998 and 1999, where anyone could raise any amount of money. The whole problem before the dot-com bust was that people were selling too much. Ideas were being sold as products, products were being sold as companies, and companies were being sold as revenue-generating entities that went public. This whole structure had no foundation, so when it was shaken up, it crumbled and destroyed those phantom companies.

The extent of this bust was so great that it had a significant psychological impact on society. The general public started having huge doubts about the future of Internet-based companies. The prevailing idea at the time was that the Internet was finished. There was nothing profitable remaining and now the entrepreneurs and venture capitalists had to work on something else like clean technology. Even though investors became cautious of the stock market and Internet companies, the browser was still going strong. The heavy hitters of the technology industry continued to experiment with new features such as AJAX and ActiveX. Their main objective was to show that the Internet was not done; in fact, it was just getting started. This was a sort of renaissance period where all the old ideas from Web 1.0 were reexamined and the engineers started to realize that most of them could be made to work.

The main problem was not that the ideas were radical or impractical, but instead, most of them were just too early. We weren't ready for them: The general public and the markets had no idea how to interact with those products and how to value them. All of that has changed since. The landscape has become much more difficult for a public company today: It is much more hostile and the regulations are far more intense. That might be why so few Internet companies have gone public in this brave new world. Then again, in Web 2.0, just as the focus on the Web changed to enabling a greater number of content creators, the focus of the companies changed from selling products to building strong technological cores. The common advice for companies going public now is to build a fortress before they ever think about going public, filling all the key positions having a solid revenue trail along with predictability. Once the company can accomplish that much, then it can think about going public.

Interestingly, there has been plenty of research done on the idea of bubbles in the technology realm, especially after the 2000 crash. The most influential line of research has been undertaken by Carlota Perez, who has studied the bubbles in terms of technological revolutions and their impact on financial capital markets. A simplified model of Perez's research is presented in Figure 2-2. At this point, the previous discussion about the bubble and the crash might make more sense: We needed to cover some background to talk about blogging emerging as a response to the things that went wrong with the old Web. The exponential increase in the number of content creators, blogging engines, and new platforms is the result of the Internet finally maturing to a very stable stage. The division between the old Web and the new Web can be understood in terms of technology cycles, and a very brief sketch is presented here. Perez's idea is that we divide technological revolutions (e.g., the steam engine and the Internet) into two phases: the installation phase and the deployment phase.

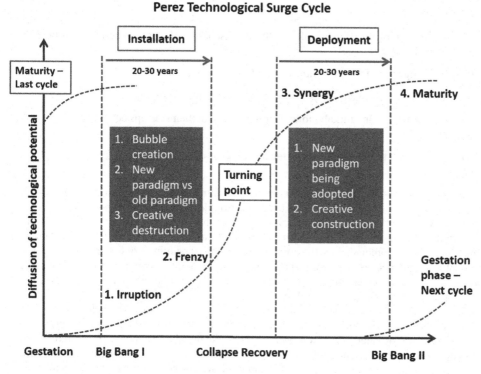

Figure 2-2. *Boom and bust cycle for technological revolutions such as the Internet. Web 2.0 has emerged in the maturation phase of the Internet. The turning point for this revolution was the dot-com crash.*

The installation phase includes the early development and deployment of a new technology. As was the case with the early map makers, the new technology is unstable and not well tested but we use it regardless, in hopes that the future use will provide great benefits. Wearable technology is going through this cycle right now. The technology starts to mature and gain widespread use, but there are still fundamental problems with the infrastructure powering it. There is finally more capital available when investors and public realize the importance of this new technology. This is followed by a financial bubble that propels the irrationally rapid installation of this new technology and its early applications. Then there is a crash, followed by a recovery and then a long period of productive growth, as the new technology is deployed throughout other industries, as well as society more broadly. Eventually the revolution runs its course and a new technological revolution begins. This is the general course of technological revolutions according to Perez, but let's discuss Figure 2-2 in a little more detail.

Figure 2-2 describes the Perez technological surge cycle. This cycle is a model for how an idea can become a technological revolution and eventually mature into a product used by the masses. The cycle starts with a gestation period with a lot of promising ideas, most of which generate a lot of hype but never make it out of this phase. The rare ideas that do make it have to pass the test of time. The first phase is installation, where the basic infrastructure for a technology is rolled out. Financially, a lot of venture capital funding and even government support fuels the development of the required infrastructure. The beginning of the installation phase is also known as the big-bang period because high availability of funding creates new jobs and economic progress. In this phase, a bubble is created where the hype around a technology clouds the real progress, but money from investors keeps flowing in. Socially, this new paradigm has a lot of opponents who are proponents of the already established ideas. This leads to the eventual downfall of the old incumbents as the jobs and the economy flow toward the new paradigm. The installation phase is also characterized by a forceful irruption of new ideas surrounding a new technology, followed by a frenzy of startups and businesses trying to grab a piece of that pie.

This frenzied chaos gains critical mass until the bubble is exposed as hype and generally dismissed; that is, until it picks up again. This period between installation and deployment is called the turning point, which usually indicates renewed interest. This period of collapsed recovery allows the skilled workers involved in the installation phase to find flaws that caused the industry to collapse and determine how it can be rebuilt. When the rebuilding starts, it involves a strong focus on the technology that was originally ignored. The public and investors have had time to reconsider, but now they are much more cautious. They expect solid results; when entrepreneurs deliver them, a synergistic relationship builds between the public and investors. Socially, the new paradigm is not as strange anymore because it shows the inefficiencies of the old ideas. It becomes widely accepted and gains more support.

This is the second phase of a technological revolution, deployment. In this phase, new technology is deployed on top of the infrastructure rolled out previously and the developments that have happened since then. At this point, the technology that entered this cycle has become stable and is ready for serious development. It reaches maturity and the cycle ends here, leaving the future of that technology to the developers. Then, a new idea arrives on the scene and the cycle starts anew.

The deployment phase really is the best of times and the worst of times, as Charles Dickens said in the opening to *A Tale of Two Cities*. This second phase signifies maturation of the technology: It is not as risky as it used to be, and now stable development can take place, pushing this new technology into the future. It must be noted that a technological revolution in the deployment phase already has a critical mass, and the users will ultimately determine the future application of this technology to their own lives. Their response often aligns with the developers who designed the applications, but often they surprised us with the ingenious, unintentional, and sophisticated uses for the technology.

Connecting the Dots

What does this all mean for blogging? How does our story of blogging as a response to the old Web fit into this whole discussion of the bubble and technological advancements? The answer is multifaceted. Blogging emerged as a solution to one of the biggest problems with the old Web: not having enough people to create content. It is very difficult to get more people to follow or like a new technology if they remain consumers and cannot personalize their experience. New ideas don't spread far when only a small percentage of the population or consumers can put forth those ideas.

The freedom to express oneself in a creative manner has been a cornerstone of the Internet, and Web 2.0 directly answers that with the advent of blogging and social media. There are a handful of social platforms now that dominate our lives, and one perspective on this is the Twitter firehose. This term describes the tremendous amount of content present, shared, and created among users on Twitter. It is safe to say that the data generated by other social networks is just as vast in quantity, if not greater. Most alternative blogging engines today have evolved in this new ecosystem where creating, sharing, and reposting are the basic features.

It must be noted that it was not just the different blogging software, but also the computer languages used to program the Web itself that evolved. The dynamic nature of the web was encoded through support for techniques like AJAX that promised to be dynamic, but a lot of work needed to be done before that promise could be fulfilled. AJAX was a catalyst for that type of dynamic web development and in time it was achieved through advancements in JavaScript. Eventually, web development accelerated with the advent of extensions that arose as a part of the modern languages, such as Python getting new packages to develop web applications (e.g., django and Flask).

This new addition of web development packages has allowed developers from different backgrounds to use the languages with which they are familiar to discover new ways of creating web sites and applications. Additionally, the rapid pace of add-on development has allowed for an incredible number of standard packages to become languages in their own sense. A great example of this is jQuery, which has become a whole new language to rapidly prototype web projects, but in the end it is based on JavaScript. On that note, JavaScript is positioned today to become the most powerful language for web development. The number of packages and libraries in JavaScript has become so large that we need package managers, as shown in Figure 2-3, just to maintain and update a directory of all the packages. With frameworks like Node.js and MEAN stack, this dream is ever closer to being realized and we spend more time on those ideas later in the book. Jeff Atwood at CodingHorror gave a humorous description of the relationship between the Web and JavaScript that has become strikingly close to the reality of of JavaScript's influence on web applications: Atwood's Law states that any application that can be written in JavaScript will eventually be written in JavaScript.

Figure 2-3. *The Jam package manager and Node.js: Two very interesting package managers for JavaScript packages*

This idea of packages is not only applicable to package managers, but also to blogging in general, a concept we discuss later on as integration. Now let's revisit the question of the role of blogging in this technological revolution: In the grand scheme of the Internet, which has already profoundly changed our lives, blogging almost serves as a historical record of the changes in the era. We can very easily see the progression of the underlying technology such as the blogging engines and protocols through time, becoming more sophisticated and easier to use. It's a story of not just the technology, but also the people using it. In the beginning, there were only a few content creators and the reason was simple: The Internet was just too difficult to use for the average Joe. Much has changed since then, though. Today, creating new content could be as simple as taking out your phone and taking a picture. The new technology will make creating content and engagement even easier, but both elements are needed to provide the full story: the technology and the people growing with it.

We will see profound changes in the blogging ecosystem in the next few years with the way blogging engines and posting protocols are constructed, thereby making it easier to share the created content along with easier methods of engagement. The hallmark of this paradigm shift has been the emergence of these content repositories. These are places on the Internet that democratically sort the most read story or the most interesting article through some sort of an upvote system. Reddit and Hacker News are both perfect examples of this type of sorting where an incredible amount of content gets shared and then evaluated by the users who might like reading them.

Content repositories and easier means of engagement are massive paradigm shifts that in combination will make it even easier to reach out to audiences and express yourself. This phase between installation and deployment is where blogging can have incredible influence on the world, making it easier for anyone to create and share good content. This is not to say that once the Internet matures, blogging will die out: It will simply take on a new form. Storytelling is never complete, it only changes with time and those who are telling the new story.

Summary

This chapter covered the big transition from the old static Web to the Web 2.0. The biggest emphasis was on why Web 2.0 became the next big thing: It allowed more users to become content creators and not just consumers. This made it possible for the explosion of new content and the massive adoption of the Internet with new services and platforms that have now become content hubs of their own. A major point of discussion was the evolution of bubbles in technological revolutions and what the place of blogging is in the major turning point. There is more to it than just recording history, though. We have seen this happen in numerous cases and the best ones include cases of a security vulnerability. The scenario often plays out as follows: A vulnerability is identified and reported on some random mailing list. The world is only slowly finding out about it when experts who blog also learn about it. They dissect the subject matter and create a post series describing the problem in detail and what a possible fix should look like. This type of immediate response is not something any other form of written media, such as newspapers and so on, can do.

It seems that blogging is playing a major role in communicating the history of the world: As the Internet matures, so do the people that use it.

Further Reading

1. *Corporate Alliances Matter Less Thanks to APIs.* https://hbr.org/2015/06/corporate-alliances-matter-less-thanks-to-apis

2. *Are You Using APIs to Gain Competitive Advantage?* https://hbr.org/2015/04/are-you-using-apis-to-gain-competitive-advantage

3. *Web 2.0.* http://www.web2summit.com/web2009/public/schedule/detail/10194

4. *Technological Revolutions and Techno-economic Paradigms.* Carlota Perez. http://technologygovernance.eu/files/main/2009070708552121.pdf

---

REVIEW

In this review, let us talk about the dot-com bubble and some lessons that we could learn from it.

1. **Search Task:** How long did the bubble last?

2. **Search Task:** What were some of the ideas from the dot-com bubble era that work very well today?

3. **Search Task:** When did the first wave of Web 2.0 companies come on the scene?

4. **Search Task:** What programming languages were prevalent as the static Web was transitioning into the dynamic Web 2.0?

We end our story of the changes in the Web and pick it up in the next chapter, which covers in detail the particular focus on blogging and the evolution of blogging platforms.

■ ■ ■

## CHAPTER 3

Static Site Generators

Which way you ought to go depends on where you want to get to ...

—Lewis Carroll, *Alice in Wonderland*

In the previous chapters, we talked about the static Web and the emergence of a new type of web called Web 2.0 or the dynamic Web. This would eventually turn out to be a major paradigm shift, but what were the implications of this transition from static to Web 2.0? In this chapter, we explore the impact of that transition and particularly how it would come to influence the world of blogging. The dynamic Web had far-reaching consequences for what it meant to be an Internet company, and how people interacted with the Web itself to tell a story. The history of blogging deeply intertwines with the development of content management systems that people were using during that time to blog and write. We review how content management systems came about and some of the common problems associated with using them. Out of those frustrations, one developer decided to switch over entirely from content management to static web sites and thus Jekyll was born. We explore his rationale behind creating a static generator and why blogging with a static web site makes sense. Finally, this chapter ends by showcasing a few of the most popular static site generators presently in use.

The Maturing Web

There was a gradual progression of developments that led to the maturation of the Internet and made it more secure. A comprehensive list of those advancements is beyond the scope of this book. However, the most important of those updates led to evolution of the Web into a stable platform for services that could take people as the input and generate interaction as the output. The Web was becoming more reliable for acting as an interface between people and computer applications. What this meant, more concretely, was that you could actually do things over the Web now. As simple as this might sound, this completely revolutionized whole new industries like e-commerce. Over time, the number of people that could access the Internet increased exponentially. To put this in perspective, more than 3 billion people are now using the Internet, according to the United Nations. With more and more people using the Internet, it quickly turned into a tool for social discovery. The idea of user-based profiles and profile-based platforms was starting to emerge; this was essentially the beginning of web services and social media. Some of those nimble web services have evolved into tech giants with billions of users (e.g., Facebook). The platforms they offer are based on rapid updates, animations, videos, and constant updates of information, all of which simply could not be achieved with the static Web.

The evolution of programming languages was central to the profile-based platforms and Web 2.0 technologies. The new web languages allowed developers to create platforms that can process user requests in parallel and increase the speed with which content was served to those users. Web applications could now be loaded in parallel chunks based on user feedback and usability. The early profile-based platforms were limited in user personalization options and provided a very small selection of core services for their users. Today, all of that has changed: Most social platforms offer several interconnected services that are reaching out to millions, if not billions, of users. One consequence of being able to reach large audiences at a fraction of the cost is that it becomes very easy to share information and turn some of those users into paying customers. Blogging in turn has taken on an ever-changing form in the maturing Web, incorporating social media to engage with larger audiences and build a loyal following or their own user base. Looking at popular blogs such as FiveThirtyEight, it is easy to see that they have become a microplatform in their own sense. These microplatforms serve a very important function to the niches in which they operate: curation of interesting information relevant to that niche along with the added opinion of the blogger. Each of these blogging microplatforms has the following three commonalities:

- A large user base or reader base with which the original poster can engage.

- A type of commenting system where the readers can interact with other readers.

- A low barrier for maintenance and posting on that platform.

■ **Note**   Web 2.0 has had many iconic companies that started small and seemed radical, but most of them eventually succeeded. Notable examples include Twitter, Facebook, Myspace, YouTube, and LinkedIn.

Blogging in Web 2.0

The art of blogging, along with its tool set, has progressed tremendously in just a few years. Today, sophisticated bloggers have a much richer set of tools for curation, automation, and posting. The different tools that a blogger uses eventually become part of his or her workflow. The blogger becomes proficient at this workflow and simply repeats this cycle of gather–synthesize–publish to continue posting great new content (we cover workflows more in later chapters). Along with the tools, we now have a comprehensive system to manage the blogs called a content management system (CMS).

There are several popular CMSs in use currently, and the three most popular are WordPress (which powers at least one third of the Web), Joomla, and Drupal. There are many other CMSs that are smaller and niche-specific (e.g., TinyCMS), used by hobbyists or others who need the additional functionality.

The three most popular CMSs just mentioned are also open source. This implies that the source code behind those blogging engines is open for anyone to review and contribute to, if they have the appropriate knowledge. This has helped improve the code tremendously at an incredible rate that would never have been possible if a company was developing those engines. New features can be added very easily, and because it is an open community, often new or creative uses of the tools that were not imagined by the creators are added. If these new use cases seem convincing, they are eventually incorporated in the system itself.

Another interesting aspect of this type of open development is that if security problems or bugs are discovered in the blogging engines, they get fixed much faster. Imagine that a problem is reported to the community about a coding error that causes the blogging engine to behave in a malicious manner. The community that gets built around the open source tools will notice that a problem arose and work toward a fix. In some cases, a patch (a solution to fix the bad code) gets released in less than a day.

Let's review very briefly what we have talked about so far: We have painted a picture of the transformation of the Web from static to dynamic. In this new dynamic Web, blogging also underwent changes, including the use of CMS to make the mundane tasks of managing posts easy. More important, the time spent to get a blog up and running got shorter and shorter until it was only a matter of minutes before someone could put up a blog of their own. As generally happens with widely used tools, CMSs also started to become more powerful with new features. Many of the new features were built to help with customization and personalization of the blog or the web site. The exact settings to personalize a web site are left to the user to decide.

Writing a new theme from scratch to style a blog or a web site might provide the best user experience, but it certainly does not address all the security gaps. As CMSs became larger and more complex, so did the components that were a part of them. Common plug-ins emerged for blogging engines like WordPress that allowed the administrator to complete easy tasks such as management of posts, comments, and other associated blog settings. This CMS management eventually turned into a comprehensive admin panel that many CMSs now offer. The admin panel provides a higher level overview of the blog and all of its components to the user. The users slowly discovered that some custom add-ons on their blog were more prone to getting compromised if not well maintained and updated.

The entire process of keeping the admin panel and the CMS updated was getting very time consuming, but the costs of not doing so could be rather embarrassing and take days to clean up. Developers were starting to get frustrated because the whole idea of blogging was becoming bogged down with more maintenance and less focus on writing and creating new content. Many developers tried to think of possible solutions and after much tinkering, a few options emerged. The easiest solution was to use a blogging engine that was being hosted online for you, instead of self-hosting something like WordPress. Blogger falls into this category of hosted blogs that did not require much maintenance, and the back end would be managed at large by the company behind the efforts. This is an incredibly lucrative option, because the user can purchase add-ons such as a custom domain that points to their own blog and circumvent the hosting issue entirely.

There are limitations of this approach in terms of customization: Self-hosting allows for more modifications that might not otherwise be possible. Increasingly, it was becoming clear that there was a need for a self-hosting service for the developer who can customize the blog to his or her own needs and still be able to spend time creating great content instead of spending it on updating and maintenance.

■ **Note** Problems often arose because the user did not update his or her CMS to the latest version in which a known problem has been fixed. Hackers took advantage of outdated software to compromise a system and defaced a web site, although the problem could have been very easily avoided.

Looking Back

As a response to the ever-complicated CMS landscape, new solutions were emerging in the form of hosted blogs, which were catching on very fast. Today, incredibly sophisticated blogging engines that are hosted in the cloud are becoming popular and many people are turning to them as a substitute to avoid maintenance. Not all developers arrived at the same solutions, though; some reached out in a different directions keeping, the blog based on hosting but removing the complexities out of it. Let's talk a little bit about how this was accomplished. Developers are always interested in workflows. That means they like to see repetitive patterns that can be automated to save them time so they can focus on the few things that matter to them. If blogging could be reduced to something like that where most of the maintenance could be automated, we could have an easy-to-use system that can allow the user to do the one thing a blog should be focused on: writing great content.

The static Web was made from a few native components: hyperlinking, documents, and pictures. That was about all it had, but it was very good at a few things. One of those was displaying text. This became the foundation for the next generation of blogging engines, which all focused around the idea that content is king. More important, these new engines are focused on removing the dynamicity to some extent and making blogs or web pages minimal to leave a minimal fingerprint. This allows for incredibly fast loading times, distraction-free reading, and automation of as many components of the blog as possible to meet the workflow considerations.

Jekyll came about as a result of these frustrations, and it is the main focus of this book. Jekyll was created by Tom Preston-Werner as he was figuring out why he had stopped blogging a few times after he started. He realized exactly what the problem was: He wanted to write great posts, not style template pages, moderate comments all day long, or constantly lag behind the latest software releases. He needed something simple to use and easy to maintain, and he thought hard about how to fix this problem from the bottom up. The following was the result of his reflection:

> *On Sunday, October 19th, I sat down in my San Francisco apartment with a glass of apple cider and a clear mind. After a period of reflection, I had an idea. While I'm not specifically trained as an author of prose, I **am** trained as an author of code. What would happen if I approached blogging from a software development perspective? What would that look like?*

> *First, all my writing would be stored in a Git repository. This would ensure that I could try out different ideas and explore a variety of posts all from the comfort of my preferred editor and the command line. I'd be able to publish a post via a simple deploy script or post-commit hook. Complexity would be kept to an absolute minimum, so a static site would be preferable to a dynamic site that required ongoing maintenance. My blog would need to be easily customizable; coming from a graphic design background means I'll always be tweaking the site's appearance and layout.*

We can already notice many of the design principles behind Jekyll being described in this note. The core issues are addressed and a simplified model for a blog is proposed to be created with Jekyll. This was only the beginning of static site generators, and Jekyll was the first one.

Components of a Static Generator

A static site generator is essentially a converter: It takes a template directory (representing the raw form of a web site), runs it through template converters, and spits out a complete, static web site suitable for serving through a web server like Apache. Jekyll was designed with a few key ideas in mind, but before we can get to those, we need to discuss what makes up a static site generator. Here are the three generalized components found in most static site generators today:

- **Core language**: The language a static generator is written in, for example JavaScript or Ruby.

- **Templates**: The templating language to be used through the blog and posts.

- **Plug-ins**: All static site generators allow for additional functionality through some sort of a plug-in system.

Having listed the three components, the next logical step seems to be discussing their purpose. Let's spend a little bit of time addressing why those three components are important to every static generator and what the implications are of switching one of them out.

The core language is the foundation of converting a raw markup of the Web site into an elegant blog. This component is the most fundamental (of the three) to how the blog elements will ultimately be structured and defined. Often, we are not concerned with lower level definitions of our blogging engine. However, it must be noted that if we need to extend the engine itself to include something new, it can only be done in a manner that is consistent with the core language. In practical terms, the extensions can only be written in the same language as the core language. This is one reason many static-site generators are simply ports of existing ones in a new language. This allows developers to work in a language with which they feel comfortable and design new extensions or functionality. Most of these static generators are open source as is, so enthusiasts often end up making their own version if need be.

The next component is the templating language. This is a level above the core language, but it is just as important because it automates and allows programmatic access to many of the key components of your blog. A templating language essentially allows the user to set forth rules for how a particular section of the blog should look. In doing so, the templating language provides the programmatic capabilities to accomplish a repetitive task, for instance, loop over all the posts in the blog tagged with a particular tag and display them in a given category.

The final component is the plug-ins, which allow for the most interesting functionality. Plug-ins play a very important role in that they allow for additions that the developers have not thought about or integrations with new technologies. Plug-ins are different from extensions to the core language as they do not actually change anything about the engine. Plug-ins only modify the representation of data that the blog has access to or that it has generated. On the other hand, extensions can modify deeper constructs such as adding a new data source to give the blog access to new information that it did not have access to previously. Plug-ins and extensions are incredibly important to a complete blog, but these are advanced concepts that are discussed more thoroughly in a later chapter.

The design of a static generator is such that any of the three components described earlier can be switched out and replaced with an equivalent from another programming domain. This is generally done to gain access to new features or allow for greater familiarity to the developers working on the core language. There are many static generators that are almost clones of each other with just one component swapped, for instance Jekyll and Octopress.

■ **Note**   Static site generators are often developed with many variations, aside from just the three components listed here. In a few cases, the final product is so different from the original generator that it serves a completely new purpose in a different language.

Static site generators like Jekyll often have a very interesting file structure, discussed at length later. However, it is worth noting now that static blogs often evolve to have custom data added, such as image assets, that are not accounted for in any standard framework. Coming back to the design principles of a static site generator, the rest of this chapter focuses on the most popular static generators and the developments that have made them popular. A few examples of the top generators are also included for the reader as a showcase.

Before we get into the static generators, one important concept to discuss is that of licensing. The various static site generators have different licenses for very good and valid reasons. These licenses are well established in the open source community and serve an important purpose: protecting the developer of the project from involvement in potential legal issues and protecting his or her reputation. The three main licenses that most static site generators fall under are MIT, BSD, and GPL. These licenses have a long history of use and establishment that is beyond the scope of this book, but the interested reader can learn more in the chapter notes. Functionally, the MIT and BSD licenses allow another developer to release derivatives of the original project under different licenses including closed source work. GPL is strictly against turning open source software into closed product, making it a requirement to release all derivatives under the GPL license. On a historical note, the GPL license had a significant impact on the development of the Linux kernel in the early stages. To this day, much of the code is licensed under GPL, even though the kernel is widely implemented. The BSD license has a few interesting provisions making it attractive to developers, such as the nonendorsement clause that, along with the nonadvertisement clause, allows the project to not be slandered while being advertised publicly, preserving the integrity and the online identity of the developers. Interestingly, there have been several derivatives of these licenses themselves that tackle issues of how to deal with code libraries and APIs, but we do not spend much time on those.

Static Generators Showcase

This section focuses on some of the most popular static generators and the features that they offer. These are all open source tools that you can use to compile your web site, but Jekyll is the easiest one with which to get started. For each generator, the details of its core components along with an image of the home page is provided. This allows you to become familiar with the different generators and what to look for when you are exploring the different options to try aside from Jekyll.

Jekyll

The first one is also the most popular one, which is the subject of this book: Jekyll, shown in Figure 3-1.

Figure 3-1. *Jekyll home page*

Jekyll is one of the most popular platforms, with about 200,000 favorites on GitHub and about 4,000 forks. It also has the best documentation and a great community associated with it, not only other bloggers who use Jekyll, but also hundreds of developers answering questions and issues on Stack Overflow regarding Jekyll. Here is the breakdown in terms of the three core components:

- **Core language:** Ruby
- **Templating language:** Liquid
- **License:** MIT

Octopress

The second widely used generator is Octopress. It is like Jekyll's cousin but with very important differences, shown in Figure 3-2. Octopress in a sense comes included with several sophisticated features that would be of use to someone who wants to customize to a greater extent. For instance, it comes with 19 preinstalled plug-ins out of the box, a dozen dependencies (ruby gems), it uses Sass by default, and so on. This is useful for someone who is willing to put in the time and create something more complex. Octopress actually has the exact same breakdown as Jekyll for the core components, but the big differences come in the form of plug-ins and add-ons that are available with Octopress that are not found elsewhere in Jekyll.

Figure 3-2. *Octopress home page*

It must be noted that because both Octopress and Jekyll are written in Ruby, any blog in one framework can be extended to the other one without many portability issues. In addition to that, any add-ons developed within the framework of one engine can easily be ported to the other.

Hexo

The third static site generator is also the first deviation, as it is based around Node.js. Hexo is a powerful blogging engine with a lot of plug-ins and features that one would find in Jekyll and Octopress, shown in Figure 3-3. Hexo is one example of a blogging engine created in a different language (JavaScript) for developers to easily contribute in a language with which they are familiar, as opposed to Ruby.

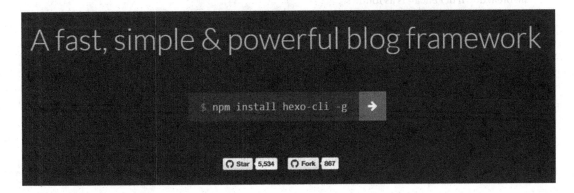

Figure 3-3. *Hexo home page*

The breakdown of Hexo can be described as follows:

- **Core language:** JavaScript, Node.js more precisely
- **Templating language:** EJS or Swig
- **License:** MIT

Pelican

The next most popular framework is written in one of the most popular languages, Python. Pelican is a powerful static site generator that imports from WordPress if needed and offers support for many different localizations other than just English. In this way, the blogger can write blog posts in his or her own native tongue. Aside from Jekyll, Pelican is one of the few static site generators that comes with a Theme repository with which new users can get started. The Pelican development blog is shown in Figure 3-4.

Pelican Development Blog

documentation   news

Pelican Static Site Generator, Powered by Python

Pelican is a static site generator, written in Python, that requires no database or server-side logic.

Figure 3-4. *Pelican Development Blog*

The breakdown of Pelican is as follows:

- **Core language:** Python
- **Templating language:** Jinja2
- **License:** GPL

To make it easier for the reader to see Pelican in action, two showcase examples are also provided:

- Kyle Fuller's blog: `http://kylefuller.co.uk/`
- Open messaging stack buddycloud: `http://buddycloud.com/`

These are the top four static site generators. As we start to dive into the next few generators, it is interesting to note that they incorporate a unique mixture of recent technologies.

Hugo

The next generator is Hugo. Hugo is a fast and flexible static site generator written in Go, which is a web programming language developed at Google around 2007. It is interesting to note that Hugo is one of the few static site generators that highlight the wide applicability of static generators to web applications beyond a blog, including portfolios, and so on. Hugo also comes with a theme repository for the blogging engine and a guide on how to customize themes, which is available at the Hugo development home page shown in Figure 3-5. The breakdown of Hugo can be described as follows:

- **Core language:** Go
- **Templating language:** Go Templates
- **License:** SimPL-2.0

Figure 3-5. *Hugo home page and quick start guides*

Just as with Pelican, to see Hugo in action, visit the following showcases:

- Steve Francia's blog: `http://spf13.com/`

- GopherCon's web site: `http://gophercon.com/`

Brunch

The next static generator is Brunch, which has been described as an ultrafast HTML5 build tool that can automate the generation of HTML5 ready sites. Brunch is different from the showcase thus far because it is fundamentally a build tool. That means Brunch can take directions and the ingredients and cook up a delicious meal for you. However, by the same logic, Brunch can also generate static sites because a similar set of instructions can be adopted from HTML5 builds to generate static blogs, too. Some of the features of Brunch are shown in Figure 3-6.

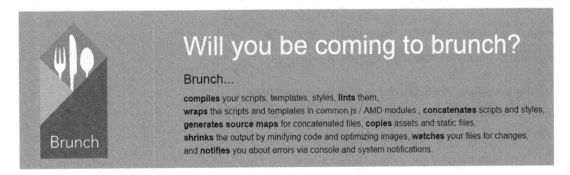

Figure 3-6. *Brunch home page and features*

The two main competitors of Brunch that are commonly used are Gulp and Grunt, both of which are discussed later in this book as crucial components of the integration to a static blog.

The breakdown of Brunch is as follows:

- **Core language:** JavaScript

- **Templating language:** Any JavaScript-based templates would work

- **License:** MIT

Given the feature set of Brunch applies more to the back end, it is hard to see it in action visually. However, there are several apps built on it and two showcase examples are also provided:

- Get Blimp: `http://www.getblimp.com/`

- Code Combat: `http://codecombat.com/`

After Brunch, the next two static generators that we will talk about are interesting in their own categories. We will be focusing on modularity and the crucial need for a modular static blog later on, but the following two generators have this principle built in.

Middleman

The next static site generator is Middleman. This generator has been described as a hand-crafted static generator for modern web development. Middleman is actually written in Ruby but uses a different templating system than Jekyll or Octopress. One of the main premises of Middleman is the ability to integrate new web technologies very easily. The home page of Middleman and the quick start guide is shown in Figure 3-7.

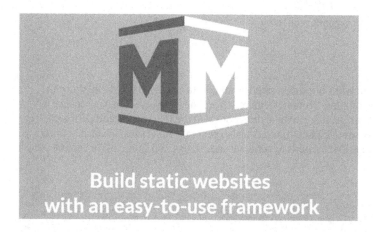

Figure 3-7. Middleman home page and development guide

The breakdown of Middleman can be described as follows:

- **Core language:** Ruby

- **Templating language:** ERB or Tilt

- **License:** MIT

Interestingly, popular companies such as MailChimp are using Middleman for static content hosting. To see Middleman in action, visit the following showcases:

- FronCube: `https://frontcube.com/`

- Lauren Dorman's blog: `https://laurendorman.io/`

Metalsmith

The second generator in the category of modularity is Metalsmith. This static generator takes modularity to an extreme where everything is a plug-in. From the simplest tasks to the complex ones, all the logic in Metalsmith is handled in small chunks of code called plug-ins. This static generator might be one of the most elegantly designed from a technical standpoint because everything is written in a modular fashion. However, for beginners, this would be a little complicated because it requires a deep understanding of the blog engine infrastructure. The home page for Metalsmith is shown in Figure 3-8.

METALSMITH

An extremely simple, *pluggable* static site generator.

Figure 3-8. *Metalsmith static site generator home page*

The breakdown of Metalsmith is as follows:

- **Core language:** JavaScript (Node.js to be more accurate)

- **Templating language:** HBT or any JavaScript-based templates would work

- **License:** MIT

There are a few enthusiasts who have used Metalsmith to completely refactor their blogs:

- Rob Ribeiro's blog: `https://azurelogic.com/`

- Robin Thrift's blog: `http://www.robinthrift.com/`

It must be noted that in the past few static site generators, the blogs or web applications are not what stands out as much as the back end, which is hard to see. Developers often have preferences, which we explore later in this book, in terms of picking a static site generator. The one that best fits their needs might not be the simplest to use, but the hope is that through this book, the reader gets the general idea behind most if not all static generators.

Nanoc

The last generator to be discussed in this section is Nanoc. Nanoc is not a very well-known static site generator, but it powers a few incredible web sites, so it is definitely worth mentioning. Nanoc, much like Jekyll, is also written in Ruby, which might be one of the many reasons it powers the developer's pages for GitHub. The home page for the static generator Nanoc is shown in Figure 3-9.

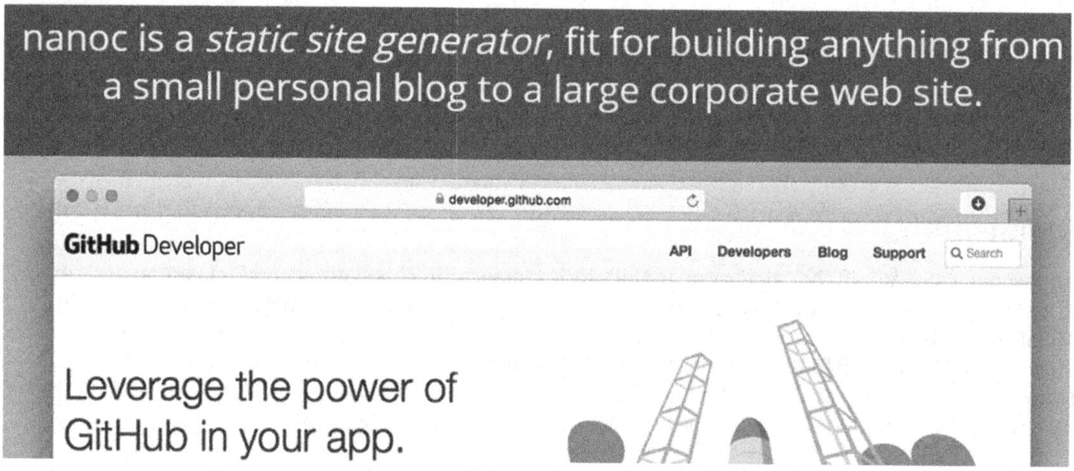

Figure 3-9. *Nanoc static generator home page*

The breakdown of Nanoc can be described as follows:

- **Core language:** Ruby
- **Templating language:** eRuby
- **License:** MIT

There are a few enthusiasts who have used Nanoc to completely refactor their blogs:

- FOSDEM 2015 page: `https://fosdem.org/`
- GitHub Developer page: `https://developer.github.com/`

Summary

In this showcase, several of the most prominent static site generators were presented and the key objective in doing so is to show the reader what is out there in the broader landscape aside from just Jekyll, which is the focus of this book. We will be talking extensively about Jekyll from here on, but the interested reader can come back to this chapter after going through some of the advanced concepts to decide if they want to make their own blog with a different static site generator.

The amazing side effect of having so many static site generators is that for those who come from a different programming background than Ruby, there is definitely a generator out there to match their tastes. Moreover, most of the principles discussed in this book can be translated to other static generators and even made to work in a similar fashion. The most exciting aspect of having different generators is the application to various tasks for which you can use a static web site. It might be surprising to some just how widely applicable static web sites can be for simple tasks, and we explore more of those applications and use cases.

Let's briefly review what we discussed here: We started by talking about the inspiration for static site generators from the static Web. We then explored the design principles behind Jekyll as seen by Tom Preston-Werner, and finally we showcased some of the most popular static site generators available in different languages. Looking ahead, we jump into Jekyll and start with the basics required to have a static blog with Jekyll.

Further Reading

1. Different types of licenses as explained by CodingHorror:
   http://blog.codinghorror.com/pick-a-license-any-license/

2. Jekyll home page: http://jekyllrb.com/

3. Tom Preston-Werner's blog: http://tom.preston-werner.com/

REVIEW

The data for static site generators was taken from https://www.staticgen.com/

1. **Search Task:** Find a popular repository containing Jekyll Themes.

2. **Search Task:** List five of the most popular Jekyll plug-ins.

3. **Search Task:** Find which themes from Octopress are most commonly used.

4. List the three core components of a static site generator that we discussed.

5. How do these components allow for greater flexibility?

6. What are some of your concerns about Jekyll and other static site generators just from a first glance?

7. What is one personal project that you can think about right now that might benefit from a static web site?

8. Why do you think it would benefit from a static blog page?

9. Software licensing plays an important role for developers. From what we discussed, which license would you pick and why?

10. If you already have a blog, what are some services that you currently use that you think might be missing in static sites?

11. Finally, do you think distraction-free reading for your reader and distraction-free writing for you are crucial components of blogging?

This concludes the introduction to static site generators. Our journey to building static blogs with Jekyll has just begun!

PART II

■ ■ ■

The Fundamentals

In this section, we focus on learning about the three most important tools that are part of a typical Jekyll workflow: Markdown, Liquid and Git. These three combined allow for most of the funtionality present in a static web site. We go through each of those components in detail, and talk about the how these technologies are implemented in a static blog. This section is heavily focused on teaching the basic principles behind the tools that are routinely used in a blog to create new styles or content. Without this early emphasis, it would become very difficult to create new projects or apply Jekyll to an idea and learn in depth about these tools. A functional introduction to the main features of these three web technologies is provided here and the section ends with a complete overview of the Jekyll file structure.

■ ■ ■

## CHAPTER 4

Fundamentals of Version Control

These guys here … They don't practice the fundamentals anymore.

—Uncle Drew

Jekyll is the static site generator that we focus on throughout this book. It is the most popular static generator in use today, with plenty of features to create a fully functional blog. This chapter begins the process of understanding the prerequisites for using Jekyll. We focus on how Jekyll parses source files to create static pages, the need to learn Markdown, the basics of version control, and an introduction to Git. These concepts and components are the backbone of Jekyll and we will be using them regularly in projects. The main focus of this chapter is version control because it becomes crucial in managing all the code associated with Jekyll projects. One of the best version control tools available is Git. We introduce Git and provide a walkthrough of the terminology and commands used in Git. We start by talking about Jekyll as a converter, and then move to using Markdown and writing posts in it. After that, we discuss version control in depth and present a few minitutorials on how to use Git. Finally, we end the chapter with a brief explanation of developer workflow and the advantages of adopting one for a Jekyll-powered blog.

Parsing Engine

Jekyll is essentially a parser that converts plain text content written in a special formatting language called Markdown into HTML. These content blocks get inserted into one or more templates to build the final output for a static page or post. Markdown is a styling language used to prepare written content such as blog posts in Jekyll that can eventually be converted into HTML. Markdown allows us to focus on content by using an easy-to-read and easy-to-write plain text format, which can then be converted to valid HTML. Jekyll does not come with any content, nor does it have any templates or design elements. This is a common source of confusion when getting started. Jekyll does not have a default style of organizing or rendering posts, so you have to create it or borrow from other open source themes.

How exactly does Jekyll use Markdown? The full story is more involved, but a high-level overview is shown in Figure 4-1. You can think of Jekyll as a cook trying to make a delicious new dish: He needs a recipe to make the dish and then the actual ingredients to use according to the recipe. The written content is analogous to ingredients that are used in a dish and templates in Jekyll are equivalent to the recipe that will tell Jekyll (the cook) how to make the dish. The cook also has a third level of instructions, and for Jekyll, that is the configuration file included in each project. This file dictates many features, such as how the web site should link internally and how those links should work in the final web site generated by Jekyll. Aside from the configuration files, there are two more components involved in the parsing: templates and include files. Both of these components, along with blog posts, make up the input that gets compiled by Jekyll. The output from Jekyll is a collection of HTML pages that make up your static site.

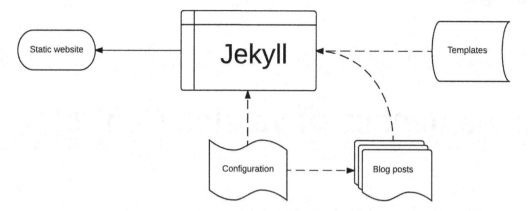

Figure 4-1. *Jekyll as a parsing engine. Three different components go into Jekyll as inputs: the configuration file for the web site, the blog posts, and the templates that organize the blog posts. The blog posts are mostly written content, the templates are mostly programmatic instructions to organize the blog posts, and the configuration file tells Jekyll how link the blog posts to each other and to the rest of the web site.*

Let's briefly talk about each of these components separately. The configuration file mostly contains Jekyll options and variables that need to be defined for compilation. The blog posts themselves are written in Markdown, which allows the blogger to write them without worrying about formatting. Jekyll converts the blog posts into HTML and renders them into a static page, as specified in the template. The template itself is mostly written in language developed for templating called Liquid, created by Shopify. Liquid is designed to provide programmatic access and to execute logic within template files without imposing any security risk on the hosting server. Jekyll uses Liquid to generate a page based on the structure specified in the template. The template leaves space for content blocks that are inserted into the static page as it is rendering. The final result is an HTML page that contains content and style elements as if the page was written from scratch. Now that we have an overall scheme of how Jekyll works, let's begin with Markdown.

Markdown

Markdown was originally created by John Gruber at Daring Fireball. The syntax was released as an open standard that GitHub adopted and then changed as they saw fit. We are not covering the original version, but instead this flavor of Markdown used by GitHub. This is also known as GitHub Flavoured Markdown (GFM), and it contains a few extra features not available in the original version of Markdown. As a consequence, some of the style conventions for formatting might not work if used outside of GitHub. Here is how Markdown fits in the bigger picture: To create style elements such as bold text, superscripts, bullet points, headings, and more, Markdown provides us with shorthand conventions that are easier to type out rather than using HTML tags. We rely on this shorthand to prepare our content and then Jekyll will render the shorthand into the appropriate HTML.

How does the conversion actually happen? Jekyll uses a markdown engine called `kramdown` that parses and converts any content prepared in Markdown into HTML, which can then be hosted. `kramdown` is itself a Ruby library, and GitHub now supports it as the official Markdown engine that Jekyll will be using. To use Markdown and learn how it works, we use an online editor called Dillinger available at `http://dillinger.io/` and shown in Figure 4-2. Dillinger uses two panes: The left pane is the source code and the right pane is the Markdown preview.

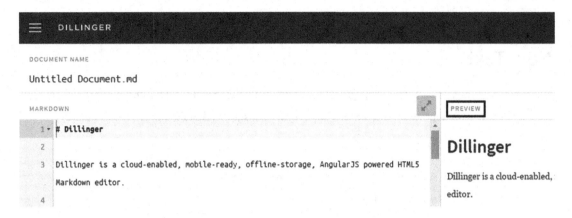

Figure 4-2. *The first section of the code is the plain text written in Markdown*

Markdown provides numerous style guidelines and conventions that can be used to format content, but the best way to understand how they are used is through an example. We first look at a passage written in Markdown, then preview what it renders and the HTML that is generated from Markdown. These three steps help illustrate just how easy it is to write blog posts using Markdown.

```
# New Text

Lorem Ipsum is simply dummy text of the printing and typesetting industry. Lorem Ipsum has
been the industry's standard dummy text ever since the 1500s, when an unknown printer took a
galley of type and scrambled it to make a type specimen book.

- Lorem Ipsum is simply dummy text (Two spaces to create bullets)
- Lorem Ipsum is simply dummy text 2
- Lorem Ipsum is simply dummy text 3

It has survived not only five centuries, but also the leap into electronic typesetting,
remaining essentially unchanged. It was popularised in the 1960s with the release of
Letraset sheets containing Lorem Ipsum passages, and more recently with desktop publishing
software like Aldus PageMaker including versions of Lorem Ipsum. As [John Gruber] writes on
the [Markdown site][df1]

> The overriding design goal for Markdown's
> formatting syntax is to make it as readable
> as possible. The idea is that a
> Markdown-formatted document should be
> publishable as-is, as plain text, without
> looking like it's been marked up with tags
> or formatting instructions.

  [john gruber]: <http://daringfireball.net>
  [df1]: <http://daringfireball.net/projects/markdown/>
```

This Markdown passage generates a preview that can be seen in Figure 4-3.

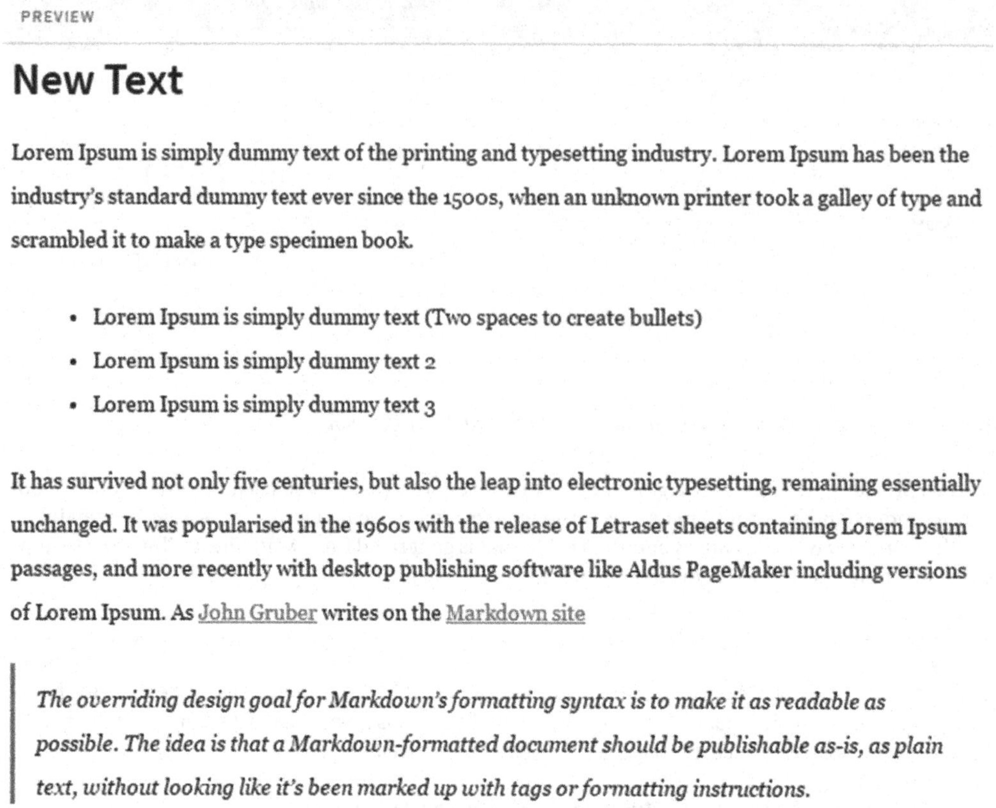

New Text

Lorem Ipsum is simply dummy text of the printing and typesetting industry. Lorem Ipsum has been the industry's standard dummy text ever since the 1500s, when an unknown printer took a galley of type and scrambled it to make a type specimen book.

- Lorem Ipsum is simply dummy text (Two spaces to create bullets)
- Lorem Ipsum is simply dummy text 2
- Lorem Ipsum is simply dummy text 3

It has survived not only five centuries, but also the leap into electronic typesetting, remaining essentially unchanged. It was popularised in the 1960s with the release of Letraset sheets containing Lorem Ipsum passages, and more recently with desktop publishing software like Aldus PageMaker including versions of Lorem Ipsum. As John Gruber writes on the Markdown site

> The overriding design goal for Markdown's formatting syntax is to make it as readable as possible. The idea is that a Markdown-formatted document should be publishable as-is, as plain text, without looking like it's been marked up with tags or formatting instructions.

Figure 4-3. Markdown preview of the content. This sample of text shows several important features such as headings, bullet points, paragraphs, hyperlinks, and block quotes. We saw the Markdown that rendered into this post and next we look at the HTML that was generated as the Markdown gets processed.

Finally, here is the HTML generated from that Markdown passage. Pay attention to the bold tags because all of those have shorthands that were used in the preceding passage. Would you really want to write all of these tags out when you just want to create a blog post? Markdown was created to write easily, without worrying about these tags.

```
<!DOCTYPE html>
<html>
<head>
  <meta charset="utf-8">
  <title>Markdown Preview</title>
  <style>
  </style>
</head>
<body id="preview">
  <h1><a id="New_Text_0"></a>New Text</h1>
  <p>Lorem Ipsum is simply dummy text of the printing and typesetting industry. Lorem Ipsum
  has been the industry's standard dummy text ever since the 1500s, when an unknown printer
  took a galley of type and scrambled it to make a type specimen book.</p>
```

```
<ul>
  <li>Lorem Ipsum is simply dummy text (Two spaces to create bullets)</li>
  <li>Lorem Ipsum is simply dummy text 2</li>
  <li>Lorem Ipsum is simply dummy text 3</li>
</ul>
<p>It has survived not only five centuries, but also the leap into electronic typesetting,
remaining essentially unchanged. It was popularised in the 1960s with the release of
Letraset sheets containing Lorem Ipsum passages, and more recently with desktop
publishing software like Aldus PageMaker including versions of Lorem Ipsum. As
<a href="http://daringfireball.net">John Gruber</a> writes on the
<a href="http://daringfireball.net/projects/markdown/">Markdown site</a></p>

<blockquote>
  <p>The overriding design goal for Markdown's formatting syntax is to make it as readable
  as possible. The idea is that a Markdown-formatted document should be publishable as-
  is, as plain text, without looking like it's been marked up with tags or formatting
  instructions.</p>
</blockquote>
</body>
</html>
```

This looks like plain HTML that we can understand and is ready to host on a server as a web page. This same type of conversion can be extended to different types of templates and one can design a layout for a blog post similar to a web page to be put in a collection of pages. In some sense, that's what a Jekyll blog is: a collection of web pages that are hosted like a static web site with JavaScript magic included.

You can see how easy it is to write content using Markdown, and you don't have to worry about using HTML or any tags to write it all. This is the real power of Jekyll: The content creator can focus on what matters to them in Markdown and the rest will be taken care of within the template. Once the template is written, there is no further need for editing each time new text needs to be converted. It must be noted here that just because a blog is static, that does not imply that the blog will be plain text and appalling. CSS and JavaScript can add a number of visually impressive features that we talk about in later chapters. Jekyll uses Markdown as the language to format text posts and it is incredibly easy to learn, so it is worth spending some time to get accustomed to the various style options available to the user.

We specifically focus on a flavour of Markdown called GFM. The reason for this will become clear later on, but in short, we will be using GitHub Pages as the publishing platform because it is incredibly easy to use. The advantages of this approach will become clear later on, but in practice, the versions of Markdown are not all that different. In the end, it is the notation that we need to focus on, and more precisely the idea that we can write posts or plain text with Markdown notation. It's more than just formatting; it becomes a natural extension of blogging once you have been using it for a long time. Once that feeling becomes natural, it is extremely easy to switch to a different flavor if needed. Let's look at the formatting features offered here.

```
Headers (The number of # determines the heading size)
# This is an <h1> tag
## This is an <h2> tag
###### This is an <h6> tag


Emphasis
*This text will be italic*
**This text will be bold**
```

Unordered List
```
* Item 1          (No spaces requied)
* Item 2
  * Item 2a       (Two spaces required)
  * Item 2b
```

Ordered List
```
1. Item 1
2. Item 2
3. Item 3
  * Item 3a       (Two spaces required)
  * Item 3b
```

Task List   (Available on GitHub and Dillinger)
```
- [x] This is a complete item
- [ ] This is an incomplete item
```

Images
```
![Cool Logo](/images/logo.png)
```

Format:

Links
```
http://GitHub.com - automatic!
```

Format: [Link name](http://website.com)

Block Quotes
```
We can all agree:
> This book is awesome
```

Format: Adding the > creates the blockquote.

Inline Code
```
def foo():
    if not bar:
        return True
```

Format: Add four spaces.

Block Code
````
```javascript
if (isAwesome){
  return true
}
```
````

Format: Use three ``` and then write the block of code.

This brief guide describes the commonly available features in Markdown as they are used to write blog posts. It might seem like a lot of complicated information, but to use Markdown, you just have to practice writing content with it. After a few times, it will become very natural. This guide is left here only as a reference so you can revisit it as you write more using Markdown.

■ **Note** A distinction needs to be made regarding the types of files where Markdown will be detected and compiled versus the types of files where Liquid will be detected and compiled.

Files that are written in Markdown are saved with the .md extension. This file extension is often interchangeable with .markdown but both extensions signify that the file contains Markdown content. Both types of files are picked up by kramdown to be compiled into HTML that can be hosted on a web server. Markdown is often used in conjunction with other technologies or libraries in Jekyll, such as Liquid. Most blog posts that are written in Markdown contain some Liquid code in the form of include files and front matter in YAML (which we talk about in the next chapter). In Jekyll you can define included files by placing them in the _includes folder. For all practical purposes, includes are not templates themselves; rather, they are just code snippets that get included into templates. In this way, you can include the code snippets in multiple templates as needed for the page overall.

On the other hand, template files are also mostly written in Liquid but saved as .html files. Even though Markdown will only be detected and compiled by kramdown if the files have an .md or .markdown extension, Liquid can work with both Markdown files and .html files in a Jekyll project.

Version Control

Version control or source control is the methodology of managing changes to a large set of documents. In the broader sense, it is the management of changes to documents, computer programs, large web sites, and other collections of information. The most important feature behind using version control is the ability to keep detailed and accurate histories. Every single change is noted and highlighted to differentiate from the previous version. Changes are usually identified by a number or letter code, termed the revision number, revision level, or simply revision. Each revision to the documents is associated with a timestamp and an ID of the person making the change. There are many popular version control software packages available, as well as different source management models, all with their own advantages, but we focus on a particular one called Git, shown in Figure 4-4. A few other popular version control systems in use include these:

- **Bazaar:** bazaar.canonical.com
- **SVN:** subversion.apache.org
- **Mercurial:** mercurial.selenic.com
- **CVS:** savannah.nongnu.org/projects/cvs
- **Perforce:** perforce.com (commercial software)

Figure 4-4. Git version control

Git was initially designed and developed by Linus Torvalds for Linux kernel development. His focus in creating it was on high-speed data queries and data integrity. For a project as large as the Linux kernel, it was absolutely necessary that the changes made be accessible for every revision possible. Another reason to pick Git is because GitHub uses it for its own back end and we use it to publish projects to GitHub. There are numerous other reasons for picking Git, but they are beyond the scope of this chapter.

To understand almost any version control system, we have to first go over some more terminology. We need to understand how the different components of a version control system work and the best way to do that is describing each one in some detail. We use most of these terms (in the context of Git) several times throughout a chapter, so they will eventually become familiar. The list of terminology is provided here just for reference.

- **Baseline:** An approved revision of a document or source file from which subsequent changes can be made locally.

- **Branch:** A set of files under version control can be branched so that two copies of those files can develop at different speeds or in different ways independently of each other.

- **Change:** A change represents a specific modification to a document under version control.

- **Change list:** A change list, change set, update, or patch refers to the set of changes made in a single commit.

- **Checkout:** A checkout is creation of a local working copy from the repository.

- **Clone:** Cloning means creating a repository containing the revisions from another repository.

- **Commit:** A commit is merging the changes made in the working copy back to the repository. The terms commit and checkin can also be used to describe the new revision that is created as a result of committing.

- **Conflict:** A conflict occurs when two or more parties make changes to the same lines of code in a particular document. When those changes are merged, the system is unable to reconcile them. A user must resolve the conflict by combining the changes or by selecting one set of changes in favor of the other.

- **Delta compression:** For efficient storage of the version control files and history, most revision control software uses delta compression, which retains only the differences between successive versions of files. Git heavily uses this to compress the files being stored or uploaded to a server.

- **Head:** Also sometimes called tip, this refers to the most recent commit, either to the trunk or to a branch.

- **Import:** The process of copying a local directory into the repository for the first time.

- **Initialize:** To create a new, empty repository.

- **Merge:** A merge or integration is an operation in which two sets of changes are applied to a file or set of files.

- **Pull, push:** These functions copy revisions from one repository into another. Pull is initiated by the receiving repository, whereas push is initiated by the source. Fetch can also be used to pull files from a remote repository.

- **Repository:** The repository is where files and their historical data are stored, often on a server or a remote location.

- **Resolve:** The act of user intervention to address a conflict between different changes to the same document.

- **Revision:** Also called version. A version is any change in form.

- **Tag:** A tag or label refers to an important snapshot in time, consistent across many files. These files at that point can all be tagged with a user-friendly, meaningful name or revision number.

- **Trunk:** The unique line of development that is not a branch also known as baseline, mainline, or master.

- **Update:** An update merges changes made in the repository by other people into the local working copy.

- **Working copy:** The working copy is the local copy of files from a repository, at a specific time or revision. All work done to the files in a repository is initially done on a working copy.

■ **Note** You are not required to know every one of these terms. The actual list of terminology from the Git documentation is much longer, but a minimal level of familiarity is needed before moving past this chapter. This shortened list is provided as a reference for you to return to at any point to look up a term as needed.

This list should provide the reader with a working knowledge of version control systems. Most of the features mentioned in the preceding list will be used in projects throughout the book. The concepts and ideas behind version control are more important than learning the terms listed. These ideas can be summarized in the following two points:

- All changes to the source code are made in small sets and accounted for in the history.

- Different versions of the same source code can be maintained independently, under the same change accountability system.

As mentioned earlier, the version control that we will be using is called Git. It is a fairly easy to use tool, and although it is tempting to cover the basics of Git here, there is a better visual resource. Before we get there, let's talk about the two different ways to access Git: The first one is through a graphical user interface (GUI) that allows one to easily see the commits and push new changes to the Master branch. The second option available for Git is through the command line. The command-line interface (CLI) is scary and confusing to many users. For that reason alone, there is a significant portion of a later chapter covering this topic and the use of the CLI. Even though it can be intimidating, the freedom that the CLI offers might far exceed what the GUI can do.

Additionally, most developers use Git through the command line. In the past, there weren't that many options available, but that all has changed, too. Now GitHub offers its own client to use Git easily and access its services, add commits, and sync them to GitHub with ease. The client is shown in Figure 4-5 and it also comes with a tutorial on how to use it effectively. It is available for both Mac OS X and Windows operating systems.

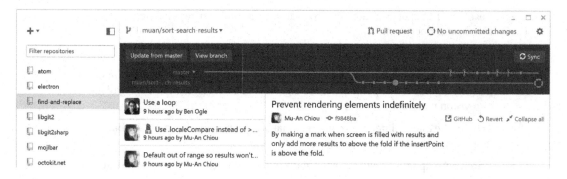

Figure 4-5. *GitHub client for desktop*

The second important resource for this chapter is the tutorial on Git, which was developed by Code School in collaboration with GitHub to teach users how to easily use Git for their personal projects. This tutorial is better than most others that are available online and the reader is strongly recommended to go through the tutorial web site shown in Figure 4-6. This tutorial allows you to put together the terminology discussed earlier in this chapter with practical exercises available through the short tutorial.

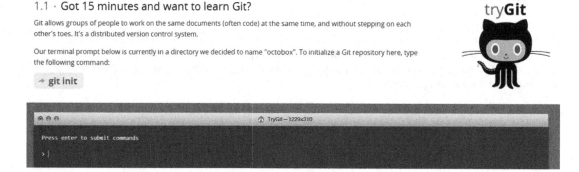

Figure 4-6. *Git tutorial available at* **https://try.github.io/**

This chapter is about mastering the fundamentals and there are three highlighted in this chapter: Markdown, version control concepts, and Git. The best aspect of these fundamentals is that you don't have to memorize anything. It's habitual, so after some practice, their use becomes natural. This is especially true for Markdown: Once you have been using it for long enough, it feels as if it is a natural extension of plain text; you no longer see formatting and plain text, you instead see output that would be generated by Markdown. Version control and Git go hand in -hand, so most of the terminology concepts discussed earlier are also directly applicable to using Git for personal projects.

Installing Git

This is a short section, but we need to talk about installing Git on your system sooner or later. We go through all three options here: Windows, Mac OS X, and Linux. Let's start with Linux because it is the easiest option: Look through your package manager in the distribution to install it. On a debian like distro, the installation would happen as follows:

```
$ sudo apt-get install git
```

This will pull all the dependencies along with Git and easily install the whole package for you, making it available.

The next platform is Windows, where you simply need to download the installer, which will install any required tools to use Git on Windows. The installer guides the user through the steps and preferences; an example is shown in Figure 4-7. The installer can be found on the Git-scm web site at `http://git-scm.com/download/win`. Finally, There is also an installer for Mac OS X available at `http://git-scm.com/download/mac`.

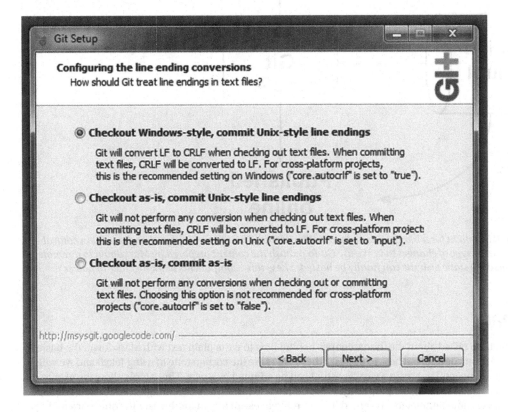

Figure 4-7. Git installation wizard in Windows

■ **Tip** The installation parameters are mostly fine as is, as we will not be using any of the advanced features. For a better visual introduction to installing Git, a good resource is available on Udacity at `https://www.udacity.com/wiki/ud775/install-git/install-git-windows`.

Jekyll Workflow

For a developer, it is important to think about workflows or find patterns that can explain a process. If we put together the three components that we talked about in this chapter, a workflow seems to emerge, as shown in Figure 4-8. The content for blog posts is written using Markdown and this content is managed by version control. This content and the whole static web site gets published online to GitHub using Git and it becomes available. Version control also maintains versions of the static web site as they are made available online one change set at a time. We will see how this interdependence becomes more technical as specific Git commands are introduced to handle this workflow in future chapters.

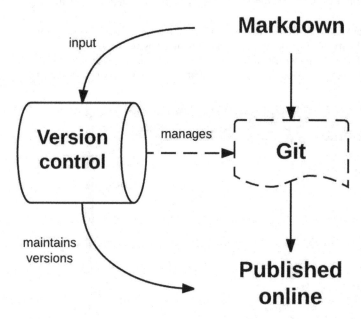

Figure 4-8. *All content for a blog post is written in Markdown. This content is placed under version control that manages any type of changes to it. We use Git to publish the content prepared by Markdown to a remote location where the static web site can finally be hosted. These three components work together to power a Jekyll blog.*

Summary

In this chapter, we talked about the fundamentals behind how to write plain text with Markdown, the basic concepts of version control, and how to use Git. These ideas are the cornerstone of using Jekyll and we will integrate these concepts later on in a workflow that can be adopted by a user. These tools allow the user to not be too focused on creating the proper styles of content and just focus on creating excellent new content. Finally, the syntax and parameters presented here as references are meant for the user to come back and revisit. After a few days of using these tools regularly, they will become very straightforward to work with for your personal projects.

Further Reading

1. **Git Documentation:** https://git-scm.com/documentation

2. **Git Reference:** http://gitref.org/

3. **Linux kernel Git Reference:** https://www.kernel.org/pub/software/scm/git/docs/user-manual.html

---

REVIEW

In this review, we focus on Markdown and Git. These are mostly small code exercises that should not take more than five minutes or so.

1. Create a numbered list in markdown, listing your favorite foods to eat.

2. Create h1, h2, and h3 headers in Markdown.

3. Read through Markdown syntax once again.

4. Read through the terminology for Git once again.

5. Work through as many Git Immersion labs as you can at http://gitimmersion.com/.

We end our journey for now with Git and Markdown, but they are not going away. In the next few chapters, we start to dive into Jekyll and revisit that template we talked about at the beginning of this chapter.

CHAPTER 5

■ ■ ■

Fundamentals of Style

Elegance is refusal.

—Coco Chanel

Well-designed user interfaces are the backbone of any personal project or blog. Whether a web site, application, or piece of software, creating the most intuitive connection between a human and a machine is key to the successful utilization of a digital product. Static generators might not seem to have the allure, but Jekyll allows for a surprisingly large amount of customization and styling.

In this chapter, we talk about how Jekyll handles various style components and the associated assets. A brief introduction to popular front-end packages such as Bootstrap, Foundation, and Sass is provided in this chapter. We also cover the compatibilities of various styles or packages and how to get started with your own projects using just those packages and using Jekyll later to put them all together in a workflow that you are already using. Finally, we analyze a few sample themes to show how the different style elements look when put together in a coherent manner with elegance.

What Is Style?

Style is what traverses through time. It becomes a personal brand that people associate with you. Over the long term, your personal style distinguishes you, even in a house full of artists. The appeal of blogs and projects built with Jekyll is the simplicity, the clean design, and the solid colors that enhance the foreground where the content is present. Additionally, the overall look is often focused on making the content stand out and removing as many distractions as possible, but that's not to say that you can't get creative with Jekyll. A huge part of the aesthetic within minimalistic styling is the reduction of distractions to give the reader the pleasure of enjoying your thoughts, visualizations, and the content you created. This removal of distractions is largely divided into two phases of blogging: distraction-free reading and distraction-free writing. Both are crucial components of the content creator's methodology and will help you discover a suitable workflow and your taste in presenting your content to the reader. Let's start with how these two ideas fit into the bigger picture of a blogging workflow.

Distraction-free writing is more important for the back end, which is to say that the content creator needs it, but the reader will not see it. For that reason, less emphasis is often given to creating an environment that a writer can efficiently navigate and feel comfortable using. The advantage of providing such an environment is that after a while, the tools used by the writer become a natural extension of his or her workflow, similar to writing blog posts in Markdown. Distraction-free writing is obviously very subjective, but the use of Markdown is critical for us in Jekyll projects to provide some additional directions to search for the right type of tools to use. Before we get into the tools, it might be beneficial to show what a great distraction-free writing interface would look like. This is borrowed from a blogging platform called Svbtle by Dustin Curtis. The interface is clean and works on a very unique yet natural idea: Write a thought down as the title of a post come back later to expand on the rest of the story and publish a full blog post. The Svbtle dashboard is shown in Figure 5-1.

V. Dhillon, *Creating Blogs with Jekyll*, DOI 10.1007/978-1-4842-1464-0_5

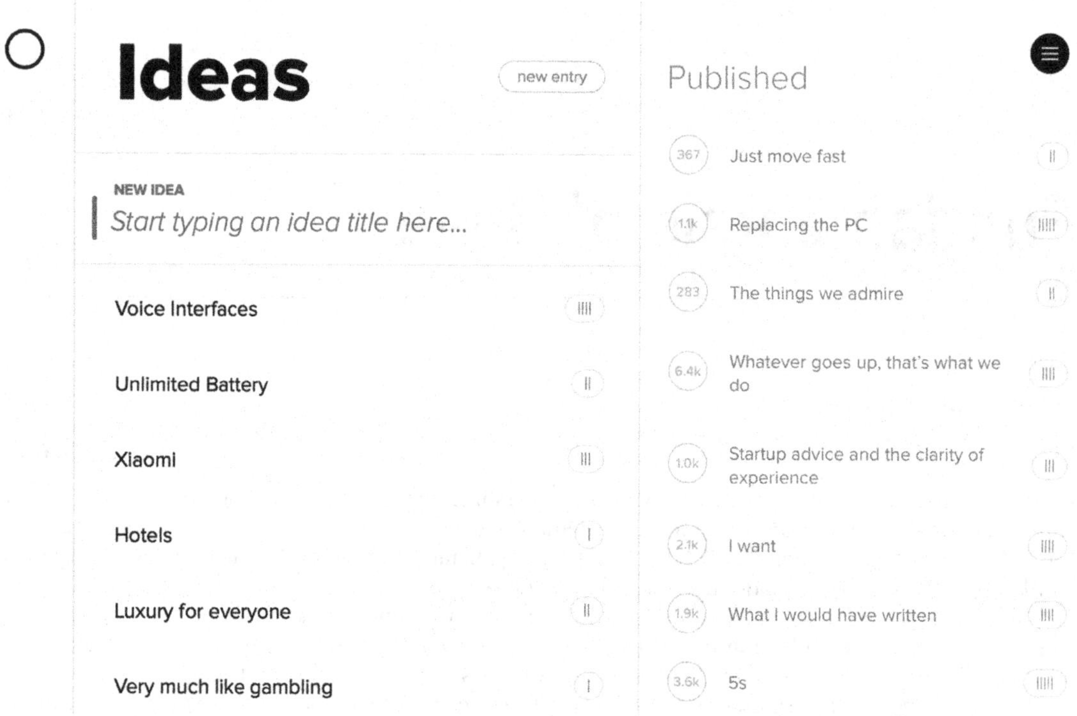

Figure 5-1. *Svbtle dashbaord providing distraction-free writing. Svbtle has this great feature but it also has many limitations, the main ones being the homogenity of the blogs: Almost all the blogs look the same, so showing off your own style is very difficult.*

In the next chapter, we will talk about how to implement a very similar feature in Jekyll. For now, this idea of writing a title and then coming back to it later to finish the post in a text editor is our main focus. In this sense, distraction-free writing can be divided into two more pieces: collecting ideas and an editor. Now that we boiled the idea down even further, we can start looking for tools. A good editor can also provide a method for collecting ideas, and superimposing Jekyll on that editor will give us a method to organize those ideas, much like Svbtle does. There are a few great editors available for writing and editing Markdown and all of them integrate very nicely into developer workflows that can be repeated to maximize the time available to create new content. We discuss the implications of this idea at length later in the book. Some of the most popular editors are listed here.

1. **Sublime Text 3:** This is a lovely text editor with a focus on ease of use and convenience through shortcuts. It has a lot of the shortcuts needed just for developers, so writing Markdown in Sublime is a very natural choice. After getting used to the basic environment of Sublime, it is easy to start working on the shortcuts and macros. Sublime can be found at `http://www.sublimetext.com/`. Additionally, a great visual guide to Sublime is present at Scotch: `https://scotch.io/bar-talk/the-complete-visual-guide-to-sublime-text-3-getting-started-and-keyboard-shortcuts`.

2. **Atom:** This editor was created by GitHub for web editing purposes. It has all the features that a modern web editor would, such as async updates, which allow one to see the updates done to code without reloading. Atom is based on Sublime so you still get all the package management goodness here. In particular, Atom has a package just for Markdown editing named Markdown-Writer for Atom. Atom can be found at `https://atom.io/`. Additionally, the full documentation for Atom can be found at `https://atom.io/docs`.

3. **StackEdit:** This editor is the simplest to use. StackEdit is an online Markdown editor with live preview of the text being written. It even lets you save the files on GitHub or Dropbox to update the blog remotely. There are some minor differences between the online editor and GFM, but the core features work almost the same. The most remarkable feature of StackEdit is that it allows you to edit on the fly and there is no need for a local install. The live preview makes it very easy to make quick edits to your blog posts if needed. StackEdit can be found at `https://stackedit.io/`.

4. **Notepad++:** This is one of the oldest and simplest code editors to use for Markdown and numerous other languages. It is similar to Notepad in terms of the interface but it is very lightweight and supports full-fledged syntax highlighting, tabbing, and all the advanced features you would expect in a resource-heavy editor. This editor does not have the same live preview as the previous three mentioned in this list, but it does provide a starting point for someone who just wants to write Markdown properly without worrying about any of the other advanced features. Notepad++ is available at `https://notepad-plus-plus.org/`.

■ **Tip**　For a novice, the best editor to start with would be StackEdit, to practice Markdown or any of the exercises from the last chapter. It's an online editor that requires minimal installation effort. Another online integrated development environment (IDE) to consider would be Codeanywhere. For the next best option, Notepad++ or Sublime would work great. Finally, for more serious web development, as we explore later in the book, the best option is to use Atom with the appropriate packages installed.

The other side to the reduction of distractions is distraction-free reading. This aspect of a project or blog is far more subjective and fewer recommendations can be made, but we critique some themes later on in this chapter. The most important part of distraction-free reading is this balance between being bland and being interesting. If a blog's appearance is too minimal, it could look like the blogger is just being lazy. If there is too much theming, it risks confusing the reader, causing them to just leave the site. A clean interface is crucial to surviving that first contact, but distraction-free reading is mostly reflected in the theme choice or theme construction. With some exceptions, it is not always difficult to remove clutter from a blog theme that was forked from an original design. In some cases, a theme has certain parameters for frame sizes or sidebars that make it incredibly difficult to remove those design flaws, but crafting a theme from scratch gives you the most freedom and control. Making a theme from scratch is a difficult and time-consuming process, but definitely worth the effort. In the upcoming sections, we introduce a few frameworks that can be used to create a new theme to be used as the front end for Jekyll. Although this discussion is short, it does aim to provide a functional introduction to the frameworks so that the reader could pick them up with ease in the future.

So where can front-end frameworks be used for style elements in Jekyll? Two out of three main components of the blog can be powered by stylistic front-end frameworks, as shown in Figure 5-2.

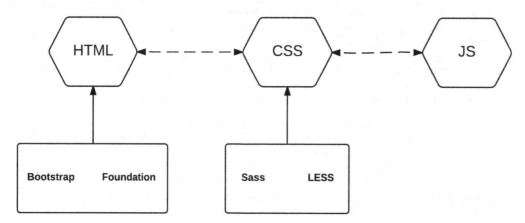

Figure 5-2. *The three components of a blog: HTML, CSS, and JS. HTML is the core element of the web site and both Bootstrap and Foundation are large libraries that work directly with HTML. The second component is CSS, which tells the HTML elements how to look. Sass and LESS are two preprocessors that can be used to power it. Finally, the last component is JavaScript (JS), which offers interactivity to a web site. We won't be using any style elements with the JS.*

Bootstrap

The first set of front-end packages that we examine is Bootstrap, built by Twitter. This package is a very powerful framework that makes rapid prototyping very easy. Rapid prototyping is the practice of reducing an idea to a tangible mockup in a short time, and Bootstrap has all the features necessary to make this happen. In this section, we cover how to use Bootstrap and the background magic that makes this framework so powerful. The other frameworks use similar principles, so we only cover them for Bootstrap, which is arguably one of the most widely used front-end frameworks. The purpose of this section is to provide a short tutorial so that the reader can understand the fundamentals of using Bootstrap to create a theme. In essence, Bootstrap is extending HTML to do more complex tasks such as making a drop-down menu as in just a few lines of code.

```
<div class="dropdown">
  <button class="btn btn-default dropdown-toggle" type="button" id="dropdownMenu1" data-
toggle="dropdown" aria-haspopup="true" aria-expanded="true">
    Dropdown
    <span class="caret"></span>
  </button>
  <ul class="dropdown-menu" aria-labelledby="dropdownMenu1">
    <li><a href="#">Action</a></li>
    <li><a href="#">Another action</a></li>
```

```
      <li><a href="#">Something else here</a></li>
      <li><a href="#">Separated link</a></li>
    </ul>
</div>
```

The result of this small segment of code is in Figure 5-3. Notice the related style elements to the div class were imported automatically. This is one of the most powerful features of Bootstrap: The default styling provides a fast solution to completing a first-version mockup of a project. The previously noted small segment of code is called a component in Bootstrap, where each component is a small template of code that can pasted as is from the components example to create an instance on a web page. The components documentation is available at http://getbootstrap.com/components/.

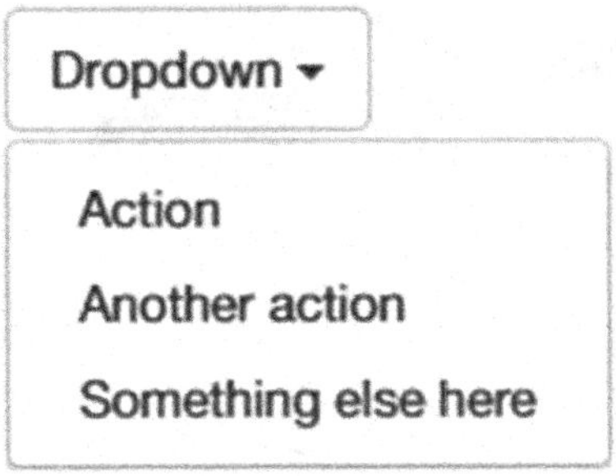

Figure 5-3. *Drop-down element generated by the code in Bootstrap. The default package comes preinstalled with several new templates and icons that can be easily used just by calling different class names.*

In the preceding code, it is easy to see how the Drop-down button and the menu are created in just a few lines of code. The div class drop-down and the drop-down-menu class are predefined snippet templates that come with Bootstrap. The interesting aspect of Bootstrap is the documentation available on the web site, which provides the code snippets for these small templates so a user can simply copy and paste the HTML template snippets into a blank page with the Bootstrap files to get a new project up and running in a very short amount of time. Bootstrap is available as an archive that can be downloaded from the web site to be used as a template. This template contains all the code snippets available to Bootstrap. A complete page showing the features and templates in Bootstrap is shown in Figure 5-4. These templates are available at http://getbootstrap.com/components/.

■ **Tip**   New front-end components might become available soon with the release of Bootstrap 4.

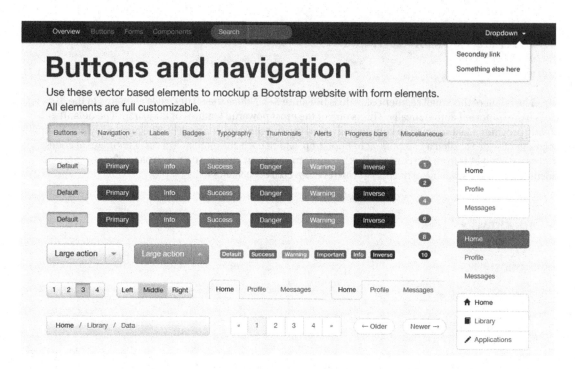

Figure 5-4. *Bootstrap template and all the features available presented on a single page*

To get the started with this new framework, let's create a theme for a blog. This will be a very simple theme only using a few components of Bootstrap. In the next few chapters, we revisit this theme to show you how to apply Jekyll to it and use it. There are two ways to download and start working with Bootstrap:

- To download the compiled version of Bootstrap, use this link: http://getbootstrap.com/getting-started/#download

- The second method is to import the required files directly into your HTML. MaxCDN hosts the latest compiled versions of Bootstrap that can be used. We will be using this approach.

Create a new empty file and save it as bootstrap.html. Let's get the basic HTML structure going for starters:

```
<html>

<head>

<!-- Bootstrap imports will go here -->

</head>

<body>

</body>
</html>
```

This is the initial template. Now we can start filling this out with the magic of Bootstrap and the components available within. Here are the MaxCDN import statements that we need to access the components.

```
<html>

<head>

<!-- Latest compiled and minified CSS -->
<link rel="stylesheet" href="https://maxcdn.bootstrapcdn.com/bootstrap/3.3.5/css/bootstrap.
min.css">

<!-- Optional theme -->
<link rel="stylesheet" href="https://maxcdn.bootstrapcdn.com/bootstrap/3.3.5/css/bootstrap-
theme.min.css">

<!-- Latest compiled and minified JavaScript -->
<script src="https://maxcdn.bootstrapcdn.com/bootstrap/3.3.5/js/bootstrap.min.js"></script>

</head>

<body>

</body>
</html>
```

From here on in this tutorial, the rest of the code will go in the <body> tag. Let's start with a simple top bar to title this blog.

```
<p class="navbar-text">First Test Jekyll Blog</p>
```

Now let's add some navigation elements to this top bar.

```
<ul class="nav nav-tabs">
  <li role="presentation" class="active"><a href="#">Home</a></li>
  <li role="presentation"><a href="#">About</a></li>
  <li role="presentation"><a href="#">Contact Me</a></li>
</ul>
```

After the top bar, let's make an introductory banner; Bootstrap calls it a jumbotron. The jumbotron in its original form will take up the entire page, but this makes the banner look uneven, so we need to constrain it using the container class. This will force the jumbotron to appear within a nice rounded corner container.

```
<div class="jumbotron">

  <div class="container">

  <h1>Hello, world!</h1>
  <p> This is our first blog theme that we will be using to practice how to use Bootstrap
  and put it together with Jekyll. </p>
  <p><a class="btn btn-primary btn-lg" href="#" role="button">Learn more</a></p>

  </div>

</div>
```

Now that we have an intro banner, let's add some placeholders for the blog posts. We can use the panel components to organize the blog. We will be using the panel component that has a heading in it.

```
<div class="panel panel-default">
  <div class="panel-heading">Daily Blog Posts</div>
  <div class="panel-body">

  <a href="#">Unread Posts <span class="label label-primary">40</span> </a>
  <h3>Example heading <span class="label label-default">New</span></h3>

  </div>
</div>
```

This component gives us a panel, and we can have as many panels on the page as we want. All we need to do is add a new component and change the parameters accordingly to fit the new panel.

```
<div class="panel panel-default">
  <div class="panel-heading">Resources</div>
  <div class="panel-body">

  <a href="#">Useful Links: <span class="label label-primary">2</span> </a>
  <h3> <a href="http://jekyllrb.com/">Example heading </a> <span class="label label-
default">Jekyll Docs</span></h3>

  </div>
</div>
```

Finally, with the second panel done, we will add pagination to allow for an easy reading mode and organization of the posts.

```
<nav>
  <ul class="pager">
    <li><a href="#">Previous</a></li>
    <li><a href="#">Next</a></li>
  </ul>
</nav>
```

This completes our tutorial of the sample blog page. The best part of it all is that all the components that were presented in this tutorial were available almost directly line-by-line on the Bootstrap web site. Only minimal edits were needed. The final result of the Bootstrap code is shown in Figure 5-5.

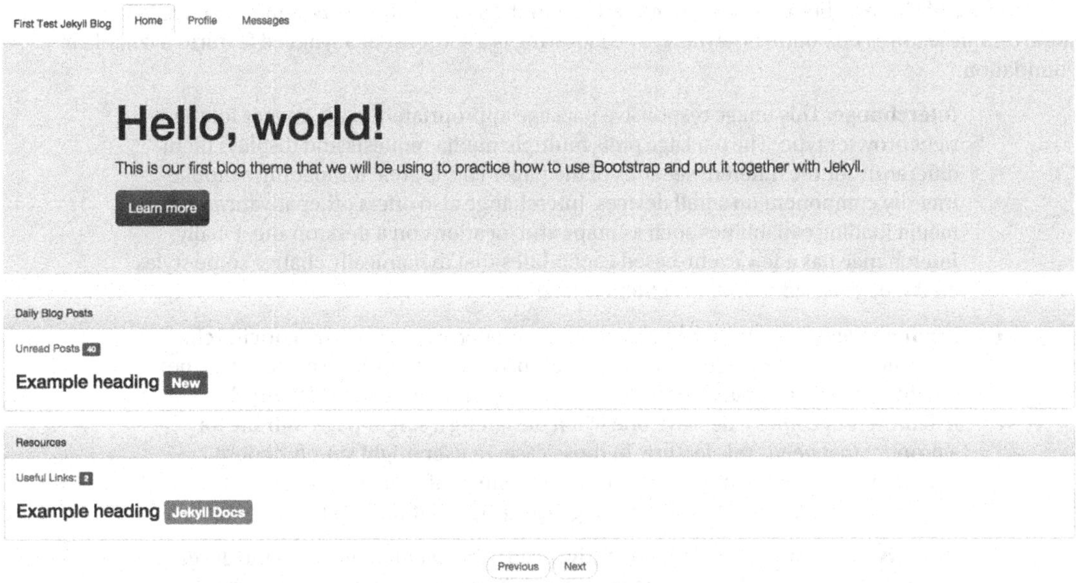

Figure 5-5. *Completed Bootstrap blog page created from basic components available with the framework*

The completed code for this sample web page is available with this chapter for ease of access, but readers are encouraged to replicate the components directly from the Bootstrap web site to use them in their own projects.

■ **Note**   To answer the question of how the sample web page we created will actually become a Jekyll theme, we have to consider some more details about how Jekyll works, particularly handlebars. We discuss these at length in the following chapter. In brief, we need a block of code to allow some sort of programmatic access to all the blog posts made and then we can loop through the collection of blog posts and show them under the appropriate panel. This block of code is a handlebars component that can turn a normal theme into a Jekyll-injectable blog template.

Foundation

The second framework that we cover is Foundation by Zurb. In some sense, Foundation is a more stripped down framework as compared to Bootstrap. It provides the user with all the essentials that one can find in Bootstrap, but there are some minor differences. Choosing between Bootstrap and Foundation is like choosing between dark and milk chocolate: One framework isn't necessarily better than the other, they just pair well with different things, and people tend to develop personal preferences. One of the most crucial parts of a front-end framework is an easy-to-use grid system. It's the core feature that enables designers and developers to rapidly prototype layouts and make quick changes without moving other elements in the grid. Foundation comes with built-in form validation from Abide, whereas Bootstrap doesn't have this feature. Foundation has always had a slightly more advanced grid layout and grid system. It was the first major framework to go responsive and was also the only big mobile-first framework until other packages caught up. It might be a matter of personal preference but even to this day, Foundation does have a more efficient grid system.

In terms of features, both the frameworks are about the same; however, Foundation does have some unique features not found elsewhere. The following is a short list of advanced features available in Foundation.

- **Interchange:** This image responsive package appropriately loads images for the right browser type. The package pulls multiple media requests and displays them differently for the different sections of the page. This is great for loading a mobile-friendly component on small devices. Interchange also offers other advanced media loading capabilities such as maps and locations on a desktop site. Finally, Interchange has a few event-based capabilities that dynamically change some styles on the page based on which content is loaded.

- **Pricing charts:** For any product or service with tier-based pricing, a pricing chart is perfect. Foundation allows you to make a pricing table with ease in a `container` for any subscription-based product. This is not a unique or novel feature, but it definitely becomes a decisive one when designing a single-page web site for a product that needs this feature. In those cases, a user might simply choose Foundation over Bootstrap when picking a theme or if designing a new theme, because it allows them to make the single-page application faster.

- **Grid system:** Foundation has a very advanced grid system that allows the developer to place elements on the web page responsively and with ease. A great example of the grid system is the Skeleton theme. This is a bare-bones theme written in Foundation that can be extended for use in personal projects and is available as a plug-in for various blogging engines like Jekyll.

- **Page tours (Joyride):** This is a feature unique to Foundation, and it would be incredibly difficult to replicate in Bootstrap without extensive coding. Joyride allows the user to provide a guided tour of a particular page along with all the noteworthy sections where the user can stop and be provided specific instructions on how to continue. This can extend to modals, as well, for providing on-screen instructions and navigation. An example of Joyride in action can be seen on the Foundation sample documentation at `http://foundation.zurb.com/docs/components/joyride.html`.

- **Off-canvas navigation:** This is another unique feature that many blogs have available. In these off-canvas elements, the navigation menus are positioned outside of the normal view of the web page and they slide in when activated, often by a click trigger as shown by the box in Figure 5-6. This type of off-canvas navigation is often very attractive in allowing for distraction-free reading of the blog post or the content. The navigation is easily available to the reader at any time, without the distraction of being a sidebar.

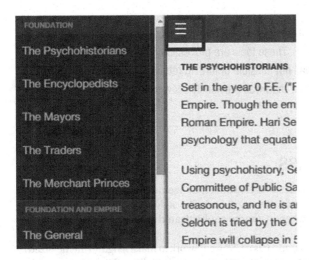

Figure 5-6. *Off-canvas navigation being demonstrated in Foundation.The sidebar only becomes active once the button shown in red is clicked. A second click makes the sidebar vanish, allowing for more reading real estate.*

These features not only make Foundation an attractive platform, but also incredibly well suited for various single-page showcases. If one of the previously mentioned features is suitable for a project, it would make a lot of sense to just start the project with Foundation. Much like Bootstrap, this framework also comes with a package that can be downloaded and used as a starting template. In the remainder of this section, we spend some time talking about the applications and practical uses of Foundation.

The mobile responsiveness and fast loading speed of Foundation-based assets make it very suitable for e-mail templates and mass e-mailing. In fact, MailChimp actually offers several Foundation-based templates in the mass e-mailing designer to send quick and easy messages. Foundation has been instrumental in creating many other e-mail templates. The team behind Foundation, Zurb, is also very serious about creating functional and responsive e-mail. Recently, Zurb released a special CSS framework called Ink to write HTML e-mails compatible across all the e-mail clients. This is usually not a problem for small or personal projects. However, alternative e-mail clients become a relevant concern when the user base grows large enough and a significant portion of the audience uses an e-mail client. Ink can make the process of supporting different clients a breeze by providing a uniform language that the various clients can all understand. The documentation for Ink can be found at Zurb's web site at `http://zurb.com/ink/docs.php`.

Here is a short list of the clients supported by Ink:

- Apple Mail (Desktop and iOS)

- Outlook (2000, 2002, 2003, 2007, 2010, 2011, 2013)

- Thunderbird

- Android

- Gmail (Desktop, Mobile, iOS, Android)

- AOL Mail

- Hotmail and Outlook.com

■ **Note** In the following two sections, we do not talk about styling frameworks, but instead tools used to manage the implementation of styling elements in CSS. These tools are processors that allow us to write manageable CSS in a more advanced fashion that was not possible before. In return, we can implement new functionality and control it in a more fine-tuned manner than was previously allowed. The two processors we discuss are Sass and LESS.

Style Sheet Management: Sass

The purpose of this section is to discuss the importance of style sheet management using Sass, which has been adopted by many Jekyll themes, in favor of writing plain CSS files. The style elements available to a blog are present in the CSS files, but they can be written in a more sophisticated and easy to read manner using Sass.

Sass stands for Syntactically Awesome Style Sheets, and it is a CSS framework to make lengthy (theme-sized) CSS manageable. Sass is actually a preprocessor for CSS, much like PHP to the Web. It allows the use of many features that are not well defined in CSS such as variables, nesting, and inheritance. These properties are mostly found in object-oriented programming to modularize a project and make it manageable, and in Sass, they exist for the same purpose. The following example illustrates the use of Sass.

CSS code

```
body {
  font: 100% Helvetica, sans-serif;
  color: #333;
}
```

The Sass implementation

```
$font-stack:    Helvetica, sans-serif
$primary-color: #333

body
  font: 100% $font-stack
  color: $primary-color
```

It is easy to see the value of global variables that can be reused throughout the following CSS code. This is only one small feature of Sass, and already it makes the implementation easier to read and manage. Along with global variables, another very useful feature present in Sass is nesting of code. This allows for reduction of tags in the CSS with additional readability and management of large projects.

CSS code

```
nav ul {
  margin: 0;
  padding: 0;
  list-style: none;
}
```

```
nav li {
  display: inline-block;
}

nav a {
  display: block;
  padding: 6px 12px;
  text-decoration: none;
}
```

Sass code

```
nav
  ul
    margin: 0
    padding: 0
    list-style: none

  li
    display: inline-block

  a
    display: block
    padding: 6px 12px
    text-decoration: none
```

■ **Tip** It must be noted that Sass uses two types of syntax. The main syntax of Sass is known as SCSS (for Sassy CSS). SCSS files use the extension `.scss`. The second, older syntax is known as the indented syntax (or just Sass). Instead of brackets and semicolons, it uses the indentation of lines to specify blocks. This is the syntax we use in the code shown here to demonstrate the concepts in an easy-to-read manner.

In the preceding code, just the proper use of indentation allowed us to nest the ul, li, and a tags. This not only makes the CSS more readable, but the style elements also start to make intuitive sense, just as they would apply to the HTML page in a similar hierarchy. The next feature in managing CSS is modularity, especially dividing long code into smaller and manageable files. There is an option already in CSS to split files and write the code in that manner, but it has a drawback: When the split of files happens in CSS, it creates a new HTTP request to be served. This could slow down web page loading speed if there is a large enough number of files. Sass introduces the notion of modularity somewhat differently: It uses the import function currently available through CSS, but instead of requiring several HTTP requests, Sass takes the files requested to be imported and combines them all into a single CSS file before serving it to the web browser. This is simply a design feature inherent to the job of a preprocessor like Sass. The single file can be served easily without any noticeable delays; at the same time, it allows the user to manage the code in an organized manner. This preprocessing capability does not actually introduce any new CSS for the most part; it only makes what is currently available easy to write and manage over the long term. Many developers have switched over their core CSS to Sass, which is processed to generate the new CSS as needed. The development cycle is also has a faster turnaround rate with Sass. The following example illustrates the import function.

Filename: _reset.sass

```
html,
body,
ul,
ol
  margin:  0
  padding: 0
```

Filename: base.sass

```
@import reset

body
  font: 100% Helvetica, sans-serif
  background-color: #efefef
```

Generated complete CSS

```
html, body, ul, ol {
  margin: 0;
  padding: 0;
}

body {
  font: 100% Helvetica, sans-serif;
  background-color: #efefef;
}
```

In this example, we can see the two files reset and base.sass containing separate code written in Sass syntax were merged together to generate a single file containing the appropriate code. The file to be imported needs the file name of the _filename.sass format. In the same manner, several smaller files can be created to hold the appropriate CSS, which can then be put together in a single file before serving them to a web server. This feature is used frequently in themes such as Skeleton, which was previously mentioned, and many other popular ones. Finally, in this section let's talk about inheritance. In object-oriented programming, this is often the most powerful feature, allowing for abstraction of a large project into smaller code files. In Sass, inheritance allows us to write fewer lines of code for the same elements and condense redundant code into fewer lines. The following example illustrates that.

Sass code
```
.message
  border: 1px solid #ccc
  padding: 10px
  color: #333
```

```
.success
  @extend .message
  border-color: green

.error
  @extend .message
  border-color: red

.warning
  @extend .message
  border-color: yellow
```

CSS generated

```
.message, .success, .error, .warning {
  border: 1px solid #cccccc;
  padding: 10px;
  color: #333;
}

.success {
  border-color: green;
}

.error {
  border-color: red;
}

.warning {
  border-color: yellow;
}
```

The use of global variables, nesting, modularization, and inheritance are only few of the advances available in Sass, but they make writing CSS easy, manageable, and fun. Many Jekyll themes have embraced the use of Sass by refactoring the current CSS. This allows for a more dynamic writing style and long-term management of the web site. The compartmentalization offered by Sass also allows the developer to reflect any changes in style elements over a smaller scale and not across the whole web site. Sass is also more broadly preferred over LESS simply because Sass allows you to write reusable methods and use logic statements like conditionals and loops.

Style Sheet Management: LESS

A variant of Sass, LESS is also a preprocessor compiling modified CSS into regular CSS. The purpose of this section is to showcase how an alternative to Sass can be used in place of CSS to manage the style elements for the Jekyll-powered blog. The main objective of LESS is to make the user write less CSS as compared to before. The syntax and features are similar to Sass, but the two differ in the packages built by the open source community. The core advantage of using Sass versus LESS is the installation procedure: Sass uses Ruby gems, whereas LESS uses JavaScript so it can easily load in the browser without any additional software. We cover Ruby and the gems both in great detail later in this book. One of the most favorable aspects of using LESS is the documentation. Many developers prefer the documentation for LESS as a compiler over the docs for Sass. The two preprocessors are very much alike and syntactically, one of the major differences is the use of @ for defining variables in LESS, whereas Sass uses $ for variables. The syntax is largely the same in both of them, as the following example illustrates.

LESS syntax

```less
@darkblue: #00008B;
    @border-color: #CCCCCC; //gray
    @base-font-size: 16px;

    body {
        font-size: @base-font-size;
    }
    header {
      border-bottom: 1px solid @border-color;
    }
    a {
      color: @darkblue;
    }
```

Compiled CSS

```css
    body {
        font-size: 16px;
    }
    header {
      border-bottom: 1px solid #CCCCCC;
    }
    a {
      color: #00008B;
    }
```

LESS is great for beginners because it's really easy and quick to set it up. It's very similar to plain CSS, so writing it is intuitive. Compared to CSS, everything about LESS is very easy and user-friendly. However, when a project starts to become more complicated, new features that might be more difficult to implement in LESS require a more powerful preprocessor like Sass. The biggest advantage provided by Sass is actually another package called Compass, which is an open source library of common tasks that are needed to run and maintain CSS assets. Compass also lets you add an external framework like Foundation or Bootstrap on top. This means you can easily harness all the power of your favorite framework without having to deal with the mess of using multiple tools.

■ **Tip** It must be noted that both Sass and LESS work at the level of style elements and managing CSS assets. Neither of the frameworks is specific to front-end packages such as Bootstrap or Foundation. They work equally well with either package, but preferences guide developers into making different choices. In the case of Compass, the tool only allows pulling in different packages with ease. That being said, LESS is a great framework to learn the basics; for more serious projects, it makes more sense to use Sass because of the packages available.

In larger projects, a tiny error can cause chaos for the entire project. An advantage of using LESS as training wheels is the ability to debug errors easily through the code. Sass does not have the same debugging features as LESS and often the debugging messages returned are not helpful. LESS notifications are well-presented and also appear to be spot on with the errors. The main difference between LESS and other CSS precompilers is that LESS allows real-time compilation via less.js by the browser. The syntax of LESS is similar to writing CSS itself and the framework keeps closest to the same conventions. The compilers involve some sort of download and setup for installation, and these tasks might intimidate a beginner, especially if the setup is more extensive. One alternative is to use an online service that can use the preprocessors in the cloud, without any need for local downloads or installs. CodePen is a popular service that offers many other code-demo services along with offering both Sass and LESS preprocessors accessible online. The user can configure the proper settings to use the appropriate preprocessor as shown in Figure 5-7. This allows for the compilation and generation of the complete CSS that can be served as a web asset.

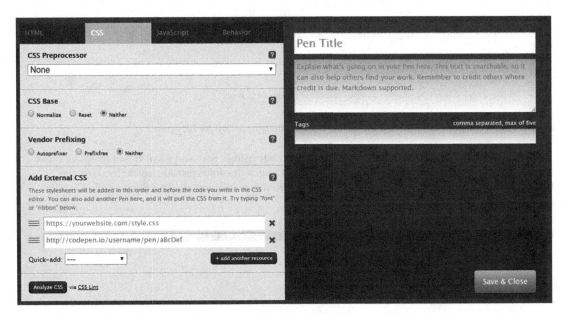

Figure 5-7. *CSS configuration panel on CodePen. In the CSS Preprocessor drop-down list, LESS, Sass, and SCSS syntaxes are all available. More details are available at* http://blog.codepen.io/documentation/editor/using-css-preprocessors/.

Jekyll Themes

So far in this chapter, we have seen a lot of style elements that create different themes but not a complete product. In the upcoming chapters, we dive deeper into the code presented in this chapter and complete that Bootstrap theme. In this section, we look at some completed themes and try to dissect the various elements being used to create those themes. These themes are simplistic, but they accomplish both our original goals: distraction-free reading and writing. All the themes covered in this section are open source and available for readers as inspiration to use later on in their own themes. One of the best repositories of Jekyll themes is available at http://jekyllthemes.org/.

The web site contains several themes created with an intricate combination of many frameworks that we cover in a later chapter. We examine a few themes that are similar to the projects that we will be working on later in the book. These themes not only provide inspiration for new features, but also give hints as to what style elements should be kept in mind while designing a Jekyll theme. The first theme examines what a Bootstrap-based finished product would look like. This theme, called Whitepaper, is shown in Figure 5-8.

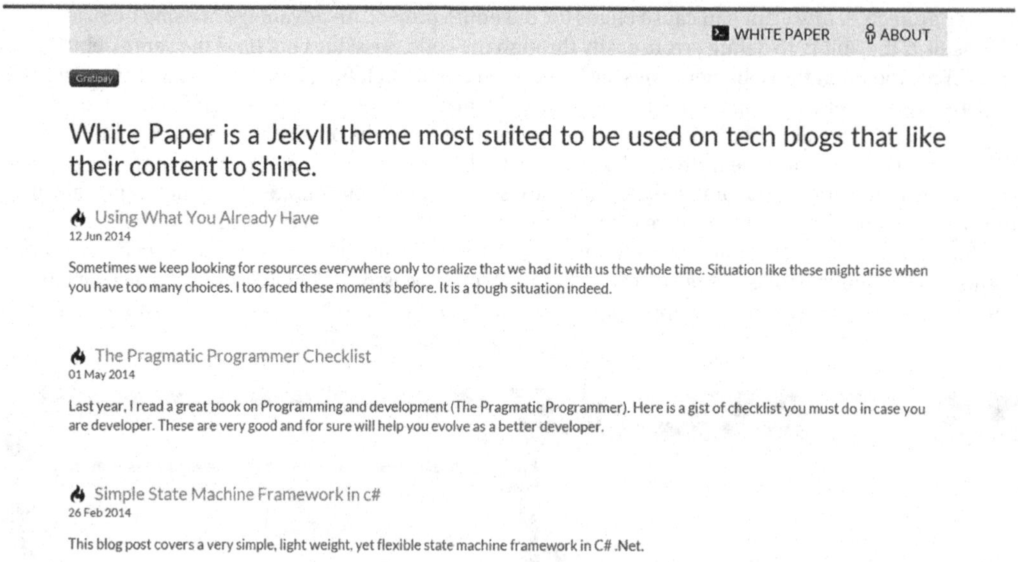

◖ WHITE PAPER   ◍ ABOUT

Gratipay

White Paper is a Jekyll theme most suited to be used on tech blogs that like their content to shine.

🔥 Using What You Already Have
12 Jun 2014

Sometimes we keep looking for resources everywhere only to realize that we had it with us the whole time. Situation like these might arise when you have too many choices. I too faced these moments before. It is a tough situation indeed.

🔥 The Pragmatic Programmer Checklist
01 May 2014

Last year, I read a great book on Programming and development (The Pragmatic Programmer). Here is a gist of checklist you must do in case you are developer. These are very good and for sure will help you evolve as a better developer.

🔥 Simple State Machine Framework in c#
26 Feb 2014

This blog post covers a very simple, light weight, yet flexible state machine framework in C# .Net.

Figure 5-8. *Whitepaper theme showing Bootstrap simplicity in action for blogging*

The next theme is also very simple, but this one is made using a Sass and Jekyll-based template called Muffin. This theme is well suited for distraction-free reading, as the fonts provide a clear focus on the content and the entire theme has very few elements to minimize distractions. This theme, called Vanilla Bean Crème by Richard Bray, is shown in Figure 5-9.

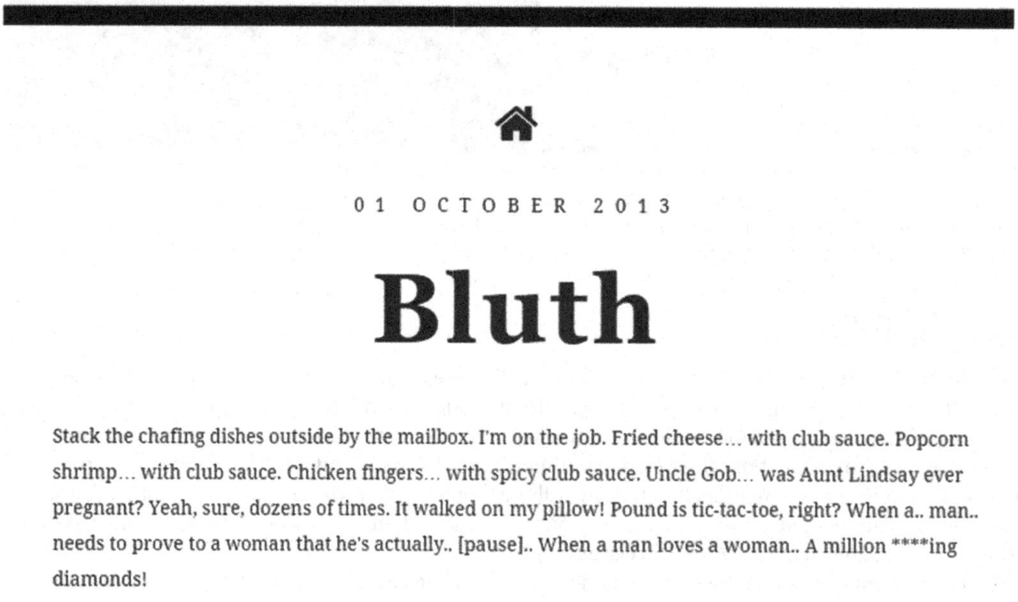

01 OCTOBER 2013

Bluth

Stack the chafing dishes outside by the mailbox. I'm on the job. Fried cheese… with club sauce. Popcorn shrimp… with club sauce. Chicken fingers… with spicy club sauce. Uncle Gob… was Aunt Lindsay ever pregnant? Yeah, sure, dozens of times. It walked on my pillow! Pound is tic-tac-toe, right? When a.. man.. needs to prove to a woman that he's actually.. [pause].. When a man loves a woman.. A million ****ing diamonds!

Figure 5-9. *Vanilla Bean Crème theme made from the template Muffin showing the distraction-free reading interface. Notice the simplicity and direct focus on the created content.*

The emerald theme is another minimal theme with a clean, responsive layout and an off-canvas menu that we discussed in the Foundation section. This theme is great as a starting point to get writing, as it has all the features that any other Jekyll theme would for the back end. On the front end, it has a clean and crisp interface to work with. The off-canvas menu along with the blog posts are responsive, so on mobile devices, they adjust to the screen requirements very easily. This theme by Jacopo Rabolini is shown in Figure 5-10.

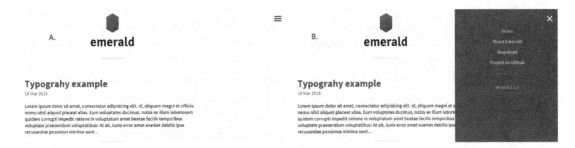

Figure 5-10. *The emerald theme shown in two panels with the off-canvas menu. Panel A shows the plain theme without the menu activated and panel B shows the activated menu.*

The final theme to be considered in this section is one that can be used for single-page applications or project demos. This theme is easy to set up and can be used as a landing page for any sort of personal project. Compass is a very straightforward theme covering just the bare bones for building a quick landing page, and this is the only theme surveyed here that does not have inherent blogging features. Therefore, making a blog using Compass would be somewhat difficult, although the same Jekyll principles apply to this theme that are found in all the themes thus far. This theme is shown in Figure 5-11.

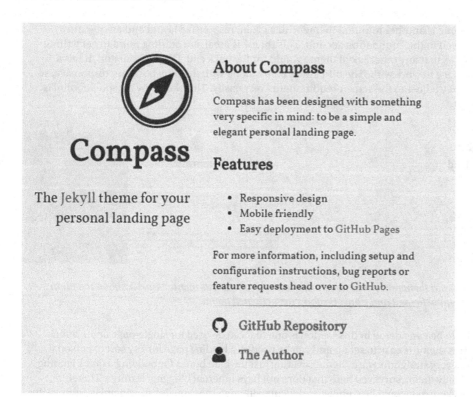

Figure 5-11. *Compass theme being used as a landing page. This theme has all the features needed to show off a personal project or single-page demos.*

Summary

Elegance is the refusal to be satisfied with bad design or lack of choices. The choices in the Jekyll ecosystem roughly translate to packages and frameworks that can be used to build a blog. In this chapter, we covered two of the most popular choices, Bootstrap and Foundation. Both frameworks have immense potential that the user can unlock with some experience with either one. We talked about the management of style elements using a preprocessor that makes the job easier in some sense, and the differences between Sass and LESS. Finally, we looked at a few finished Jekyll themes that use the frameworks we previously mentioned and what the application of such a finished product would be. There are numerous themes available for Jekyll, with more features than we covered here (e.g., automation) that we return to later in this book. The community around these frameworks is constantly evolving and incorporating new web technologies, making it possible to do more in a shorter amount of code. The style of blogging and storytelling is a living "thing"; it lives and grows just as the people who develop it do. As the times change, so will the meaning of terms like elegance and design, but the refusal to settle for anything less than elegant will always remain an inflexible choice. Our adventure through the style of Jekyll comes to an end here. In the next chapters we start to explore Jekyll more thoroughly, look at its folder structure, and learn how to complete the theme that we started building in this chapter.

Further Reading

1. **Foundation documentation:** http://foundation.zurb.com/

2. **Bootstrap complete components:** http://getbootstrap.com/components/

3. **Bootstrap snippets:** http://bootsnipp.com/

4. **Bootstrap Tutorial Lab:** http://www.tutorialrepublic.com/twitter-bootstrap-tutorial/

5. **Foundation 6 is coming:** http://zurb.com/article/1403/foundation-6-prototype-to-production

6. **Compass style documentation:** http://compass-style.org/

REVIEW

In this review, we focus on the frameworks covered in this chapter and the process of creating a theme using the two tools.

1. **Coding Task:** Import Bootstrap files from MaxCDN. Have a file skeleton prepared and then make a simple Web page with gylphicons of a barcode and a qrcode.

2. **Coding Task:** Create a four-column and three-row table using Bootstrap on the same page with the icons.

3. **Coding Task:** Download the Foundation template and create the same table as the second task. Notice the differences here.

4. **Coding Task:** Find the corresponding Foundation components for all the Bootstrap components used in the sample web page covered in the Bootstrap tutorial.

5. **Coding Task:** Find a simple e-mail template being used in Foundation from the web site at http://zurb.com/playground/responsive-email-templates and try to replicate it to some extent in Bootstrap.

CHAPTER 6

■ ■ ■

Fundamentals of Jekyll

Know thyself.

—Socrates

Understanding how a project is organized and constructed can provide deep insight into the principles that make it work. Organization is critical for a project of any scope, this can be true for something as simple as a Java applet to something as complex as a full mobile application back end. For that reason, most projects follow some established conventions. These conventions are kept uniform across most projects with minor modifications, which allows a new developer to get up to speed in a very short time. They know exactly where to look and find the appropriate code. In this chapter, we talk about the organizational principles used within Jekyll to manage a blog. More specifically, we talk about how Jekyll organizes a blog and what conventions should be used while working with a Jekyll blog. We discuss the implications of this organization in the context of more complex features such as inheritance for the blog theme files. We also cover the handlebars templates and how the use of handlebars allows for Jekyll magic to be added to a blog theme. Finally, we talk about whether it is practical to install Jekyll locally on your computer.

Folders

Much like any app project, Jekyll also creates a folder structure where it holds all the files. This allows the user to group files in a specific manner and as the project grows large, the structure is the only factor making it manageable. To understand the operational principles behind Jekyll, we discuss the folder structure in detail here. It must be noted that even though each project is different, there is a well-defined convention that most projects follow. Let's introduce some notation to read the folder structure chart. The top level is given by a single period . and it is also known as the **root**. The root is generally where the entire project is stored. Every other folder underneath is tabbed once and the files under those folders are tabbed twice. The folders that contain information pertaining to the blog settings by Jekyll are named in the following format: `_folder-name`. Within this format, we can get an overview of the entire project folder and also learn about what kind of blog style assets are being used and stored. A well-designed folder structure can give a great deal information about the project at a glance; that's why knowing how Jekyll creates them is so important.

Let's start by looking at a simple folder structure for a new blog. The only folder that we do not discuss is the assets folder, as it is not part of the standard Jekyll structure. The assets folder represents any generic folder you happen to create in your root directory. Images, documents, and files that are not properly formatted for Jekyll will be left untouched here so that they can be served normally.

© Vikram Dhillon 2016
V. Dhillon, *Creating Blogs with Jekyll*, DOI 10.1007/978-1-4842-1464-0_6

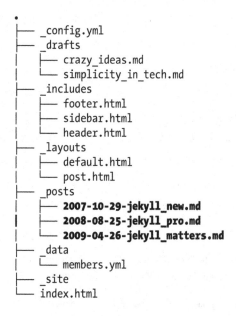

```
.
├── _config.yml
├── _drafts
│   ├── crazy_ideas.md
│   └── simplicity_in_tech.md
├── _includes
│   ├── footer.html
│   ├── sidebar.html
│   └── header.html
├── _layouts
│   ├── default.html
│   └── post.html
├── _posts
│   ├── 2007-10-29-jekyll_new.md
│   ├── 2008-08-25-jekyll_pro.md
│   └── 2009-04-26-jekyll_matters.md
├── _data
│   └── members.yml
├── _site
└── index.html
```

■ **Tip**   A short note about file extensions is in order here. The .yml file extension is the YAML front-matter, the HTML files are Jekyll-associated HTML files with content and templates, and the .md extension is the Markdown format that contains the blog posts. We talk about the .yml files in depth shortly.

Drafts and config

This seems like a complex structure, but it is actually not that difficult to follow along. Let's break it down from the top level. The first file, _config.yml, is a Jekyll-associated file that specifies some global variables that will be used throughout the site. A good example of this is site color preference. Jekyll themes are often based around single colors that are overlapping in the theme, so changing that color for the whole site in _config.yml is the best design choice.

The next folder is _drafts. This folder can have multiple uses, but one recommended use borrowed from Svbtle is using it as a list of ideas that can be developed further over time. In this way, the names of the files in this folder are just ideas, and the files can be left blank, to be developed and then saved into the appropriate folder.

Includes

_includes is one of the most useful folders in the project. This folder contains modular blocks of code that can be reused in several different posts and contexts. Generally, the _includes folder is a nice place to throw in and test new web technologies without any major impact on the project. The files from _includes are matched to the post by using a Liquid tag: {% include file.html %} and if any of the newly added technologies are incompatible, simply remove the Liquid tag. That's all. We discuss Liquid tags later in this chapter.

Layouts

The next folder is _layouts, which contains layouts for the entire blog. A layout is essentially HTML infused with Liquid and handlebars to create a full web page. The layout is actually a template that determines how each page of the blog will render, once that particular layout is applied to it. Some layouts take priority over others. For instance, the default layout is much like a master layout, which can be applied to every web page in the blog, and even other layouts. The default layout is a perfect place to store code that needs to be used globally. A perfect example of this type of code would be using font-awesome. Font-awesome is an incredibly rich source of vectorized icons available free of charge to use. The icons render as true font elements that can be manipulated with CSS. To use font-awesome, the recommend methodology is to include import the files in the <head> tag of an HTML file. The default layout can be the perfect place for this. The following code is an example of font-awesome implemented in a default layout file.

```
<head>
  <meta charset="utf-8">
  <title>{{ site.data.theme.name }} - {{ page.title }}</title>
  <meta name="author" content="{{ site.data.theme.name }}" />
  <meta name="description" content="Sample blog of John Smith: Tech, startups, design -
  connected. " />

  <link rel="stylesheet" href="//maxcdn.bootstrapcdn.com/font-awesome/4.3.0/css/font-
  awesome.min.css">

  {% include analytics.html %}
  {% include mixpanel.html %}

</head>
```

Here is an example of importing the font-awesome style elements from MaxCDN into working web sites or HTML pages. The most powerful aspect of this default layout is that other layouts can inherit from this default layout and extend it as needed for different applications. We discuss this feature of the inheritance shortly. Font-awesome is, well, pretty awesome for personal projects. Additionally, it is very easy to get started.

```
<html>
  <head>
    <link rel="stylesheet" href="https://maxcdn.bootstrapcdn.com/font-awesome/4.4.0/css/
    font-awesome.min.css">
  </head>

  <body>

      <p> <i class="fa fa-amazon fa-4x"></i> </p>
      <p> <i class="fa fa-firefox fa-4x"></i> </p>
    <p> <i class="fa fa-battery-half fa-4x"></i> </p>

  </body>
</html>
```

That's all you need, and the result is shown in Figure 6-1.

Figure 6-1. *A sample of font-awesome icons implemented in the preceding HTML code*

▓ **Tip**   The font-awesome web site has a lot more information on advanced techniques with the icons such as stacking icons and increasing the font sizes. See the web site and the Getting Started page for more information at `https://fortawesome.github.io/Font-Awesome/get-started/`.

A few features of the preceding sample code must be brought to the reader's attention. The font-awesome web site includes a list of all the icons, along with a single-line code that calls a particular icon. For instance, the Amazon icon was given by `<p> <i class="fa fa-amazon fa-4x"></i> </p>`.

In this line of code, fa-amazon is the call to the Amazon icon, however the fa-4x is a feature within font-awesome to increase the size of the icon four times. This is an immensely useful feature, allowing us to increase the size of any required icons up to five times. After that, we have to perform some CSS magic, and treat the icon as a single font character and just increase it as we would for an alphabet. This short passage demonstrated font-awesome and the unique ability of the default layouts to modularize code. Now let's move on to the rest of the folder structure.

Posts, data, and site

The next folder after _layouts is the _posts folder. This is arguably the most important folder for your blog, as it contains all the posts and also the content that will be filling up the templates and layouts designed for the blog. The _posts folder has a very specific format for each of the files being kept in it. The file name has to be in the date-filename format—year-month-date-complete_filename.md—and this post date will be shown as the date on which this post was made to the blog in Jekyll. One important feature to note is that all the files in the _posts folder are not necessarily blog posts, and therefore not required to follow the post layout. Any file can follow any layout, but it has to be specified in the front matter, another topic that we discuss shortly.

The portion of the folder structure that we have covered so far can be classified as content-based categories; that is to say, these folders contain the content that will be rendered to the final blog. The remaining folders contain web site data that are generated from how the blog content interacts with the layouts and templates. The next folder is the _data folder, appropriately titled as such to contain any JSON or CSV formatted blog to be made accessible to the blog. This data can be accessed by the Liquid templating system and a good example for the _data folder is accessing different authors who write for the same blog, and pulling their related information programmatically. The data on those authors, such as their Twitter handles or other social media, can be stored in as shared data, and then accessed appropriately as needed.

The next folder is `_site` in our folder structure. This is actually the only folder in the project that becomes populated automatically. Generally, Jekyll compiles the web site, integrating the various components and storing the compiled web sites in the `_site` folder. The web site contained in this folder is ready to be served through a web server such as Apache. We use this folder extensively in the later chapters of this book to create custom additions to our blog. The last remaining file is `index.html`; as with any other web site, this one holds the front page to the blog. However, in comparison to most other platforms, the index file usually contains very little information. Most often, this information is limited to helping organize the posts to render on the blog and paginate in case there are too many blog posts on a single page. This concludes our introduction to file structure in Jekyll, so let's spend a bit of time talking about the intervening topics before returning to a code-level overview of all the major files in the file structure.

YAML

Jekyll is powered largely programmatic access to various elements connecting the blog as a project. One of the connecting threads in Jekyll is YAML. The YAML language was developed as a way to create simple hierarchical documents. The YAML syntax was created as a computerized format of storing and relating metadata to content. It exists as a serializing structure that is the process of translating data or an object state into a format that can be stored in memory or a data structure like an array.

■ **Note** At one point, YAML was called Yet Another Markup Language, however, eventually in the later versions, it was renamed as a recursive acronym for YAML Ain't Markup Language. This more appropriately reflected its purpose as a data development language, rather than simply marking up documents as in the case of Jekyll blog posts. More information on YAML is available at `http://yaml.org/`.

In Jekyll, YAML is used for maintaining metadata for the page or post and its contents. For Jekyll, YAML is used as front matter, which is defined by being the first thing in the file and set between triple-dashed lines as follows:

```
---
title: YAML Front Matter Demonstration
description: A very simple way to add metadata descriptor to a page
---
<h1> {{ title }} </h1>
<p> {{ description }} </p>
Add page content here...
```

In the preceding example, the first `---` denotes the start of YAML front matter and the second set of dashes signifies the ending of the metadata. The HTML below the dashed lines uses Liquid tags, which are covered in the next section. Generally in YAML, the user can set predefined variables to values such as the `title` and `description`, or even create custom ones. Essentially, in Jekyll, YAML is one of the few ways that data can be stored about the blog. The extension `.yml` denotes a YAML file, and if you go back to the file structure under `_data`, the `members.yml` file is actually a YAML file that would contain data in a specific format as shown next in the `_data/authors.yml` file. The front matter is not only important for blog posts, as it contains the title and other post-related information, but it is also used by all pages in a Jekyll project to provide context about the file and its function in the whole project. As such, any file with front matter within the dashes will be processed as metadata by Jekyll. In YAML, there are numerous predefined variables and some of them are crucial to all the blog posts:

- `layout`: This specifies the layout file to use, and this variable is how different posts or pages can use different layouts. The layout files must be placed in the `_layouts` directory.

- `permalink`: This allows the blog post URLs to be more meaningful and more useful than Jekyll's default standard of giving each post a `site-address/year/month/day/title.html`. This variable allows you to create more meaningful short permalinks to your blog posts when published.

- `category/categories`: Blog posts can be categorized into different categories in the YAML front matter. When the site is generated, the `index.html` is often used to actually render the grouped posts under the respective category.

- `tags`: Blog posts can also be tagged with multiple tags and often these tags are displayed at the end of a post to allow the user to see related searchable posts with the same tag.

Using just these four predefined variables, there is a lot of information that can be provided about a post. Jekyll will process that information and render the blog post, place it in the proper categories, and make sure it links to other posts with the same tags. Let's see a more complete example of a YAML front matter.

```
---
layout: post
title: My new post
comments: True
permalink: my-new-post
categories:
- blog
- 2016
---
```

A lot is going on in this short snippet. It must be noted that all the metadata here is simply directing Jekyll on what to use and how to use it in the context of this post. The layout variable tells Jekyll what type of layout should be used for this post. The title specifies the title of the blog post to be shown on the blog itself. The next variable is not technically predefined, but it is used so often that it might as well be considered a predefined. The comments variable is used to add blog comments, and this is done through Disqus which we will talk about in the later chapters. The next predefined is permalink, which gives your blog-post a meaningful link or shortcut to remember by the last variable is categories. As the name implies, this variable allows you to organize and categorize the blog posts in a systematic manner. This is mostly helpful in the index file to allow for proper display of the appropriate categories.

This is how simple it is to use YAML: Just a few lines describes the blog post as Jekyll requires it completely. Let's go over another example of YAML that is more practical for a blog. Imagine that your blog has multiple authors. Sometimes they want to coauthor a post and you want to show who the author is for each post. By default, Jekyll will default to a predefined in `_config.yml` but we can change that. In this example, we use two authors and write their information in YAML, saving it in the `_data` folder.

```
_data/authors.yml
authors:
  hanzou:
    name: Hanzou Hattori
    display_name: Hanzou
    email: hanzou@company.com
    web: http://company.com
    twitter: company
    github: hanzou
  jorgen:
    name: Jörgen Mortensen
    display_name: Jörgen
    email: jorgen@company.com
    web: http://company.com
    twitter: company
```

Here the information about the two authors is classified under the authors tag, along with the reference name for each of the authors, followed by his information. This is the type of data representation at which YAML excels. The next file will be the actual implementation. This can be done anywhere in the layouts, but the recommended location is the <header> or the default layout.

```
{% assign author = site.authors[page.author] %}
  <header>

    <h1>{{ page.title }}</h1>
    <p>
      by {{ author.display_name }}
    </p>

  </header>
```

Here the author.display_name is a reference by Liquid to the _data/authors.yml file. Another important tag is the assign author one, which sets the author tag for a page equal to one of the authors given in the list of the site.authors data. Now that we have an implementation, all we need to do is to update YAML to let Jekyll know of the changes and exactly what type of data to pull out.

```
---
layout: post
title: New Post Using Jekyll
author: jorgen
tags: Tumblr, Jekyll, tutorial
---
```

This post will pull out only the information related to the author jorgen, and Jekyll can use that in the post. This concludes our introduction to YAML, as the information presented here should be enough in the case of using YAML for Jekyll. Additionally, there will be some more links for further reading at the end of this chapter.

Liquid and Handlebars

We have been skirting around the topic of Liquid templating language and handlebars, but we finally address it in this section. Liquid is a Ruby-based template language created by Shopify to be used in their e-commerce products, but it can also be used as an independent library. It is heavily used in Shopify themes and therefore it fits well with the templating system in Jekyll. Liquid and handlebars offer similar functionality: to add programmatic access in themes to site data. The previous example involving the use of site data involving multiple authors is a perfect use case for Liquid. Handlebars adds extensibility and minimal logic, such as #if, #unless. Liquid takes this a step further and offers a more complete feature set. In addition, Liquid is Ruby-based, the same as Jekyll, therefore the two are very compatible. This section provides a thorough introduction to Liquid and how Jekyll takes advantage of it. This templating language can be broken down into three main components: tags, objects, and filters. In the upcoming sections, we focus on the first two components.

Tags

Tags are the programmatic logic that provides access to simple statements like if and for. The tags available in Liquid can be further broken down into four categories, depending on the type of access they provide to the user. The tags used in Liquid are wrapped in {% insert-tag %}. The first category is control-flow tags; this is the set of tags that allow Jekyll to determine which block of code should be executed and in what order. There are four types of control-flow tags and the first type is the if tag. As the name implies, an if tag executes a block of code only if a certain condition is met. Here is an example of the if tag in action.

```
{% if product.title == 'shoes' %}
    These shoes are awesome!
{% endif %}
```

This generates the statement These shoes are awesome! only if the product.title matches the declared title shoes. This is a very simple application of control-flow, but the if tag is also used as conditional for showing or hiding blog elements. The next tags are elseif and else, demonstrated here.

```
{% if customer.name == 'joe' %}
  Hi Joe!
{% elseif customer.name == 'anonymous' %}
  Hey Anonymous!
{% else %}
  Hello!
{% endif %}
```

The next tag is the case/when tag, which compares a statement to the provided possible alternatives and evaluates them. In some sense, this tag is an easier version of the if tag.

```
{% assign food = 'cake' %}
{% case food %}
  {% when 'cake' %}
    This is a cake
  {% when 'cookie' %}
    This is a cookie
  {% else %}
    This is not a cake nor a cookie
{% endcase %}
```

The last tag that we discuss is actually much like a do-while loop, but it's called the unless tag. As the name implies, this block of code executes only if certain conditions are not met. This tag might not be used much, but for the sake of completeness, the following is an example of an unless tag in action.

```
{% unless product.title == 'shoes' %}
    These are not shoes
{% endif %}
```

This was the first type of tags, the control-flow tags. The next category is the iteration tags. These tags allow for programmatic access through iteration or looping. We only cover the three most commonly used iteration tags: for, break, and continue. The for tag repeatedly executes a task until exhausted by another condition, as this example shows.

```
{% for author in site.authors %}
  {{ author.display_name }}
{% endfor %}
```

This snippet of code allows us to iterate through each of the authors and obtain their display_name. However, the for loop tag is nondiscriminant. If there is a need to make the loop stop, or prevent it from going on, a condition is required, and this is where the break and continue tags come into play.

```
{% for i in (1..5) %}
  {% if i == 4 %}
    {% continue %}
  {% else %}
    {{% break %}}
  {% endif %}
{% endfor %}
```

This snippet of code actually does not generate any output because the loop would break at each runtime. That is not of much consequence because the snippet simply demonstrates the use of break and continue tags. This was the second category of tags, the iteration tags. The next type of tags are variable tags, which, as the name suggests, allow programmatic access to variables. There is only one tag among the variables that gets frequently used, the assign tag. As the name implies, the assign tag allows the user to create a new variable as shown in this example.

```
{% assign new_variable = false %}
{% if my_variable = true %}
Hooray!
{% endif %}
```

In this snippet, the new_variable was assigned the Boolean value of false and the if statement logically verified it. This was the third of the tags, the variable tags. Finally, the last type of tag is the theme tags. These are a collection of tags that help Jekyll decide which components of the layout and the template to use. The most commonly used theme tag is the include tag. As the name implies, the include tag allows the user to include unique, modular components in a theme or a template. Most of these elements are stored in the _includes folder. This tag is immensely useful in almost every single Jekyll theme file, as it allows for modularization and includes only the components that are needed in a particular layout. This tag is ubiquitous in layouts as well because it allows for advanced features such as inheritance to be used in Jekyll files. Let's spend some time talking about the topic of inheritance in the next section. We have finally completed the first of the Liquid components: tags. The next category is objects.

Objects

There are more than 20 different types of objects in Shopify's Liquid that make possible an incredible amount of customization and provide granular access to a theme. In this chapter, we cannot address all of those objects, but we discuss a few of the most popular ones. Before we delve into the properties of objects, we need to define what an object is. Objects are crucial to understanding object-oriented programming. There are numerous examples of real-world objects: your desk, your laptop, and your bicycle, to name just a few. The objects present in an environment all share two characteristics: They all have a concrete state and some defined behavior. If loosely defined, a state is the physical characteristic and the behavior is the result of the input or interaction with the object. Identifying the state and behavior for real-world objects is a great way to begin thinking in terms of object-oriented programming.

Software objects are conceptually similar to real-world objects: They also consist of state and related behavior. An object stores its state in terms of variables contained within the object. It also makes the possible behavior available through functions that can be used on objects. Functions or methods, as they are called, operate on an object's state and serve as the primary mechanism for object-to-object communication. The use of methods to manipulate an object allows the developer to hide the internal state of the object or how the object itself is being constructed. All the interactions with the object are performed through methods, in a technique called data encapsulation. In a sense, this is also how APIs work. Bundling code into individual objects provides a number of benefits, including the following.

1. **Modularity:** The code for an object can be written and maintained independently of the source code for other objects.

2. **Reuse:** If an object that you require in your project already exists, you can simply use that object in your program.

3. **Debugging:** If a particular object turns out to be problematic, you can simply remove it from your application and plug in a different object as its replacement. This is analogous to fixing mechanical problems in the real world. If a bolt breaks, you replace that bolt, not the entire machine.

Liquid objects are also often referred to as Liquid variables. Just like any programmatic object, these objects have state and behavior (also known as an attribute). To output an object's attribute on the page, wrap it in {{ and }}. For example, the product object contains an attribute called title that can be used to output the title of a product:

```
{{ product.title }}
```

Let's try to focus on the objects available in Jekyll, as those will be more pertinent to us in theme files and while creating smaller include files. The three most commonly used objects that we focus on are site, page, and paginator. In the remainder of this section, we review these objects and the associated variables. The first object and associated variables we cover is the site object.

■ **Note**   Handlebars.js is a templating language (much like Liquid) that offers programmatic access for templates to access site data. However, it had a limited feature set that could not be extended easily. That's why Shopify came up with its own templating language called Liquid, which is now the backbone of Jekyll. Liquid is very similar to handlebars in terms of using the same {{ some code }} syntax. Currently, Liquid has surpassed Handlebars.js and therefore Jekyll switched to using Liquid as well. As a result, we only see the handlebars notation, not the feature set.

Site Variables

The `site` object refers to the entire Jekyll blog. The attributes of the `site` object are often globally applicable to the blog. The following are some of the most commonly used attributes of the `site` object in a Jekyll blog:

- `site.pages`: A list of all pages.

- `site.posts`: A listing of all posts in the blog, in reverse chronological order.

- `site.related_posts`: If the page being processed is a post, this contains a list of up to ten related posts. By default, these are the ten most recent posts.

- `site.data`: A list containing the data loaded from the YAML files located in the _data directory.

- `site.categories.sample`: The list of all posts in the category sample.

- `site.tags.newtag`: The list of all posts with tag newtag.

Page Variables

The next of the objects to consider is the page object. The `page` object refers to a single page under consideration. Therefore, the attributes of the `page` object refer to the content of that page and provide programmatic access to the post in the context of all the posts in the blog. Here are some of the most commonly used attributes of the `page` object:

- `page.content`: This method returns the content of the page.

- `page.title`: This method returns the title of the page.

- `page.excerpt`: This method returns the excerpt of a given page.

- `page.url`: This method returns the URL of the post without the domain, but with a leading slash; for example, `/2009/10/10/test-post.html`.

- `page.date`: This method returns the date assigned to the post.

- `page.categories`: This method returns a list of categories to which the post belongs. The categories can either be specified in the YAML front matter and also from the directory structure. Categories are derived from the directory structure above the _posts directory. For example, a post at `/new/code/_posts/2008-12-24-testing.md` would have the categories `['new', 'code']`.

- `page.tags`: The method returns a list of tags to which this post belongs. These are specified in the YAML front matter.

- `page.next`: This method returns the next post relative to the current post in `site.posts`.

- `page.previous`: This method returns the previous post relative to the current post in `site.posts`.

Paginator Variables

The last of the objects to consider is the `paginator` variables. The `paginator` object allows for the use of pagination in the blog, to create multiple pages for a reader. The `paginator` object helps to dynamically update the page counts and provide intelligent pagination. Here are some of the most common attributes of the paginator object:

- `paginator.per_page`: This method returns the number of posts per page.

- `paginator.posts`: This method returns the posts available for that page.

- `paginator.total_posts`: This method returns the total number of posts.

- `paginator.page`: This method returns the number of the current page.

- `paginator.previous_page`: This method returns the number of the previous page.

- `paginator.next_page`: This method returns the number of the following page.

The purpose behind selecting these variables for the three objects and presenting them here is to allow the reader to be familiar with them. All of the variables in Liquid cannot be covered here, but hopefully the pattern behind the variables can be exposed to the reader to the point where they can read the documentation and figure out which of the objects and the associated variables to use in their own projects.

■ **Tip**   The methods and objects presented here were limited by space and scope. To learn more about Liquid, a great reference is the Shopify pages. Again, the purpose of presenting that material here was to get readers familiar with the tags and objects, so that they can use different variables as they need more comfortably. The web site for the objects is available at `https://docs.shopify.com/themes/liquid-documentation/objects`.

Inheritance

Inheritance is an advanced object-oriented programming concept where a base-level object with a general feature set is constructed. This common base is used to construct other objects by adding features to them and obtaining the desired object. In this manner, all objects inherit from a basic object. Jekyll allows for inheriting previously defined files in two ways. The first one is using the `include` tag, which is shown the next example, and the other method is using the YAML front matter for inheriting layouts.

```
{% include header.html %}
<h1> Testing below the header </h1>
```

Here, the `include` tag is being used to bypass rewriting all the code of the header, as it is simply imported here. The analogy of the inheritance can be used here in that this new file simply inherits the properties of the header and extends them in a new direction. The more direct observation of inheritance is through the YAML front matter. In this example, individual pages can inherit from other pages. A perfect example of this is in layouts: The `default` layout is the base object, and every other layout inherits from it. Therefore a page layout can use the `default` for the header and extend that layout to add new features to create a page. This type of inheritance is usually carried out as follows:

```
---
layout: default
---
<h1> Testing out a new page </h1>
... More code ...
```

Although inheritance might seem like a simple concept as it is used in Jekyll, it is an incredibly powerful tool that we will be revisiting and using often throughout the book. Often in themes, many elements are inherited to ensure that the code is clean and maintainable. This also allows for reusing previously written code in an efficient manner.

Installing Jekyll Locally?

In this section, let's briefly talk about whether installing Jekyll locally is practical. Most of the development that we undertake will be happening on GitHub, which already offers automatic compilation of Jekyll-powered blogs and web sites. Performing the compilation locally will not make much of a difference because the end result will still have to be pushed to GitHub. The primary advantage of not installing Jekyll locally is that you do not have to worry about installing or maintaining all the dependencies that come along with Jekyll. This can be a particularly difficult problem on a Windows machine. Most of the projects that will be covered in the following chapters use GitHub as a code hosting platform and we push our Jekyll projects to GitHub. Each push to the online platform will automatically trigger a Jekyll recompile of our static web site to keep it updated. As a result, for a Windows machine, there are hardly any advantages to installing Jekyll locally. We perform an in-depth installation of Jekyll later in the book.

For the interested reader, here we provide some resources and ideas on how to use Jekyll in Windows. Installing Jekyll on Windows is perhaps the most time consuming. Using Windows, no libraries are installed, so everything needs to be installed from scratch. Julian Thilo has created an excellent guide to installing Jekyll on Windows alongside Ruby and the other needed tools. His tutorial has tested several versions, so following his tutorial to install Jekyll is highly recommended. The tutorial is routinely updated with new versions of Ruby and Jekyll as they become compatible to run on Windows. The general process for installing Jekyll is as follows:

1. Installing a compatible, stable version of Ruby on Windows.

2. Installing a stable version of the Jekyll gem.

3. Installing the Rouge gem for syntax highlighting.

4. Installing the optional syntax highlighting through Pygments and Python.

5. Running Jekyll.

The reason for not including an entire tutorial in this chapter itself is that although this book might be recent, new versions of Jekyll, Ruby, and Rouge are constantly coming out; therefore a tutorial presented here would become outdated for later versions. On the other hand, Thilo's guide is a smaller, self-contained project that can be updated with each release, making it more reliable and up to date. The entire tutorial is available at `http://jekyll-windows.juthilo.com/`.

Installing Jekyll on Linux is actually very straightforward:

```
$ sudo apt-get install ruby ruby-dev make gcc nodejs
$ sudo gem install jekyll --no-rdoc --no-ri
```

The first line installs the prerequisites for Jekyll, and the second one installs Jekyll itself through a gem. Installing Jekyll on an OS X machine can be done in a simple manner as well. The only tool needed to install Jekyll is Xcode, as OS X already comes preinstalled with Ruby and gems, at least Yosemite. The terminal will do the rest:

```
$ sudo gem install jekyll
```

■ **Tip** A very nice tutorial on how to install Jekyll on a Mac OS X machine is available at `http://internet-inspired.com/wrote/install-jekyll-in-osx-mavericks/`.

Summary

In this chapter, we talked about the folder structure of a Jekyll project. We went into depth about the types of folders and the conventions used in Jekyll. In addition, we explored the various components that make up each of the files. This includes the three packages font-awesome, YAML, and Liquid. We talked about each of these packages in the context of their use in Jekyll and provided some background on each one. These packages are very powerful when used together in a blog, but they are only a small part of the larger Jekyll ecosystem that we discuss subsequently in the book. In this chapter, we also talked about two advanced concepts: inheritance and objects. Both of those are used extensively in Jekyll but only abstractly. The proper implementation is generally obscured and the idea behind presenting it here was to more concretely point to the fundamental concepts behind those ideas. We are only starting to scratch the surface of the files present within a Jekyll structure, and although this introduction was not exhaustive, it was meant to help the reader understand the basics. Once a reader is familiar with the material, it is easy to know what else he or she needs to seek out and learn to complete his or her understanding. Our journey ends here with the Jekyll folder structure. In the following chapters, we pick up the remaining components of a folder structure such as static assets and how they integrate into the remaining Jekyll ecosystem.

Further Reading

1. **Liquid for Designers**: `https://github.com/Shopify/liquid/wiki/Liquid-for-Designers`

2. **Shopify's Liquid cheat sheet**: `http://cheat.markdunkley.com/`

3. **Font-awesome**: `https://fortawesome.github.io/Font-Awesome/`

4. **Portable Jekyll**: `http://www.madhur.co.in/blog/2013/07/20/buildportablejekyll.html`

5. **Liquid filters**: `https://docs.shopify.com/themes/liquid-documentation/filters`

REVIEW

In this review, we focus our attention on using the objects and variables learned in the context of YAML.

1. **Review Task**: Go through the YAML section quickly and then the page object.

2. **Review Task**: Go through the folder structure again and be able to explain all the components accurately.

3. **Search Task**: Find a new folder structure from a theme in a previous chapter and elucidate its folder structure.

4. **Interpretation Task**: Interpret the following _include file along with the following YAML front matter.

_include file

```
{% if content and page.related %}
    <h2>Related Posts</h2>
    <ul>
    {% for post in site.posts %}
        {% if page.related contains post.title %}
            <li><a href="{{ post.url }}">{{ post.title }}</a></li>
        {% endif %}
    {% endfor %}
    </ul>
{% endif %}
```

YAML front matter

```
layout: post
title: "Jekyll related posts"
category: blog
permalink: /blog/jekyll-related-posts
related: [
    "A tiny rant: Jekyll vs. Octopress",
    "6 Weeks of Daily Blogging",
    "Bash Productivity Tips"
]
---
Blog post content here.
```

PART III

■ ■ ■

Projects

This section is all about application: We take on several projects and modify them completely to fit a problem that we are trying to solve. Some of those are just hobby projects, but others are focused on social issues and how technology can affect them. Each of these projects is focusing entirely on a web technology that is crucial to Jekyll and pushing it to the limits. In each of these projects, we use the resources offered by the last section and apply them here. The idea here is to simply build on those tools and just keep adding features until a theme that we picked for Jekyll to edit looks similar to the desired final result. There are several limitations of modifying a theme instead of just creating a new one from scratch, but the biggest advantage is to save time from developing all the style assets and more. The later chapters also have a social theme that can better showcase the use cases for the technologies and how it can be helpful. I hope that you enjoy these projects just as much as I did selecting and preparing them. Good luck!

CHAPTER 7

■ ■ ■

Blog-awareness

Great ideas don't need approvals, they need application.

—Amit Kalantri

We have talked about a lot of concepts pertaining to Jekyll in the previous chapters, but all of them were presented in an isolated manner. In this chapter, we go through a simple Jekyll theme to learn how those ideas come together to create a static web site. A very in-depth overview of the code used in the theme along with helpful comments to understand that code are provided here. Our discussion is focused on blog-awareness, which is also the central theme of this chapter. This is the idea that Jekyll has built-in support for features that are needed in a blog such as permalinks, categories, pages, and custom layouts. In addition, these simple features can be further customized and configured in a number of ways to support new ideas. Being blog-aware makes it easier to add new features to Jekyll and inherit the same rules or layouts that apply to the rest of your blog. New pages or posts can be added seamlessly and they still follow the same fundamental rules and conventions. We show how a theme takes advantage of blog-awareness and more important, how this property makes Jekyll themes modular. This modularity, along with the theme configuration, allows for us to recycle working code and reuse it in different parts of a project. We spend the majority of our time in this chapter talking about how to download a Jekyll theme, how to extract it, and how to get ready to start editing. Finally, we methodically go through each file in a code editor and explain how the code works.

Getting the Theme

The example used in this chapter is a fairly straightforward theme and it also has a very simple design. We focus on various aspects of Jekyll by studying this theme. The theme is called Kactus, developed by Nick Balestra and available on GitHub at `https://github.com/nickbalestra/kactus`. Later we look into more themes that can be found at `http://jekyllthemes.org/`.

We review the specifics of GitHub in much more detail later on in the book; our focus for now is to download the theme and start editing it locally. Any Jekyll themes available on GitHub are open source and freely available so that developers and users may use and modify them. The theme can be downloaded directly (as a zipped file) from GitHub, as shown in Figure 7-1. The project page on GitHub also provides a very nice overview of the folder structure of the theme. Generally, a project on GitHub is not simply downloaded, but rather cloned for editing purposes. GitHub allows this by forking the project. By forking, the developer also carries over the history of previous developments to projects that were checked in. The check-ins are in the form of commits, and keeping a history of them might become necessary in case the developer wants to contribute those changes back to the project. In those cases, cloning preserves the previous history and simply adds new code on top. For now, we are not concerned with cloning the theme or maintaining histories. We won't be adding new features to the theme that enhance functionality, but rather

© Vikram Dhillon 2016

V. Dhillon, *Creating Blogs with Jekyll*, DOI 10.1007/978-1-4842-1464-0_7

using the theme as a foundation to apply it toward our ideas and projects. Once the theme is downloaded from GitHub to your computer, it's time to extract the files and then we can start navigating through the folder. In Windows, extracting files is very straightforward.

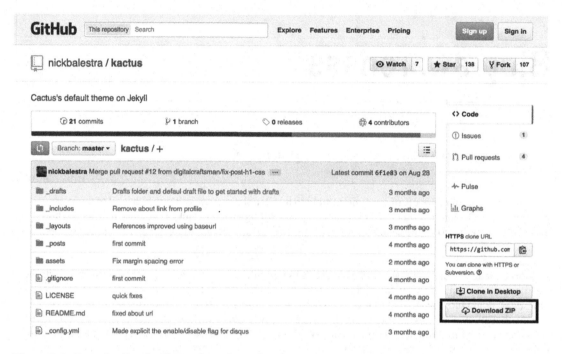

Figure 7-1. *Downloading the Kactus theme by Nick Balestra. Once the theme is downloaded, we can start exploring it and working with the code.*

The initial folder structure after downloading the theme and extracting is shown in Figure 7-2. Let's dive into the folder structure and rely on the most commonly used conventions to understand the files and folders here.

- Every folder with a `_folder-name` is a folder storing information about the blog. In this theme, the folders include drafts, layouts, and posts.

- The `assets` folder contains the styling assets associated with the blog.

- The `LICENSE` and `README.md` files are both instructional files for the developer or the user to understand the terms under which this project has been open sourced and how to get this theme running in Jekyll.

- The only `HTML` file present in the folder structure is `index.html`.

- There is only one page aside from the home page in this theme, named `about.md`.

- The `feed.xml` files contains the ATOM feed of blog posts and other related changes synchronized over the Web.

- Finally, the `.gitignore` file contains a list of files that will not be recorded in version control. This is generally done for files that change frequently, but their internal state is not of much importance to the overall project.

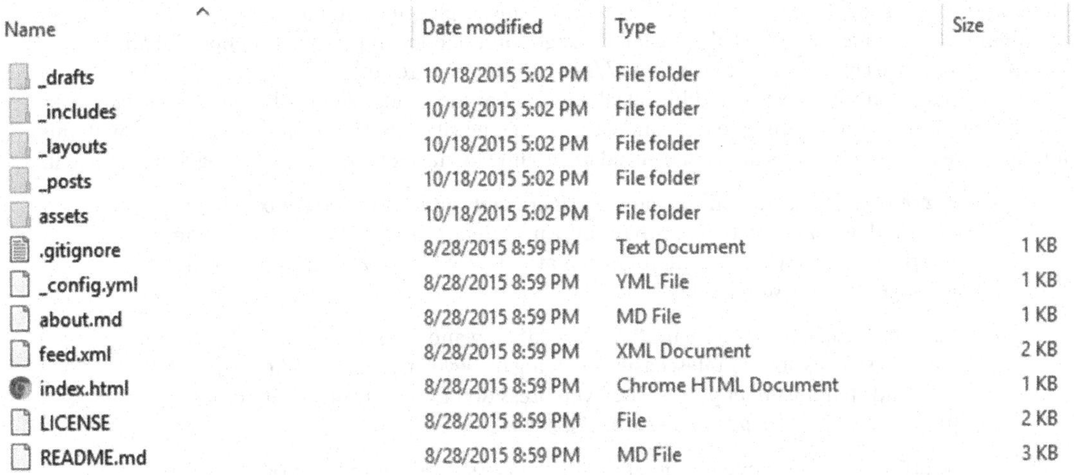

Name ^	Date modified	Type	Size
_drafts	10/18/2015 5:02 PM	File folder	
_includes	10/18/2015 5:02 PM	File folder	
_layouts	10/18/2015 5:02 PM	File folder	
_posts	10/18/2015 5:02 PM	File folder	
assets	10/18/2015 5:02 PM	File folder	
.gitignore	8/28/2015 8:59 PM	Text Document	1 KB
_config.yml	8/28/2015 8:59 PM	YML File	1 KB
about.md	8/28/2015 8:59 PM	MD File	1 KB
feed.xml	8/28/2015 8:59 PM	XML Document	2 KB
index.html	8/28/2015 8:59 PM	Chrome HTML Document	1 KB
LICENSE	8/28/2015 8:59 PM	File	2 KB
README.md	8/28/2015 8:59 PM	MD File	3 KB

Figure 7-2. Folder structure of the downloaded theme Kactus. A brief explanation of the folders and files shown here is provided in text.

Now that we have briefly reviewed the folder structure, let's spend a little time on the one folder that we did not cover in detail previously: the style assets folder. This folder contains four subfolders:

- Css: Stylesheets.

- fonts: Fonts specific to the blog.

- images: Storing images to be used in the web site.

- js: JavaScript for interactivity.

It is easy to see how the assets folder works: It stores mostly static assets and style files that are being used in the blog. The Css folder contains the stylesheets for the entire blog, the fonts folder contains any special fonts being used on the web site, the images folder is a repository for images being used in blog posts or pages, and finally the js folder contains JavaScript files pertinent to the theme or layouts. These assets allow interactivity in a Jekyll blog, but the files inside or the frameworks chosen for each blog could be very different. Generally, the layouts being used decide which styles to use.

■ **Tip** The Kactus theme does not have very complex style sheets, so it might be worth the time to look through the entire stylesheet (style.css). This will provide the reader a refresher on manipulating HTML elements using CSS. On the other hand, the js assets will be available as downloadable libraries (in most cases) that need to be implemented in the blog to become actionable.

Installing a Code Editor

The code editor that we use throughout this book is called Sublime. It's free to use, user-friendly, and incredibly powerful with the proper customizations. The current version is Sublime Text 3, available at http://www.sublimetext.com/3. The Sublime web site also gives easy instructions to follow on how to install Sublime 3 for Windows, OS X, and Linux. One of the best features in Sublime is the integration of plug-ins, and there are thousands of plug-ins available. The plug-ins are managed as packages and can be added to Sublime using the package control system. The terms plug-ins and packages are interchangeable for Sublime. To use plug-ins, we need to install package control following the instructions that are provided through the package control web site at `https://packagecontrol.io/installation`.

The package control has an incredible Jekyll plug-in that can be loaded in Sublime and used for tasks such as new post shortcuts, template tags, and easily saving Jekyll posts in the date format. Along with this plug-in, there are several others that can be used in Sublime to make life easier while blogging with Jekyll.

- **MarkdownEditing**: An amazing add-on, it arguably adds the best syntax highlighting to Markdown files, even better than some proprietary apps. It also simplifies the interface by removing line numbers. It is available at `https://packagecontrol.io/packages/MarkdownEditing`.

- **SmartMarkdown**: It supplements `MarkdownEditing` and adds a variety of other useful features such as smart tables, easily changing the level of headlines (i.e., h1, h2, h3, etc.) and creating bullet points when you press Return. It is available at `https://packagecontrol.io/packages/SmartMarkdown`.

- **WordCount**: As the name implies, this add-on adds word count functionality to the Sublime Text status bar. It can be very useful in certain situations, especially if it is used in conjunction with estimated reading time to allow the reader to know how long the post will take to read. It is available at `https://packagecontrol.io/packages/WordCount`.

- **Markdown Preview**: Markdown Preview renders the Markdown written either with original Markdown or via Github API and generates the result through output methods. The output can be opened in a browser, sent to a new Sublime Text document, sent to the Clipboard, or saved to an HTML file. It is available at `https://packagecontrol.io/packages/Markdown%20Preview`.

- **Jekyll**: As mentioned earlier, this package makes it easier to write Jekyll blog posts. It is available at `https://packagecontrol.io/packages/Jekyll`.

■ **Note** All the relevant code from the Kactus theme will be provided within the chapter and any modifications to it will be available with the book. However, readers are encouraged to follow along with the changes being made to the code within their own editor to get familiar with browsing a Jekyll theme in Sublime.

In addition to plug-ins, Sublime has a few very nice features such as tabs and a distraction-free mode. To enable the distraction-free mode, select the option from the View menu or press Shift + F11 on your keyboard (in Windows). In this mode, the word-wrap length shortens, menu interface elements disappear, and there's nothing left to distract you. It certainly helps to focus on what Jekyll is intended to do: help you write great content.

A Kactus in the Desert

Digging into a new theme and understanding it can be like a traveler looking for water in the desert. If you keep looking around without a plan, you will not make any progress and might run out of time. In the beginning of this chapter, we started to look at the folder structure to obtain a few fundamental clues on how this theme is organized. In this section, we examine the Kactus theme in depth, going through every file in the theme. You are encouraged to open the files and follow along or just open the whole theme folder in Sublime, as we present only the relevant snippets. The first folder in the theme is the _drafts folder. To refresh your memory, the purpose of this folder is to store unfinished drafts of blog posts. There is only one file available in this folder: a-draft-post.markdown.

```
---
title:  "A Draft Post"
description: Work in progress
## date: add a date when publishing
---
```

[...]

```
Check out the [Jekyll docs][jekyll] for more info on how to get the most out of Jekyll. File
all bugs/feature requests at [Jekyll's GitHub repo][jekyll-gh].

[jekyll-gh]: https://github.com/mojombo/jekyll
[jekyll]:    http://jekyllrb.com
```

This file starts off with the YAML front matter, as we would expect from a Jekyll post. The notation right below the front matter [...] is being used to show that some of the text or code in the file was omitted. It is not an artifact in Jekyll. We covered Markdown fairly thoroughly earlier in the book, but the way in which the hyperlinking works is very unique. In this case, the second [bracket] refers to a footnote that is actually a link. This is different from the usual GFM, where the link is simply inserted in the [text](link) format.

The _includes Folder

The next folder in the theme is the _includes folder. This folder contains seven files; let's start with disqus. html. Disqus is actually a very popular commenting system available as a freemium service. For our purposes, the free version would be more than sufficient. The file contains some JavaScript embedded code provided by Disqus to be pasted into that file and saved in _includes to obtain a functional commenting system. The Disqus web site provides instructions on how to obtain a functioning instance on your own blog at https://help.disqus.com/customer/portal/articles/472138-jekyll-installation-instructions.

The next file is footer.html, which creates the footer of the blog, as the name implies. This is also a very simple file:

```
<footer id="footer">
    <p class="small">© Copyright {{ site.time | date: '%Y' }} {{ site.author }}</p>
</footer>
```

This snippet of code defines a footer class and starts it on a new line using the paragraph element. Within the copyright notice, the Liquid variables time and date are used, along with the name of the author who owns the copyright. This was a very straightforward example of how to implement a modular component and then import it within the different layouts. The next file we examine is navigation.html, and this file generates the top bar:

```
<nav class="main-nav">
    {% if page.url != "/index.html" %}          # If current page is not home page
        <a href="{{ site.baseurl }}"> <span class="arrow">←</span> Home </a>
    {% endif %}                                  # Show an arrow to return to home page
```

```
{% if page.url != "/about/" %}              # If current page is not the About page
    {% if site.aboutPage %}                 # And the site has enabled an About page
        <a href="{{ site.baseurl }}about">About </a>
    {% endif %}                             # Show a link to the About page
{% endif %}
<a class="cta" href="{{ site.baseurl }}feed.xml">Subscribe</a>
</nav>
```

This code might seem intimidating because it is using a lot of the advanced Liquid features, but we can break it down into simpler pieces. The snippet starts off by defining a navigation class. The logic behind this snippet is in the if-tag from Liquid. It is being used to inquire about the page.url property. If the current page is not the home page, then it would make sense to provide an option to return to the home page. This snippet does so by using the back arrow in the span tag. That is the purpose of the first if statement. The second if statement applies the same logic to show the About page: If the current page is not the About page, provide a link for the user to see the About page. Finally, it doesn't matter which page the user is on; this code snippet will always show the Subscribe button in the top bar, as shown in Figure 7-3.

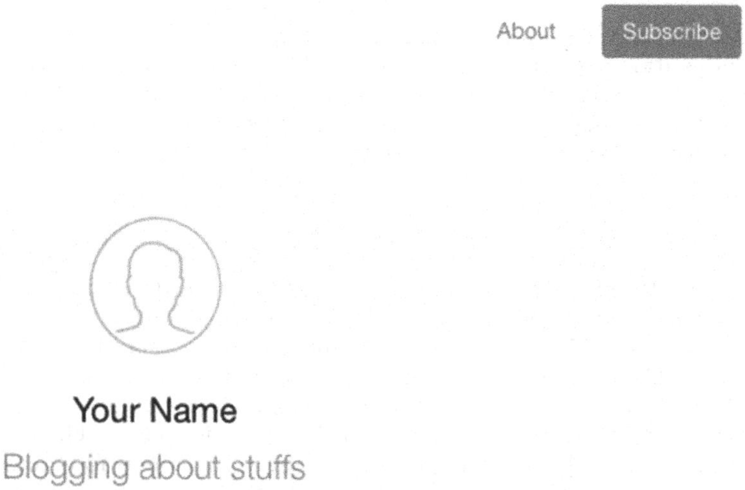

About   Subscribe

Your Name

Blogging about stuffs

Figure 7-3. The top bar shown in the Kactus theme. The Home button is not displayed in the top bar because the site is on the home page; therefore the if statement would not execute. The other two buttons have not satisfied the if statement requirements so they continue to be displayed.

We return to the site.baseurl variable shortly. The next file that we examine is a bit more complex. This is the pagination.html file and its purpose is to provide Jekyll with the logic on how to spread blog posts across multiple pages to keep the home page from overflowing and listing everything. Pagination has two basic features: previous and next pages. The trick is to understand how to dynamically move posts to the next page after a certain number of them have been listed. A minor detail to keep in mind with pagination is that it starts numbering the pages from 0, so the first page is 0 and the following page is 1. Let's look at the code for this file.

```
<nav id="post-nav">
    {% if paginator.previous_page %}
        <span class="prev">
            {% if paginator.previous_page == 1 %}
                <a href="{{ site.baseurl }}" title="Previous Page">
```

```
                    <span class="arrow">←</span> Newer Posts
                </a>
            {% else %}
                <a href="{{ site.baseurl }}page{{ paginator.previous_page }}/">
                    <span class="arrow">←</span> Newer Posts
                </a>
            {% endif %}
        </span>
    {% endif %}
    {% if paginator.next_page %}
        <span class="next">
            <a href="{{ site.baseurl }}page{{ paginator.next_page }}/">
                Older Posts <span class="arrow">→</span>
            </a>
        </span>
    {% endif %}
</nav>
```

There is a lot going on in this file, but breaking it down into smaller pieces makes it easier to examine. The file starts off by defining a nav class, more specifically a pagination-type object. The first part of this code is the previous_page property and it can be best explained with the following example. Let's say we are on page 1 and look through the first if statement; if the current page is page 1, then we have moved past the home page (which is page 0) and we have also moved past the first few posts that can be displayed. In that case, it makes sense to give an option to move back to the home page (which essentially takes the user to the home page or page 0). If that current page is page 2, then the previous_page property can be used to give the user an option to move back to page 1. Let's look at this visually:

```
(A)     *0              1
        Home    Next Page
(B)      0      <--     *1
        Home    Go back to home page

(C)      0              1       2       3       <--     *4
        Home                                    Go to previous page
```

In the first case (A), we have two pages and currently we are on the home page, shown by the asterisk. In the second case (B), we want to navigate to the previous page, but we only have two pages, so the previous page is the home page and we can simply hyperlink paginator.previous_page to site.baseurl. In the third case (C) we are several pages down and we want to navigate one page back. Here, we have to call paginator.previous_page to get the appropriate link because we can't use the site.baserul anymore. That was the previous_page property, but how do we move to the next page? That's the next if statement, the next_page property. This is actually far simpler than previous_page logic: On any given page, if there are more pages remaining, provide a link to go to the next_page.

■ **Tip** It might help to look at how Jekyll blogs are organized to understand the contradictory nature of previous_page pointing to newer posts, and next_page pointing to older posts. In a paginated Jekyll site, the newest posts appear first. This implies that page 0 will have the latest posts. Now if we are on page 2, the previous page actually contains more recent posts; that's why it points to newer posts. At the same time, if you want to go to the next_page, this page will contain older posts, therefore next_page points to older posts.

The next file to examine is the `post_list.html` file. As the name implies, this file generates a list of posts that will be displayed on the home page. Generally, this code is present in `index.html`, but it doesn't always have to be the case.

```
<ul id="post-list">
    {% for post in paginator.posts %}

        <li>
            <a href="{{ site.baseurl }}{{ post.url | remove_first: '/' }}"><aside
            class="dates">{{ post.date | date:"%b %d" }}</aside></a>
            <a href="{{ site.baseurl }}{{ post.url | remove_first: '/' }}">{{ post.title }}
            <h2>{{ post.description }}</h2></a>
        </li>

    {% endfor %}
</ul>

{% if paginator.previous_page or paginator.next_page %}
    {% include pagination.html %}
{% endif %}
```

The logic behind this code snippet is to create a list of all the posts with a hyperlink. This hyperlink is between the `post.date` and the post title to the Jekyll path of the blog post or page. This is done by using a `for` loop on the list. This list actually functions like an ordered list with the `<li>` tag. The hyperlinking is done by URL concatenation where `site.baserul` is added on top of `post.url` to get the full link to the blog post. There are two parsing operations needed to obtain the URL. The first one is using `remove_first` to get rid of the trailing slash (applied to `post.url`) and the second one is applied to `post.date` to get the date in the appropriate format. This format is typical for a blog post where the date is on top, followed by the post title, and finally the description of that post. There might be some confusion with the use of the `post.url` and `baseurl`, but Figure 7-4 clarifies how a URL is broken down into the two variables. The last `if` statement in this file ensures that the previous or next page also contains the paginator from `pagination.html` as we discussed earlier.

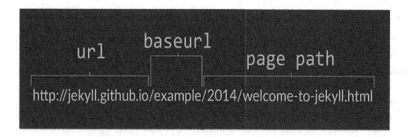

Figure 7-4. *The breakdown of a URL created by Jekyll pointing to a page on the Web site or blog. Note that the property* `site.baseurl` *simply accesses the site variable* `baseurl` *and* `site.url` *accesses the site variable* `url`.

These two files were complex files as they involved a deep understanding of concepts that we have not applied before. The remaining two files in this folder are fairly straightforward. The next file that we examine is `profile.html`. This file creates the author's profile that would go on top of the page, as shown earlier in Figure 7-3. There are a few global variables used as site properties, but the code itself is very straightforward. One thing to note is that this file is included in every page, which is possible due to the layouts that we discuss in the next section. Let's look into the code for the author profile.

```
<div class="profile">
    <section id="wrapper">

        <header id="header">

        {% if site.aboutPage %}
            <a href="{{ site.baseurl }}about">
                <img id="avatar" class="2x" src="{{ site.baseurl }}assets/images/avatar.png"/>
            </a>
        {% else %}
            <img id="avatar" class="2x" src="{{ site.baseurl }}assets/images/avatar.png"/>
        {% endif %}

            <h1>{{ site.author }}</h1>
            <h2>{{ site.description }}</h2>
        </header>

    </section>
</div>
```

In this code snippet, the author profile is being wrapped inside the <header> tag where it passes through a conditional statement: If the site is configured to have an About page in _config.yml, then hyperlink the avatar picture to the URL of the About page with the site.baseurl. Otherwise, simply display the avatar without any hyperlinking. That is the logic behind the if statements: After the if loop, the rest of the code displays the name of the author with site.author and a small description of the web site using site.description. This snippet is behind the code being used to display the author image shown at the top of Figure 7-2.

The last file in _includes is share.html, which allows the reader to share an article on Twitter or Facebook. There are many ways to share a post, and some are simpler than others. We look at three different ways to share on social media. The simplest way is to use the embed code for a share button, as most social media sites have an easy-to-use code. Let's look at Twitter, for example: It provides various sizes and types of share buttons, along with the code for how to use them. This code can then just be turned into an include file that can be referenced from a layout. The Twitter share buttons are available at https://about.twitter.com/resources/buttons.

The second method of sharing involves the use of a third-party service such as AddThis or Flare by Filament that offers multiple share services embedded in a single plug-in. These plug-ins work in a similar fashion to the embed codes, but they take it a step further. To use AddThis or Flare, the pages of the blog or web site have to be linked through an admin panel and then an embed code can be obtained. The biggest advantage of this method is that the web site is completely modular: The appearance or the types of social media sharing services that are available to the blog or site can be controlled completely independently of the site itself. This allows the code to remain small, yet functional and customizable. The final method of sharing posts involves creating custom code involving a link to open the social media site and share the post or page. This is the approach Kactus took; let's examine only the Twitter share code being used in share.html.

```
<a class="twitter" href="https://twitter.com/intent/tweet?text={{ site.domain_name }}
{{ page.url }} - {{page.title}} by @{{ site.authorTwitter }}"><span class="icon-twitter">
Tweet</span></a>
```

This piece of code seems very complicated, but it is actually a clever way of getting someone to tweet your page.url, and it works using Liquid properties. The logic here is to append the site domain and the post URL to post on Twitter along with the author of the article. This hyperlinks to the text tweet with the intent of sharing the post or page. This was the last file in the _includes folder. Now we move on to the folder that integrates all these files in a meaningful manner to display on the blog, the _layouts folder.

The _layouts Folder

Layouts are templates that tell Jekyll what to draw from the _includes folder and how to integrate it into a cohesive web site. Layouts are generally written in Liquid combined with HTML to make the best use of all the _includes. The first layout is the default layout, from which every other layout inherits. Let's look at the code for default.html in small segments. The first segment is the <head> tag.

```
<!DOCTYPE html>
<html lang="en">

<head>
  <meta charset="utf-8">
  <meta http-equiv="X-UA-Compatible" content="IE=edge,chrome=1">
  <meta name="viewport" content="width=device-width, initial-scale=1">

  <title>{{ site.name }}{% if page.title %} - {{ page.title }}{% endif %}</title>
  <link rel="shortcut icon" href="{{ site.baseurl }}assets/images/favicon.ico">
  <link rel="stylesheet" href="{{ site.baseurl }}assets/css/style.css">
  <link rel="alternate" type="application/rss+xml" title="My Blog" href="{{ site.baseurl }}
rss.xml">
  <link rel="stylesheet" href="{{ site.baseurl }}assets/css/highlight.css">
</head>
```

Here we can see the meta-information in the <head> tag present at the opening of the file. The initial meta tags are browser compatibility checks. They can be obtained from a reference guide or any theme. The interesting snippet following the meta tags includes the title of the web site by referencing the page.title property. Following the title, the next link is referencing the favicon of the blog, the second link is loading up the style.css files, and the last link is referencing the RSS feed feature available in the blog. Finally, there is another call to load up highlight.css, which serves the purpose of syntax highlighting in the posts. Now let's look at the second section of this layout.

```
<body>

  {% include navigation.html %}

  {% if page.profile %}
      {% include profile.html %}
  {% endif %}

  <section id="wrapper" class="{% if page.profile %}home{% endif %}">
    {{ content }}
  </section>
```

This segment of the code calls to various files that should be included in the default layout and the page. The first one, include, integrates the top bar through navigation.html, and the second one checks to see if the current page is the profile page, in which case the profile elements should be incorporated here. The third portion would show the rest of the profile data for the author if the current page is indeed the profile page. This segment of code integrated a few of the _includes. Let's move on to the next segment of code.

```
<script src="https://ajax.googleapis.com/ajax/libs/jquery/2.1.1/jquery.min.js"></script>
<script src="{{ site.baseurl }}assets/js/main.js"></script>
<script src="{{ site.baseurl }}assets/js/highlight.js"></script>
<script>hljs.initHighlightingOnLoad();</script>
```

This segment is actually very straightforward: These few lines are importing or loading scripts necessary to run the blog. The first one points to loading jQuery, which is immensely helpful in front-end tasks. The second one loads the local `main.js`. The third statement loads another local file called `highlight.js`, and the last `<script>` tag is initializing a function called `initHilightingOnLoad()`. As the name implies, this function starts code highlighting when the page is loaded. This was the third segment covering loading the JavaScript files into the blog. There is actually one last tidbit in the default layout, which is a Google Analytics code. It is also an embed code, and there is nothing for us to review in that segment. We talk about Google Analytics in much more depth later in the book. There is only one more layout left in this folder, the post layout. This layout is specific just for blog posts, but it inherits from the default and it builds on the missing pieces.

■ **Tip** While reading through `post.html`, pay careful attention to how the default layout carves out a basic structure but leaves the specifics for other pages to inherit and define. This is the true power of object-oriented programming: A single core can power all sorts of different objects, and once the default object has been constructed, other objects can inherit from it and develop it further.

The next layout is `post.html`, the layout that every post will follow; more precisely, any file that has the layout YAML front matter variable set to post. This time, the code won't be broken down into segments. Instead, this time, try to work through the code on your own and then we discuss it in detail.

```
---
layout: default
archive: true
---

<article class="post">
    <header>
        <h1>{{ page.title }}</h1>
        <h2 class="headline">{{ page.date | date:"%B %-d, %Y" }}</h2>
    </header>
    <section id="post-body">
        {{content}}
    </section>
</article>

<footer id="post-meta" class="clearfix">
    <a href="http://twitter.com/{{ site.authorTwitter }}">
        <img class="avatar" src="{{ site.baseurl }}assets/images/avatar.png">
        <div>
            <span class="dark">{{ site.author }}</span>
            <span>{{ site.description }}</span>
        </div>
    </a>
```

```
        <section id="sharing">
            {% include share.html %}
        </section>
</footer>

<!-- Disqus comments -->
{% if site.disqus %}
    <div class="archive readmore">
        <h3>Comments</h3>
        {% include disqus.html %}
    </div>
{% endif %}

<!-- Archive post list -->
{% if page.archive %}
    <ul id="post-list" class="archive readmore">
        <h3>Read more</h3>
        {% for post in site.posts %}
            <li>
                <a href="{{ site.baseurl }}{{ post.url | remove_first: '/' }}">{{ post.title
                }}<aside class="dates">{{ post.date | date:"%b %d" }}</aside></a>
            </li>
        {% endfor %}
    </ul>
{% endif %}
```

There are at least four distinguishable segments in the code just presented: the post section, the footer, the Disqus comments, and the archive post list. Let's break each of them down.

- The first section is the header, which contains the post title, followed by the post date and then the content. It must be noted that this is different from the home page, where the post.date preceded the post title.

- The second section is the footer, which contains the share to Twitter button, along with the site author's name and his or her description or bio.

- The third and fourth sections are related by the same class, but they have different purposes. The third section configures the comments section and Disqus is enabled if it is configured in the YAML code.

- The comments will be displayed by using the include import. Notice that each section calls to the appropriate includes to fill in the layout as needed.

- The final section of the code enables a related posts section under the blog post itself. This is accomplished by using an if loop to confirm whether an archive is enabled. If archive is enabled, then a for loop is used to go through the posts available and list them out with the date and title. The post name is hyperlinked to the actual blog posts, creating a Related Posts section at the end of each blog post.

The _posts Folder

We examined both the layouts available in the Kactus theme, and the next folder is the _posts folder, which contains one sample post. We do not examine this folder because the information about how to write a Jekyll post in Markdown was presented previously. This covers the folder structure in the theme, but we are still left with a few key files in the theme. These files, _config.yml and index.html, are both absolutely critical to the entire blog. Index.html follows more naturally after covering layouts and includes. This file is generally used to generate a list of posts and the styles for how to display them, but in Kactus, this was done by post-list.html much earlier. Here's index.html.

```
---
profile: true
---


{% include post-list.html %}
{% include footer.html %}
```

The YAML front matter enables the author profile to be shown on the home page as seen earlier in Figure 7-2. The other two includes create the post list and also add a footer to the blog. There are several instances like this file covered in the chapter where using the proper include allows for code to be reused; more important, it allows for the code to become modularized. The last file in Kactus is _config.yml, and the code is shown here.

```
name: Your New Jekyll Site
description: Blogging about stuffs
meta_description: "Your New Jekyll Site, Blogging about stuffs"

aboutPage: true

markdown: redcarpet
highlighter: pygments

paginate: 20
baseurl: /
domain_name: 'http://yourblog-domain.com'
google_analytics: 'UA-XXXXXXXX-X'
disqus: false
disqus_shortname: 'your-disqus-shortname'

# Details for the RSS feed generator
url:            'http://your-blog-url.example.com'
author:         'Your Name'
authorTwitter:  'YourTwitterUsername'

permalink:      /:year/:title/
```

This file is crucial because it is one of the only files where all the parameters that we have been using thus far can be defined. All the entries shown with the variable: value are either site, page, or YAML variables. The first few lines only describe the blog and the name for it. This is important for search engine optimization (SEO), which we discuss later in the book. The following line defines the aboutPage variable to be true for the blog, followed by two lines containing interpretive code for GitHub where the blog will be hosted. This code sets a compiler for Markdown called redcarpet and selects a code highlighter to be

103

pygments. The pagination is also defined here, following the baseurl convention of defining the baseurl to be the URL. The domain name is defined as the web site's home address, and the variables following define the analytics and Disqus. The information about these variables will be obtained from the various third-party services. The following three lines of variables define the properties of the blog for an RSS generator that syndicates the blog. Finally, the permalink is defined as the URL followed by the year and the title of the post. This is a very important setting, as it will carry through to every post or page made with the blog. The remaining code in the config file is actually site-wide defaults that can be defined here. Often in a Jekyll blog, we repeat many of the same configuration options in YAML and other sources. The use of defaults in the config file can allow us to apply them to a majority of the blog posts or pages; for instance, setting the same layout in each file, adding the same categories to a majority of posts, assigning the same author to all the posts in the same folder, and so on. This type of configuration allows for even more reuse of code and it works as shown here.

```
defaults:
  -
    scope:
      path: "amazing-posts"
      type: "posts"
    values:
      layout: "my-site"
      author: "Mr. Hyde"
```

In this example, everything that comes under scope has the same values applied to it. That's the whole purpose of using defaults in a site-wide configuration file. In this example, the layout my-site is being applied to all posts under the folder amazing-posts/ and the author name is defined as Mr. Hyde. This covers the last of the files, and the entire Kactus theme. We made it!

■ **Note**   The latest release of Jekyll (Jekyll 3.0) has made some of the _config.yml in Kactus outdated. There are two instances that need to be updated: The default Markdown compiler now is kramdown, not redcarpet, and the syntax highlighter in use now is rouge, not pygments. Both of these changes need to be applied to this file before hosting on GitHub.

Summary

In this chapter, we broke the entire Kactus theme down into small components that we could examine to see how Liquid and Markdown interacted within the context of Jekyll in this theme. This chapter was more about the application of concepts that we have been learning on and off about previously. We started with a few general principles about the folder structure and then looked further into each of the folders and the files present in them. We talked more about the ideas behind the code through each of the sections as we examined the code. This simple theme is a very powerful guided exercise and it was an opportunity to see the code behind a full theme in action. It might be worth the time to go through this chapter again with fresh eyes to understand any snippets of code that weren't very clear. In the end, the application of concepts is the easiest way to show how the components such as Markdown and Liquid give rise to inheritance and reusable code that can make Jekyll aware. Blog-awareness is an emergent phenomenon that results from the use of object-oriented principles, making Jekyll incredibly powerful and an easy tool to use for prototyping. Our journey breaking down Kactus ends here. Review this chapter well because we will be using Kactus again in the next chapter to create a very cool small project!

Further Reading

1. **Popular Jekyll themes**: GitHub Themes, https://github.com/jekyll/jekyll/wiki/Themes

2. **Jekyll Now home page**: http://www.jekyllnow.com/

3. **Smashing Magazine tutorial**: http://www.smashingmagazine.com/2014/08/build-blog-jekyll-github-pages/

REVIEW

In this review, we focus on a few interpreting tasks reviewing code similar to our Jekyll themes.

1. **Interpretive Task**: The following piece of code creates a footer. What would the output be like? Just draw it out on paper.

```
<footer class="center">
  <div class="measure">
    <small>
      Theme crafted with &lt;3 by <a href="http://johnotander.com">John Otander</a>
      (<a href="https://twitter.com/4lpine">@4lpine</a>).<br>
      &lt;/&gt; available on <a href="https://github.com/johnotander/pixyll">Github</a>.
    </small>
  </div>
</footer>
```

2. **Interpretive Task**: The following piece of code creates social media icons. Which icons would be seen on a page? Use the font-awesome cheat sheet if necessary.

```
<div class="social-icons">
  <div class="social-icons-right">
    {% if site.github_username %}
      <a class="fa fa-github" href="https://github.com/{{ site.github_username }}"></a>
    {% endif %}

    {% if site.stackoverflow_id %}
      <a class="fa fa-stack-overflow" href="https://stackoverflow.com/users/{{ site.stackoverflow_id }}"></a>
    {% endif %}

    {% if site.twitter_username %}
      <a class="fa fa-twitter" href="https://twitter.com/{{ site.twitter_username }}"></a>
    {% endif %}
  </div>
</div>
```

3. **Interpretive Task**: The following piece of code creates pagination. Review the
    pagination covered earlier and then interpret this piece of code.

```
<div class="pagination clearfix mb1 mt4">
  <div class="left">
    {% if paginator.previous_page %}
      {% if paginator.page == 2 %}
        <a class="pagination-item" href="{{ site.baseurl }}/">Newer</a>
      {% else %}
        <a class="pagination-item" href="{{ site.baseurl }}/page{{paginator.previous_
        page}}/">Newer</a>
      {% endif %}
    {% else %}
      <span class="pagination-item disabled">Newer</span>
    {% endif %}
  </div>
  <div class="right">
    {% if paginator.next_page %}
      <a class="pagination-item" href="{{ site.baseurl }}/page{{paginator.next_
page}}/">Older</a>
    {% else %}
      <span class="pagination-item disabled">Older</span>
    {% endif %}
  </div>
</div>
```

■ ■ ■

Git It Done

Don't let your dreams be dreams.

—Shia LaBeouf

We covered the Kactus theme in detail in the last chapter, but now it's time to make something using Kactus. In this chapter, we create a news brief web site using Kactus and implementing the web technologies that we have been discussing thus far. Kactus is a good foundation for this project because it is a simple theme that yields to modifications very easily. Our finished product with new style components would be very different from the original theme. This is our first self-contained project, so we also discuss the thought process that goes into starting a project: the design thinking involved in prototyping what the project should look like, creating a wireframe of the project at different stages, and finally making a list of components that need to be integrated into the project. These additional topics should give the reader a sense of how to start a new project using Jekyll and arrive at a mental image of how the project should function. We also talk about adding new style elements that we have not covered previously. Finally, we introduce how to use Git through this project, and more specifically, how to host the project on GitHub and manage modifications to Kactus using GitHub Desktop.

Scope and Scale

Planning is crucial in the early stages of starting a new project. Even though a good plan can't account for the unexpected, it can provide us with broad milestones. We have to turn those milestones into concrete objectives that can followed throughout the project. If obstacles arise while executing the objectives, we simply have to revisit the milestones and rethink the objectives in line with what we learned from the ones that didn't work. This iterative process is known by many names, but Kent Beck provided us with a complete framework called Extreme Programming (XP): starting projects with a simple design that constantly evolves to add needed flexibility and remove complexity. There are two questions to keep in mind during the initial planning phases of this project:

- **What is the scope of this web site?** The scope spans a multitude of factors, such as the purpose of the project, the intended audience, and how that audience will interact with the web site. Finally, the scope extends beyond the project to the developer as well. How much time will a developer dedicate to maintaining and updating the project instead of creating new content?

- **What is the scale of this web site?** The scale covers the resources required to integrate new technologies with the web site in the future, reaching out to and serving a large enough audience. This might involve techniques such as creating mailing lists, which we talk about later in this chapter.

These two questions are broadly applicable to personal projects that you would like to show off, a blog that you started to write, and even professional web sites for organizations. Let's try to answer these questions for Kactus. To begin answering, we first need a concise description of our web site: This web site is going to be a news brief, where articles (roughly 140 words in length) are posted every day discussing the delicate connection between science and society. Now that's a simple yet comprehensive description of what the project will be about. Great! Once we have this description, we can start thinking about the finished product that will deliver the goals outlined in the description. To make this task simpler, the best solution is to find other projects that have a description similar to ours so that we can draw inspiration from them. An alternative method is to prototype your idea from scratch (this is sometimes the only possible way). However, if we can find another app that already does most of what we want, prototyping becomes much easier.

There are many web sites and apps for news briefs, but one of the best designed and functional apps that accurately fits our description is the Economist Espresso app, shown in Figure 8-1. Espresso is a mobile app that provides a short list of news briefs (150 words long) every morning about what is happening in the world. We want to accomplish something similar, but at a much smaller scale, with only one post per day fitting the rest of our description. We also want to do a Web-version powered by Jekyll and not a mobile app. We thus have two well-defined constraints that can point us in the right direction. Let's go back to examine the Espresso app, as we might discover some useful insights in the process that someone else has already figured out.

A   B

Figure 8-1. *The Economist Espresso app shown in two panels. Panel A is the opening screen, listing the news briefs split into different categories. Panel B shows what a single news brief looks like. The particular section shown in this panel contains multiple briefs.*

We can obtain a lot of information from Figure 8-1, and the first piece to note is the length of the briefs. They are very short and to the point, with key words shown in bold. We can use syntax highlighting to accomplish the same result, or we can simply boldface the words in Markdown. Figure 8-1 can also help us decide the features that we don't want in our app. For instance, our scope was one article a day, so we cannot have all our briefs combined in a daily summary. That is not to say that we can't use summaries, but instead of daily summaries we would have to do weekly summaries of the news briefs. Interestingly, that model works well for many publications such as *The Scientist,* which uses weekly briefings to report on the top science stories of the week. Just from examining an already existing app, we have a few ideas about how our product should look or function. To get a realistic idea of what that a finished product might look like, we need to advance our understanding of the project and how we approach it. Creating a simple prototype is a great way to start modeling behaviour that our web site will exhibit. For instance, a news brief is analogous to a short blog post. A very simple way to model a single news brief would be in a word processor, as shown in Figure 8-2.

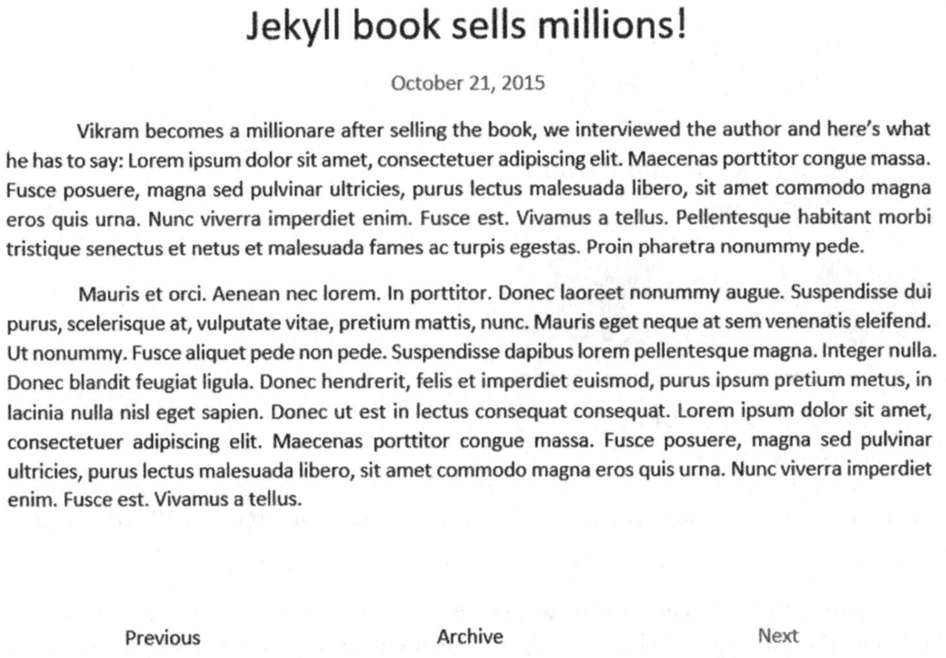

Jekyll book sells millions!

October 21, 2015

Vikram becomes a millionare after selling the book, we interviewed the author and here's what he has to say: Lorem ipsum dolor sit amet, consectetuer adipiscing elit. Maecenas porttitor congue massa. Fusce posuere, magna sed pulvinar ultricies, purus lectus malesuada libero, sit amet commodo magna eros quis urna. Nunc viverra imperdiet enim. Fusce est. Vivamus a tellus. Pellentesque habitant morbi tristique senectus et netus et malesuada fames ac turpis egestas. Proin pharetra nonummy pede.

Mauris et orci. Aenean nec lorem. In porttitor. Donec laoreet nonummy augue. Suspendisse dui purus, scelerisque at, vulputate vitae, pretium mattis, nunc. Mauris eget neque at sem venenatis eleifend. Ut nonummy. Fusce aliquet pede non pede. Suspendisse dapibus lorem pellentesque magna. Integer nulla. Donec blandit feugiat ligula. Donec hendrerit, felis et imperdiet euismod, purus ipsum pretium metus, in lacinia nulla nisl eget sapien. Donec ut est in lectus consequat consequat. Lorem ipsum dolor sit amet, consectetuer adipiscing elit. Maecenas porttitor congue massa. Fusce posuere, magna sed pulvinar ultricies, purus lectus malesuada libero, sit amet commodo magna eros quis urna. Nunc viverra imperdiet enim. Fusce est. Vivamus a tellus.

Previous   Archive   Next

Figure 8-2. *A simple prototype of what a single news brief should look like. This rapid prototype was done in a word processor, but it shows all the necessary features that we would want on a news brief web site: the heading of the post, the date it was published, the post itself, and finally navigation to see older posts.*

■ **Tip** The simplest way to prototype or storyboard an idea is to just do it on paper. It doesn't matter how poorly it is done: As long as you can get your ideas out, you can always go back and organize them on another sheet of paper methodically.

Once we have this base model of the prototype, it is easier to start adding components to it and making more modifications. We can think of Espresso as a collection of features, and then decide which ones we want to implement in our own project. The first feature we want to look at is the archive. Espresso has a very nice archive organized by days, shown in Figure 8-3. This archive can be reached from the Settings and contains the articles organized by each day. Clicking on a different day takes you to the set of news briefs published that day. We can model this archive by listing news briefs organized by the date and month of posting. We can also use labels (in the archive) to list posts that have a common theme, much like the categories in Figure 8-1.

Settings

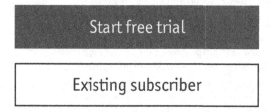

Tu	We	Th	Fr	Mo
20	21	22	23	26

To read all articles every day, log in
with your existing Economist.com
digital subscriber credentials.
Alternatively, start a one month free
trial today.

Start free trial

Existing subscriber

Figure 8-3. *The archive in the Espresso app. The days on the top correspond to the articles published on that particular day.*

Let's think about prototyping this in the simplest way possible: We can go back to the word processor that was used in Figure 8-2 to create the mockup of a blog post. Creating a hyperlink from the blog post navigation bar to the Archive page would be sufficient for the web site, at least in the prototype. An example prototype of an Archive page is shown in Figure 8-4. So far, we have a two-page prototype (from the word processor) that we can use to focus on the overall picture and answer the two questions that we posted at the beginning of this chapter. The scope of this web site is to provide news briefs on topics that deal with the connection between science and society. The web site will be a Jekyll blog with each news brief roughly the Jekyll equivalent of a blog post. These briefs will be fewer than 140 words and we will post one per day. There are two intended audiences for this web site: college students who are studying science or interested in it and the general public or layman who reads the news briefs to learn what is happening in the world of science.

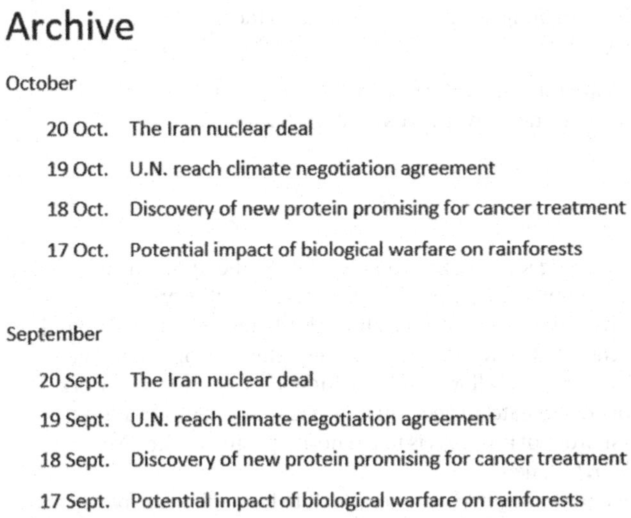

Archive

October

20 Oct.	The Iran nuclear deal
19 Oct.	U.N. reach climate negotiation agreement
18 Oct.	Discovery of new protein promising for cancer treatment
17 Oct.	Potential impact of biological warfare on rainforests

September

20 Sept.	The Iran nuclear deal
19 Sept.	U.N. reach climate negotiation agreement
18 Sept.	Discovery of new protein promising for cancer treatment
17 Sept.	Potential impact of biological warfare on rainforests

Figure 8-4. *A minimal prototype of the archive. The posts for each day are listed by the month. This is the page that users will reach after clicking the Archive link on a blog post or the home page.*

The scale of the web site is small initially and we will be hosting it on GitHub Pages for the moment. In this early testing period, you want to learn as much as you can about your audience and how they interact with the web site. Other resources required for the web site are enabling comments by readers and capturing their attention so that they come back to reading it again. Scale is all about testing and improving on the features that your audience uses. This is not something we can prototype easily. However, we talk about techniques such as creating mailing lists and integrating them into the blog to start building up a critical mass in the latter half of this chapter. It is important to understand the rationale behind the extra steps that we use in this chapter, such as drawing inspiration from the Espresso app and then prototyping the final product, instead of just implementing features right away. This chapter is structured so that you will form a mental representation of how the project should function and appear before we start coding. That's why we talked about Espresso, then moved on to a more concrete representation with a prototype, and finally defined the scale and scope of the web site. In the next section, we pick up the Kactus theme again and you are encouraged to follow the changes in code on your own code editor (Sublime).

Tools List

The scope and scale discussed earlier are actually part of a larger thought process that results in the creation of a project specification. We create a complete spec in the next chapter. After creating a simple prototype (either on paper or using a tool like a word processor), the last step before we start writing code is to make a list of web technologies that we will be implementing in this project. This list is similar to a recipe that first lists out the ingredients that you need and then the method of preparation. For now, it might be a good idea to simply make the list on a piece of paper. With some practice, as you are writing these components down, your mind will start thinking ahead in terms of concrete code snippets or the appropriate include files. The following list shows the components we need.

1. **Disqus:** This is used for comments on the news briefs. Disqus can be found at `https://disqus.com/home/`.

2. **Font-awesome:** This is used for navigation and simple stylistic additions. The home page is found at `https://fortawesome.github.io/Font-Awesome/icons/`.

3. **MailChimp:** This is used for creating a mailing list and subscription to the list. It can be found at `http://mailchimp.com/`.

4. **Social buttons:** These are used to share the news brief by using AddThis or custom-creating the icons. This can be found at `http://www.addthis.com/`.

Just Do It

We can finally get started modifying the code powering Kactus for the news brief. All the updated code from Kactus is provided here and the files are available along with the book for the reader. In this project, we use GitHub to host the final project. GitHub will convert the theme into a static web site powered by Jekyll and then host it for us. In brief, GitHub is a web interface to Git, where source code under version control can be hosted and modified collaboratively by developers. This allows multiple individuals or teams to work together on a project. To use GitHub, you first need to create an account and verify your e-mail address. Once that is done, you can start using it. The first order of business is to create a repository. Click New Repository to get started or go to `https://github.com/new`.

This repository needs to be configured in a certain way because we want it to hold the code for Kactus and also host the web site on GitHub. The naming pattern of this repository will direct GitHub to use GitHub Pages, which is the hosting tool powered by Jekyll used for processing Jekyll-based web sites. It can create static web sites from the source code present in the repository. The appropriate naming scheme for the repository is `username.github.io`, as shown in Figure 8-5. It is crucial to name the repository in this manner for it to be compiled properly by GitHub into a web site.

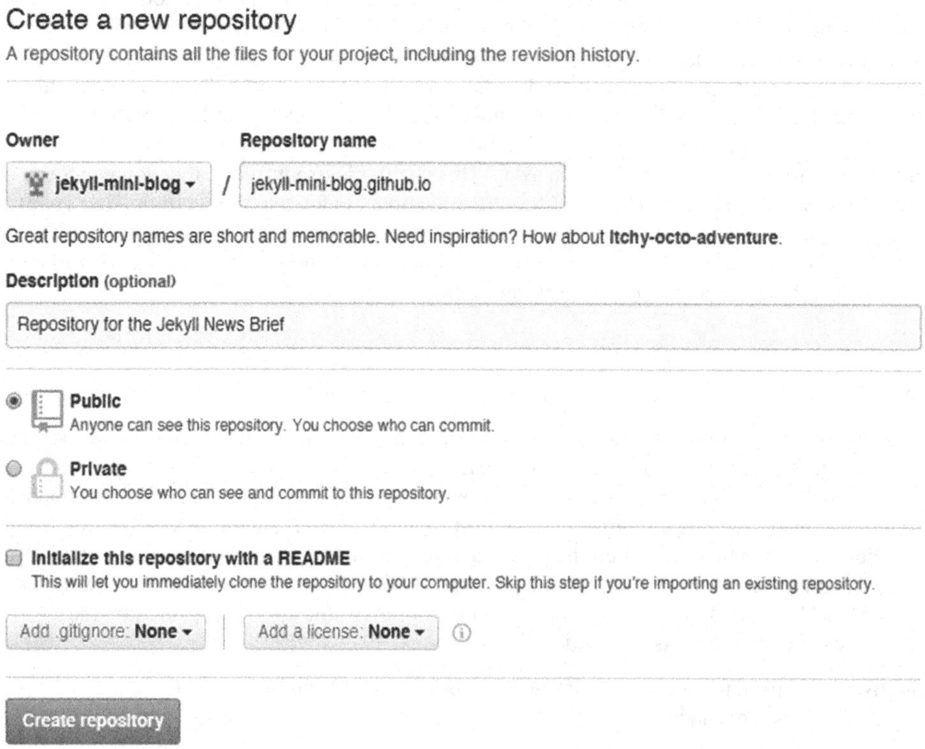

Create a new repository

A repository contains all the files for your project, including the revision history.

Owner   **Repository name**

🐙 jekyll-mini-blog ▾   /   jekyll-mini-blog.github.io

Great repository names are short and memorable. Need inspiration? How about **itchy-octo-adventure**.

Description (optional)

Repository for the Jekyll News Brief

⦿ 📖 **Public**
Anyone can see this repository. You choose who can commit.

○ 🔒 **Private**
You choose who can see and commit to this repository.

☐ **Initialize this repository with a README**
This will let you immediately clone the repository to your computer. Skip this step if you're importing an existing repository.

Add .gitignore: **None** ▾ | Add a license: **None** ▾   ⓘ

Create repository

Figure 8-5. The naming scheme for a repository to be converted into a web site: `username.github.io`

Once the repository has been created, it is ready to handle code. New code needs to be pushed to this empty repository in a process often called the initial commit, which also makes the web interface of GitHub available to us. To make the initial commit, GitHub needs a local repository to work with. This copy will be synced and made available online. We use GitHub Desktop to manage the repository locally and push code online. GitHub Desktop is a new tool built to bring the native workflow of Git to a visual application for platforms such as Windows and Mac. You can easily connect to GitHub and publish or share code with a few simple clicks. After a repository has been created as shown previously, you are given a few options to make the initial commit. We use GitHub Desktop, so the best choice is to select Set up in Desktop, as shown in Figure 8-6. This will take you to the download page for GitHub Desktop, from which you should install the version appropriate for your platform.

■ **Tip**   To review Git terminology or the need for version control, refer back to Chapter 4 and review the sections on version control.

Figure 8-6. *Downloading GitHub Desktop to set up this git repository. Notice that the username in this example is* jekyll-mini-blog *and the domain associated where the website will appear is* jekyll-mini-blog.github.io

After the installation is done, open GitHub Desktop, which shows the Tutorial by default. It is a good idea to walk through the tutorial to understand the software. To get started, click on the gear icon near the top right and go to the Options setting. In the Options setting, log in to the GitHub account with which you created the repository, as shown in Figure 8-7a. Once you have logged in, click the plus sign near the top left of GitHub Desktop to access the empty repository that we created earlier. This is shown in Figure 8-7b. After cloning the repository, you will be prompted for a location on your computer to which to save the repository, which will become our local version. Remember this folder location, as we will use it shortly. Initially, we don't see anything in GitHub Desktop because the cloned repository is empty; however, we now begin adding files to it.

⊙ Options

Accounts

You're not signed in to any accounts. Add a GitHub account for quick access to your repositories or add a GitHub Enterprise account to access repositories on your corporate network.

Figure 8-7a. *Adding the GitHub account with which you created the repository will allow you to access the repository and clone it.*

Figure 8-7b. *Cloning the repository locally after signing in. After selecting the available repository, click Clone* `repository-name` *and you are done.*

The process of adding new code, files, and images is all the same, and it revolves around three steps: add, commit, and push. In brief, new files (code and noncode) are added to the repository under Git. The files are finalized in a commit that takes a commit message as a comment on what changes are being introduced. Finally the commit containing the changes and a description of those changes is pushed to GitHub, where the code will be hosted. This process is basically repeated for every change introduced to the project. The objective is to keep those changes small and testable because in that manner, when we make a mistake, it is easy to track down which commit introduced those problems. In this fashion, we can easily diagnose problems with a project that requires long-term development and also a project that will be improved over time, such as a blog or our news brief web site.

We are ready to make the initial commit. In this first commit, we add all the files from the original Kactus theme. This can be accomplished in a few ways, but we will go with the simplest approach for now: Download the Kactus theme as a zipped file (shown in the previous chapter), extract it, and copy all the files over to the local location of the cloned empty repository. Once the files have been copied over, GitHub Desktop will be populated with all the new changes to be added. This group of changes is the commit that we will push to GitHub, as shown in Figure 8-8. Once the changes become visible in GitHub Desktop, add a commit message and then click Commit to master.

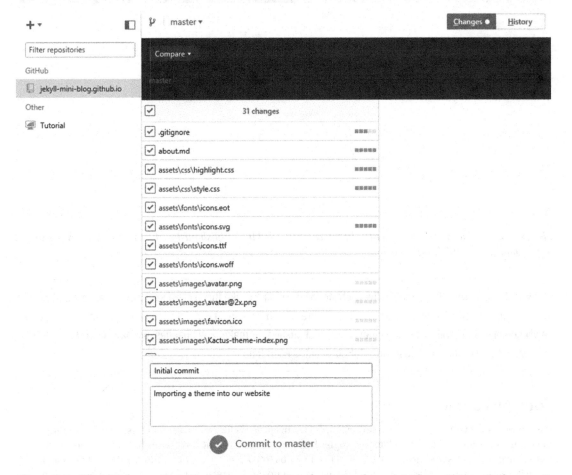

Figure 8-8. *The initial commit: A set of changes importing the Kactus theme into the repository. Each commit must be a small and manageable set of changes, so that debugging becomes easier. The exception is the initial commit.*

Once the changes are committed, it is time to push the code to GitHub. This step has many names: Sometimes it is simply referred to as pushing and other times as publishing or just committing code. GitHub Desktop calls it publishing changes to the repository, which is a functional description. In the top right corner, clicking Publish will finalize the changes to the repository and make them available online, as shown in Figure 8-9. Pushing the code to GitHub has a few other noteworthy effects: In this case, the pushed changes contain Jekyll components and Jekyll-formatted source files. We also named the repository in a way to let GitHub know to use GitHub Pages and compile the web site using Jekyll. After the code is pushed, within the next ten minutes or so, the live version of Kactus-theme (which is exactly what we pushed in the initial commit) will be available on `jekyll-mini-blog.github.io`. In the future, all changes pushed to this repository will trigger GitHub to recompile the blog, but the changes will be reflected on the live version nearly instantaneously. When GitHub finishes compiling the blog, it will be published online at the `username.github.io` address for users to access.

Figure 8-9. *Publishing changes after the initial commit. Clicking Publish pushes the changes to the repository and makes them available on GitHub.*

■ **Tip**   To make any change to the live website, we must first make those changes to the local version. After that, the changes need to be pushed to GitHub where GitHub Pages will use Jekyll to recompile the blog. The newly compiled blog will reflect the changes we just pushed. To make new changes, we have to go through the process of add, commit, and push with GitHub Desktop each time.

Font-Awesome

We can now start working through a few examples of this process for our project. Let's start implementing the features we covered in the web technologies list. The first one is font-awesome. To briefly review it, font-awesome provides a standard set of web and brand icons free for personal or commercial use. These icons make it easy to illustrate something quickly with almost no effort. The web site for the project is available at: `https://fortawesome.github.io/Font-Awesome/`.

We look at the code first before switching back to GitHub Desktop. Implementing font-awesome is very straightforward. To follow the instructions on the web site linked earlier, click Getting Started. We use the MaxCDN link to get access to font-awesome. The proper location to place the import is in the <head> tag. In Kactus, the head tag can either be in a file under _includes or _layouts. One way to tell is generally the name of the file itself; for convenience, most themes would name such files head.html or header.html. In this case, there is no such file, so we move on to _layouts, where in default.html, we find the head tag as follows:

```
<head>
  <meta charset="utf-8">
  <meta http-equiv="X-UA-Compatible" content="IE=edge,chrome=1">
  <meta name="viewport" content="width=device-width, initial-scale=1">

  <title>{{ site.name }}{% if page.title %} - {{ page.title }}{% endif %}</title>
  <link rel="shortcut icon" href="{{ site.baseurl }}assets/images/favicon.ico">
  <link rel="stylesheet" href="{{ site.baseurl }}assets/css/style.css">
  <link rel="alternate" type="application/rss+xml" title="My Blog" href="{{ site.baseurl }}
rss.xml">
  <link rel="stylesheet" href="{{ site.baseurl }}assets/css/highlight.css">
</head>
```

We add the font-awesome line to the very end as shown here.

```
  <link rel="stylesheet" href="{{ site.baseurl }}assets/css/highlight.css">
  <link rel="stylesheet" href="https://maxcdn.bootstrapcdn.com/font-awesome/4.4.0/css/font-
awesome.min.css">
</head>
```

That was it! The simplicity of font-awesome makes it absolutely delightful to use, and soon enough, we will start implementing the icons, too. One rationale behind placing this code in default.html is that every layout will inherit from this file, making the imports instantly available to every page in the theme. Once this code has been added to default.html, this should come up as a new change in GitHub Desktop because this entire project is under version control. Let's work through how to add this change, commit it, and then push the code. The commit message should be simple, yet descriptive enough to give us an idea of what changes are being pushed to the live web site, as shown in Figure 8-10. In addition, GitHub Desktop also shows the changes made to the file present in this commit. Remember that every time a change is made, it is available in GitHub Desktop. Once a series of changes are available, it is time to include all of those in a commit and push the changes. The goal is to include a small set of changes to push each time in a commit, and these commits can be derived from breaking down large project goals into small, manageable tasks. It is very easy to get lazy with commit messages, but they are critical to managing a large project with a long-term history of changes. Our first commit added font-awesome to the project, and the next series of commits will change the outlook of Kactus.

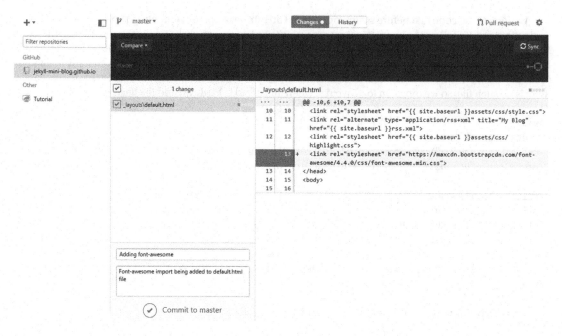

Figure 8-10. Adding a commit message to the change made in default.html *including font-awesome. The actual line of code added is visible in the panel on the right. After the change has been added through a commit, click Sync to push the changes to GitHub and update the live web site. This is essentially the process of add, commit, and push in Git.*

Navigation

Let's start by fixing the navigation bar at the top of the site. The objective here is to point the Subscribe button to an empty link that will be replaced by MailChimp later on and move the current link to feeds to an RSS navigation bar element. We also add the appropriate font-awesome icons to each of the navigation bar elements. For reference, use the font-awesome cheat sheet. The following are the appropriate font awesome icons to be used for the navigation bar.

- **Home:** Uses a unicode back arrow to be replaced with fa-arrow-left.

- **RSS:** New element, font-awesome companion: fa-rss.

- **About:** No current icon, font-awesome icon: fa-cog.

- **Subscribe:** No current icon, font-awesome icon: fa-envelope-o.

Let's see how these modifications (adding an RSS element and font-awesome icons) look in code for navigation.html.

```
<nav class="main-nav">
    {% if page.url != "/index.html" %}
        <a href="{{ site.baseurl }}"> <i class="fa fa-arrow-left"></i> Home </a>
    {% endif %}
```

```
{% if page.url != "/about/" %}
    {% if site.aboutPage %}
        <a href="{{ site.baseurl }}about"> <i class="fa fa-cog"></i> About </a>
    {% endif %}
{% endif %}

<a href="{{ site.baseurl }}feed.xml"> <i class="fa fa-rss"></i> RSS</a>
<a class="cta" href="#"> <i class="fa fa-envelope-o"></i> Subscribe</a>
</nav>
```

Once the modifications have been made in navigation.html, it is time to commit the changes and push the code to GitHub so that our live copy can be updated. This process is reviewed once again in Figure 8-11. From here on, we focus only on the code, as the process remains the same for every single change made to the local version. This second commit adds a few font-awesome icons to the navigation bar, and now we need to start changing the web site itself to get it closer to the prototype that we presented earlier in this chapter. To do so, the first element to be removed is the profile near the top.

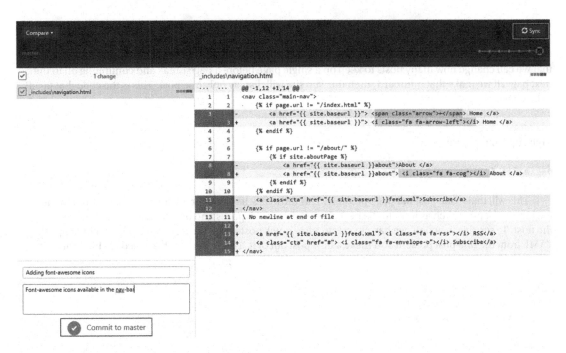

Figure 8-11. *Demonstrating a commit of changes and pushing code to GitHub. After adding the font-awesome icons to the navigation bar, a commit message is added and the changes are pushed to GitHub.*

Page Profile

The code for the page profile is found in _layouts under default.html, and under the <body> tag is the code we need to remove (shown as the bold snippet).

```
<body>

  {% include navigation.html %}

  {% if page.profile %}
      {% include profile.html %}
  {% endif %}
```

This will make the profile stop showing up at the top of the page. Now we repeat the cycle of add, push, and commit to make the change available on the live web site. We can now start changing the layout of the page itself to make it look more like the prototype that we proposed.

Pagination

One unique aspect about Kactus is that the pagination variable is defined in the config.yml file. This means that we can change how many posts to keep on a single page before a page break and continuing on to the next page. If we make that number 1, then the web site will display only one post. This is the code that needs to be changed:

```
markdown: redcarpet
highlighter: pygments

paginate: 1
```

This will make one post per page possible. This little trick has a major advantage: It lets us retain the pagination features such as links to the next page and previous pages and use them as navigation below the post. To see this in action, we have to create a few quick posts to be included on the blog. Let's copy the YAML from the one post present and make a new post out of it. This is the part that needs to be copied:

```
---
title:  "Welcome to Jekyll!"
date:    2013-11-10 10:18:00
description: Thriller Comedy Horror
---
```

The date and the description need to be changed for each post, and the newly created posts need to be saved as new files in the Jekyll format year-month-date-filename.markdown. In Sublime, there is a quick way to make a dummy post: Just type in lipsum and press Tab to get the standard dummy text on the post. Just type it again to get another paragraph, and that will be the second file. Now add these changes and push them to GitHub. In this commit, we have two new files and an edit to config.yml that will be available on the live web site. The web site now looks more like Figure 8-12; the additional bar under the navigation bar will be cleaned up later on.

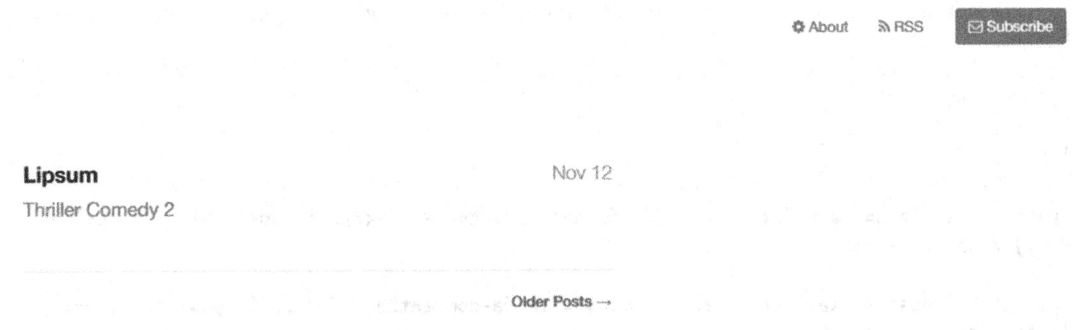

✿ About   ⟩ RSS   ✉ Subscribe

Lipsum   Nov 12

Thriller Comedy 2

Older Posts →

Figure 8-12. *The web site at its current stage. The title of the first post here depends on which post was dated most recently. That is the post that will show up first, another pagination feature, along with the Older Posts buttons that are retained by simply changing the* config.yml.

Post List

The next task is to change how the web site displays the posts: Instead of just loading up a list of the posts, we need to display the text along with the post. For this, we would have to look into post-list.html, and this file is crucial for the transformation of the Kactus theme into our news brief. The first elements we need to remove are the hyperlinks from each post to the post layout from the title and the date. We want to display the post itself on the home page. This can be done by simply removing the hyperlink <a> tag entirely, and to keep the date in the same location, we can use a <span> in the same line as well:

```
<span><aside class="dates"> {{ post.date | date:"%b %d" }}</aside></span>
<span><h1>{{ post.title }}</h1> <h2> {{ post.description }}</h2></span>
```

The next step is to actually show the content of the post as an item of the page list. In this way, the page list loops through each post and shows its name, the date it was created, and the content of the post. This is a very important distinction to make because every change that needs to be displayed on each post will have something to do with the post list. To display the content of the blog post, let's look at how the default layout shows the content of each post. The default layout uses the following code snippet:

```
<section id="wrapper" class="{% if page.profile %}home{% endif %}">
  {{ content }}
</section>
```

The section tag allows the default layout to wrap the Liquid content variable in it and display it. We can simply modify this to not include the profile each time, as follows:

```
<section id="wrapper">
  {{ content }}
</section>
```

That's it! It was very easy to do this because we could simply borrow from the default layout. Now we can add this to the post list file along with two font-awesome icons:

- **Post Description:** fa-commenting-o

- **Post Date:** fa-calendar-check-o

Let's look at `post-list.html` after the modifications. The lines of code shown in bold indicate the new changes.

```
<ul id="post-list">
{% for post in paginator.posts %}
<li>

<span><aside class="dates"><i class="fa fa-calendar-check-o"></i> {{ post.date | date:"%b
%d" }}</aside></span>

<span><h1>{{ post.title }}</h1> <h2><i class="fa fa-commenting-o"></i> {{ post.description
}}</h2></span>

<section id="wrapper">
{{ post.content }}
</section>
</li>
    {% endfor %}
</ul>
{% if paginator.previous_page or paginator.next_page %}
    {% include pagination.html %}
{% endif %}
```

After pushing this code, the web site is finally starting to look more like the prototype, and the end result is shown in Figure 8-13. Keep in mind that the post layout itself is not being used here at all; we are using a trick to show the details of a post such as the name, date, and most important, the contents of the post as a list item (or `<li>` items). This idea might be easier to conceptualize if we think of it in terms of objects. Each item in the post list is an object with multiple properties such as a name, a short description, and the blog post content. The post list is only a `for` loop that goes through each of the objects, showing it in a previously specified manner.

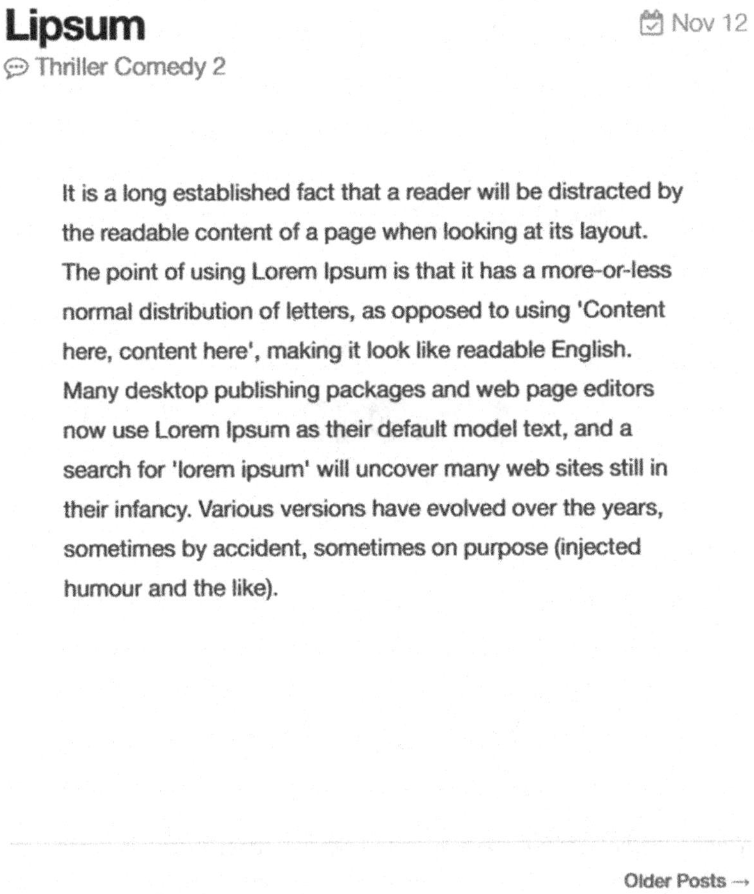

Lipsum

🗓 Nov 12

💬 Thriller Comedy 2

It is a long established fact that a reader will be distracted by the readable content of a page when looking at its layout. The point of using Lorem Ipsum is that it has a more-or-less normal distribution of letters, as opposed to using 'Content here, content here', making it look like readable English. Many desktop publishing packages and web page editors now use Lorem Ipsum as their default model text, and a search for 'lorem ipsum' will uncover many web sites still in their infancy. Various versions have evolved over the years, sometimes by accident, sometimes on purpose (injected humour and the like).

Older Posts →

Figure 8-13. *The post content present along with the post title, description, and date. At the bottom, the pagination navigation bar shows the Older Posts link. Kactus is starting to look more like the prototype discussed earlier.*

Share Buttons

Now that the post content appears on each post, we need to make it shareable by including share buttons. The post layout actually has a footer that contains share buttons that we can repurpose to our own use in the post list. The best way for us to reuse it would be to modularize the code and put it in a separate file, including it only where necessary. The original share buttons in Kactus are present in a footer shown in Figure 8-14. The code for the social buttons is present in _includes/social.html and the implementation is in the post layout shown here.

```
<footer id="post-meta" class="clearfix">

    <a href="http://twitter.com/{{ site.authorTwitter }}">
        <img class="avatar" src="{{ site.baseurl }}assets/images/avatar.png">
        <div>
            <span class="dark">{{ site.author }}</span>
            <span>{{ site.description }}</span>
        </div>
```

```
    </a>
    <section id="sharing">
        {% include share.html %}
    </section>
</footer>
```

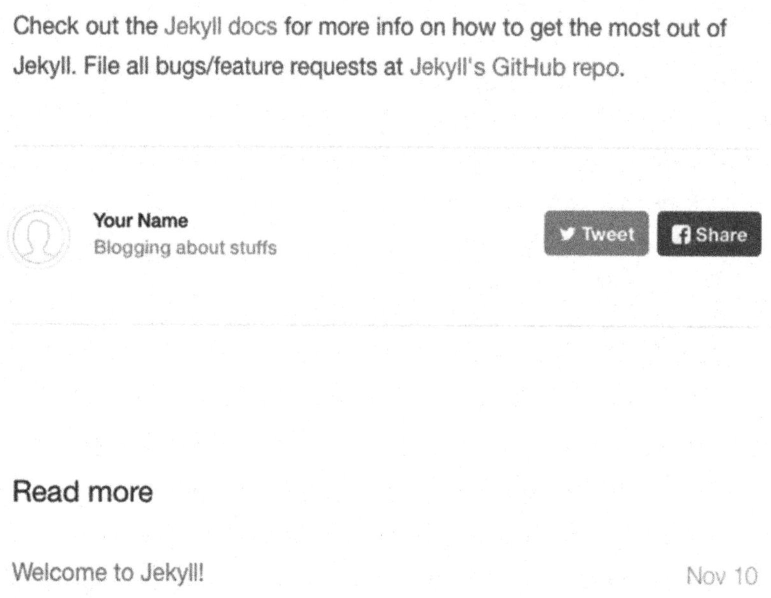

Check out the Jekyll docs for more info on how to get the most out of
Jekyll. File all bugs/feature requests at Jekyll's GitHub repo.

Your Name
Blogging about stuffs

🐦 Tweet   f Share

Read more

Welcome to Jekyll!   Nov 10

Figure 8-14. Social icons in a share bar with the author name and summary, after `foot.html` *is included*

This segment of code creates a footer containing a social profile, the description of the site, and the author's name. We need to save this snippet as a file itself so that the code can be reused in the appropriate files. The proper location to place this would be on top of the pagination navigation bar. We can copy this snippet and save it as `foot.html` for further use. We will be including this file within `pagination.html` and the rationale behind placing it here instead of the post list file is that spacing the web site would be easier later on when we clean up the news brief. This include is very easy; just add the following to the top of `pagination.html`:

```
{% include foot.html %}
```

That should do the job. Notice that we didn't write any code this time, we simply repurposed code in a different context by creating a new file. That's the power of modularity in Jekyll. We had to do no work this time to get the social buttons. The final result would include the social icons bar right above the pagination. Just ignore the extra horizontal rules for now, as we will clean them up at a later stage as we add colors to the site and also a title.

We only covered two social media icons here, but to add a larger variety of social media icons or enhance the intractability of the user with the web site, there are two other very nice tools. The first one is a third-party service called AddThis, which creates a small social share bar that loads on the side of every page. This share bar can be filled with any of the hundreds of social media sites of the user's choice on AddThis.com. The second service is more subtle, but you might have come across a blog where you could select a line and share the post by quoting the line you selected. This service is called Flare by Filament. It also works similar to

AddThis, where a script loads up the service and the users can interact with it. The main difference between AddThis and Flare is simply the subtle share options when the reader selects a line. One recommendation for this news brief site is to use custom icons to share the post along with Flare to quote and share a specific line. In general, this type of sharing increases user interactivity. A good tutorial to get started with Flare is available at `http://www.dtelepathy.com/blog/products/share-content-with-flare`.

Archive

Our prototype also included an archive feature, so let's build that into the pagination navigation bar. This one is very easy: Simply go into `pagination.html` and replicate an `<a>` tag to point to an archive page. If we look in the file, we can see remnants of unicode arrows, so let's replace those with font-awesome while we are updating the file as follows:

- **Front-arrow:** Older posts - `fa-arrow-right`

- **Back-arrow:** Newer posts - `fa-arrow-left`

- **Archive:** `fa-archive`

The code to include the archive looks like this (shown as the bold line):

```
</span>
{% endif %}

<a href="#"><i class="fa fa-archive"></i> Archive </a>

{% if paginator.next_page %}
```

The archive is not pointing to anything because the page has not yet been created. Let's work on that next.

■ **Note** The archive can be created in many ways; some are simple and others are more complex. In this chapter, we are going with a simpler approach because we have not yet covered how to use plug-ins in Jekyll. As a result, the archive created in this chapter does not look the same as the one proposed in the prototype. That is also a reality of prototyping: The features created in a prototype often don't translate well to production web sites. In this case, a beautiful archive can be created with ease by using plug-ins. You can revisit this project and upgrade the archive after learning how to implement plug-ins.

The code for generating an archive is shown here. The main idea of an archive is to display each of the posts along with the date on which it was published. All the add-ons, such as categorizing by year or even months, require more complex loops and capture statements.

```
---
title: Archive
permalink: archive/
---

<section id="archive">
  <h3>Most recent posts</h3>
```

```
{%for post in site.posts %} <!-- For loop for categories -->
  {% unless post.next %}

    <ul class="this">
  {% else %} <!-- Capture the year and compare them -->
    {% capture year %}{{ post.date | date: '%Y' }}{% endcapture %}
    {% capture nyear %}{{ post.next.date | date: '%Y' }}{% endcapture %}
    {% if year != nyear %}
      </ul>

      <h3>{{ post.date | date: '%Y' }}</h3> <!-- If the years don't match, create a new
      heading-->
      <ul class="past">

    {% endif %}
  {% endunless %}

    <li><time>{{ post.date | date:"%d %b" }}</time><a href="{{ post.url }}">{{ post.title
    }}</a></li> <!-- Listing out the date and the titles -->

  {% endfor %}
  </ul>
</section>
```

The logic in the archive loops is to go through each post available and capture the year it was published. Then the years are compared to each other. If the year for the next post is not the same as the current post, that must mean the next post was published in a different year than the current post. If the years being compared are different, a new heading is created for the year and the posts are all listed under the appropriate year. In this manner, the post date can be differentiated and organized. The rest of the code deals with creating a list of the posts with the URL linked to the title of the post. This code is a bit complex, but the main ideas can be broken down into organizing the appropriate posts within each year and then listing them on the archive page. The multiple loops make this process a little easier to categorize and display. There is an even simpler approach to creating an archive as a simple list of all the posts, which can be done with the following snippet:

```
{% for post in site.posts %}
  * {{ post.date | date_to_string }} &raquo; [ {{ post.title }} ]({{ post.url }})
{% endfor %}
```

In this snippet, one loop goes through all the posts and the * represents the Markdown character to create a bullet point. Each post is listed by its date and then hyperlinked using the title to the post URL. This creates a simple, yet functional archive. Let's spend a little bit of time on the front matter as well. In this case, the title is actually the title of the page, and the permalink gives an address for the page after the baseurl. The address to access the archive is given as username.github.io/archive and this was defined by the permalink. To create new pages, save the file as filename.md and specify the permalink to access it. Now we can update our link from earlier in pagination.html for the navigation bar.

```
<a href="http://jekyll-mini-blog.github.io/archive"><i class="fa fa-archive"></i>
Archive </a>
```

Comments

Now that we are done creating the archive, the next objective is to integrate a commenting system. We use Disqus for this web site. It is one of the most widely used commenting systems and it is very easy to implement as well. To get started, create an account on `https://disqus.com/`.

Disqus will load independently of the web site, but it works as a system that becomes embedded. After creating an account, click the gear in the top right corner to see the settings menu, shown in Figure 8-15. From this menu, select Add Disqus To Site.

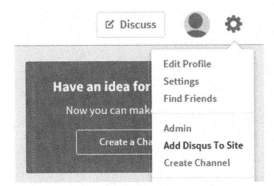

Figure 8-15. *The settings menu near the top right of the web site, with the Add Disqus To Site option*

That should take you to the Disqus Engage platform, which is the commenting system. Select Start Using Engage, which should take you to the site registration page, shown in Figure 8-16. This registration simply asks you for the name of the site, a URL where the site becomes available on Disqus, and finally the category of the web site. Click Finish registration to complete the process and get to the actual integration page. Here you are given a few options based on the blogging platform that you use. We would be using the universal code for this project, but the Kactus theme, like many other Jekyll themes, comes along with the universal code implemented with a variable used for `disqus_shortname`. This variable can be defined in `config.yml` according to what Disqus assigns you.

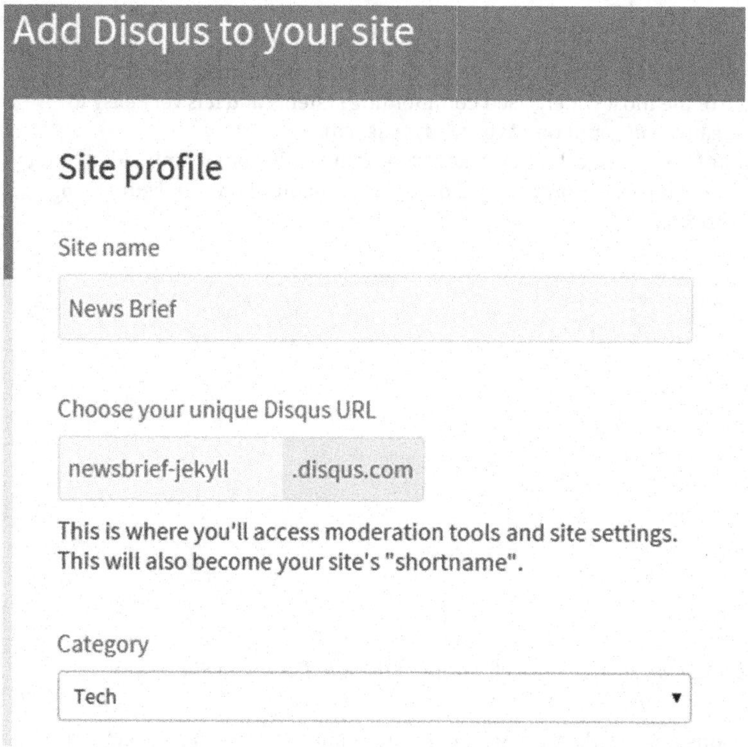

Add Disqus to your site
Site profile
Site name
News Brief
Choose your unique Disqus URL
newsbrief-jekyll
.disqus.com
This is where you'll access moderation tools and site settings.
This will also become your site's "shortname".
Category
Tech

Figure 8-16. *Registering to use Disqus on the web site. These required fields will activate Disqus on the news brief site and allow users to comment on posts.*

Once the registration is complete, it is time to set up Disqus on the web site, and for that we need the shortname. After finishing registration, Disqus takes us to the Choose a platform page, which has a sidebar containing all the settings, shown in Figure 8-17a. Select the Basic tab, and scroll halfway down the page to reach the Site Identity heading; the shortname is given under that heading, as shown in Figure 8-17b.

Installation
Basic
Advanced

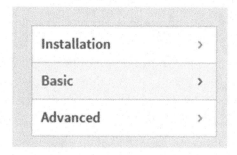

Figure 8-17a. *The sidebar containing options to install Disqus. The Basic option takes you to the site settings*

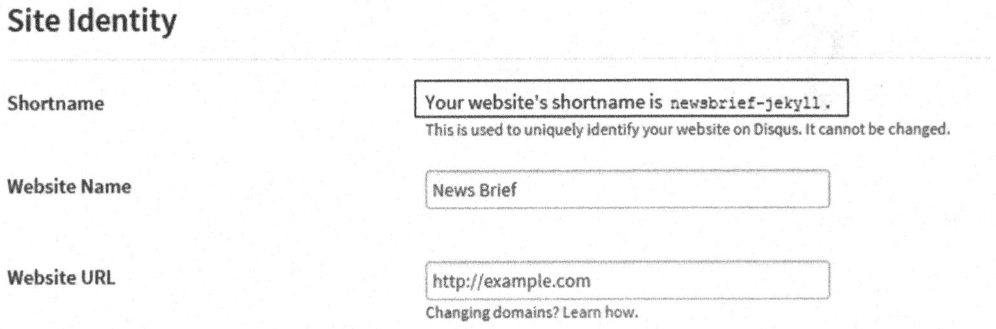

Site Identity

Shortname

> Your website's shortname is `newsbrief-jekyll`.
> This is used to uniquely identify your website on Disqus. It cannot be changed.

Website Name

> News Brief

Website URL

> http://example.com
> Changing domains? Learn how.

Figure 8-17b. The Disqus shortname revealed in the site properties. We use this in the config.yml

Once we have this code, we need to update our web site to enable Disqus and define the shortname associated with the domain that we want to use it on. To do this, let's look at the `config.yml` file for the variables.

```
disqus: true
disqus_shortname: newsbrief-jekyll
```

These variables enable Disqus, but we still have another issue: The comments are enabled for the post layout, and for that reason, they will not be present on every news brief. Conceptually, as of now, each news brief is being displayed on the web site as a post list object with blog-post-like properties. To display comments, we simply add another property to the object. The proper location of Disqus comments to be displayed for each individual news brief is right below the pagination navigation bar, shown as follows:

```
</nav>
{% include disqus.html %}
```

That completes setting up and enabling Disqus for our news brief page. Notice that adding comments was not a feature we prototyped earlier, but decided to include in production because it made sense to have it.

MailChimp

The next task is to setup MailChimp to capture an audience and keep them coming back for more. Using Mail Chimp efficiently is a lengthy endeavor, so we split our discussion of MailChimp into two phases: setting up the mailing list signup form, which is covered in this chapter, and running a campaign using the mailing list, which is covered in the next chapter. The signup form is the subject of this section because we will be including this in the top bar, which includes the Subscribe button. Here's an outline of what we will be covering: Sign up for MailChimp, set up the mailing list, set up the signup forms, and finally configure the navigation bar link for the web site. To get started with MailChimp, go to `mailchimp.com` and sign up. Once your account is confirmed, you are asked for some details about yourself, as shown in Figure 8-18.

Let's Get Started

About you

First name

Vikram

Last name

Dhillon

Email address

dhillonv10@knights.ucf.edu

Your email address will remain private. Our privacy policy

Figure 8-18. *MailChimp signup page. Fill out the required information (not shown here) on this page to get started*

The initial setup takes only a few minutes. After completing the setup, you are brought back to the dashboard, shown in Figure 8-19. From here, we can being creating a signup list.

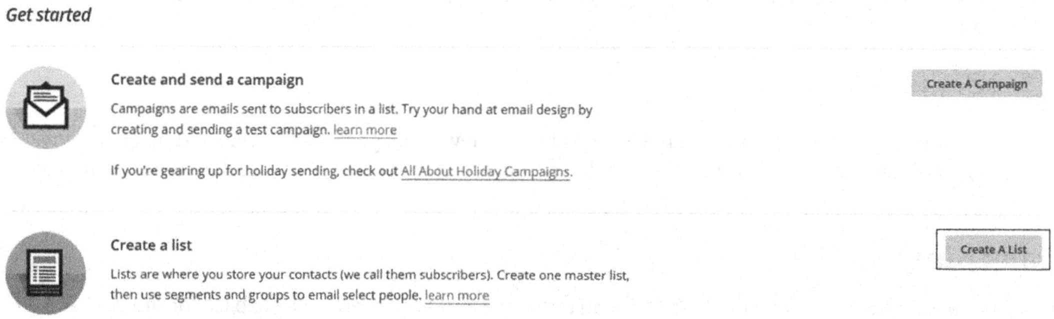

Get started

Create and send a campaign

Campaigns are emails sent to subscribers in a list. Try your hand at email design by creating and sending a test campaign. learn more

If you're gearing up for holiday sending, check out All About Holiday Campaigns.

Create A Campaign

Create a list

Lists are where you store your contacts (we call them subscribers). Create one master list, then use segments and groups to email select people. learn more

Create A List

Figure 8-19. *Creating a list in MailChimp, after signing up and providing the initial information for the mailing list*

Clicking Create a list, opens a List Details page. This page requires you to provide more information about the mailing list, such as the default from address, a reminder for people to know how they found this mailing list (which is an I-CANN antispam requirement), and a few other minor details. The mailing list is almost ready after you fill in this page, as shown in Figure 8-20.

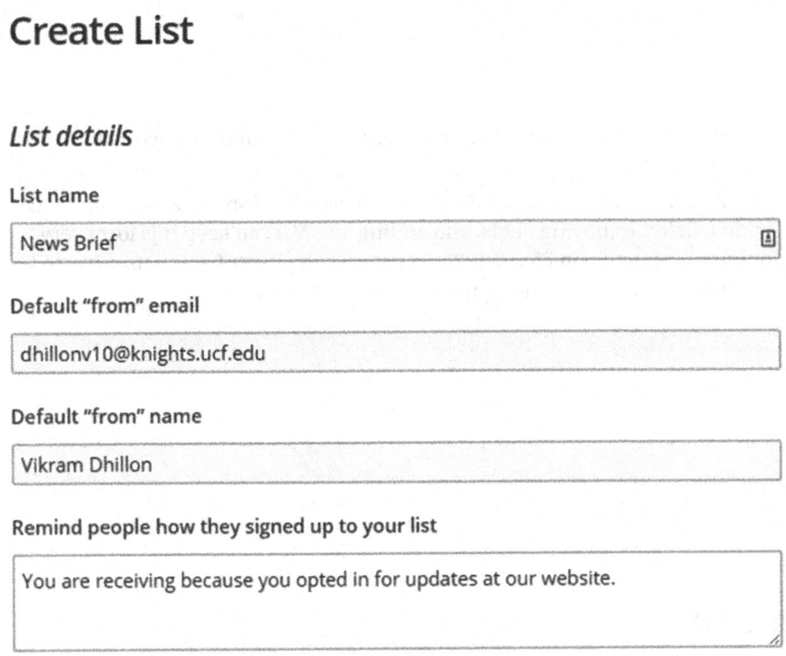

Create List

List details

List name

> News Brief ▣

Default "from" email

> dhillonv10@knights.ucf.edu

Default "from" name

> Vikram Dhillon

Remind people how they signed up to your list

> You are receiving because you opted in for updates at our website.

Figure 8-20. *Completing the mailing list details. Once completed, the mailing list is almost ready to be used*

After filling in the list details, the mailing list is almost ready, and it is time to set up the signup form. When you click Save for the mailing list, you see a confirmation on the top of the page letting you know that the mailing list was created as shown in Figure 8-21. The last step is to configure the signup form so that we can include it on the web site.

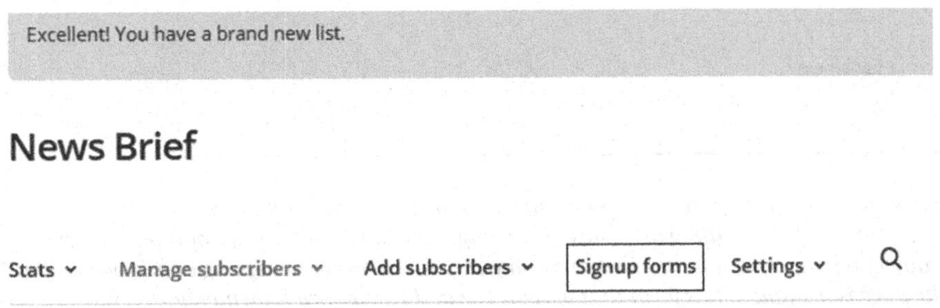

> Excellent! You have a brand new list.

News Brief

Stats ⌄   Manage subscribers ⌄   Add subscribers ⌄ | Signup forms | Settings ⌄   Q

Figure 8-21. *The confirmation on the top signifies that the mailing list is ready. Below that is the link for signup forms that we will edit next.*

The purpose of the signup forms is to start building a following with the mailing list and keep visitors coming back to the news brief page. Once you have a dedicated following, monetization strategies could help bring in revenue. Clicking on the signup forms will take you to a list of the different types of forms. We will be editing the General forms, as shown in Figure 8-22.

General forms

Build, design, and translate signup forms and response emails

Select

Figure 8-22. *The different possible signup forms available in MailChimp. We will edit the General forms*

This selection takes you to a page for editing the General forms. The page itself shows a form and it has numerous options for editing, adding fields, removing fields, and adding text. We can keep this form very simple and only ask the bare minimum, as shown in Figure 8-23. In general, the fewer fields a user has to fill out, the more likely he or she is to complete the form and sign up for the mailing list.

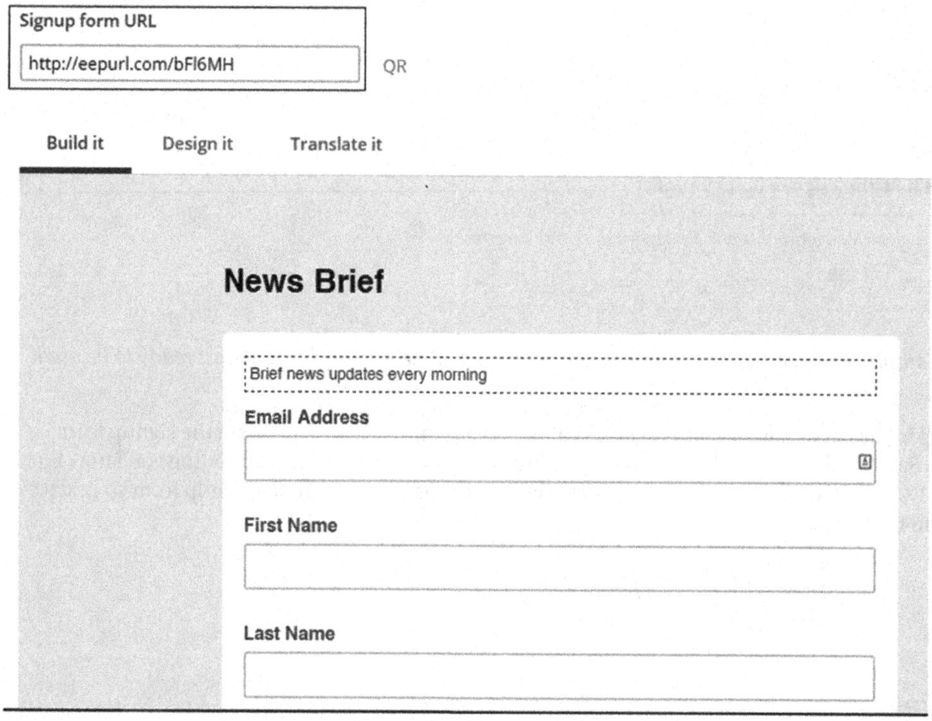

Signup form URL

http://eepurl.com/bFl6MH   QR

Build it   **Design it**   **Translate it**

News Brief

Brief news updates every morning

Email Address

First Name

Last Name

Figure 8-23. *Editing page for the signup form. This page allows us to customize what readers see if they choose to sign up for the news brief site mailing list. The editing page contains a variety of options in the right sidebar for customization of the information that we have about a reader and even theming of this page. The URL near the top of the page is the link to this form that we can use in the news brief site navigation bar.*

Cleaning Up

The previous section covered setting up the signup form and the mailing list. Now let's return to our web site and clean up the news brief site by adding colors and removing unnecessary style elements and padding. The current state of the web site is shown in Figure 8-24.

sometimes by accident, sometimes on purpose (injected humour and the like).

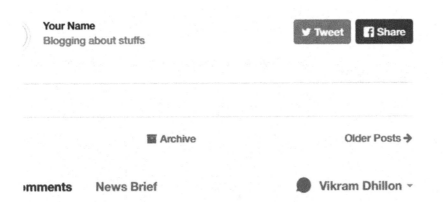

Figure 8-24. The current state of the web site. Notice the issues we need to clean up: the padding after the end of blog post content, the extra horizontal rule above the pagination navigation bar, a title for the web site, and adding color to headings.

Let's start with the title. The best placement for the title would be right under the navigation bar, which would allow the title to remain spaced in between the navigation and the news posts. The following code should do the trick, in `navigation.html`:

```
<h1 align="center" style="color:rgb(103, 65, 114)"><i class="fa fa-bolt"></i>
Science Brief </h1>
```

The bold code is actually the title. This line does three things: add a `fa-bolt` font-awesome in front of the title, provide the title itself, and color it using the style element. As another example, let's add a brick red color to the `post.title`

```
<span><h1 style="color:rgb(150, 40, 27)">{{ post.title }}</h1> <h2><i class="fa fa-
commenting-o"></i> {{ post.description }}</h2></span>
```

Now that we have added two colors, it is time to start removing elements and adjusting spacing. Given that we are editing style elements, it stands to reason that the code behind those elements would also be found in the style files. In this project, the style files are located in `assets/css/style.css` and the actual file is very lengthy, but there is an easier way to edit the file. Notice that the assets folder doesn't have a `_foldername` in front of it, which implies that this folder is not one of the folders that Jekyll processes into HTML. The implication of this is that the code present in that folder is the same as the one on the production

133

web site. For that reason, we can use the console in a browser like Chrome to edit the code as it looks. The exact same changes can be carried over to our local copy and we would have fixed all the style elements. Let's start with removing the extra hr element present above the pagination bar. One way to accomplish this is to remove the horizontal rule (border) under the sharing icons and then remove the padding to bring the two elements closer. This will allow the page to flow more naturally. In Chrome, pressing F12 launches the inspection console that can show you the code for each element as you hover the mouse over it. The inspect button is near the top, on the left side of the console, as shown in Figure 8-25.

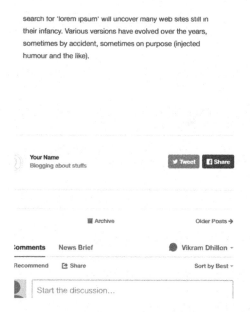
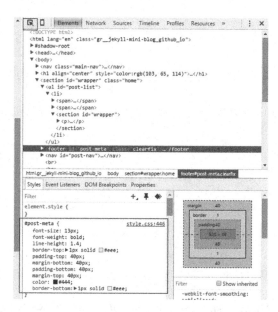

Figure 8-25. Opening the console to examine the style elements of the blog. The inspect button is highlighted at the top left of the console. When you click this button, just hovering the mouse over a style element will bring you to the HTML code in the top part of the panel, and the CSS in the bottom panel. It points exactly to the lines in the code that contain the style code.

You can edit the styles in the panel and observe their effects on the web site on the left side of the screen. In this case, to remove the border underneath the share icons, just click on the `bottom border` element and press Delete to remove that element. You will immediately see the effect of deleting the element on the web site. To close the space in between the pagination bar and the social icons, just delete the `padding-bottom` element as well. The next part is to close the spacing in between the end of the post content and the beginning of the social icons bar. To do this, let's examine that region using the Inspect element. We find the following lines as the source:

```
#wrapper {
    max-width: 600px;
    margin: 0 auto;
    padding: 60px 40px 100px 40px; }
```

The line shown in bold is the main culprit, and the largest padding space is the 100px present. If we reduce that to 10px, our gap will be gone! That removes the second gap and the cleaning up is complete. Our web site now looks ready, as shown in Figure 8-26.

sometimes by accident, sometimes on purpose (injected humour and the like).

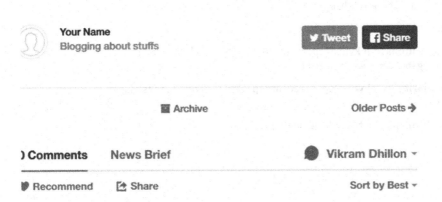

Figure 8-26. *The effects of our cleanup on the web site. The additional padding, borders, and spacing have all been removed and the web site looks better without all the gaps.*

■ **Note**   Even though we can see the effects of removing or adding elements immediately on the web site, these changes still need to be carried over to the actual `styles.css` file and applied to the exact lines stated in the console. For instance, the `wrapper` element mentioned earlier corresponds to line 141 in `styles.css`. When you browse the file, line 141 really does begin with the `wrapper` element. The changes made in the browser are only temporary, and they need to be carried over to the file. Once these changes are made, they need to be added in a commit and pushed like any other change to this web site.

Summary

In this chapter, we tackled a full-length project of creating a news brief web site and introduced a wealth of ideas by editing the Kactus theme. We applied new technologies to this project by integrating the knowledge gained and topics covered over the past chapters, implementing font-awesome, Disqus, and MailChimp. We also discussed the topic of version control, and specifically Git, in the context of this whole project. GitHub Desktop is an indispensable tool that allows us to visually commit our changes. We used it to push every change to the live web site. We also introduced a few style changes to make the web site more complete. We discussed some ideas behind project management, such as prototyping, and how to identify the scope and scale of a project. The prototype we created guided the actual coding and modifications that we made to Kactus. In most large projects, in-depth planning and creating well-defined specifications for a project saves a lot of resources and minimizes risk.

Further Reading

1. **GitHub Desktop guides:** https://help.github.com/desktop/guides/getting-started/setting-up-github-desktop/

2. **Livefyre commenting system:** http://web.livefyre.com/comments

3. **Getting started with MailChimp:** http://mailchimp.com/resources/guides/getting-started-with-mailchimp/

4. **Flare by Filament:** http://filament.io/flare

5. **Adding social buttons to Jekyll:** http://vdaubry.github.io/2014/10/20/add-social-sharing-buttons-with-jekyll/

6. **Simple post sharing in Jekyll:** http://codingtips.kanishkkunal.in/share-buttons-jekyll/

7. **AddThis social sidebar:** https://www.addthis.com/

CHAPTER 9

■ ■ ■

Photo Blogging

Photography takes an instant out of time, altering life by holding it still.

—Dorothea Lange

We just finished building our first project with the Kactus theme, and here we begin another exciting project. This time, we build a Jekyll-based photo blog with some nice add-ons. We begin this chapter with a discussion of the scope and scale for this project and then dive into the details. We make a formal project specification that details the features to be implemented in the photo blog and technologies that we will use. This is presented in a general format so that the reader can adopt the spec to any personal or hobby projects. After going over the spec, we look for a Jekyll theme that can be modified to meet our goals. We then prototype the project in the simplest way possible. Once the prototype is done, we can start making modifications to the Jekyll theme and implementing features. We also discuss web technologies related to photo blogging, such as using a content delivery network (CDN). Finally, we end this chapter by going over how to create and run a MailChimp campaign.

There can be many motivations behind building a photo blog: You can use it to track your experiences on a journey, or perhaps put together pieces from your life that you want to share with the world. In this project, we create a Jekyll blog that acts as a personal portfolio to show off your photography skills, in a manner that you enjoy. To keep readers engaged with the blog, we integrate MailChimp and use it to send a "picture of the day." There are several ways of operating and maintaining a portfolio, but a freemium blog approach would work best in the long run. Within this technique, daily content discussed by the photographer on the blog engages the readers and eventually converts them into paying users for any photography that you might want to sell. Before we go any further with this project, there are two restrictions that we must keep in mind:

- Hosting pictures on GitHub and then incorporating them in a Jekyll theme is not efficient or preferred. There will be significant lag on the web site (load time), driving users away from it.

- Selling photography on the blog itself would involve setting up a shopping cart and would create unnecessary overhead in terms of complexity, maintenance, and costs.

The best option for us would be to to offload the photography on a platform meant to share and sell photos, such as 500px. Before diving into the code, we also discuss why Jekyll is an ideal platform for the portfolio. Jekyll doesn't natively support photo galleries, but that won't stop us from trying indirectly. Compared to other blogging engines like Wordpress, implementing a photo gallery in Jekyll is slightly more difficult, but definitely very doable.

© Vikram Dhillon 2016

V. Dhillon, *Creating Blogs with Jekyll*, DOI 10.1007/978-1-4842-1464-0_9

Project Specification

Let's start by describing the technical requirements for this project. The photo blog will be built using Jekyll so we need a Jekyll theme, we need to modify the theme, and we also need to use a photo hosting service like 500px. To satisfy these technical requirements, we create a project spec. A spec is similar to a blueprint that breaks down the goals of a project into smaller tasks and then matches the tasks with the corresponding web technologies. As such, the spec is divided into three main sections: broad goals, TODOs, and technologies. The goals section also includes the scale and scope of the project. Let's create a project spec for this photo blog as follows.

Broad goals

Scope: A static blog that embeds photography hosted elsewhere, and daily blog posts about interesting pictures across the Web.

Scale: A minimal theme hosted on GitHub pages for a blog showcasing a personal portfolio, with MailChimp incorporated, which is free for the first 2,000 subscribers.

- To create a photo blog with Jekyll that can act as a personal portfolio.

- To embed photos in the blog using 500px.

- To find an appropriate theme to showcase the photography.

- To blog daily about photos, discussing their relevance or significance.

- To send a picture of the day to readers.

- To set up a method for readers to purchase your photography.

TODOs

- Find an appropriate theme for the blog.

- Edit the theme to remove any unnecessary elements.

- Create a blog layout that also contains some portfolio elements.

- Set up a 500px account.

- Learn about the 500px embed codes.

- Learn how to assign prices to 500px photos.

- Set up MailChimp to send the picture of the day.

Technologies

- Jekyll

- GitHub Pages

- Front-end frameworks in the Jekyll theme

- MailChimp

- 500px

This spec is simple enough to get us started for now, but we refine it and make it more comprehensive in later projects. The spec provided here is enough to get a full picture of what we will be building. Now that we have a spec, the next step is to create a simple prototype that can be used to guide our search when we look for a theme. The prototype shown in Figure 9-1 was created in PowerPoint to demonstrate that you can make basic drawings quickly in PowerPoint. This design is very rudimentary, but there's a reason for this: More often than not, this type of sketch is about all you would have the chance to do. Prototypes are not meant to be perfect representations, but only to place your thoughts on paper, and this sketch accomplishes that purpose.

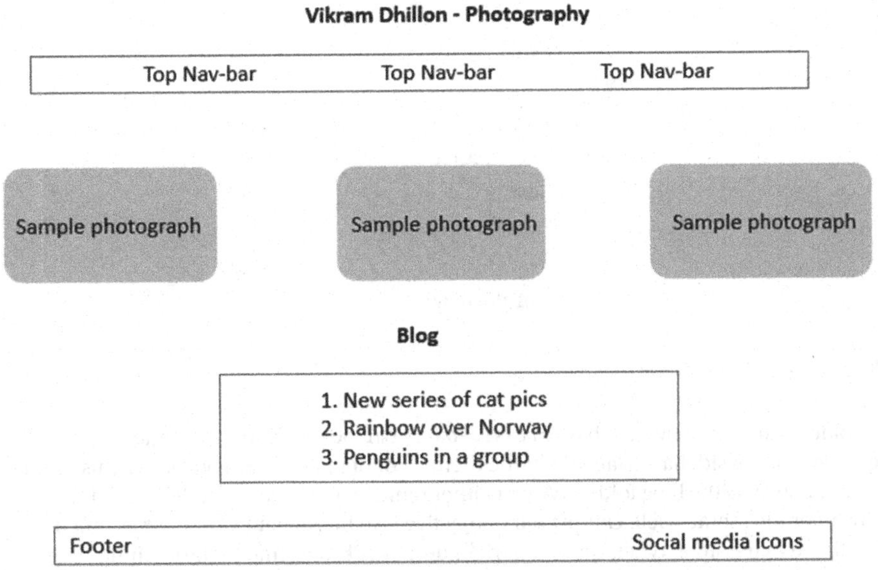

Vikram Dhillon - Photography

| Top Nav-bar | Top Nav-bar | Top Nav-bar |

Sample photograph   Sample photograph   Sample photograph

Blog

1. New series of cat pics
2. Rainbow over Norway
3. Penguins in a group

| Footer | Social media icons |

Figure 9-1. *A simple sketch of the photo blog with the core elements placed on the canvas. This sketch was made in PowerPoint to guide our search for a Jekyll-theme based around these elements. Notice the progression here: The spec translates into a prototype which guides the search for a theme and finally, we start editing the theme to obtain the desired product.*

The search for an appropriate theme begins with the prototype that we just completed. The usual leads come from the Jekyll Themes home page (`jekyllthemes.org`) or simply Google search. In this case, after looking through a few pages of Jekyll Themes, Dopetrope (`http://jekyllthemes.org/themes/dopetrope/`) seems like the perfect theme for this project. This theme is designed to be a portfolio and most elements available in the theme are responsive and photography-inclined. We can edit this theme to fit our own needs, so let's go over some of the available features. The theme has additional layouts for sidebars that can be used to display art, as shown in the top navigation bar. The footer is also extensive, containing a few lists and brief descriptions of articles, along with the date they were posted. The home page also contains a panel that can used to show the features available for the portfolio. These can be repurposed if necessary to talk about the categories of photography that you are interested in or have done in the past. Finally, for our project, it is necessary to include a Subscribe button for the mailing list. This allows us to send readers the picture of the day. Now that we have a decent idea of the theme, let's start editing it. The folder structure is shown in Figure 9-2.

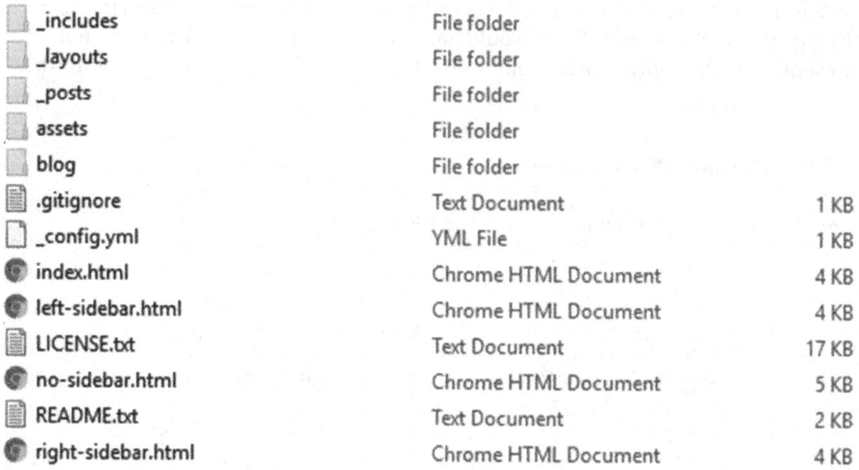

_includes	File folder	
_layouts	File folder	
_posts	File folder	
assets	File folder	
blog	File folder	
.gitignore	Text Document	1 KB
_config.yml	YML File	1 KB
index.html	Chrome HTML Document	4 KB
left-sidebar.html	Chrome HTML Document	4 KB
LICENSE.txt	Text Document	17 KB
no-sidebar.html	Chrome HTML Document	5 KB
README.txt	Text Document	2 KB
right-sidebar.html	Chrome HTML Document	4 KB

Figure 9-2. Folder structure of the Dopetrope theme

A first look at this folder structure shows us that left-sidebar.html, no-sidebar.html, and right-sidebar.html are the three types of sidebars available in the theme. For demonstration purposes, this theme has some additional folders, such as the blog folder. We can either remove or merge the code in that folder into the appropriate layout or the theme itself. Our primary objective is to be efficient and reuse as much of the code written in the theme as possible. When the usual tricks don't work, it is time to start writing code from scratch. Before we start making edits to the code, it is worthwhile considering why Jekyll is a good platform for building this portfolio.

- **Cost:** The early versions of the portfolio made with Jekyll and hosted in GitHub Pages are essentially free for the user. The up-front cost of hosting the portfolio and maintaining it is essentially zero. You don't have to buy server hosting space or worry about downtime.

- **Hosting:** GitHub Pages also brings forth one of the most important features of Jekyll: There is no need to manage complicated back ends for the portfolio and additionally the shopping cart, if you are selling the photography.

- **Platform:** Integrating well-known services such as 500px to host and sell your photography gives you another platform where you can advertise your photography and build a following. This can obviously be done on other platforms as well, but it often involves the use of plug-ins, which only add more maintenance overhead. Additionally, 500px gives you embed codes that can simply be copied into Markdown as you are writing the post in Sublime.

- **Expertise:** Finally, the best part about using Jekyll is that you get to show off your technical expertise and coding skills as well as photography. They go hand-in-hand, and could give you an edge over other people when you display your portfolio.

Although it might make sense to switch your portfolio to an advanced platform later on, Jekyll can power the early versions perfectly when your main focus is on building an audience or a following.

Using GitHub

When we start making changes to the theme, the theme files will be put under version control. Every set of changes needs to be committed to the repository and finally pushed online to GitHub where the code will reside. We use the same repository naming style as in the last chapter: creating a new repository and naming it in the username.github.io format. This naming convention will let us use GitHub Pages to compile the Jekyll source code present in the repository into a static web site. This is the second time we are using GitHub, so let's delve into some concepts before getting to the theme. We first need a clear idea of the tools being used.

- **Git:** This is the main tool that instantiates version control on a set of files. Git is actually what allows us to add files to a set of changes, commit those changes, and finally push them online to the live web site. In the last chapter, we used GitHub Desktop, which makes this process visual and easier to manage. Eventually, we will begin using Git CLI.

- **GitHub Desktop:** As mentioned earlier, GitHub Desktop is actually a visual tool that allows us to manage code using Git and interface it with GitHub, where the code is being hosted. This is what we use to push all of our changes online and in turn to the live web site.

- **GitHub:** GitHub is an online code-hosting platform that works with Git and allows developers to push their code online so that it can be shared with other collaborators and developers. GitHub actually hosts the web site and all the code that we work on. Using Git through GitHub Desktop, we push our code online to GitHub, which is the final destination.

The difference among these three tools is important to understand because it determines the limitations of what each tool can do. GitHub is primarily a code-hosting platform. Its main purpose is to provide developers the means to create multiple repositories to host their projects, manage them, and collaborate. GitHub allows us to put a full web site in the repository and then host it online using GitHub Pages. For Jekyll-based projects, GitHub Pages serves as a playground to learn, prototype, and experiment with Jekyll. There are two hosting services provided through GitHub Pages. The first one involves creating a root repository that triggers GitHub Pages to compile and host whatever Jekyll code is present in that repository. The second service is useful when you don't have Jekyll code, but still want to create a project web site for your repository. You can do that with GitHub's Automatic Page Generator, which will help you quickly create a landing page.

▪ **Tip** In this second method, GitHub creates a special branch called gh-pages to store the HTML template web site created by the Automatic Page Generator. Given that the resulting web site is already in HTML, it can be hosted directly.

Ultimately, GitHub as a platform is not meant to be a replacement for hosting, although it works sufficiently well. As such, there are some limitations associated with using GitHub Pages. The repository created in the last chapter with the format username.github.io is called a **root repository**. There can only be one root repository per account, and once it has been created, it automatically uses GitHub Pages to compile any Jekyll source code present. The reason for having only one root repository per account is due to the naming convention. As mentioned earlier, the root repository also has the corresponding web address http://username.github.io but that can be changed to a custom domain name. After the root repository has been created, any project pages (using the second method) that are online under an account are redirected by default to username.github.io/REPOSITORY-NAME or under the custom domain name.

To reiterate the point, GitHub Pages is meant to help you learn Jekyll, but it is not a hosting server. You actually can host a project or a blog for production use and GitHub will not disappoint you, but you can only have one web site at a time. There are other publishing platforms like Amazon's AWS, but using them involves advanced concepts and AWS is not as user-friendly. To continue using GitHub with a new project in each chapter, we have to delete the previous root repositories. Our old repository had the Kactus news brief, and now we have to delete it and create a new root repository. After deleting the current root repository on GitHub, we have to re-create the root repository and then copy over Dopetrope in an initial commit. Rest assured, all your old code is still safe offline in the folder location that was being used to push the code online. Additionally, you can simply download the final product as a zipped file, just as we have been downloading themes from GitHub for our own projects. In the next section, we delete the current root and make room for Dopetrope to be pushed to a new and empty root repository.

Deleting Repositories

We start by going to the repository page and clicking Settings as shown in in Figure 9-3a. On the Settings page, scroll all the way down to the bottom and find the Danger Zone, shown in Figure 9-3b.

Figure 9-3a. Settings button for a repository Figure

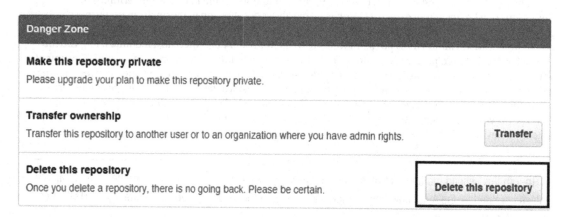

Figure 9-3b. Settings to delete a repository. Once Delete the repository is clicked, a dialog box box will open, asking you to type the name of the repository and then click Confirm to delete the repository.

This completes the deletion of the root repository. Your code is safe locally at the location you were using to push the code online. If you want a copy of the finished product before deletion, you can go to the repository page and download it as a zipped file. Now that your account doesn't have a root repository, it's time to start the process again.

Visual Tutorial

In the previous chapter, we demonstrated how to create a repository and set up GitHub Desktop with it. The process is briefly summarized here and shown in Figure 9-4.

1. Create a root repository in the form of username.github.io.

2. Once the repository is created, set it up in GitHub Desktop.

3. Download the Dopetrope theme from its GitHub repository, extract the zipped file, and copy over the code to the location of the local repository on your computer (`https://github.com/CloudCannon/DopeTrope-Jekyll-Theme`).

4. Add the files to an initial commit on GitHub Desktop and push the code online.

Create a new repository

A repository contains all the files for your project, including the revision history.

Owner		Repository name
😈 **jekyll-mini-blog ▾**	/	jekyll-mini-blog.github.io ✓

Figure 9-4a. *Creating the root repository again on GitHub*

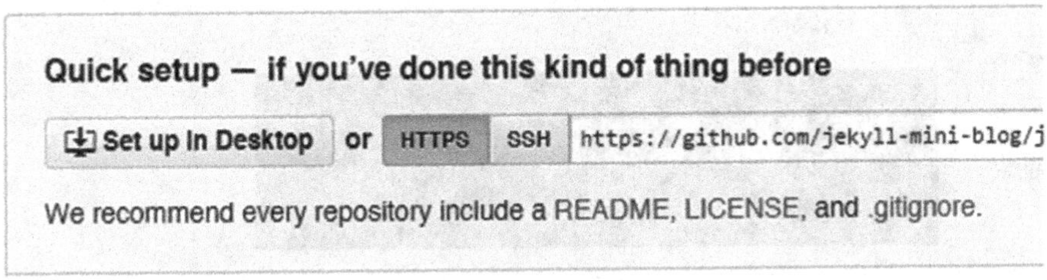

Quick setup — if you've done this kind of thing before

[⬇] **Set up in Desktop**   or   **HTTPS**   SSH   `https://github.com/jekyll-mini-blog/j`

We recommend every repository include a README, LICENSE, and .gitignore.

Figure 9-4b. *Confirmation that the root repository has been created. Now we need to configure it in GitHub Desktop.*

■ **Tip** This visual tutorial is a very quick walkthrough of the steps needed to create a repository and set it up in GitHub Desktop. It does not show the initial commit, which includes the changes made by copying over the source code for Dopetrope into the local GitHub repository. For a more detailed overview, please revisit the previous chapter.

The root repository has been created. To set it up in GitHub Desktop, click the plus sign in the top left corner to reveal all the repositories in the account. Pick the root repository and click Clone, which will prompt you to pick a local location to save the code, as shown in Figure 9-5.

Figure 9-5a. *Browsing for the folder location in which to clone the repository. The location in this case is* Documents/GitHub/repo.

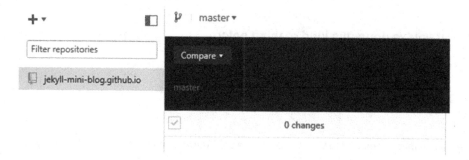

Figure 9-5b. *After clicking OK in the preceding dialog box, the repository has been cloned in GitHub Desktop*

Dope Editing

Let's start editing the theme. You might notice that after you push the initial commit, the theme renders terribly when you actually visit the domain username.github.io, as the issue resides in the _config.yml file. The actual problem is that of routing, in the last line:

```
baseurl: '/DopeTrope-Jekyll-Theme'
```

To fix this issue, simply delete the baseurl definition and _config.yml should look like the following:

```
name: DopeTrope
description: DopeTrope template for Jekyll
paginate: 10
```

Now that the web site is live, let's start editing it from the top. The first element is the name of the theme, and your personal portfolio should have your own name. The first file to look into would be index.html, and we immediately see the include, which has the theme name:

```
<body class="homepage">
{% include header_landing.html %}
```

Let's look at _includes/header_landing.html. The beginning of the file shows us the name of the theme. We can edit that and the final result would look like this.

```
<div id="header-wrapper">
<div id="header">

<!-- Logo -->
<h1><a href="index.html">Vikram Dhillon</a></h1>
```

Navigation Bar

The next element to edit is the top navigation bar, which is a bit complicated to edit because it is not clear where the code resides. When we examine header_landing.html, we see a navigation layout; on the other hand, the _includes folder also has a nav.html file that seems to be similar. The difference between the two files is actually the layouts in which they are being used. The header_landing template is used for index. html, but most other pages such as sidebar layouts use nav.html, which doesn't contain the extra image elements. For our purposes, we would edit header_landing.html and change the nav bar to contain only the following.

```
<!-- Nav -->
<nav id="nav">
        <ul>
                <li class="current"><a href="index.html">Home</a></li>
                <li><a href="#">Blog</a></li>
                <li><a href="#">Specialties</a></li>
                <li><a href="#">Subscribe</a></li>
        </ul>
</nav>
```

This slims down the navigation bar and also gives us all the elements that we need. The links will all be placed here once they are ready. Now that the top nav bar is ready, let's move on to the banner. The banner gives a first impression of your portfolio, so feel free to edit it in any way that seems fit. The code resides in header_landing.html.

```
<!-- Banner -->
<section id="banner">
        <header>
                <h2>Howdy. This is my portfolio.</h2>
                <p> Check out my dope art.</p>
        </header>
</section>
```

Photography Specialties

Below the header there is a collection of features, which you can use to highlight your special talents or interests in photography. However, a visitor on the portfolio needs to see the best of your images as soon as possible, to have a **moment of inspiration**. This is a term defined by Google and Amazon as the moment when a visitor is inspired by a visual to take action, which is often a sale. That's part of the reason the Amazon one-click button is crucial to the web site. This features section needs to be moved to a separate page that can be easily accessed through the top navigation bar. To do this, we need to consider what elements are suitable for a page showcasing the features. We can carry over the title, nav bar, and the banner from the landing page and truncate the page after the features have been discussed. This can be accomplished by editing the layouts, which decide what should render on a page. The index.html page uses the landing layout, and if we examine the layout, it has a few includes:

```
{% include header.html %}
        {{ content }}
{% include blog.html %}
{% include footer.html %}
```

We actually don't need the last two includes, as they become unnecessary for the page showcasing the features. The index page included header_landing.html, which made the banner, navigation, and title possible, so we can modify this layout to look like this:

```
{% include header.html %}
{% include header_landing.html %}
```

This creates a layout that will truncate right after the features are displayed. Now we can't just modify the landing.html layout because it is already being used, so let's save our edits into a new file under _layouts as feature_layout.html. This file name denotes the layout that the features page will be using. Once the layout is saved, it can now be referenced by a new page. A layout by itself can't do much, because a page needs to define a layout in the YAML front matter to access it, and then the page can inherit all of its properties and add more elements to it. Essentially, a layout provides basic elements that all pages belonging to a certain category can benefit from. Once a page inherits a layout, it extends the layouts to a specific goal and the page is rendered to meet that goal. In the preceding case, the two includes are self-sufficient components and we actually don't need to extend the page at all. A new page called features.html can be created and saved in the top directory (the same location as the sidebar pages). This page will simply contain the following:

```
---
title: Features
layout: features_layout
---
```

That's all we need to create a new page showcasing the features. Now that we have them in a separate location, we need to remove them from the index page. There is a slight problem with this approach: You might notice that the index page includes header_landing.html to show those features. If we try to edit the header_landing page to remove the features, we won't be able to display them on the features page either. There are a few ways to fix this problem, but in these situations, the best approach preserves the greatest amount of code. Here's one way to solve this problem: Create a second layout cloning header_landing.html and use this new layout in index.html. Then, we can delete the features section from the original header_landing file and save the day. More concretely, here's the change made to index.html:

```
<body class="homepage">
{% include header_landing_new.html %}
```

This tells the index page to use a new layout called header_landing_new, which will not contain the features. In this fashion, the header_landing page remains unchanged and is used to display the features. A clone of the header_landing page without the features is used to render the index page. Here is what the clone page header_landing_new.html contains:

```
<!-- Header -->
<div id="header-wrapper">
        <div id="header">

<!-- Logo -->
        <h1><a href="index.html">Vikram Dhillon</a></h1>

<!-- Nav -->
<nav id="nav">
        <ul>
                <li><a href="index.html">Home</a></li>
                <li><a href="#">Blog</a></li>
                <li><a href="#">Specialties</a></li>
                <li><a href="#">Subscribe</a></li>
        </ul>
</nav>

<!-- Banner -->
<section id="banner">
        <header>
                <h2>Howdy. This is my portfolio.</h2>
                <p> Check out my dope art.</p>
        </header>
</section>

<!-- Features section removed -->

</div>
</div>
```

Notice that in the original navigation, the Home hyperlink included a class <li class="current">, which has been removed here. We are no longer on the home page, so the current class does not have any purpose for the features page. Additionally, notice the section where the code for the Features was removed. Making a new file to include the features code in this sense allows us to keep the same code and modularize it.

Portfolio

The next step is the actual portfolio. We actually don't need to edit anything here. The portfolio, as designed, gives you the perfect opportunity to explain your photograph in a title followed by a short description. The photos can essentially be thumbnails of the actual pictures, and this theme gives you a great chance to highlight yourself at your best. While working with Jekyll, there will be numerous occasions when you feel like a crucial component is missing from a theme; you have two options at that point. The first is to code it yourself and use it as you intended, and the second is to adapt whatever is available. In this portfolio, a small section to showcase your photography is already available, so let's use that. It does require some level of preparation and strategy. The portfolio section displays images that are present in: assets/images/, so that's where you would need to go and replace the images with your own so that they show up in the portfolio. To edit the subtext for each one, we need to go back to `index.html`, which contains the code for the portfolio under the appropriate section:

```
<section>
<header class="major">
        <h2>My Portfolio</h2>
```

Underneath this `<section>` there are descriptions for each of the pictures. Let's change the Find out more button to Learn More.

```
<footer>
<a href="#" class="button alt">Learn More</a>
</footer>
```

This highlights a disadvantage of having everything hard-coded here: The button text has to be replaced six times for consistency. Even though this might seem intensive, it actually saves you more time in the long run because of how simple the process is: You just need to update the caption and subtext along with the picture under the assets folder to update your portfolio.

So what goes in the link that points to the Learn More button? In this portfolio, we want to offload the photography to another platform that is better suited for it; some practical reasons for doing so were discussed earlier. The recommended platform is 500px, but Flicker might work as well. The simplest reason for hosting the photography on 500px is because that service has been created to share and sell photography, and it has some additional security features for the photographer to prevent pictures from being stolen. Once you have created a 500px account, you can upload the pictures along with all the EXIF information. After an image has been uploaded, you can simply point the Learn More button to the link for the image. This strategy for managing the portfolio might be effective, if that you update the thumbnails every month or so with new and refreshing pictures. We talk more about embedding your own photography in those posts later on in the chapter.

■ **Note**   In the editing thus far and the remainder of this chapter, we are not using font-awesome icons for the buttons or headings, but feel free to add them as necessary. The appropriate file into which the font-awesome style sheet should be imported would be `header.html` under `_includes`. After that, you can add fa-icons anywhere in the web site that you wish.

The Blog

The next component to edit is the blog. Currently, the large photos on the blog are only taking up space and not providing much value to the portfolio. The blog itself is an essential component, but just like the features, we need to move it out of the way. The blog won't entirely be gone because of the footer, and we talk about that shortly. To move the blog onto its own page, we need to make a new page. Luckily, the templates that already came with Dopetrope might come in handy, especially the `no-sidebar.html` page. On this page, we can basically remove everything after the `<header>` comment.

```
<!-- Content -->
<article class="box post">
<header>
        <h2>The Blog</h2>
</header>
... <!-- Blank space -->
</article>
```

Now this page is ready to contain and render the blog. The way posts were being displayed with a large picture is not very efficient, so we follow a simple method of listing the title of the blog posts with a brief post.excerpt for each listed post. This is actually very easy to do.

```
<ul>
  {% for post in site.posts %}

  <li>
    <a href="{{ post.url }}"><strong> {{ post.title }} </strong></a>
    <p> {{ post.excerpt }} </p>
  </li>

  {% endfor %}
</ul>
```

This gives us a very nice listing of the blog posts. Notice that we are still making all these edits with no-sidebar.html, but we need to save our changes as a new file. Let's call this file posts.html; it will reside in the top directory (where the index.html file is). This serves to fix one side of the issue, but now we need to remove the blog from the landing.html layout. This actually turns out to be somewhat tricky because of the formatting of the theme. If we remove the {% include blog.html %} from the layout, this renders the theme completely white near the bottom, and all the elements in the footer have their color overwritten. The problem starts in the index.html file near the beginning with two extra <div> tags. They should be closed at the end of the file, but in this theme they are left open. To fix this, two closing </div> tags were added to _includes/blog.html at the end of the file. The layout integrates blog.html and footer.html into the home page so the tags matched up, but once we remove the blog.html include from the layout, this mismatch causes the footer color issue. The way to fix this is very straightforward: Just add two </div> tags to the end of index.html to close the tags. The layout now doesn't need to rely on blog.html to close the tags for the theme, and we created a new blog page.

Footer

Now that the blog has been set up, let's get started with the footer. It looks cluttered, so the first order of business is to clean it up. Let's remove the two lists at the bottom with the headers Tempus conseqat and Ipsum et phasellus. To do that, under _includes/footer.html, remove the entire code within both of the 4u classes:

```
I.
<div class="4u"> <!-- Start removing from this line -->
<section>
        <header>
        <h2>Tempus conseqat</h2>
        </header>
```

```
...  <!-- Remainder of the code -->

</section>
</div>

II.
<div class="4u"> <!-- Start removing from this line -->
<section>
        <header>
        <h2>Ipsum et phasellus</h2>
        </header>
...  <!-- Remainder of the code -->

</section>
</div>
```

This should remove the lists from the page. Incidentally, the next 4u class is the social icons, so let's label it correctly:

```
<header>
        <h2>Social:</h2> <!-- This header used to say Vitae tempor lorem -->
</header>
```

Below the social icons, there is the address. It's up to you if you want to delete it, and the contents of the address reside in the contact class.

```
<ul class="contact">
        <li>
...  <!-- Remainder of the code -->
</ul>
```

The footer has room for a lot of other delicate modifications. Let's start with changing the title.

```
<section>
        <header>
                <h2>The Blog</h2> <!-- This header used to say "Blandit nisl adipiscing"
-->
        </header>
```

This footer contains a small snapshot of the blog, up to five posts as declared by the for loop offset. Let's change that to three, and we discuss later how to change what posts show up here.

```
{% for post in site.posts offset: 0 limit: 3 %}
```

After this, the next change is actually the date of posts being shown in the footer. Currently, the date filter displays the full month on the top, which becomes a problem if the post was in November, because the date arrow element gets distorted very easily. To fix this, we need to switch over to the three-character abbreviations for the month:

```
<span class="date">{{ post.date | date: "%b"}} <strong>{{ post.date | date: "%d"}}</
strong></span>
```

The %B shows the full month and the %b displays the shortened month name. On the right side, the footer contains a small section titled "What's this all about?" where you could briefly talk about the purpose of this blog and what you hope to post about. While we are on that topic, how can you optimize your blog to try and sell your photography? The idea here is that your blog will eventually build a following to whom you can sell the photography. The best way of building this following is to create interesting content that relates to the photography that you do. In this manner, you can embed your own photos in the blog post and pitch them to the readers. This is the essence of the freemium model: You attract readers to your blog with free content and embed your own pictures at the end of the post. The readers are eventually converted into paid users of that photography.

Blog Post Layout

We talk at length about how to embed the proper way, but before that, we need to change the layout of the blog posts themselves. Currently, a blog post is rendered on a page with a top image, followed by the title and the date, then a featured image for that particular post, and finally the post content. We need to streamline this layout so that the main focus is the text that you write; for that reason, we will remove the top image and the featured images. Additionally, we need to add the categories variable in the YAML front matter, which allows us to selectively call on the category pinned posts to show them on the home page. Let's start looking through the post layout. At the very beginning of the file, we see a {% include nav.html %} statement. This was the other navigation in this theme designed for all the pages that are not the landing page. We should start here and sync this navigation with what we have in the header_landing.html page. This implies that we need to remove the contents of <!-- Nav --> and replace them with the navigation in header_landing. We also need to remove the banner image at the bottom. Here's what the new nav.html looks like after removing the code.

```
<!-- Header -->
<div id="header-wrapper">
        <div id="header">

        <!-- Logo -->
        <h1><a href="index.html">Vikram Dhillon</a></h1>

        <!-- Nav -->
        <nav id="nav">
                <ul>
                        <li><a href="{{site.baseurl}}/index.html">Home</a></li>
                        <li><a href="#">Blog</a></li>
                        <li><a href="#">Specialties</a></li>
                        <li><a href="#">Subscribe</a></li>
                </ul>
        </nav>

        </div>
</div>
```

This is a much shorter version of the navigation available to the blog posts. Now that the top image is done, the next part is the featured image in the post. To remove that one, we need to remove the line that hyperlinks the images, which is shown in bold here.

```
<section class="box">
        <a href="#" class="image featured"><img src="{{ site.baseurl }}{{ page.featured }}"
alt="" /></a>
        {{ page.content }}
</section>
```

The resulting segment is shown as follows:

```
<section class="box">
        {{ page.content }}
</section>
```

The featured image has been removed and now it's time to discuss the blog posts themselves and their format. The posts are crucial to convert readers, and we talk about a few techniques that make this process easier. We need to modify the contents of the post itself and format the post in a manner that can promote sales. We use the following format: Start with an introduction to a genre of the photograph, followed by a brief history or some interesting facts about that genre or picture that will be the subject of this post. This will be followed by the photograph itself and the story it tells, in your own perspective. That's what gives your blog a personal touch that differentiates your blog from others in the blogosphere. Finally, after talking about the photograph, you need to link it to your own work and embed a picture that you have put up on 500px into the blog post. Underneath the post there will be space for comments powered by Disqus. Let's start with the YAML front matter.

```
---
title: Sunt in culpa qui
featured: /assets/images/pic05.jpg
layout: post
---
```

The line shown in bold points to the featured image section that we removed from the layout. This line should also be removed from the front matter. Notice that we will use this image, just not from the front matter. There are a few reasons for this, but the main reason is that putting an image in as a tag in the front matter limits how you can manipulate it. This tag has an associated style component or a rule attached to it in the layout (post.html) that defines how the picture should render. Jekyll will apply that rule to every image referred by the featured tag without exceptions. This "cookie-cutter" approach takes away any ability to manipulate the image or add any additional HTML tags to it. Now this might work for images that are all exactly the same size, but it will not work out of the box for any image taken from the Internet. The simpler approach is to display the image by using an <image> or <a> tag, which gives you a much higher degree of control over the image. This might involve a few extra lines of code written among the beautiful Markdown, but that is a totally acceptable trade-off to get full control over the image. We will show an example of the blog post following the format that we discussed earlier, but before we get to that, let's make another addition to YAML for categories. Currently, the first three blog posts appear on the home page, but if we add categories to them, we can simply list the posts that belong to that particular category.

```
---
title: Sunt in culpa qui
layout: post
categories:
- pinned
---
```

This adds the category pinned to the post, and now we can be more specific about this category in the footer. We will be editing the same line that controls how many posts show up in the footer:

```
{% for post in site.categories.pinned offset: 0 limit: 3 %}
```

Embedding Photography

The last component in the blog post is embedding your own photography from 500px into the blog post. This seems very simple because for each image, 500px provides you an embed code and you can simply use that in the post. However, there are some complications with this method, the main one being if the image being used is larger than the box container used in the post layout, the image will extend beyond the box and appear out of proportion. This will definitely happen for many images out of the box. The situation is the opposite from last time, where the use of a rule or style component limited the amount of manipulation we could do to the image. Here we actually need a rule to contain the size of this embedded image from 500px. The best tool for this job is a platform called Embedly available at `http://embed.ly/code`.

Embedly creates cards that can embed components of a web site along with a small excerpt that describes the component, in most cases. The cards look absolutely beautiful and better than an embedded image manipulated with CSS style options. The web site just mentioned allows the user to create cards that are followed by an embed code that can be used within the blog post. The rationale here is to upload the image to 500px, and then use Embedly to control the size of the pictures we want to embed. To see an example of this, we use an article from the *New York Times,* "Blood Pressure, a Reading With a Habit of Straying," which is available at `http://www.nytimes.com/2015/12/01/health/blood-pressure-a-reading-with-a-habit-of-straying.html`.

Now if we put that link in the Embedly bar on the Cards page, a beautiful embed is generated, as shown in Figure 9-6.

Figure 9-6a. Putting a link in the Embed bar on `http://embed.ly/code` *to obtain a card along with an embed code shown in Figure 9-6b*

■ **Note** Embedly is a freemium platform to create cards from URLs that are free until the first 5,000 cards created per month. This is more than enough for most personal projects, so we can safely use it. For more information on pricing, please visit `http://embed.ly/pricing`.

This embed card also comes along with code that can be copied to the blog post where the embedded image should be displayed, as shown in Figure 9-6b.

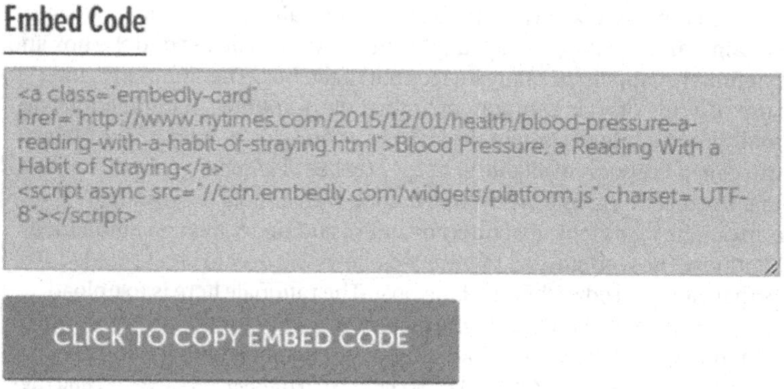

Embed Code

```
<a class="embedly-card"
href="http://www.nytimes.com/2015/12/01/health/blood-pressure-a-
reading-with-a-habit-of-straying.html">Blood Pressure, a Reading With a
Habit of Straying</a>
<script async src="//cdn.embedly.com/widgets/platform.js" charset="UTF-
8"></script>
```

CLICK TO COPY EMBED CODE

Figure 9-6b. *Embed code for the card generated by Embedly*

Let's do a complete example of a blog post following our own guidelines.

```
---
title: Awesome picture post
layout: post
categories:
- pinned
---

Integer volutpat ante et accumsan commophasellus sed aliquam feugiat lorem aliquet. Ut enim
rutrum phasellus iaculis accumsan dolore magna aliquam veroeros.

<img id="center_image" src="assets/images/pic5.jpg">

<style>

#center_image{
 position: absolute;
 top: 50%;
 margin: -50px auto 0;
}
</style>

Lorem ipsum dolor sit amet, consectetur adipisicing elit, sed do eiusmod tempor incididunt
ut labore et dolore magna aliqua. Ut enim ad minim veniam, quis nostrud exercitation ullamco
laboris nisi ut aliquip ex ea commodo consequat. Duis aute irure dolor in reprehenderit
in voluptate velit esse cillum dolore eu fugiat nulla pariatur. Excepteur sint occaecat
cupidatat non proident, sunt in culpa qui officia deserunt mollit anim id est laborum.
```

```
<a class="embedly-card" href="https://500px.com/photo/127469533/full-homemade-thanksgiving-
dinner-by-brent-hofacker">Full Homemade Thanksgiving Dinner</a>
<script async src="//cdn.embedly.com/widgets/platform.js" charset="UTF-8"></script>
```

In this post, we covered the fundamentals that we talked about previously, and this completes our editing of the Dopetrope theme to obtain the portfolio. In our example, any of the missing links can be referenced to the top navigation bar by using {{ site.baseurl}}/page_name.html. The created page such as the blog page or the features page can be linked to fill out the top navigation bar. The picture portfolio is ready for action!

```
<!-- Nav -->
<nav id="nav">
        <ul>
                <li class="current"><a href="index.html">Home</a></li>
                        <li><a href="{{site.baseurl}}/posts.html">Blog</a></li>
                        <li><a href="{{site.baseurl}}/features.html">Specialties</a></li>
                        <li><a href="#">Subscribe</a></li>
        </ul>
</nav>
```

Content Delivery Network (CDN)

In our photography blog, some of the images that we have used in the blog posts reside locally in the assets folder of the repository. This folder eventually gets pushed to the cloud where it resides on GitHub and is rendered into a web site by GitHub Pages. For a regular web site hosted on a shared server, the web site would be far too slow if the photos were simply being loaded from a directory. The loading time for professionally taken pictures would be much longer because those photos have a high resolution and are large in size. In this sense, professional photography needs a boost so that it can be hosted on a server. The best option generally is to offload the photos and in our case, we offloaded the professional pictures onto 500px. There are a few other methods that professional photographers use to keep pictures on their own portfolios entirely. The most effective of those methods is the use of a CDN.

The goal of a CDN is to serve static content to the users with high performance. When a user makes a request to a web site that is using a CDN, the web site loads itself and a request to load the static content is sent concurrently. The CDN resolves to an optimized server based on location of the user and availability of the server that will handle the request. The requests for content are algorithmically directed to a collection of servers (called nodes) that are optimal to handling that request. The performance optimizations are based on location that is best used for serving content to the readers. As you can understand, a CDN is a very large service provider, and using a CDN is generally cheap, too, so most portfolios rely on some kind of CDN. If you recall, even font-awesome uses MaxCDN. There are numerous benefits in doing so, including reducing bandwidth costs, improving page load times, and increasing availability of the content. GitHub itself sits behind a massive CDN known as Fastly; that's why the load times for web sites hosted through GitHub Pages are very fast. Another aspect of using a CDN such as CloudFlare is the added protection against attacks. Many CDNs provide a feature set that protects the web site against denial-of-service (DoS) attacks in which thousands of bots make millions of requests to a server and bring it down so that no traffic can access it. Smart security solutions such as DDoS protection, SSL encryption, and other web application firewalls keep the threats to a minimum. Most of these services recognize the extraneous requests during attacks and deny them while keeping the web site alive.

A new portfolio doesn't yet need to set up an extensive CDN, but it might need one at a stage with high traffic. Later in the book, we discuss web site publishing in detail and cover how to set up a CDN. Now that we have talked about the CDN and its relation to a portfolio, let's get to the last topic of this chapter: setting up MailChimp. We covered the first half of using MailChimp, which is setting up the signup form. Here we discuss the second half, which is how to run a MailChimp campaign.

MailChimp Campaign

In the last chapter, we created a MailChimp account and set up a sign up list that was linked to the Subscribe button. We use the same list here again to link the Subscribe element of the top navigation bar. Let's assume we already have some users signing up for our mailing list. In this section, we discuss how you would actually run a campaign to send a picture of the day to your users. Log back into your MailChimp account and follow along. After logging in, the first page you see is the Dashboard, shown in Figure 9-7.

Dashboard

Create Campaign ▾

Get started

Create and send a campaign

Campaigns are emails sent to subscribers in a list. Try your hand at email design by creating and sending a test campaign. learn more

Create A Campaign

If you're gearing up for holiday sending, check out All About Holiday Campaigns.

Figure 9-7. Dashboard of MailChimp after a signup form has been created. Click the drop-down list to show the campaign options

We use a Regular Campaign in this case, and selecting that brings us to the next page, where we select which mailing list to use for this campaign. We only have one that belongs to our blog, as shown in Figure 9-8.

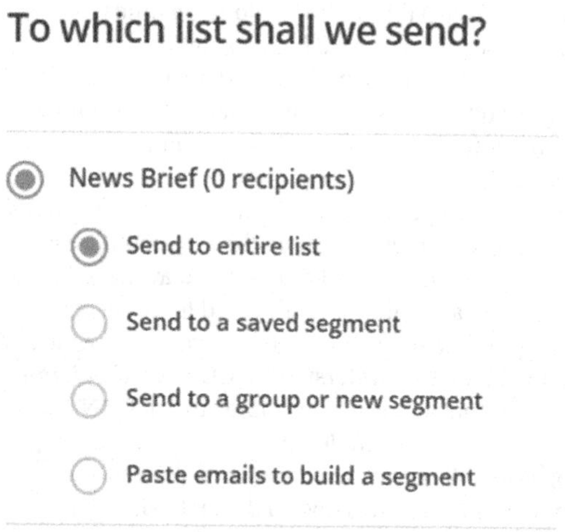

To which list shall we send?

- **News Brief (0 recipients)**

  - **Send to entire list**

  - Send to a saved segment

  - Send to a group or new segment

  - Paste emails to build a segment

Figure 9-8. Selecting which mailing list to use for this campaign

Once the mailing list has been selected, click Next to move to the next page. This is the Campaign info page, shown in Figure 9-9. On the Campaign info page, we set up some basic information, such as the return e-mail address for the campaign newsletters and the e-mail subjects. Most of this information is very straightforward to fill out, and for the tracking options and the rest, the defaults work perfectly fine. This will help your readers connect the source of the e-mails to the blog and the rest of your portfolio.

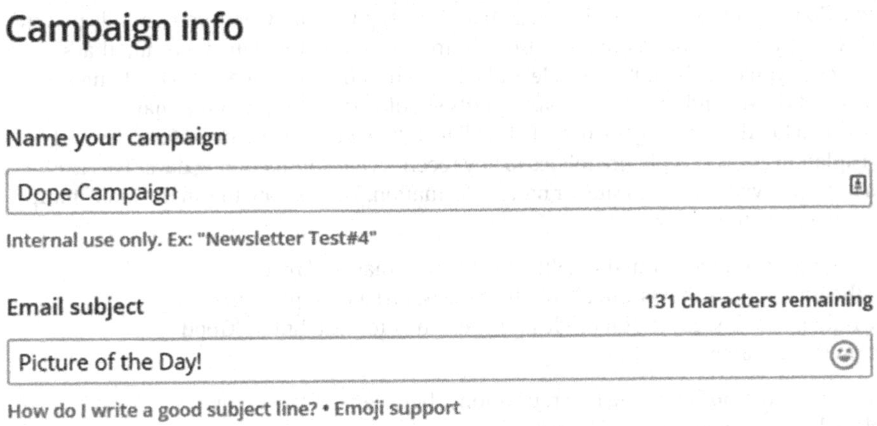

Campaign info

Name your campaign

| Dope Campaign | 🗒 |

Internal use only. Ex: "Newsletter Test#4"

Email subject   131 characters remaining

| Picture of the Day! | 😊 |

How do I write a good subject line? • Emoji support

Figure 9-9. *Campaign info page*

After completing the campaign information, we arrive at the page where we need to build the e-mail template, as shown in Figure 9-10. There are numerous templates being showcased, so let's think about what our requirements from this e-mail campaign are. We only need a very simple e-mail template where a picture is the focus, and a description under it takes the reader either to your blog or to your 500px page. For that reason, we pick the 1 Column layout.

Select a template

Basic   Themes   Saved Templates   Campaigns

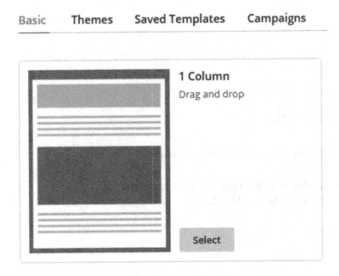

Figure 9-10. *Selecting the 1 Column layout for the e-mail campaign*

After selecting the 1 Column template, you will be taken to the design wizard where you actually design the e-mail. This wizard actually allows you to drag and drop components from the right pane, and that's the method we use. However, you can also edit the code and fix any components if needed. The themes are all written in straightforward HTML and CSS. What components should we include in our e-mail? To keep things simple, we start with a header greeting the user. This will be followed by the picture of the day and a text box very briefly explaining how this picture relates to any recent events or upcoming days. This text box should end with a button to visit your web site for more information. To replicate this in the MailChimp wizard, you would need to follow these steps.

1. Start by dragging a text block from the right pane to the e-mail and place it at the top of the image block that is already on the canvas. Just as you place the block, the right pane changes to edit mode and you can enter text. Enter, "Good Morning!" in the text area.

2. Hover over the picture box and drag it to reposition it between the header and the text block below it, as shown in Figure 9-11.

Figure 9-11. *The drag icon shown on the left side*

3. Move the already existing text block below the image and click the edit pencil icon to edit that text block, as shown in Figure 9-12. Remove the header text in it because we already have the header, and the remainder of the block would serve as the description area for the picture of the day.

It's time to design your email.

Figure 9-12. *Removing the default heading 1 text because we already have a header*

4. Scroll past the text block and add a button from the right pane below the text block. Edit the button text to "Visit my Portfolio" and the link to your web site, as shown in Figure 9-13.

Button text

Visit my Portfolio

Link to:

Web Address

Web Address (URL)

jekyll-mini-blog.github.io

Figure 9-13. *Editing the button to display your web site*

That's all you need for designing the e-mail. The full template is shown in the two parts of Figure 9-14. This is the e-mail that we will be sending out through this campaign. You have to run the campaign every day to send a picture of the day.

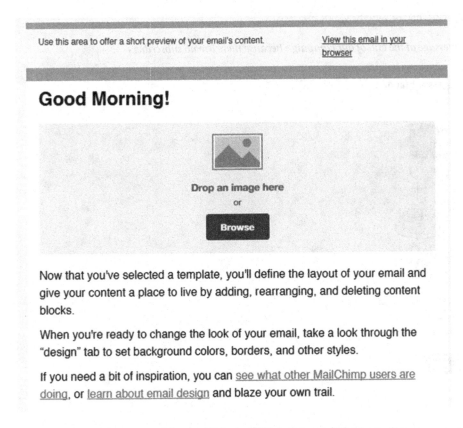

Figure 9-14a. *The top part of the e-mail that will be sent through the campaign*

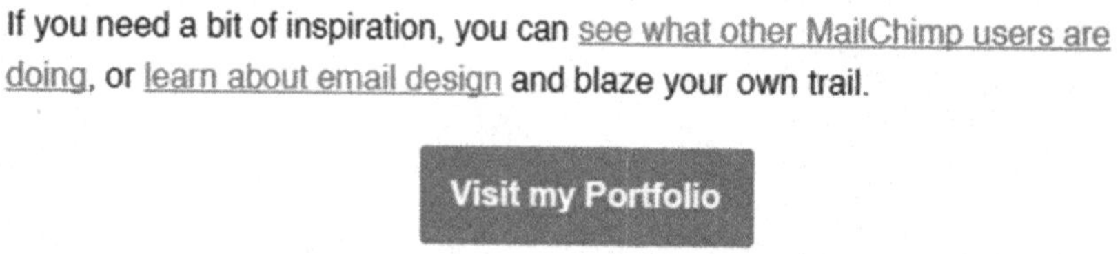

If you need a bit of inspiration, you can see what other MailChimp users are doing, or learn about email design and blaze your own trail.
Visit my Portfolio

Figure 9-14b. *The lower half of the e-mail to be sent through the "Picture of the Day" campaign*

■ **Note** The designer allows for the addition of numerous other components to the e-mail, such as dividers to organize the e-mail, social share and follow icons, and even videos. Use them once you become more familiar with the designer and the basic theme.

Once the e-mail has been designed, we can go to the last step, which is a checklist of the campaign (as shown in Figure 9-15), and then you can click Send. Here, we actually run into a bit of trouble because our list doesn't actually have a subscriber. Besides that, at this stage, MailChimp asks you to confirm once more and the e-mail gets sent out to all the subscribers of that mailing list, as shown in Figure 9-16.

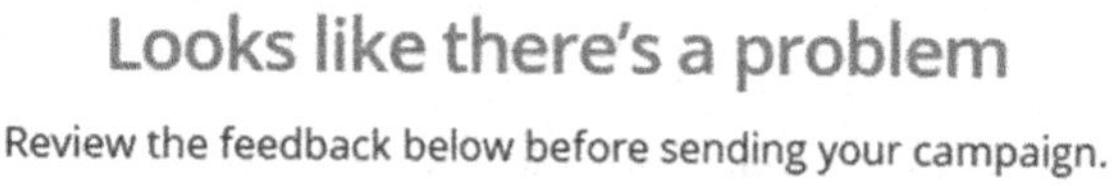

Looks like there's a problem
Review the feedback below before sending your campaign.

Figure 9-15. *Error message at the end of our campaign because there are no subscribers*

Prepare for launch
You're about to send a campaign to:
The Best List Ever
126 subscribers
Send Now
Cancel
This is your moment of glory.

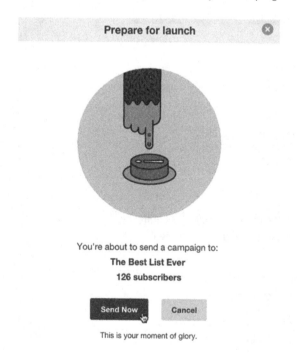

Figure 9-16. *Last confirmation before sending the mass e-mail*

This finishes up our discussion of MailChimp, as we have created a mailing list and also run a campaign. Most of the campaign information that was entered for the first time can simply be reused if you start a new campaign. After running a campaign once, you can rerun it the next day to send out a new picture. All you would have to do is add a new picture to the designer. The rest will all carry over from the last campaign run. Now add the signup form for the mailing list we created last time and complete the last element of the top navigation bar.

Summary

In this chapter, we started editing the Dopetrope theme to create a personal portfolio that can showcase your photography and interests in art. We started off by understanding some basic limitations of Jekyll and by creating a project spec that detailed the technologies that we needed to accomplish our goals. The spec translated into creating a simple prototype, which gave us further direction into the nature of the web site. We found the appropriate theme to work on and modify into a final product that can be used as a portfolio. Then, we identified all the problem areas for the theme and fixed each one, manipulating several layouts and creating new pages to fix the blog. We also edited the layout of the blog posts themselves to make the images easy to manipulate and confer to the freemium model better. Finally, we talked about how to run a MailChimp campaign and send the picture of the day. Over time, using this as a personal portfolio and creating great content on the blog will lead to successful conversion of readers into long-term paid users of your photography.

Further Reading

1. **500px support center:** https://support.500px.com/hc/en-us

2. **MailChimp Campaign:** http://kb.mailchimp.com/campaigns/ways-to-build/create-a-campaign-with-campaign-builder

3. **Embedly docs:** http://embed.ly/docs

4. **CloudFlare:** https://www.cloudflare.com/overview/

CHAPTER 10

■ ■ ■

Open Debates

Those who stand for nothing fall for anything.

—Alexander Hamilton

Technology has fundamentally changed how we communicate with each other. New tools and platforms allow us to share our stories more vibrantly than ever before. In this chapter, we focus on a cornerstone of discourse: debates. We build a Jekyll-based debate platform that can leverage the full capabilities of GitHub to host open debates. We begin with an introduction to the debate platform and the rules of an Oxford-style debate. After that, we provide an in-depth overview of GitHub and all of its features, including some features of GitHub Pages that we have not yet had a chance to cover. We then create a prototype based on the rules to help us find a theme. When we have found a suitable theme and understood the requirements for this project, we can start editing the theme to obtain our final debate platform. Finally, we end this chapter with a discussion of how our platform can take advantage of the open standards and use them in conducting the debates.

A common theme that many new nonprofits are aiming for is creating a platform to have intelligent and candid conversations about the problems facing our society. A discussion involving strong opinions often breaks down into slander and flame wars, but a sophisticated platform can control the chaos that ensues during a debate. In these debates, controlling the flow of information becomes crucial and being able to direct the participants and users in a meaningful way adds value to the debate. An online platform can make this process smoother and more efficient. The focus of this platform is Oxford-style debates involving two speakers, one moderator, and participants. Each debate has a central theme and an associated statement that one of the speakers defends and the other speaker opposes. The inspiration for this platform came from The Economist, which often hosts Oxford-style debates on a wide variety of issues at http://debates.economist.com/ and has a very good functional understanding of how to carry out a debate. Their platform is very well designed and polished, but closed. We will be designing an open source alternative powered by Jekyll and integrating third-party tools where necessary in our project. There are several benefits to creating an open platform, but the biggest one is that anyone can implement this project on GitHub and use it with minor modifications to host their own debates. Keeping the project open source also plays to several advantages that we discuss shortly. Before we get any deeper into the project itself, we have to change some of the rules for an Oxford debate and modify them to fit Jekyll as a platform.

Rules of the Game

Let's talk about the structure and the rules of an Oxford-style debate. In some cases, the debate lasts over a span of ten days or more, but we modify some of the rules here to fit our Jekyll theme. We use the The Economist debates as a basis to develop our own rules.

© Vikram Dhillon 2016
V. Dhillon, *Creating Blogs with Jekyll*, DOI 10.1007/978-1-4842-1464-0_10

- The debate will be conducted in five phases: briefing, opening statements, rebuttal, closing statements, and results.

- Guest opinions will be interspersed within the debate, not to take sides, but to provide context to the debate from fresh perspectives.

- The home page of the debate should contain the briefing. This provides a summary of the issue at hand, briefly discusses the problem statement for the debate, and gives the reasons why this debate fits in the context of modern society. It should provide a timeline for the debate.

- From that point onward, every page in the web site actually represents each of the five phases, so let's dive into what elements each page should include.

- The briefing page was already discussed, but it should also provide a mechanism for voting that is easily accessible on the home page.

- The opening statements page should be distraction-free and start with opening statements by the moderator. Here, the moderator will introduce the two speakers participating in the debate, along with a brief summary of how their backgrounds play a role in this debate. After introducing the speakers and providing the context for this debate, the moderator should inform the audience why the issues in this debate are relevant to the audience. Following the moderator's statements, the two speakers will provide their sides and support them with evidence and additional links for further study. At the end of the page there is room for comments, which allows the readers to ask questions after reading the opening statements.

- The next phase is the rebuttal, which gets very interesting. At this point, the debate has been going on for a few days, so the moderator would start off this section and summarize the points made by both the speakers and the top comments or comment threads. This is followed by the speakers examining each other's opening statements and using them to provide support for their own positions and leaving a note as their rebuttal statement. Most of the guest notes should be provided by now during the opening and rebuttal phases. Comments are still allowed in the rebuttal phase on the speaker's positions.

- The next phase is the closing phase. The debate has run its time and the speakers, along with the participants, have provided their input. In the closing statements, the speakers examine how their views changed after being influenced by the other speaker and how their positions have evolved. The moderator also summarizes the whole debate with the key turning points and his or her own opinion on the issue. This phase is very similar to the opening statements, the only difference being that this phase is the ending.

- The debate has now come to a conclusion. The results phase is a summary of the entire debate. There are a few components here, the first one being the results from voting by the participants. The second one is an analysis of the debate by the moderator along with the decision made by the participants. This could simply be a short summary of the points made by the speakers and the winner of the debate as decided by the participants.

■ **Note**   The reader might wonder why we covered the structure and the rules of the debate in such detail. This time, instead of creating a project specification, we simply discussed the structure and rules pertaining to a project. The main reason is that often in real projects, you would have nothing more than a set of ill-defined ideas to start from; this is great practice for building a full-fledged project from a simple structure.

We just discussed the structure and the rules of this debate, but how can we distinguish ourselves from The Economist debates? An important theme we have for this chapter is to use open standards and provide transparency in the debates, to keep them "open." For that reason, GitHub will turn out to be our best friend here. To use GitHub effectively, we need to understand its components. In the next section, we do a deep walkthrough of the platform, describing all of its features.

Navigating GitHub

Previously, we covered how to create a new repository on GitHub, but we have not yet covered all the features and components offered by GitHub in detail. Let's start after you sign in to your account. The first page after logging in is the home page, which contains several feeds of information, some of which are taken from other projects that you follow. We talk about followed projects momentarily. Underneath the + New repository button, there is some information about types of repositories, as shown in Figure 10-1. Recall that in Git, repositories are functional units that contain your code for a project. All the changes that you make to the code are pushed to the corresponding repository for that project. A single account can hold any number of public repositories.

Figure 10-1. *The different types of repositories that can exist under your account*

So what is a public repository? In Figure 10-1, we can see a few other types as well. The All view lists all the repositories under the account. Under your account, public repositories are the ones that anyone can access. To clarify what access means, they can see all of your code and reuse it if they want. With public repositories, any code or static elements pushed to the repository are available to anyone else who might access them. On the other hand, private repositories are only accessible to you and other collaborators to whom you provide access (there's an option to provide access that we cover shortly). The Sources tab lists the repositories that contain source code from your projects. This is important because not every repository that you create would have to be based on code; you can create simple text-based repositories as well to share text and use version control to collaborate with developers. Finally, the last tab is Forks. GitHub allows you to clone other public repositories in a process called forking. This creates a clone of the available repository that you wish to fork under your own account. Now you can make as many modifications to it as you like and eventually even contribute back to the original project. From this dashboard, let's open the repository and start exploring.

Repository Overview

The next page is the repository overview, shown in Figure 10-2, which provides a plethora of information.

Figure 10-2. *The repository view. In this view, several other features located in the top bar become available*

This is the repository view. It shows all the functionality and features available for this repository. Within this repository view, we are in the code section. Let's start unraveling this information from the top. The first thing to notice is the three buttons on the top: Unwatch, Star, and Fork. These buttons show how popular a repository might be in GitHub among developers. A very hot project might have a lot of stars, which is the way other developers keep up with updates from your repository. The fork count in a repository is the number of times other developers have cloned this repository to make their own edits. The name of the account and the repository are presented next, followed by the features of this repository. We examine each of these features individually. Underneath this list is a description of the code base; in this case, we haven't provided one to the repository. Next is a quick view of some numbers on the repository, the most important of which include how many branches exist, the number of commits, if this repository has produced any releases, and how many people have contributed to the code. Following the stats is the quick access bar, which gives you the link to clone the repository locally, switch between branches, download the code as a zip, and so on. Finally, after the quick access bar is the source code for the repository itself. Here, we can see the folder structure, the latest commit that was made, and any readme files underneath the code, if present at all.

That was a lot of information for a single feature, but as you start using Github more often, all of this will seem familiar to you. Additionally, most of your work is not really done on GitHub; it's generally offline. For the purposes of this debate, however, we use the next feature, which is Issues.

Issues

In brief, each repository that contains code might also have bugs associated with it. When a commit causes other code to break, one of the contributors to the blog or a user can open a bug with the repository. The Issues tab is essentially a way to track these bugs. We use this bug tracker in a different way: The Issues tab is publicly accessible, so we can take advantage of it to keep the conversations between the moderators and speakers open. More concretely, we can open a new issue and ask the speakers to reply to the issue, which the participant can see. The moderator simply copies the replies by the speakers into the debate. Aside from transparency, this method greatly reduces the complexity involved on the speaker side. It allows them to reply in a very straightforward manner as a comment to the issue created. The Issues feature is shown in Figure 10-3a and creating an issue is displayed in Figure 10-3b.

Figure 10-3a. *Issues feature in GitHub. Clicking New Issue allows you to create a new issue for the repository. We use this feature to keep the conversations between the moderator and the speaker transparent*

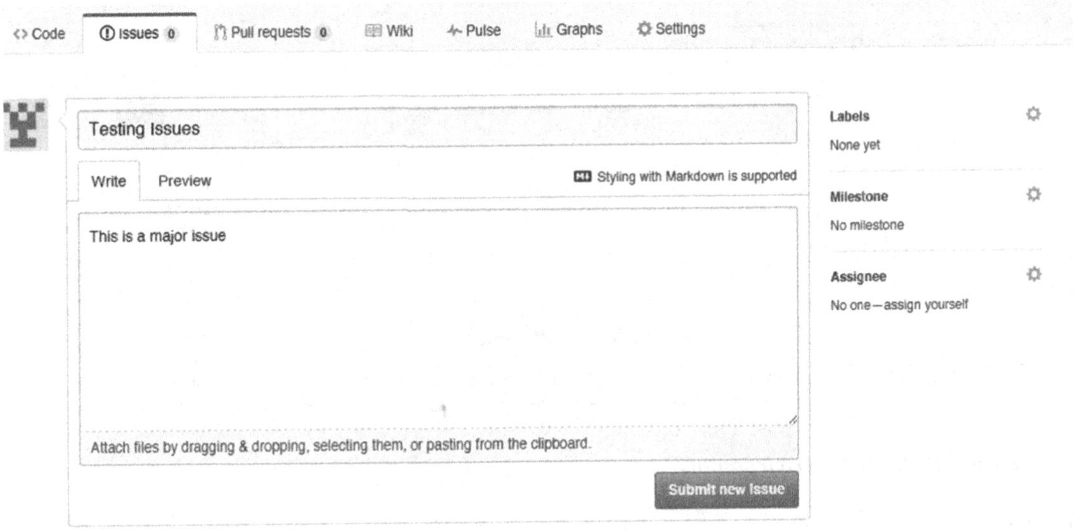

Figure 10-3b. *Creating a new issue within a repository. The issue statement can be written in Markdown*

The issues act as task manager for the repository and allow us to manage and fix any problems that arise. The issues are not limited to just code; you can create them for any sort of repository. In our case, we will be using them to obtain statements from the speakers through each phase of the debate. We will be creating new post layouts that can be inherited to format the statements properly. The issues can be designed to reflect which debate they originated from, and one easy way to distinguish the issues is by using a naming scheme: *[Debate-name] Opposing-Speaker Opening Statements*. This method would work nicely to organize the debates on the GitHub side.

■ **Note**   We are only discussing one Git hosting solution in this chapter, GitHub. However, there are several other platforms for Git. Some of the most popular ones include Bitbucket, GitLab, Gerrit, and Perforce. Not all these platforms are open or free to use, however; in some cases the requirements for enterprise-level development are different than for personal projects.

Pull Requests

The next feature is pull requests, which goes back to the idea of forking repositories. Once you have cloned a repository, you also have the entire history of that repository. There can be many reasons to fork a repository, and a common one is to learn how the code works and play with it on your own. However, another reason for forking a repository is to make a change and contribute back to the original project. In those cases, after forking a repository and making the changes that you desire, it is time to push the changes back to the original project using a pull request. Essentially, a pull request is a summary of the commits and exactly what changes are you proposing to make. This is also the only proper way to contribute back to open source projects on Git. The pull request feature is shown in Figure 10-4.

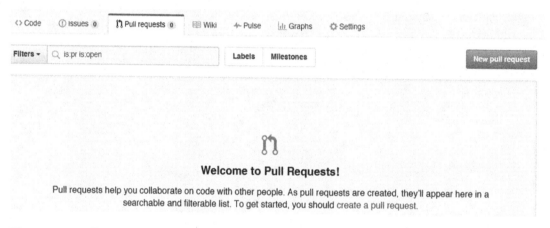

Figure 10-4. Pull requests to a repository

Wiki

The next feature is the wiki for a repository. This feature simply allows you to create pages and use them as tutorials or status updates on your project. The pages can really be used for anything as necessary, and creating them is very easy because the pages can be formatted with Markdown. This feature can be useful in our project if the moderator of the debate chooses to rephrase the rules discussed in the previous section and show them to the speakers. Another interesting use of the wiki that will have to be ported into the debate would be a further reading section that would allow interested readers to learn more about the context in which the debate is happening. The wiki feature is shown in Figure 10-5.

Figure 10-5. *Wiki feature for the repository*

The next two features are more for the purposes of obtaining data on developers and less for the project itself. As a result, they might be used more often within an organization developing an open source product.

Pulse and Graphs

The next feature, Pulse, gives you an overview of the repository. It tells you the interactions developers have had with it in terms of commits or merges, and also how many interactions the repository has had with the "outside" in terms of the pull requests. It also details the number of open or resolved issues. This feature is handy when a project grows large enough to accommodate many developers and a large code base. At that time, it is crucial that some level of accountability and a measure of repository health is present. The Pulse feature is shown in Figure 10-6. The next feature is Graphs, and as the name implies, this is another analytics feature for the repository. Just as Pulse provides data on the repository, Graphs provides data on the developers interacting with the repository. This feature is shown in Figure 10-7, and the data tabs show the seven prominent metrics on the developers. The particularly important ones are number of commits made be the developers involved and the contributors. For personal projects such as this debate project, most of this data will show one developer or one contributor, so this data is not very insightful to us. On the other hand, it might be a good idea to use this data for personal goals and improvement. Recently, there has been a push to centralize the contributions made by developers so that they can include them in their own achievements. One path forward has been to use Mozilla Open Badges, which seems like an interesting alternative, and the data from GitHub certainly makes it easier to link and identify developer contributions.

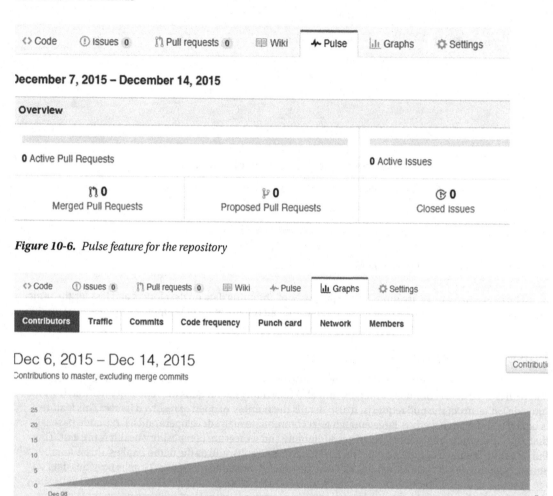

Figure 10-6. *Pulse feature for the repository*

Figure 10-7. *Graphs with data on the developers interacting with the repository*

There are more options available in each of the two features than we covered here, but most of those options are not useful for small projects. The last feature is the settings. This is what we used previously to delete an older repository and then create a new one. Launching this feature takes us to the Settings page, and the sidebar helps the user navigate through the various settings available for the repository. The most practical settings are on the Options tab of the sidebar and we focus on them. The Options page is split into four zones. The first zone provides the option to rename the repository. This is easy to do, but you have to be very careful that any other variables in the code using that repository name are also updated, or it might break links. The next zone shows the features of the repository. Remember the issue and wiki views we discussed earlier? Those can be disabled for a repository if needed. This is generally done to restrict the repository strictly to a code base. We need these features so we will leave this section untouched. Let's skip ahead to the danger zone. This is the zone where you can upgrade your GitHub plan to get a private repository if need be. In addition, you can also transfer the ownership of your repository to another user so they can manage it for you. This could be useful if someone managing the repository cannot do it for the near future and you need a new manager. Finally, this zone contains the option to delete your repository and all the information associated with it. This allows you to create root repositories again to host new code.

GitHub Pages

The last zone that we'll talk about is GitHub Pages, which contains an automatic page generator. Let's start with the page generator, and then we cover some features of GitHub Pages. Essentially, the page generator uses predefined templates to create a Jekyll-based landing page for your project. The code generated from the template is a fully functional web site stored in the same repository under a new branch called gh-pages. The branch is hosted on a web address provided by GitHub as username.github.io/project_name. This can be incredibly useful if you want to make a landing page for your finished project. The auto-generator wizard will create a beautiful layout for you where you can provide a download link to your executable. There are two types of web sites that GitHub Pages will generate for us, and we have already briefly covered both of them. The first type is a user or organization site. This option is automatically selected when the repository is created with the name username.github.io and GitHub Pages automatically compiles that repository into a web site using any Jekyll components available within the repository. For our purposes, this is the type of web site that we are creating within this project. The other type of web site that GitHub Pages will create is a project site. This option allows you to make a project page for any of the repositories under your account and you can hold multiple landing pages within your repository using this method. GitHub Pages is simply creating a Jekyll-based landing page that you can modify for every project that you launch with the auto-generator. The auto-generator is shown in Figure 10-8.

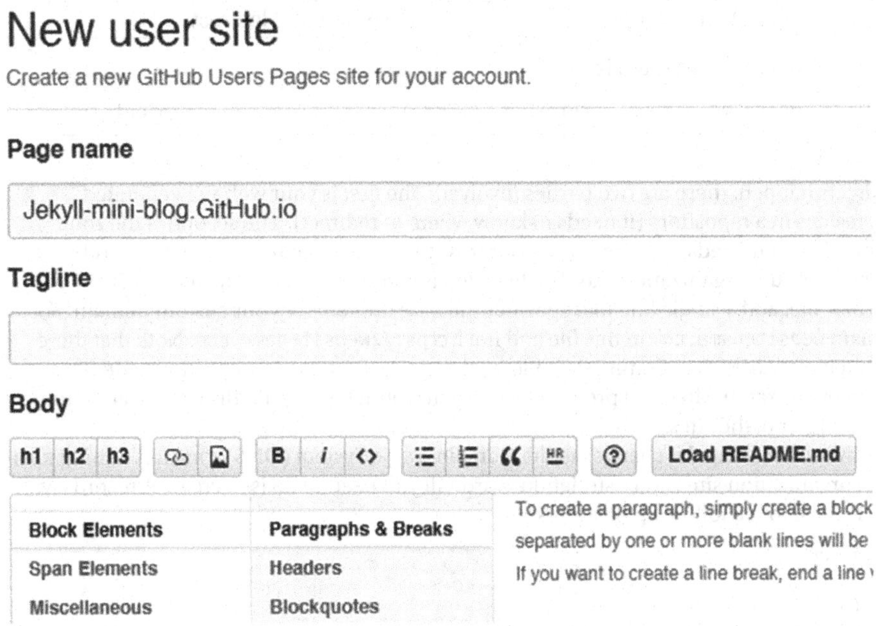

New user site

Create a new GitHub Users Pages site for your account.

Page name

Jekyll-mini-blog.GitHub.io

Tagline

Body

| h1 | h2 | h3 | ⌘ | 🖼 | B | *i* | <> | ☰ | ☷ | 66 | HR | ⑦ | Load README.md |

Block Elements	Paragraphs & Breaks	To create a paragraph, simply create a block
Span Elements	Headers	separated by one or more blank lines will be
Miscellaneous	Blockquotes	If you want to create a line break, end a line '

Figure 10-8. GitHub Pages auto-generator for project pages

The organization web site created by GitHub Pages using the username.github.io naming format not only compiles automatically, but it also has a few other interesting features. The most practical feature is that you can configure a custom domain for this web site that was compiled by GitHub Pages. This allows you to redirect from the username.github.io web address to a custom domain that you like. There are two types of redirects for GitHub Pages sites: subdomains and apex domains (top-level domains). It is important that we discuss the terminology first before moving on to avoid any confusion.

- **Primary domain**: A web address pointing to the location of a web site on a server. Generally given in the form of example.com and also known as a top-level domain or simply domain.

- **Subdomain**: A domain that is part of the primary domain. Generally given in the form of subdomain.example.com.

- **Project directory**: A web-accessible directory present on a server. Generally given in the form of example.com/project. This should not be confused with GitHub's project sites, which are given the web address of username.github.io/project.

- **Apex domain**: Top-level domain, much like a primary domain. The only difference between the apex domain and the primary domain is the use of terminology. Domains are used normally to refer to web sites and apex domains are being used by GitHub to refer redirects to top-level domains.

So how does GitHub Pages actually do the redirects for project sites and organization sites? Essentially, these redirects work as shown in Table 10-1.

Table 10-1. *Redirects for GitHub Pages*

Type	Given Web Address	Custom Domain Redirect
For organization sites	username.github.io	example.com
For project sites	username.github.io/project	project.example.com or project.com

To make the redirects happen, there are two parties involved: The first is your web site generated by GitHub Pages that resides in a repository (it needs to know where to redirect). The second is the zone file of the custom domain (which needs to know the web address to which it can redirect). Let's start by creating a custom domain for the organization site. The first step is committing a text file named CNAME to the repository. In the new file, add a single line that specifies the bare domain for your custom domain. For example, use the domain websitename.com in this file and not https://websitename.com. Note that there can only be one domain in the CNAME file. Commit this file, and that takes care of the repository side. This step is common to both organization sites and project sites, so you would have to do this if you were setting up a custom domain for either of the sites.

The second step involves making the changes to the Domain Name System (DNS) zone file. Setting up a domain redirect for an organization site is very straightforward: All you need to do is to create A records with your DNS provider to resolve to the following IP addresses:

- 192.30.252.153

- 192.30.252.154

Following this method and editing the A records with the DNS provider, we can redirect an organization site to a custom apex domain. Redirection for project sites is very similar, but it involves a few more steps in certain cases. A sample DNA zone file with an A record that points to GitHub is shown in Figure 10-9.

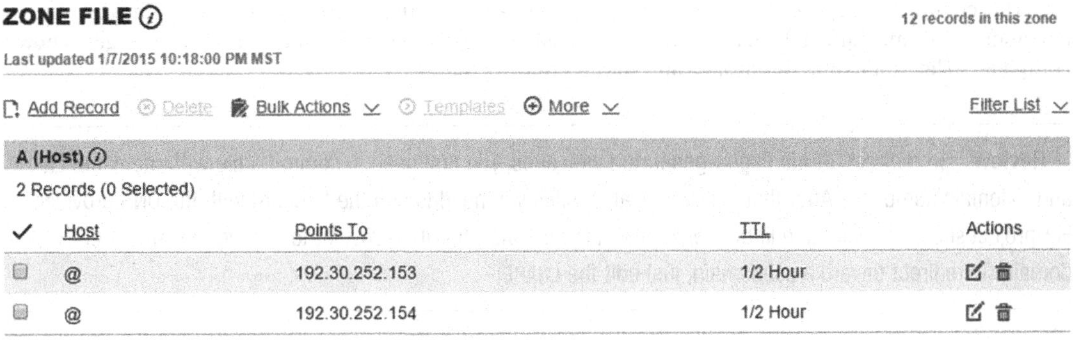

ZONE FILE ⓘ   12 records in this zone

Last updated 1/7/2015 10:18:00 PM MST

⌐ Add Record   ⊗ Delete   ▧ Bulk Actions ⌄   ⊙ Templates   ⊕ More ⌄   Filter List ⌄

A (Host) ⓘ

2 Records (0 Selected)

✓	Host	Points To	TTL	Actions
☐	@	192.30.252.153	1/2 Hour	☑ 🗑
☐	@	192.30.252.154	1/2 Hour	☑ 🗑

Figure 10-9. A sample zone file on GoDaddy for an apex domain redirection

---

■ **Note**   For DNS providers such as GoDaddy, setting up redirects with GitHub Pages can be done by committing the CNAME file to the repository and then editing the zone file by clicking Manage Domain and then the DNS Zone File tab on the GoDaddy dashboard.

The process of redirecting project sites is slightly more involved because you have two options: Either create an independent domain for the project site or redirect it as a subdomain of a custom domain. If an organization site has been created (or there exists a repository under your account using the format username.github.io), then any project site that you set up will default to being a subdomain under that organization site. If you use the GitHub Pages auto-generator, the resulting landing page will also be created as a subdomain. The project sites can be kept as subdomains of the organization site or redirected to independent custom domains following roughly the same process as before.

For the project sites, the first step is exactly the same: Add a CNAME file with the domain name to the repository. Here you get to decide what you want to do with this project site. One option is to redirect the site to an independent domain, using example.com in the CNAME file. This is on the repository side; on the DNS side, side, you have to add a CNAME record and an A record as follows:

```
CNAME
Name = blog
Type = CNAME
Value = yourusername.github.io. (Yes, there is a . at the end!)

A record
Name = (blank, nothing)
Type = A
Value = 192.30.252.153
```

If you want to redirect the site to a subdomain, then put subdomain.example.com in the CNAME file. The next step is different: Instead of adding an A record and CNAME record in the DNS zone file, we simply add the CNAME to the zone file as follows:

```
Name = blog
Type = CNAME
Value = yourusername.github.io. (Yes, there is a . at the end!)
```

173

This completes the process of redirecting the project site to a custom domain. A visual guide to changing CNAME and editing the A records is referenced later in the chapter. Our tour of GitHub Pages is now complete, so let's jump into this project and start editing the theme.

■ **Review**   To redirect GitHub Pages-generated web sites, you first need to commit a file with the name CNAME and a domain name in it. After that, for organization sites you need to edit the A record with the DNS provider. For project sites, you need to edit the CNAME and A record with the DNS provider to redirect toward an apex domain. To redirect toward a subdomain, just edit the CNAME.

Prototyping

We have prototyped our projects before, but the approach we took was largely to create a model for what our blog should look like. The model then guides our search for a theme that we can edit. So why do we start with a built theme and then edit it? Well, the answer is a practical one: Whenever you want to start with a new task or project at hand, starting from complete scratch might be a waste of time. You want to start at a solid foundation and then keep changing it or adding elements to give it a personalized feeling. In development terms, you almost never want to start from absolutely nothing, which can be a huge setback. Selecting a theme to use as a base greatly helps to visualize the end product. That's the main objective of prototyping: providing a tangible representation to aid our visualization of the final product. Another approach to the same problem is to model the behaviour of the web site or the way users would interact with the web site and their workflow. Given that our debate has multiple phases and a workflow to it, we can storyboard our prototype. In this approach, the main focus of the model is to try and capture the transition that users face while going from one phase to another. In this section, we model the home page for Open Debates and the transition into the briefing phase for the debate. The storyboard will first show the home page and detail the features available on the home page, and then transition into the briefing phase of the debate. This allows us to capture the interaction between the linking page and the beginning of the debate itself.

Figure 10-10 shows the Open Debates page. This page starts with a top navigation bar containing the name of the web site and two navigation options. Beneath the navigation bar are a few options to share the ideas from the debate to social media. After the social bar there is a summary of the current debate, along with a picture relating to the debate. This allows the readers to understand the motion being debated and the positions of the speakers. There must also be an easily accessible and distraction-free button to access the current debate. Underneath the current debate is an archive of the past debates that have happened on this platform.

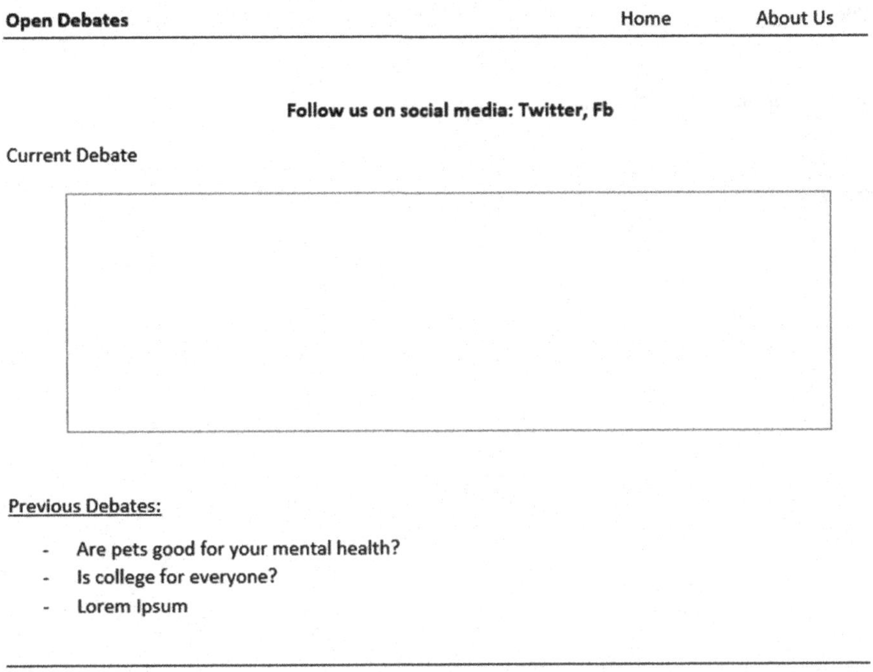

Open Debates   Home   About Us

Follow us on social media: Twitter, Fb

Current Debate

<u>Previous Debates:</u>

- Are pets good for your mental health?
- Is college for everyone?
- Lorem Ipsum

Figure 10-10. *The Open Debates home page*

Figure 10-11 shows the results of the transition from the home page to the debate briefing page. This page would be the entry page for the user, and it shows a brief summary and description of the debate. The page starts with the same top navigation bar, but instead of the site name, this navigation bar provides the name of the current debate. Underneath this bar, instead of social media, we have a debate specific navigation bar that takes us from one phase of the debate to the next. Under the debate phases is the content of the debate. This is a briefing page, so it contains a summary of the debate along with the two speakers. Finally, after providing a brief introduction to the debate, there is a voting option. This first vote gauges the initial reactions of the crowd tuning in for this debate.

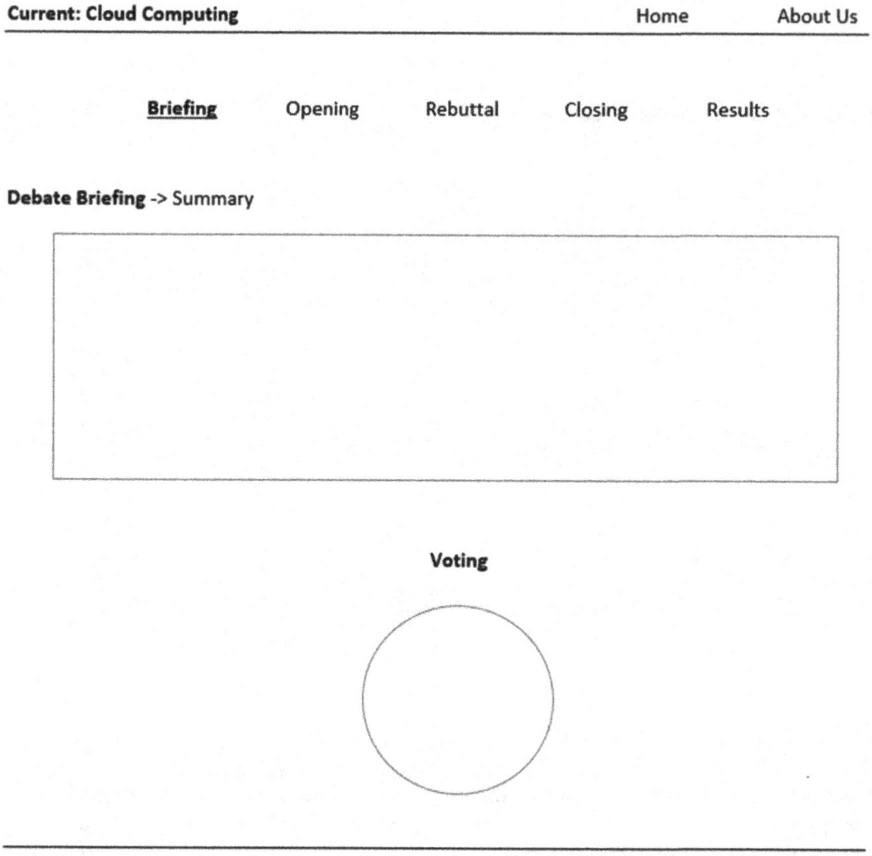

Current: Cloud Computing   Home   About Us

<u>**Briefing**</u>   Opening   Rebuttal   Closing   Results

Debate Briefing -> Summary

Voting

Figure 10-11. *Transition into the debate itself*

Jekyll Collections

Before we get into editing the theme, there is one more problem that comes to light after making the storyboard. The issue we face is organizing the pages created through the debates. It is clear that each debate will require five or six different pages and the total number of pages will grow very fast. We need a method for organizing these pages from each debate, and more important, we need a way to dynamically reassign and automatically update links throughout the theme using some global variables. This becomes important for elements such as navigation bars, which are generally created with hard-coded links to defined pages. It is not sensible to hard-code the links to pages associated with a debate when they will become obsolete in the next debate. We can't simply ask the maintainer of the theme to update the links each time for a new debate. The links in a navigation bar need to be such that they can be automatically updated with a single switch. If we can create a template for navigation that has the property of dynamically updating links each time a new debate happens and preserving the old links, we can properly direct the user to any debate and its associated pages. This problem is commonly known as routing, and to solve it, advanced front-end frameworks such as Ember.js and Angular.js use sophisticated mechanisms called routers. The sole purpose of a router is to help guide user workflow through a web application and make it easier on the developer to create new routes. These routes can essentially be understood as links that can be dynamically updated.

Jekyll has two types of routing mechanisms that provide the most basic functioning to a blog. The first one is a primitive-type routing preset within Jekyll, which creates the links to every post and page once the site has been compiled. The second one is a derived-type routing relying on components of Jekyll such as YAML and Liquid. Two examples of the latter include the permalink YAML variable, which allows for some level of routing to individual blog posts, and Liquid tags that provide support for inheritance and includes. Recently, a much more sophisticated mechanism for routing was included in Jekyll 2.0 called collections. A collection allows you to define a new set of documents that behave much like a post or a page, but have their own properties. Collections bring all of Jekyll's features to custom sources of data or information that are not chronologically organized posts, but have a set relationship with one another. Everything that's not a post or a page can be represented as a collection. Using collections allows for an organization scheme to be applied to the custom sources (posts or pages). We rely on this ability of organizing new pages to provide us with the routing features needed for the debates. To implement a collection and tell Jekyll to read in your collection, create a new folder with the name of the collection. This folder name needs to be specified in the _config. yml file along with some optional variables and that's it: Your collection is ready. Now we can add all sorts of pages in the folder and the configuration added to the _config.yml file will take care of routing the files properly for us. Let's take a look at what this configuration is.

```
collections:                      # What comes next pertains to a collection
  new_debate:                     # Name of the collection
    output: true                  # Convert every page in the collection to an html file
    permalink: /awesome/:path/    # Routing and permalink for each of the pages
```

These four lines of code implement the collection and routing that we need for this project. The first line denotes that the following configuration is related to a collection. The second line is the name of the collection. For this collection to be processed by Jekyll, there needs to be a folder in the format _foldername containing the pages or posts under this collection. The third line specifies an output for Jekyll to convert every post or page into a corresponding HTML file. The last line here actually gives us the routing. This permalink specifies that all the files from this debate should be listed under the /awesome/ path. For instance, if we had a file _new_debate/debate_briefing.md, it would be converted to jekyll-mini-blog. com/awesome/new_debate/debate_briefing.html. Each debate will become a functional unit for this blog. In that sense, we consider each debate as a collection of posts or pages that correspond to the phases of the debate. To add new debates to the collection, simply add the next collection underneath the debate and the associated configuration for it. This is shown as follows:

```
collections:
 first_debate:
   output: true
   permalink: /awesome/:path/

 second_debate:
   permalink: /two/:path/
```

We will see this in action in the upcoming section, so let's get started with selecting a theme and editing it.

Theming the Debate

It should be noted here that the actual theme for this debate doesn't matter as much as the concepts being brought in and used to edit the theme. The only requirement for a theme is that it needs a navigation bar on the top of the page. Looking through Jekyll Themes for a minimal theme with a navigation bar, the Type theme seems a very interesting choice (http://jekyllthemes.org/themes/type-theme/). Download the zipped file and set it up as we have done previously on GitHub and use GitHub Desktop to manage and commit changes. Let's start by editing _config.yml. The baseurl has been set to root, so we don't need to edit anything. Here is the metadata for the site:

```
theme:
  # Meta
  title: Open Debates
```

Add a description fitting to the web site, and edit the header.

```
# Header text - Link the current debate here
header_text: >
    <p>Oxford style debates on issues that matter.</p>
    <p>Current debate topic: Cloud Computing.</p>

header_text_feature_image: img/debate.png # A cover-image for the header
```

Make sure that the image is not distracting, because the header text will appear in front of that image. A few lines down, there's also a feature to add Disqus-enabled comments to pages, and we will use that, so remember to come back to this later and add your shortname.

```
# Scripts
google_analytics: # Tracking ID, e.g. "UA-000000-01"
disqus_shortname:
```

Let's start adding the first debate. We also add some metadata with the collections code.

```
collections:
  first:
    output: true
    permalink: /first/:path/
    thumbnail: /thumbnails/first.png
```

This creates a collection called first, with an associated permalink variable that points each page of the debate under site.baseurl/first/page and we also have a thumbnail custom variable. Each collection can have some metadata associated with it, and here, the variable points to a newly created folder that contains a thumbnail image representing the debate. The output: true option tells Jekyll to convert any Markdown files present in the collection into HTML files that can be normally accessed. We can use this on the home page to list all the previous debates. There is some clutter with social icons that can be removed from the page if necessary, but most of the variables need to be assigned to be active, so if we leave them alone, they will not cause any issues. Now let's get to the home page. There are plenty of edits we need to make, so a list might help.

- Edit the top navigation bar.
- Make sure the header featured image displays with the appropriate text.
- Show the current debate.
- List previous debates.

The navigation bar is a bit convoluted in this theme. Instead of just having a list of links to form the navigation, the theme loops over every page available and makes the navigation bar from the pages that have a title and page.hide disabled. Note that in our case, each debate needs to have a navigation bar that is different from the one present on the home page. We need to create two separate navigation bars and replace the loop with hard-coded links to actual pages. The first step in this process is to take the navigation code from header.html and put it in a separate file.

```
<!-- Code to be moved from header.html to nav-bar.html -->
<nav class="site-nav">
        <ul>
                {% for page in site.pages %}
                {% if page.title and page.hide != true %}
                <li>
                        <a class="page-link" href="{{ page.url | prepend: site.baseurl }}">
                                {{ page.title }}
                        </a>
                </li>
                {% endif %}
                {% endfor %}
                <!-- Social icons from Font Awesome, if enabled -->
                {% include icons.html %}
        </ul>
</nav>
```

This code needs to be saved in a new file. Let's call it nav-bar.html, and to make the navigation appear on the home page, let's include this file in header.html as {% include nav-bar.html %}. Let's start editing the navigation bar to link to defined pages. We will be editing the previously mentioned code, now present in nav-bar.html.

```
<nav class="site-nav">
        <ul>
                <li> <a class="page-link" href="{{ site.url }}"> Home </a> </li>
                <li> <a class="page-link" href="{{ site.baseurl }}/about"> About </a> </li>

                <!-- Social icons from Font Awesome, if enabled -->
                {% include icons.html %}
        </ul>
</nav>
```

This snippet of code allows us to control what goes in the navigation bar of the home page while preserving the social icons that were defined. Now save the nav-bar.html file and remember to commit the changes. For the Home link to work properly, we have to use site.url instead of site.baseurl because the value of site.baseurl actually changes for different parts of the web site. If you are browsing the About page, site.baseurl will evaluate and return a link that is the subsection of the site. For instance, site. baseurl will return jekyll-mini-blog.github.io/about from evaluating {{ site.baseurl }} for the About page. That's why defining site.url in _config.yml is the right course of action: That variable will evaluate to an absolute for the whole site.

```
# SITE CONFIGURATION
baseurl: "" # the subpath of your site, e.g. /blog/
url: "http://jekyll-mini-blog.github.io" # Your username.github.io url here
```

So how do we create the second navigation bar that auto-updates the links each time? We need to use a global variable that can be changed each time to reflect the name of the current debate. This variable can be placed in _config.yml, underneath the collections definitions to make the editing easier:

```
current: first
```

The current becomes the global variable that will update the links for us in each debate. Using this global variable, and the fact that all the phases for the debate would be the same, we can construct the navigation to follow a pattern like {{ site.baseurl }}/{{ site.current }}/briefing. Let's see how this works for navigation.

```
<nav class="site-nav">
<ul>

<li> <a class="page-link" href="{{ site.baseurl }}/{{ site.current }}/briefing">
Briefing </a> </li>

<li> <a class="page-link" href="{{ site.baseurl }}/{{ site.current }}/opening">
Opening </a> </li>

<li> <a class="page-link" href="{{ site.baseurl }}/{{ site.current }}/rebuttal">
Rebuttal </a> </li>

<li> <a class="page-link" href="{{ site.baseurl }}/{{ site.current }}/closing">
Closing </a> </li>

<li> <a class="page-link" href="{{ site.baseurl }}/{{ site.current }}/results">
Results </a> </li>

        <!-- Social icons from Font Awesome, if enabled -->
        {% include icons.html %}
</ul>
</nav>
```

This allows us to rely on just the global variable to auto-update the links each time within the debate. This file is a clone of the original navigation bar, but this one is special for debates, so save it as nav-bar-debates.html. Each time, simply editing the current variable in config.yml will automatically generate new links for the navigation. This navigation bar by itself is just one component; eventually we will have to create a series of new layouts for each of the five phases of this debate. We return to this topic shortly, but for now we have to organize the collections and display them on the home page. This can be done in a number of ways, but we will do a simple loop through the collections to display them all, along with a thumbnail. That's what the thumbnail variable in the config.yml file was for. First, a folder with the name thumbnails needs to be created. After that, place images in the folder corresponding to each of the debates and make sure that the names of the images match with those specified in config.yml so that Jekyll lists them out. Before that, we need to clean up the home page a bit and remove the posts. All the code within <div class="posts"> is safe to remove along with the pagination code under

```
{% if paginator.total_pages > 1 %}
  <div class="pagination">
```

You should be left with just a </div> tag in the end that closes off the initial home class. That will remove the posts from the home page, and now we can start adding the debates. The logic here is to consider each collection as a unit or an object, and on the home page, we are simply listing each object using a simple <li> tag. The way to do this would be through a for loop: Loop through all the collections and list their names.

```
{% for collection in site.collections %}g
<p> {{ collection.label }} </p>
{% endfor %}
```

The new updates to Jekyll 3.0 allow you to simply use collections.label to get the name of the collection. This is essentially the logic that we are using to list all the collections on the home page. As you keep adding more collections, this home page list will automatically grow. This code needs some style elements so that we can list the collections in a visually appealing manner, so let's look at the code for the full index.html.

```
---
layout: default
---

<!-- Old code -->
<div class="home">
  {% if site.theme.header_text %}
  <div class="call-out"
  style="background-image: url('{{ site.baseurl }}/{{ site.theme.header_text_feature_image }}')">
    {{ site.theme.header_text }}
  </div>
  {% endif %}
<!-- Old code -->

<br> </br> <!-- Line breaks -->

<strong><p align="center"> Our debates: </p> </strong>

<style> <!-- Styling the list to center it and remove the bullets -->

.test{text-align:center}
ul{list-style-type: none;}

</style>

<div class="test"> <!-- A class using the style we just specified -->

<!-- The current debate in session being displayed on top of the page -->

<p>
The debate in session currently is - <a class="page-link" href="{{ site.baseurl }}/{{ site.current }}/briefing"> {{ site.current }} </a> </p>

<small><strong> {{ site.curr_description }} </strong></small>

<br> </br>
```

<!-- For loop: List a thumbnail and hyperlink the label of the collection to the briefing page for that debate-->

```
{% for collection in site.collections %}
<ul>
  <p> <img align="center" src="{{ collection.thumbnail }}"> </img>
  <li> {{ collection.label }}:<a href="{{ site.baseurl}}/{{ collection.label}}/
briefing/">  Briefing </a></li></p>
</ul>
{% endfor %}                              <!-- End for loop -->

</div>

</div>
```

There is quite a lot happening in this file, so let's break it down into a few simpler components.

- The old code leftover from the edits starts the home class and makes the header appear with the featured header image.

- The <br> tags just add horizontal breaks. These tags are dispersed throughout the theme to make it appear clean and not cluttered. The technically correct way would be to put everything in a <div> and then put the spacing in CSS, but this was just a quick way to do that.

- The next block is actually the style elements, which centers the list of objects and also removes the bullet from the <li>.

- The next block of code is another measure to make the debate platform clean. This one lists the current debate explicitly, along with a link to the briefing page for that debate based on the current variable in the config.yml file. There's also a new variable called site.curr_description, and this variable corresponds to a definition in config.yml for curr_description. The purpose of this variable is to enter a short description for the current debate and the way this would be done in config.yml is as follows:

```
curr_description: >
    Lorem ipsum dolor sit amet, consectetur adipisicing elit, sed do eiusmod
# There must be one tabbed spacing on the line after the > character.
```

- Finally, the last block of code is simply extrapolating from what we discussed earlier with the collections. This block does two things with the listing. Remember that even if this code looks complex, it just lists each collection as an object or a unit. The first element to list is an image or a thumbnail for each of the collections. The second element is the label of the collection along with the word "Briefing" hyperlinked to the briefing page of the debate.

This fixes up the home page for us, so right now the home page shows a list of debates and highlights the current debate. We only added minimal style elements, but a few simples ones such as creating a box around the current debate with a dashed green border can be implemented with ease. Now what's left for this project is actually designing the layouts for each of the six phases. There will be significant repeats across the phases, but each phase will have some unique features. Let's start with the first one, the debate briefing.

Phases

The first element needed in the briefing page is a voting mechanism. The Economist debates use a beautiful miniature voting mechanism, but in Jekyll, we can't do any server-side programming so we have to rely on third-party services to provide us with a polling capability. Recently, Twitter announced the ability to create polls with multiple choices, so what if we used Twitter polls in our debates? There is one limitation of these polls: The voting period only lasts for 24 hours. That might seem like a serious disadvantage because we want to capture the votes through the entire debate. Arguably, that's just one way to gauge what the audience thinks. Another possibility is to capture the change in their thoughts over the period of 24 hours. In this case, we have to create new poll every 24 hours, but that offers a very high degree of control and granularity on audience input. The difference here is that instead of capturing the feedback from the audience over the whole debate, we capture how their minds changed as the new phases expose them to different ideas and information that they might not have considered before. Creating a poll on Twitter is actually very simple. A sample poll is shown in Figure 10-12. There are two distinct advantages of creating a poll on Twitter and using that instead of creating it on the Open Debates platform.

- The first one is the simplicity of creating and maintaining the poll. There is absolutely no overhead in terms of development on our end: The poll is hosted elsewhere and it can be embedded very simply just as a normal tweet would be embedded in a web page. Being able to embed the poll is one of the best features, and the results from that poll are displayed after the 24-hour window. The moderator can take note of those or even save the old polls as images, and then update the briefing page each time for the 24-hour window. This allows the audience to see the results of the poll and more important, they get to see the changes in mindsets as the debate progresses.

- The other realistic advantage is that most debates on The Economist are already using social media to some extent, either to ask questions or spread awareness about the issue. Incorporating social media as a central component of the debate allows us to reach our followers on social media easily. The use of another platform also makes it possible to reach a larger user base, which follows the same principles mentioned previously in the choice of using 500px for hosting photography.

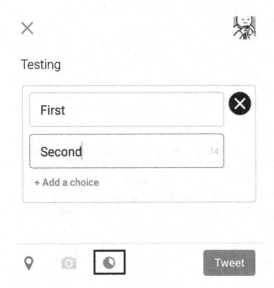

Figure 10-12. Creating a poll on Twitter using the mobile app. A poll can also be created easily on the web app using the same method as shown here

The major disadvantage within this scheme is having the moderator present the results from every polling window. More specifically, this would mean that the briefing file would have to be edited daily. Being aware of this shortcoming, though, can make it easier for us to accommodate the editing from the moderator and keep it minimal.

To make the editing pain-free for the moderator, we rely on styles that can make the text visually appealing and standardize them through the theme. This allows us to include the styles in a layout and then implement them using a `<div class="style">` tag. For this debate platform, we will need five styles:

- **Bios:** The style being used to display the bios of the speakers and the moderator on the briefing page.

- **Moderator talks:** The style being used to show the statements made by the moderator.

- **Speakers talk:** The style being used to show the speaker statements.

- **Guests talk:** The style being used to show the statements by guests.

- **Poll results:** The style being used when the moderator presents the results from a polling window.

Each of these styles will turn into an individual file present under _includes. In this way, we can include all of the styles in a layout and then inherit that layout for the phases that are actually pages themselves. The styles being presented here are not always the best visual choices and they are not very sophisticated, but they illustrate the phases accurately and minimally. Most of these styles are font changes and other CSS-based elements designed to distinguish among the various participants in the debate. The logic here is to design style classes such that the moderator only needs to use basic HTML during the editing. So where should the styles be stored? The obvious solution is that we would put them as individual files that we can then include in a layout. Let's look at the _layouts folder, where three layouts are present. Both the posts and pages inherit layouts from the default, which has a few lines of code.

```
<!DOCTYPE html>
<html class="no-js">
  {% include head.html %}
  <body>
    {% include header.html %}
    <div class="content">
      {{ content }}
    </div>
    {% include footer.html %}
  </body>
</html>
```

Most of the interesting code is in the includes, as the header.html file contains the top navigation bar code edited earlier to modularize the code and create a new nav-bar.html file. We need to revisit that file because the navigation is still not fixed for the debates. We created two files, nav-bar.html and a second one called nav-bar-debates.html for the debates. So how do we make Jekyll switch the navigation bars? Let's use an if statement with the logic that if we are not at the home page, then the other navigation bar should display.

```
{% if page.url == "/index.html" %}
    {% include nav-bar.html %}
{% else %}
        {% include nav-bar-debates.html %}
{% endif %}
```

This code replaces the single line {% include nav-bar.html %} in the header.html file. Going back to the default layout, the page layout inherits from this one, so the page layout might be the better place to store the styles. The styles should be entered near the top of the file, after the front matter, shown as follows:

```
---
layout: default
---
{% include bio_style.html %}
{% include guest_style.html %}
{% include mod_style.html %}
{% include speaker_style.html %}
{% include results_style.html %}
```

This will ensure that any page that inherits the page layout will have access to any of these style elements if necessary. In the remainder of this chapter, we cover each of the phases along with the corresponding styles. The first phase is the briefing, stored in briefing.md in the location _first-collection/briefing.md. This file has three elements: mod style for introducing the debate, bio style for the bios of the guests, and finally the poll embedded from Twitter. The poll created on Twitter can be embedded with ease, as shown in Figure 10-13.

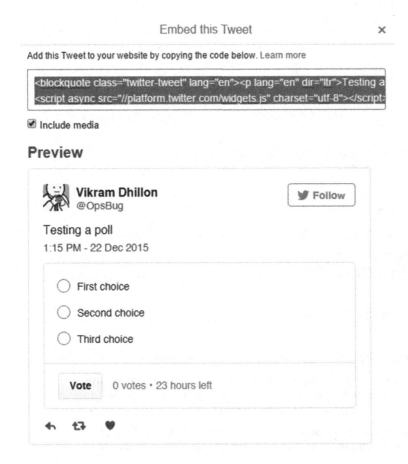

Figure 10-13. *Embedding a poll created on Twitter. The embed code provided by Twitter and selected here can be copied over to an individual file,* twitter_poll.html, *and then included in the briefing page.*

Let's start with the full code of the phases, the first one being `briefing.md`.

```
---
layout: page
title: Debate Briefing
---

<div class="mod">
Consectetur adipiscing elit. Donec a diam lectus. Sed sit amet ipsum mauris. Maecenas congue
ligula ac quam viverra nec consectetur ante hendrerit. Donec et mollis dolor. Praesent et
diam eget libero egestas mattis sit amet vitae augue.
</div>

<!-- Embedding the twitter poll -->
{% include twitter_poll.html %}
<!-- Biographies for the mod and the speakers -->

<p style="text-align:center;">
<img src="http://www.placehold.it/70x70" />
<span> Vikram Dhillon (Moderator) </span>
</p>

<div class="bio">
<p> Biography of the moderator </p>
</div>

<hr>

<img src="http://www.placehold.it/70x70" />
<span> John Smith (Opposing) </span>

<div class="bio">
<p> Biography of John Smith </p>
</div>

<img src="http://www.placehold.it/70x70" />
<span> Benjamin Franklin (Favoring) </span>

<div class="bio">
<p> Biography of Benjamin Franklin </p>
</div>
```

Let's break down what is happening in this file, along with the styles being used.

- We are using the page layout for this page in the debate. We also saved all of our style includes in the page layout, so it makes sense to use that. This layout also has an additional style feature of making the title appear in the h1 tag.

- Right away, the first block of text is contained within the `<div class="mod">` and this corresponds to the moderator style. We discuss exactly what is in the style shortly.

- Following the mod style is the include for embedding the Twitter poll. This code is being kept in a separate file to make the polling modular. That is to say, this code will have to be changed each 24 hours, so if we keep the code in an isolated file, all you need to do to edit the code is to paste the embed code in the `twitter_poll.html` file. The integration of this poll in the appropriate place is already taken care of.

- After the poll, we start listing the biographies. This is the last part of the code. Here we are using the `bio` class and there are some style features associated with the `span` and `img` classes, too. These features allow us to edit without having to worry about how the pictures or bios will render on the page. The CSS in the background takes care of this automatically with the styles we specified. Notice that the trend of hiding style details is common in this file. This is due to the fact that editing can be done simply using HTML tags; any other styles and related features can be stored elsewhere and used in the page as needed.

All of the styles corresponding to biographies can be contained in `bio_styles.html` and the moderator style can be stored in `mod_style.html`. Let's look at both of them, starting with `bio_styles.html`.

```
<style type="text/css">


img { /* The style applies anytime an img tag is used */
  vertical-align: middle;
  margin-bottom: 0.50em;
}

span { /* The style applies anytime a span tag is used */
  font-size: 1em;
  padding-left: 0.5em;
  padding-right: 5em;
  font-variant: small-caps;
}

.bio { /* The style applies only to div class bio */
  font-size: 15px;
  font-family: 'Roboto', sans-serif;
  padding-bottom: 1em;
}

hr { /* The style applies anytime a hr tag is used */
  border: 0;
  border-bottom: 1px dashed #ccc;
  background: #999;
}

</style>
```

The code here applies to both custom `div` classes and HTML tags. This allows us to ensure that any instance of a tag can inherit the proper style. This is what allows us to just use `<img>` tags and not have to worry about whether the images will be placed appropriately. Let's look at the `mod_style.html` next.

```
<style>


.mod { /* The style applies only to div class mod */
  font-size: 12px;
  font-family: 'PT Sans Narrow', sans-serif;
  padding-bottom: 1em;
}


</style>
```

This is a simple custom style implementing a new font. Where are these fonts coming from? We are using Google Fonts for these custom styles. To use custom fonts properly, Google Fonts tells us that we have to import the fonts into the header of an HTML page. In this theme, all the imports are handled in head. html. Let's create a new file called fonts.html in _includes where we can store import links to any fonts that we want to use. This file should be included in head.html (line 23) under the Google Fonts option.

```
<!-- Google Fonts -->
{% if site.theme.google_fonts %}
<link href="//fonts.googleapis.com/css?family={{ site.theme.google_fonts }}"
rel="stylesheet" type="text/css">
{% endif %}
```

{% include fonts.html %}

Now the fonts stored in fonts.html will be imported automatically and made available to the whole theme. The contents of fonts.html for our debate platform are shown here.

```
<!-- For bio styles -->
<link href='https://fonts.googleapis.com/css?family=Roboto:300italic' rel='stylesheet'
type='text/css'>

<!-- For results styles -->
<link href='https://fonts.googleapis.com/css?family=Montserrat' rel='stylesheet' type='text/
css'>

<!-- For speaker styles -->
<link href='https://fonts.googleapis.com/css?family=Droid+Sans' rel='stylesheet' type='text/
css'>

<!-- For mod styles -->
<link href='https://fonts.googleapis.com/css?family=PT+Sans+Narrow' rel='stylesheet'
type='text/css'>

<!-- For guest styles -->
<link href='https://fonts.googleapis.com/css?family=Slabo+27px' rel='stylesheet' type='text/
css'>
```

These link statements are all taken right from Google Fonts and stored here to allow for easy addition of any new fonts and a modular structure. In this manner, we can now design any styles with these fonts, and the fonts will become available automatically.

The next file to cover is the opening phase, which should be named opening.md in the debate collection folder. This file is actually very simple, as it only contains three styles: the mod style for when the moderator discusses the issue, the opening statements from the speakers, and any input from guests. Here's the full code for opening.md, and a discussion of the code follows.

```
---
layout: page
title: Opening Statements
---

<div class="mod"> <!-- Moderator comments -->
Consectetur adipiscing elit. Donec a diam lectus. Sed sit amet ipsum mauris. Maecenas congue
ligula ac quam viverra nec consectetur ante hendrerit. Donec et mollis dolor. Praesent et
diam eget libero egestas mattis sit amet vitae augue. Nam tincidunt congue enim, ut porta
lorem lacinia consectetur.
</div>

<div class="speakers"> <!-- Speaker #1 opening statement -->

<img src="http://www.placehold.it/70x70" /> <!-- Speaker #1 picture -->
<span> John Smith (Opposing) </span>

<p> Duis aute irure dolor in reprehenderit in voluptate velit esse cillum dolore eu fugiat
nulla pariatur. Excepteur sint occaecat cupidatat non proident, sunt in culpa qui officia
deserunt mollit anim id est laborum. </p>

</div>

<div class="speakers"> <!-- Speaker #2 opening statement -->

<img src="http://www.placehold.it/70x70" /> <!-- Speaker #w profile picture -->
<span> Benjamin Franklin (Favoring) </span>

<p> Duis aute irure dolor in reprehenderit in voluptate velit esse cillum dolore eu fugiat
nulla pariatur. Excepteur sint occaecat cupidatat non proident, sunt in culpa qui officia
deserunt mollit anim id est laborum. </p>

</div>
<hr> <!-- Speaker statements done -->

<div class="guest"> <!-- Guest input -->

<p class="input"> Lorem ipsum dolor sit amet, consectetur adipisicing elit, sed do eiusmod
tempor incididunt ut labore et dolore magna aliqua. </p>

</div>
```

- The front matter tells Jekyll that this is the opening page. Additionally, with the page layout, the "Opening Statements" title also gets the <h1> property.

- From the start, this page has some comments from the moderator in <div class="mod">, which we discuss shortly. This class has some font updates for the moderator comments.

- After the moderator statements, there are two instances of `<div class="speakers">` that are the opening statements from both the speakers. In each instance, the first line is actually their photos following the same code as the debate briefing. The next are their names, again following the same logic as the briefing. After the name and image come the opening statements from the speakers put into new paragraphs to give ample spacing.

- Once the opening statements from the speakers are done, there's a horizontal rule to indicate the completion of the opening statements.

- Following the opening statements is some input from guests who are experts in the areas being discussed in the debate. The guest statements are introduced in `<div class="guest">` and the statements themselves are put into another paragraph class called `input`.

This code actually uses three style classes: `guest`, `input`, and `speaker`. The other elements are being inherited from the `bio_style.html` file for the bios. The `input` class is being used for the guests, so we can store them together in one file. Let's start looking at these files to see what elements they bring in for the `opening.md` page. The first is `guest_style.html`, which contains the guest class.

```
<style>

.guest {
  padding-top: 0.5em;
  font-size: 22px;
  font-family: 'Slabo 27px', serif;
  padding-bottom: 1em;
  color: rgb(108, 122, 137);
}

.input:before {
    content: "Guest Input: ";
}

</style>
```

The `guest` class provides the guest input with the Slabo font and also a peculiar `rgb(108,122,137)` color. This helps distinguish the guest input from the rest of the page. This class also provides the input text with some padding. The `input` class just exists to provide the words "Guest Input" before the input text is displayed. The content property is the only way to add text in CSS, but it only works with pseudo-elements `:after` and `:before`, which decide the placement of the text. We used this tag as `<p class="input">` Lorem ipsum … `</p>` and therefore the content "Guest Input" was inserted right before the Lorem ipsum text. The next file to be examined is the `speaker` class, contained in the `speaker_styles.html` file.

```
<style>

.speaker {
  font-size: 12px;
  font-family: 'Droid+Sans', serif;
  padding-bottom: 1em;
}

</style>
```

This is also a very simple style file providing the Droid Sans font to the statements from speakers. These two files add the style elements to the opening page and make it easier for the moderator to simply add the content provided to them by the speakers or guests within the proper classes.

■ **Note** It must be noted that the moderator only adds the content provided by the speakers in the appropriate areas designated to the speakers. This content should also be requested through GitHub via opening an issue. We discussed how to open issues with a GitHub repository and now we can finally use them to obtain feedback from speakers and guests.

The next file is for the rebuttal phase, which would be stored in the `rebuttal.md` file. It looks the exact same as the opening file, as it contains the same three elements: moderator summary, the rebuttal by each speaker examining the other's statements, and guest comments on the issue. The only difference would be the front matter.

```
---
layout: page
title: Rebuttal
---
```

The next file is for the closing statements, saved as `closing.md`. This file has two components that are already covered: the moderator summary and closing statements by the speakers. The full code is shown here.

```
---
layout: page
title: Closing Statements
---

<div class="mod">
Consectetur adipiscing elit. Donec a diam lectus. Sed sit amet ipsum mauris. Maecenas congue
ligula ac quam viverra nec consectetur ante hendrerit. Donec et mollis dolor. Praesent et
diam eget libero egestas mattis sit amet vitae augue. Nam tincidunt congue enim, ut porta
lorem lacinia consectetur.
</div>

<div class="speakers">

<img src="http://www.placehold.it/70x70" />
<span> John Smith (Opposing) </span>

<p> Duis aute irure dolor in reprehenderit in voluptate velit esse cillum dolore eu fugiat
nulla pariatur. Excepteur sint occaecat cupidatat non proident, sunt in culpa qui officia
deserunt mollit anim id est laborum. </p>

</div>

<div class="speakers">

<img src="http://www.placehold.it/70x70" />
<span> Benjamin Franklin (Favoring) </span>
```

```
<p> Duis aute irure dolor in reprehenderit in voluptate velit esse cillum dolore eu fugiat
nulla pariatur. Excepteur sint occaecat cupidatat non proident, sunt in culpa qui officia
deserunt mollit anim id est laborum. </p>

</div>
```

There is nothing new in this code, as the style elements being used and the code itself were discussed previously in the opening statements. Finally, the last phase of this debate is the results, which is stored in `results.md`. This phase involves just comments from the moderator. Let's look at the full code of `results.md`.

```
---
layout: page
title: Results of the Debate
---

<div class="mod">
Consectetur adipiscing elit. Donec a diam lectus. Sed sit amet ipsum mauris. Maecenas congue
ligula ac quam viverra nec consectetur ante hendrerit. Donec et mollis dolor. Praesent et
diam eget libero egestas mattis sit amet vitae augue. Nam tincidunt congue enim, ut porta
lorem lacinia consectetur.
</div>

<div class="results">
Sed sit amet ipsum mauris. Maecenas congue ligula ac quam viverra nec consectetur ante
hendrerit. Donec et mollis dolor.
</div>
```

This file uses a new style class that we have not covered. The idea here is for the moderator to summarize the debate on both sides and announce the results of the debate. The first mod class is just for a summary and the `results` class later on is the polling results from the debate. This is where the moderator shows the data on how the mind-set of the audience changed over the course of the debate and if any interesting shifts happened. The `results` class is also very straightforward, stored in the `results_style.html` file.

```
<style>

.mod { /* The style applies only to div class mod */
  font-size: 13px;
  font-family: 'Montserrat', sans-serif;
  padding-bottom: 4em;
}

</style>
```

This segment of code gives the poll results the Montserrat font and some padding on the bottom. That was the last section of the debates, and this finishes up the first debate collection. There are still a few finishing touches left for this Open Debates platform, the first one being the use of comments. We discussed how to implement Disqus previously, so in this case, we would want to put the Disqus embed code in a file under _includes and then manually include the embed file in the appropriate areas. It must be noted that comments should not be posted under the page layout because we don't want comments on the briefing or results. Therefore the include has to be done manually for the `briefing.md`, `opening.md`, `rebuttal.md`, and `closing.md` files. The next feature is actually about the content of the statements made by the moderator and speakers: To encourage the readers to actively participate in the debates, speakers should end their statements with something like, "If you agree with my statement, please vote for my side." This last line can hyperlink to the poll on the briefing page, and in this manner, we can at least try to ensure that the polling happens frequently in each window. The last feature is about the navigation bar. When a new debate starts, each of the links to the debate navigation bar will be present but not active because the pages have not been created. This is simply an artifact of the sidebar, and users will be redirected to a 404 page if they click on the inactive link. In a later section, we can try to fix this inactivation through the use of plug-ins. For now, though, the 404 page will be perfect for the debate platform.

Summary

In this chapter, we created an Open Debates platform that uses the GitHub platform to promote open standards in communication between the moderator and the speakers. We talked about how an Oxford-style debate happens and after listing out the rules for the debate, we started constructing our prototype. Based on the rules and our prototype, we found a matching theme and started editing until our platform satisfied all of the features required by the rules. This type of behavior-driven development is crucial for large projects, and we relied heavily on our ideas about the platform to create the final project. Our debate platform used some advanced features such as collections and using a collection as an object to create lists. These lists were presented on the home page, and we used a lot of Liquid tags for routing alongside conditionals like if statements to route the user workflow. We also leveraged the open standards of GitHub to collect input from the guests and speakers by opening issues. A new approach in capturing the change in mind-sets of the audience was used here in terms of the Twitter poll, and we discussed how to best embed and take advantage of the polling mechanism.

Further Reading

1. **Jekyll collections docs:** http://jekyllrb.com/docs/collections/

2. **Google Fonts:** https://www.google.com/fonts

3. **GitHub Pages: User and organization pages:** https://help.github.com/articles/user-organization-and-project-pages/

4. **GitHub Pages: Custom domains:** https://help.github.com/articles/setting-up-a-custom-domain-with-github-pages/

5. **GitHub Pages basics:** https://help.github.com/categories/github-pages-basics/

6. **Twitter polls:** https://blog.twitter.com/2015/introducing-twitter-polls

7. **DNS zone file editing:** https://www.godaddy.com/help/manage-dns-for-your-domain-names-680

8. **Adding CNAME records and A records:** https://www.godaddy.com/help/add-a-cname-record-19236

9. **GitHub Issues:** https://guides.github.com/features/issues/

10. **GitHub video guides:** https://www.youtube.com/user/GitHubGuides

11. **GitHub text guides:** https://guides.github.com/

CHAPTER 11

■ ■ ■

Open Research

What we find changes who we become.

—Peter Morville

Following the theme of this section, we build another open resources platform. The open dissemination of research data has been a boon to the community because it allows for cross-verification and a more cohesive understanding of the topics being studied. In this chapter, we return to using Jekyll as a blogging platform, but with new tools commonly used in academia. These power tools are enabled as modular includes so that they can run in the background to add several interesting features to the blog. We begin by picking a simple theme to use and then design a prototype for how we will integrate the services within that theme. After the prototype has been completed, we take on in-depth overview of Git and the CLI for it. We talk about the foundations of Git, followed by a tutorial on the most commonly used Git commands. Finally, we apply all the changes necessary to integrate all the tools that we previously discussed and end the chapter by discussing how those tools can be beneficial at large.

A New Platform

When the heartbleed vulnerability was made public, the most reliable sources of information were the bloggers examining the source code and the details themselves. They blogged extensively about it by going into the details of the bug and explaining its implications. Often, they were using variables and symbols to explain broad ideas, and more important, they were extending the logic they discovered to show how widespread the problem was. The open distribution of their findings was crucially helpful, and that's what we replicate in this chapter.

In designing products, keeping the end user in mind is very important, and there are three gradations of this.

- The best case is the founders designing a product for themselves. They are solving problems that matter to them, and ultimately they are the users themselves.

- The second case is that of building products that other users will use as intermediate components in their product.

- Finally, the hardest case is that of building a product that you don't have any intention of using (health care and most human resources software falls into this category). This project is an example of the last case.

Technical blogging is the theme of this chapter, but every tool being used here has broad applications, even outside of technical subjects. The main topic for application here is the Git command line and we are pairing it with the application and implementation of some JavaScript-based tools. It is the actual

V. Dhillon, *Creating Blogs with Jekyll*, DOI 10.1007/978-1-4842-1464-0_11

implementation of these technologies that holds more far value than just using all those tools. This chapter is not straightforward or easy to go through, but learning how to integrate diverse web technologies and maintain a theme is a formidable skill that you will gain from reading this chapter.

There are several components going into this blog, and most of them might be new to the reader, so we introduce each one and go over its usage in detail.

KaTeX

The first tool is KaTeX, which is a minimal port of LaTeX for the Web. LaTeX is a document markup language, in the same category as Markdown, but created for a very different purpose. LaTeX uses the design philosophy of separating presentation from the actual content. This allows authors to focus on the content of what they are writing, rather than the visual appearance. LaTeX is widely used in academia to prepare documents and for publication of scientific documents in many fields, including mathematics, physics, chemistry, bioinformatics, computer science, statistics, and economics.

LaTeX is actually a high-level language that uses the power of TeX in an easier way for writers. In short, TeX handles the layout side and LaTeX handles the content side for document processing. In that respect, LaTeX and TeX are much more exhaustive, whereas KaTeX is a web port of LaTeX and only offers a few necessary features. Instead of using the complete language, we are interested in using only the features that enable the rendering of math fonts and symbols. This limited typesetting is much easier to perform and KaTeX does it with incredible speed as well. A sample document prepared by LaTeX and rendered by TeX is shown in Figure 11-1. Our implementation of KaTeX is accomplished by downloading and including the `katex.css` and `katex.js` files from the publicly available release. Once the files are included in the repository, the files can then be imported into the relevant locations.

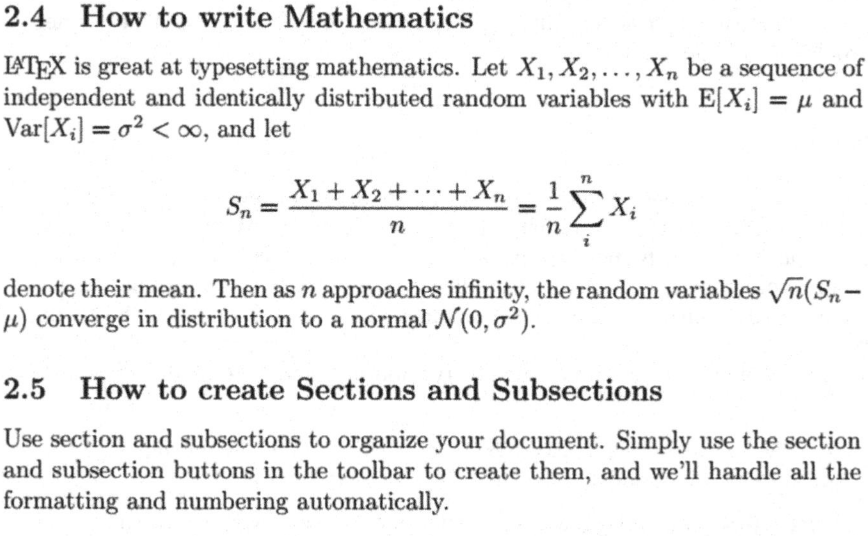

2.4   How to write Mathematics

LaTeX is great at typesetting mathematics. Let $X_1, X_2, \ldots, X_n$ be a sequence of independent and identically distributed random variables with $E[X_i] = \mu$ and $\mathrm{Var}[X_i] = \sigma^2 < \infty$, and let

$$S_n = \frac{X_1 + X_2 + \cdots + X_n}{n} = \frac{1}{n} \sum_i^n X_i$$

denote their mean. Then as n approaches infinity, the random variables $\sqrt{n}(S_n - \mu)$ converge in distribution to a normal $\mathcal{N}(0, \sigma^2)$.

2.5   How to create Sections and Subsections

Use section and subsections to organize your document. Simply use the section and subsection buttons in the toolbar to create them, and we'll handle all the formatting and numbering automatically.

Figure 11-1.   *A rendered document prepared using LaTeX*

There's a lot more that can be done using LaTeX, although displaying equations or symbols is a big portion of what we would be using online. Notations and symbols across subject areas can take advantage of KaTeX. A common use case has been developers blogging about breaking down a complex algorithm where they need to symbols or notation to explain how the algorithm would behave given an arbitrary set of initial conditions or input. KaTeX can format and render them very easily, and with enough practice, it might seem like a natural extension of Markdown.

The next two tools are related in the function that they perform: to create a presentable and graphical display of data. This can be immensely useful in many different situations, especially if you are trying to provide an example of your own point of view and then you can present data that you either collected or borrowed from a particular source. A perfect example of this can be you representing data taken from an organization with custom views that help you showcase your own points better.

Plot.ly

The first tool in this set is Plot.ly, which we use to create interactive graphs within blog posts. Plot.ly is a graphing library built for large data set visualizations; however, we will only be using its JavaScript API. The use of an API will allow us to use Plot.ly as a rendering engine that will create our graph off-site and just display it on our blog posts. That's essentially how APIs work: A company builds an incredible tool and wants developers to use its service without exposing the secret sauce. To that end, the company develops commands and functions that let developers pass their own data as an argument to the secret sauce, which will produce the desired result. In this manner, the developer only gets to a black box that can do the processing and provide the results. A graphical representation of this relationship between the developers and the APIs they use is provided in Figure 11-2.

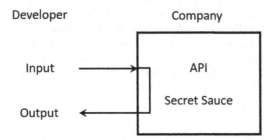

Figure 11-2. *The developer is allowed special access to the secret sauce, but only if he or she sends her data through a bridge constructed by using the methods that the company provided.*

Plot.ly is the same way for us through their JavaScript API that we will be using: Essentially it gives us the tools to draw a graph and represent data, but the actual functioning of the methods or functions used to draw that graph are hidden from us. One thing to note is that we're specifically using the JS API for Plot.ly because the JS inports work out very nicely on static blogs. Using Plot.ly will feel very similar to using font-awesome, except that here you actually have to write a bit of code to render the graph. A sample graph made by the Plot.ly JS API is shown in Figure 11-3. Our implementation will simply import the Plot.ly JS API file through their CDN into the theme and then we can rely on Plot.ly features to make a graph using JavaScript.

Here's a simple Plotly plot - <u>plotly.js documentation</u>

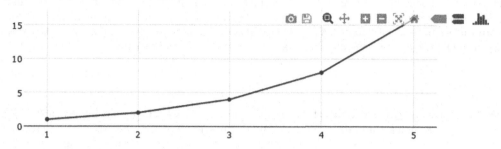

Figure 11-3. *A sample graph produced by Plotly.js API*

There is a notable open source alternative to Plot.ly called D3 (Data-Driven Documents), a JavaScript library that allows you to make high-quality graphics and render them on the Web. The JavaScript D3.js library uses prebuilt JavaScript functions to select elements, create SVG (Support Vector Graphics) objects, style them, or add transitions. The final result is embedded within an HTML web page. Incidentally, Plot.ly is also built using the D3 library, but it adds several new features that make it easier to use with a static site generator like Jekyll. It renders very smoothly, as compared to D3, which takes a little longer to produce the desired graphic. Using D3 within Jekyll is a bit convoluted and requires some fixes that make it impractical. The effort put into building a D3 graphic alone is considerable, and then to have to work on displaying it properly within HTML makes the process very time-consuming. The page load speeds are also different with both Plot.ly and D3, as the former loads a little bit faster and is less resource intensive.

IPython

The second of the two tools for data visualization and sharing is IPython. Originally designed to be a feature-rich and interactive development environment for Python, the project evolved into a web-based interactive computational environment for creating IPython notebooks. These notebooks allow you to combine Python programming with interactive prewritten programs and even text and equations for documentation. The concept of a notebook is very powerful for the notion of open research: Being able to share data and, more important, the methodology behind those results is crucial for increasing reproducibility in research. A notebook essentially guides a reader on the steps being followed to obtain a certain result. It can document the methodology being used very precisely, and at the same time it demonstrates the computations being done, all in one notebook. Currently, the lack of reproducible research is debilitating the confidence of researchers, and there are several efforts in the research community to create notebook-like interfaces where anyone can follow and verify the methods being used in a study. The notebook document format actually stores all the information and the input and output cells in JSON format, which can contain code, text, interactive media, and plots. An example notebook session (in the browser) is shown in Figure 11-4.

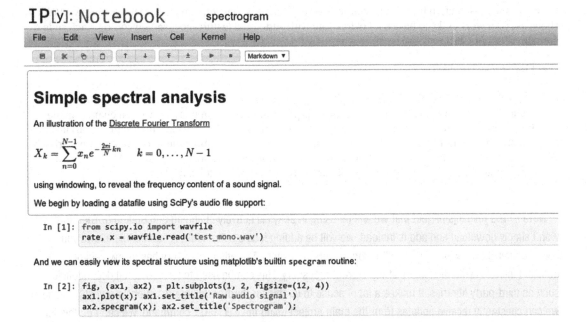

Figure 11-4. IPython Notebook. Notice the top half describing the problem and some background information, followed by input and output cells that implement the theory described.

The IPython project now comes under the Jupyter organization, and they have created a fantastic notebook viewer, called nbviewer, that can render your IPython notebook on the Web from a GitHub repository. The notebook viewer already has several demons that can be found at `http://nbviewer.ipython.org/`. Because the viewer pulls information from GitHub, sharing your notebook is as simple as sharing your code on GitHub. You can also share segments of your code in Gists and have the nbviewer render the Gist into a web notebook. Some books have taken advantage of the nbviewer as a book companion where the code for each chapter is presented in one large notebook. One distinct advantage to hosting your own work in GitHub and then sharing it through the notebook viewer is that you can reference yourself easily in a blog post through compiling site data. This is a feature of Jekyll much like collections, but it is easier to implement. Site data creates globally accessible data in JSON format that can be shared across the web site; that way, you can always call on your work using a shortcut and the notebook viewer will be linked. There are two main ways to share your work, the first one being uploading the files to a file-sharing server and then linking to them from within your blog, and the second being using a notebook viewer such as the one mentioned here. We go over how to do both, but the second strategy is much more effective, and we will be using a similar idea for sharing slides, too.

Reveal.js

The topic of sharing slides brings us to our last tool to be used in the blog: Reveal.js. Again, the use of JavaScript falls within Atwood's law. It just makes development much easier to accomplish in a static blog. Reveal.js is a framework for creating beautiful presentations using HTML. It has a number of slick features like Markdown content, code highlighting, nested slides, PDF export, and so on. In this project, we host reveal.js presentations on the Jekyll blog, so that the presentations become a natural extension of the listing of posts. In this manner, linking to a blog post would be replaced by linking to a presentation. In an

HTML-based presentation framework, the greatest advantage is that you don't need Microsoft PowerPoint to showcase your work and you have a lot of freedom with additional features focused on coding. Each slide is contained within <section> tags as shown here.

```
<section data-markdown>
</section>
```

There is a lot of configuration used in a reveal.js presentation, and in this case we can change all the variables in the YAML front matter. In exchange for being able use YAML, we have to design a smart layout that can pull information from the variables we just defined and then supply them to reveal.js appropriately. We can create a simple layout to show how to accomplish this. In addition, we use the YAML front matter to make presentations just as you would make a normal blog post, in a regular .md file.

■ **Note**　The reveal.js project that we will be using in Jekyll is actively changing and updating. Therefore we won't simply download and add it. Instead, we will be adding it as a submodule. A submodule allows you to keep another Git repository in a subdirectory of your repository. The other repository has its own history, which does not interfere with the history of the current repository. This can be used to have external dependencies such as third-party libraries. It makes a lot of sense to do this for third-party libraries such as reveal.js because we can constantly receive updates from the main project using the git pull command. We can't do this for themes because once we start editing a theme, the end result is sufficiently far away from the original theme that any updates to it might end up breaking our theme and causing more issues for our projects.

Planning the Theme

Before we start adding these features and editing a theme, we need to have an idea of what we are about to do with the theme. We will make a simple prototype, but let's focus first on the concrete details for each of the components.

- **KaTeX**: Import the source files from the latest release, place them in the Jekyll theme, and include the files within the theme to allow KaTeX implementation throughout the blog.

- **Plotlyjs**: Import the CDN file in the head of the theme, then use the provided tags to create a drawing area for the graph on a canvas. Finally, use JavaScript to actually draw a sample graph.

- **Bibliography**: Use a bibtex file to create a sample bibliography within the theme on a separate page, use a JavaScript parser to parse the bibliography, and finally show a possible alternative with site.data.

- **IPython**: Show how to make an IPython notebook available on the blog and also on the nbviewer.

- **Reveal.js**: Import the release files into the theme, include them within the theme, create a layout that can take configure reveal.js in the front matter, and use the layout to create a sample presentation as a blog post.

- **Wrappers**: Any tool that is imported in the theme to be used requires instantiation. The JavaScript does all the processing necessary in the background, and after that your objects and elements are ready to be used on the HTML canvas. Now, to actually use the objects, you need to instantiate them. This is generally done using a simple `<div>` tag to denote the beginning of a class associated with the JavaScript objects. We will have to use wrappers for all of the elements listed here, and very often, the wrappers are provided along with the tool being used.

Let's create a simple storyboard that features a blog post that uses KaTeX and a model page containing the bibliography that will be made using a JavaScript parser. The storyboard prototype is shown in Figure 11-5.

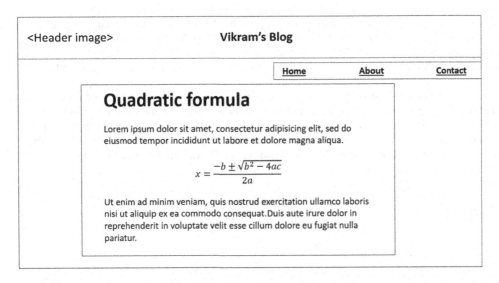

Figure 11-5a. *Prototype of a blog post, containing the quadratic formula in TeX typesetting*

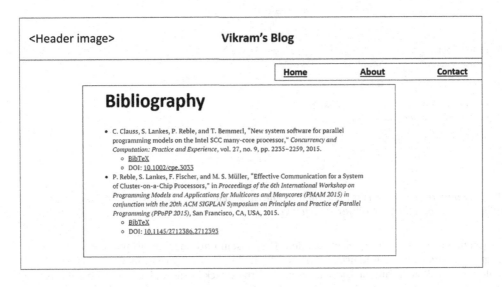

Figure 11-5b. *Prototype of a bibliography, rendered on the page by a parser*

Exploring Git

We have been talking about GitHub in the past few chapters and have used it extensively to push all of our changes online, but let's review some of that information. In this chapter, we will be talking about yet another way to push code online through the command line. This is the way Git was intended to be used, but it is much easier to understand and introduce the concepts after you've already been using the tools.

Recall that GitHub is the front end to hosting code using version control with Git. GitHub has numerous projects hosted on it in the form of repositories, which are essentially project folders that can be edited locally and then synced online. Each repository in turn can have several branches, where each branch is just a different version of the same code held in the repository. The primary branch (or the trunk) is called the master branch, and this is usually the branch that gets synced online to GitHub. Now Git is actually the tool being used in the background to make all of this magic happen, and GitHub Desktop is just a nice graphic interface that simplifies the task for new users. This is not to say that GitHub Desktop is limited, as it does almost everything you would need to use in this book, but the CLI does provide more options and advanced features not available within GitHub Desktop. Here, we go into detail covering the command line and the convenience it provides to the user.

When you installed GitHub Desktop, you also installed Git, but you can download and install the latest version from the project web site at `https://git-scm.com/downloads`, where it also explains how to download for all the platforms. On Linux, this is much easier to do, as you can simply install it using the preferred package manager for your distribution. For OS X, just clicking the Mac OS X web site will start the download for the latest release. The same applies for Windows: The Downloads page provides a link to start the download, as shown in Figure 11-6.

Downloading Git

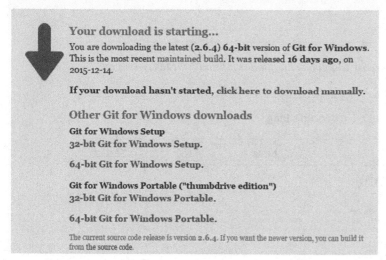

Figure 11-6. *Downloading the latest version of Git from the Git-scm web site. The version you download might be a different one than the 2.6.4 release shown here.*

You can accept the defaults during the installation. The most important of those options is Windows Explorer Integration, which allows us to use Git from any folder location. After downloading and installing Git, you should see it working within the shortcut menu. Just right-click in any folder and you should see the new Git options, as shown in Figure 11-7.

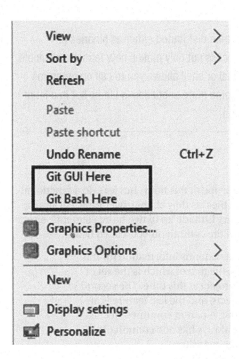

Figure 11-7. *Git shortcut menu options integrated into Windows Explorer*

Once Git is installed on the computer, we can start playing around with it, but before we start using Git and the command line, it is more important to understand the tool just installed. What you installed just now is not actually Git in the true sense; rather, it is a collection of tools that form a bare minimum development environment called MinGW (Minimalist GNU for Windows). MinGW is essentially a wrapper for a few essential Linux tools (e.g., the GCC, or GNU C-compiler) that are carried over to Windows. MinGW operates on Windows but provides access to tools like GCC that are normally found in a Linux-like environment.

MinGW has grown to include more packages, such as a component derived from the Cgywin project that provides the command shell called bash to Windows. Git is actually used within this environment, on the command line shell (Bash) on Windows. The shell (or terminal, as it is called in many Linux distributions) is one of the most important components of a Linux distribution. It is a user interface that allows access to the services or commands available within the operating system. It takes input from the user and gives the commands to the operating system to perform. The command line is called just that because it can execute either commands that are predefined statements or applications that are called by their name as if they were commands available within the operating system. Git is an example of the latter; once it is installed, it's an application available to the system that be loaded by typing its name.

One of the most popular shells available on Linux machines is the bash shell, and the MinGW environment packaged along with Git brings us a bash shell to execute commands on Windows. These commands are limited to a small subset of what would be available on a Linux machine, but they are enough for our purposes. In brief, the main purpose of a shell is to execute commands, and we review how to use the commands for Git shortly. Now that we understand what a shell is, let's talk about Git CLI. As the name implies, this version of Git is used from the terminal and there are some very good reasons behind it.

The advantage of using the command line is that you can use the same knowledge and skills to manage any Linux distribution. Although Git is available with a GUI, many developers prefer to use the command line. The primary reason behind using the CLI is that you can string together a series of tools to manage your Git workflow in the terminal. Often the GUI is limited by the features that are available within it and the application can't talk to other tools; therefore, customization is very difficult.

■ **Note**   In Linux, most programs are compiled from source and then distributed either as binaries or packages to be installed from the package manager. The install process not only makes new features available, but it also lets you call on the installed binary. Therefore, the terminal or shell allows you to call on programs just as it would let you call the commands themselves. There are some more subtleties in Linux, but in a lot of cases, installed programs and commands become roughly the same.

Git Internals

So how does Git itself work? An in-depth overview is outside the scope of this book, but let's do a functional overview of Git internals. The purpose of Git is to manage a set of files, as they change over time. Git stores this information in a data structure called a repository. A repository is made up of two basic elements: a set of *commit objects* and a corresponding set of *references* for each of the commit objects called heads.

- A **commit object** can be thought of as one object that contains information for the current commit. More precisely, it has a few features, the first of which is the set of *files* included in this change reflecting the state of a project at this time. The second feature is a set of *references* to the parent commit objects, and the last feature is an SHA1 *unique key* that identifies this particular commit. A parent commit object is a commit made before the current one. A repository always has one commit object with no parents, as this is the first commit made to the repository.

- A **head** is a reference to a commit object. Each head has a name, and by default, there is a head in every repository called master. Each time a new commit occurs, the default head now points to the latest commit object generated from that commit. The concept of commit objects and a head are displayed visually here.

```
----> Time ----->           (As time passes, new commits get added to the repository)

(A) <-- (B) <-- (C)         (Each commit object refers to the previous one)
             ^
             |
          Master            (Head)
```

We've used these components of Git, but never looked this far into the actual magic happening behind Git. This is a simplified explanation of how Git works, but essentially addition of commit objects and the head referring to a new commit object is what we're doing when we add new code. Let's dive into the most commonly used commands in Git and then we'll use them on the command line. Recall that a folder containing your code initially needs to be put under version control. To do that, you have to use the command git init, which tells Git to treat the current directory as a Git repository. In this instance, a .git folder is created that actually contains all the revision history; this folder is where all the references are contained. In large projects, the history alone could become very disk-space-consuming. Create a new directory in a suitable location and let's look at how the Git commands work in the terminal. Once you've created a new directory, open up Git Bash from the shortcut menu by right-clicking. The shell should look something like Figure 11-8.

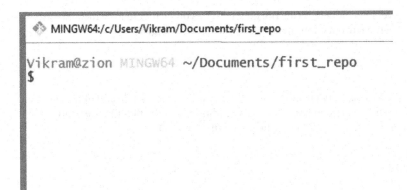

Figure 11-8. *Git Bash console. Your console window might look different, but the differences in appearance are irrelevany. The console has a prompt, the $ sign, for taking commands from the user, and the commands will work for all types of shells.*

The first command we will use is the `git init` command, so let's see how it works in the command line.

```
$ git init
Initialized empty Git repository in C:/Users/Vikram/Documents/first_repo/.git/
```

The result from the terminal is displayed in the following line. Here it tells us that a Git repository has been created in the specified location. Let's create a text file called `my_info.txt`, and to see if the file really has been created, we can use this:

```
$ ls
my_info.txt
```

`ls` lists the files and folders in the current working directory. Notice that when we used it, the output did not list the `.git` folder because it is a hidden folder. Now that we have created a file, let's take a look at the repository.

```
$ git status
On branch master                               [Current branch]

Initial commit

Untracked files:
  (use "git add <file>…" to include in what will be committed)

        my_info.txt                            [The file we just created]

nothing added to commit but untracked files present (use "git add" to track)
```

The `git status` command tells us about the current status of the repository. This command is very important because it tells us exactly what will go in the next commit and what files are being changed. In this manner, if your commit breaks something, you know exactly what you did and how to reverse those changes. The actual message is quite verbose. It starts by telling us that we are currently on the branch master, and that this is the initial commit to the repository. In this commit, there is one untracked file. Untracked simply means that the changes have not yet been added to Git. The message goes on further to list which files are untracked and how to add them to the current commit. Let's add the file we changed now.

```
$ git add -A :/
$
```

The command to add files is git add, but here, the -A and the :/ options recursively add new files anywhere in the repository to Git. This ensures that we don't miss adding any of the files that we changed or added in our repository. Finally, after adding the files, it's time to commit the change.

```
$ git commit -m "Initial commit, adding the first file"
[master (root-commit) 1d8382d] Initial commit, adding the first file
 1 file changed, 1 insertion(+)
 create mode 100644 my_info.txt

$
```

This is the commit message, which starts with the command to commit the changes, git commit. The -m parameter is to write a commit message so that you would know exactly which changes were made. After the command is issued, Git responds with a lot of information. The first line starts with a head named master (the default head) pointing to the first commit. This first commit is also called the root commit and the second line also assigns a commit ID with the commit message. After the commit message, we see the total number of changes made; here it was just one file changed and this file had an insertion of data. Finally, the commit message states that a new file was created under mode 100644, which is a mode of file permissions in Linux. This particular mode implies that the file being created is a regular nonexecutable file. Some of the common modes are shown for reference as follows, as you might encounter them during your commit messages.

```
(040000): Directory
(100644): Regular non-executable file
(100664): Regular non-executable group-writeable file
(100755): Regular executable file
(120000): Symbolic link
```

Recall that once the changes have been committed, there must be no outstanding changes left. Especially with the -A :/ switches used with git add, every change made should have been added to the commit. To check this, run git status once again.

```
$ git status
On branch master
nothing to commit, working directory clean
```

This tells us that there are no new changes that were made since the last commit. Now what if you were to look for who made the last change? Git keeps a very detailed log of what changes were made and by whom, which allows large projects to carefully manage changes. The command to look at this log is git log and it works as follows:

```
$ git log
commit 1d8382d2e9ae4c678e3dd165dcbbb959b54850fc
Author: Vikram Dhillon <dhillonv10@gmail.com>
Date:   Mon Jan 4 21:27:58 2016 -0500

    Initial commit, adding the first file

$
```

This log is very descriptive, and generally for more involved projects, this log would be several lines long. The first line contains the SHA-1 hash that uniquely identifies this commit, and the part shown in bold is a shortened commit ID that showed up earlier in the commit message. After the hash is the name of the author who made the changes that went into this commit, along with a timestamp. Finally, the log entry has the commit message. This is another reason why it's crucial that commit messages be descriptive. Generally a log file has a lot more entries, but this one contains just the commit we made.

Distributed Development Model

So far, we have only used Git in a local environment on our own computer but it was designed to do much more. Originally, Git was designed to be a tool for distributed development for large teams. What does that mean? Basically, in a distributed development environment, multiple developers work on a project and then send their changes back to contribute to the project. The power of Git-based distributed development is in its ability to manage multiple versions of the same code and show exactly what changed and where. Let's explore a few more of the common Git commands in the context of the distributed development model. In this scenario, the main repository would reside on a server, and everyone contributing to the project downloads (clones) a copy of that repository. This is exactly what we do on GitHub when we click Fork a repository. After the repository has been cloned, you might see multiple branches within the repository. Those branches can be different versions of the same code or different releases, but you can't just start editing those branches. Essentially, you have to make changes locally, and then create a patch that contains your changes that can be sent so that other developers can look at your changes and test them, too.

It might seem a bit complicated, but the process is very intuitive. Here's a concrete outline of what you would have to do: First, you have to create a new branch and make all your changes to the code in that particular branch. Once you are done, commit your changes to this branch. Now you would need to see how your changes differentiate from the code in the master branch. These changes are compiled in a patch that you can then send off to other developers for them to examine and apply. The process of branching and creating new ones is displayed graphically here.

```
(A) -- (B) ------- (C)            [Commits]
     |       |
  master(HEAD)  new-branch        [New branch created]
```

The terms branch and head are nearly synonymous in Git. Every branch is represented by one head, and every head represents one branch. When you create a new branch, what you are really doing is creating a head that points to a different set of commit objects, which in turn represent the state of the project at a different time. Let's go through an example of branching, as we discussed earlier. In this example, we go up to creating a patch. We don't have a remote repository where the code is located but let's assume we know the URL for it. We would have to clone it using `git clone <repository address>`, which will create a folder for us. The `clone` command allows us to create a local copy of the remote repository, but this clone is also synced with the remote repository. Now there might be multiple branches in this repository, so let's check what they are.

```
$ git branch
* master
  testing
  testing2

$
```

The command `git branch` by itself lists all the branches available under a project. The * next to the master branch shows us that currently, we are on the master branch. In a distributed environment, you never want to make changes to the master, so we have to create our own branch.

```
$ git branch testing_local_vikram
$
```

Using the command `git branch <branch_name>` creates a new branch with the specified name. Now if we check again, we should see the name in the list of branches.

```
$ git branch
* master
  testing
  testing2
  testing_local_vikram
$
```

The `clone` command allows us to create a local copy of the remote repository, but this clone is also synced with the remote repository. This means that if there are more changes made to the master branch elsewhere, you can import those changes and keep your local version updated. This is done through the `git pull` command, which can just be used as such because `git clone <repo address>` also defines the remote repository URL variable that the `git pull` command can use to pull new information or changes. This is yet another reason we need to create local branches: Our local code can always be synced with the remote version. Now that we have created the branch, we need to switch to it and start making edits. Here's another way to think about it: Currently you are on the master branch and any changes you make will be saved to that (master) branch. If you do that, then you lose a frame of reference to compare your end results, which is why we needed to create this new branch. Let's switch to our newly created branch.

```
$ git checkout testing_local_vikram
Switched to branch 'testing_local_vikram'
$
```

Here Git tells us that now we are on this new branch we just created. The changes we make at this moment will all be saved to the new branch and not interfere with the master branch. Let's make some more changes in this new branch, so create a new file called `my_info2.txt`. Add some contents to the file; now it's time to commit those changes. The same two commands are used here, `git add -A :/` followed by `git commit -m "Adding the second file to a new branch"`. Finally, if you had a remote location to push the changes, you'd issue `git push` to push the changes. We will be doing this shortly with GitHub. After adding this new file, there's something interesting that happened to our repository. We added the `my_info2.txt` file in this new branch, so if we check the master branch again, that file will disappear entirely. Try it out on your own.

Now let's move on to examining the differences between the master and this new branch. We expect to see the differences being limited to this new file that we just added. To see the differences, we can use the following:

```
$ git diff master..testing_local_vikram
diff --git a/ducks.txt b/ducks.txt
new file mode 100644
index 0000000..dd93ec9
--- /dev/null
+++ b/ducks.txt
```

```
@@ -0,0 +1 @@
+"Do ducks still come to this campus pond, when it's spring break?" - CL
diff --git a/my_info2.txt b/my_info2.txt
new file mode 100644
index 0000000..01a59b0
--- /dev/null
+++ b/my_info2.txt
@@ -0,0 +1 @@
+lorem ipsum
$
```

Reading diffs is not that straightforward, but let's break it down to make it simpler to understand. The command to get a diff is `git diff master..<branch name>`. This lets you compare the master branch to any other branch that you want. When you issue this command, the output is verbose, but actually very simple to follow. The first line, shown in bold, indicates what was being compared. Here the diff command is trying to compare two versions, a and b, of the `ducks.txt` file. Git tells diff that this file was just created so the command outputs the file permissions of this new file. After the permissions, the `---` and `+++` signs show what happened to the repository. Notice that the location is `/dev/null`, which implies that previously there was nothing and now there is a version `b/ducks.txt` created. This is how Linux shows a new file was created. After that, the next line is shown in bold because this tells you exactly how many insertions, edits, and deletions happened to the file that we are comparing. As expected, we see that only one addition was made to this file, which is displayed next. This exact same layout is repeated the second time to show that the file `my_info2.txt` was created and what its contents are.

This diff is the end result in distributed development; basically it is a summary of all the work that you have done locally. After you compared the state of the project following your changes to the master branch, you need to submit your code to other developers so that it can be examined and finally incorporated into the master branch. A submittable version of a diff is also called a patch. These patches get submitted by developers, and others can apply them to their own Git tree and test the outcome of your change. Git is very nice about creating patches, and there's even a command to do all of this for you.

```
$ git format-patch -1 HEAD
0001-Adding-two-new-files.patch
$
```

[Normally, you need to provide the 40-letter long SHA-1 id, but here HEAD is a reference to the latest commit so you can use that as a shortname]

The command to create a patch is `git format-patch`, but the options provided here turn the last commit we made into a patch. This is useful for us at this moment only because we know that we only made two commits, and the first one was to the master branch, so including that in the diff would provide us with nothing useful. When creating patches, you really have two main options.

- Create a patch from the latest commit, which is what we did in the preceding command. The format of creating a patch from any N number of commits is shown as follows.

  ```
  git format-patch -<N> <SHA1>
  ```

- Create a path from a particular diff comparing branches, which can be done by piping the output from diff into a patch file. To pipe an output is a Linux operator that allows you to send the output of one command as an input to the second one; in this case, the output is sent to `stdout`, which redirects to the `mypatch.diff` file.

  ```
  git diff master..testing_local_vikram > mypatch.diff
  ```

The first option seems to be a better one here because it already creates a very sophisticated patch that is ready to be sent as an e-mail. Here's what the patch looks like.

```
From d75e079c180bf9cd27fe4799a5c8f67ca14f6429 Mon Sep 17 00:00:00 2001
From: Vikram Dhillon <dhillonv10@gmail.com>
Date: Tue, 5 Jan 2016 15:52:30 -0500
Subject: [PATCH] Adding two new files

---
 ducks.txt     | 1 +
 my_info2.txt | 1 +
 2 files changed, 2 insertions(+)
 create mode 100644 ducks.txt
 create mode 100644 my_info2.txt

diff --git a/ducks.txt b/ducks.txt
new file mode 100644
index 0000000..dd93ec9
--- /dev/null
+++ b/ducks.txt
@@ -0,0 +1 @@
+"Do ducks still come to this campus pond, when it's spring break?" - CL
diff --git a/my_info2.txt b/my_info2.txt
new file mode 100644
index 0000000..01a59b0
--- /dev/null
+++ b/my_info2.txt
@@ -0,0 +1 @@
+lorem ipsum
--
2.6.2.windows.1
```

This patch can roughly be broken into three parts: the header, the summary, and finally the diff. In all practicality, a diff is not so much different from a patch, except for the formatting. The header contains the e-mail components To, From, and a subject, which is the same as the commit we made. After this header and above the `---` present in the patch is where you would write your e-mail summarizing the changes that you made. Below the `---` is a summary of all the changes made with this patch. This format is very intuitive because it clearly summarizes what files were changed, whether additions or deletions were made, and finally if new files were created. The diff below the patch is still the same as before, with nothing new added.

Just as there was a workflow with with GitHub Desktop, there's a very simple workflow that we follow while using Git. It comes down to roughly the following four simple steps:

1. The first step in the workflow is to actually make the changes to the code and save the files. This lets Git know that you made some changes but those changes haven't been included in version control yet.

2. The next step is adding the changes using `git add -A :/` command. This recursively adds any new files or any changes that were made to the code.

3. The third step is to commit all the changes. This ensures that a small set of changes are made in each commit, so that if something breaks, it is easy to point to and figure out which changes caused the code to break. As a result, it is essential that every commit is made with a descriptive commit message.

4. The final step is to push the changes online to GitHub or a remote repository. This is what will ultimately allow you to make your code available online. Otherwise, you have to use format-patch to send your changes to other developers.

This workflow is cyclical using the three commands after making a set of changes. These three steps are fundamental to Git-based development and will be followed in almost every repository, regardless of how large the project is or how many branches you have. The last topic to discuss in this section is the protocols that Git uses to clone a repository or pull or push changes. This becomes important when we start to use Git CLI with GitHub, as we see shortly. You have two choices of protocols—HTTPS and SSH—and the protocol that you choose while cloning repositories will also become the default protocol of choice for pulling and pushing changes. Both of the protocols are perfectly safe to use and will not result in more or less secure projects. The only difference is that HTTPS will require you to enter your GitHub credentials each time you want to commit to the remote repository.

■ **Note** In the past themes, we have encountered the file `.gitignore` in the repositories. We only talked about that file briefly in the appropriate content, but now we can revisit that topic in more detail. If you have multiple releases of a product being managed in different branches, it becomes difficult to test the product without creating more noise for Git. To avoid such an issue, the `.gitignore` file can be programmed to ignore all binaries, compile files, or makefiles being generated. That way, anyone can make test cases or compile the files without influencing the repository.

Let's Git Coding

To get started, let's delete our last repository on GitHub and start fresh. Create a new repository, in the same format, `username.github.io`. Once the repository is created, you should see the Quick setup page shown in Figure 11-9.

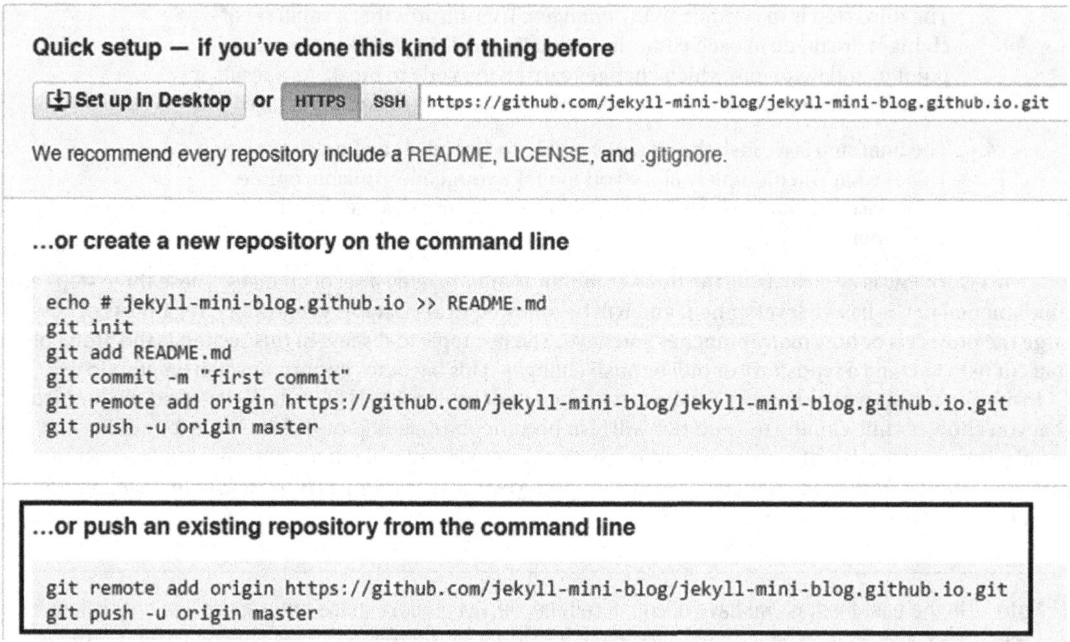

Quick setup — if you've done this kind of thing before

⬇ Set up in Desktop   or   `HTTPS`   `SSH`   `https://github.com/jekyll-mini-blog/jekyll-mini-blog.github.io.git`

We recommend every repository include a README, LICENSE, and .gitignore.

...or create a new repository on the command line

```
echo # jekyll-mini-blog.github.io >> README.md
git init
git add README.md
git commit -m "first commit"
git remote add origin https://github.com/jekyll-mini-blog/jekyll-mini-blog.github.io.git
git push -u origin master
```

...or push an existing repository from the command line

```
git remote add origin https://github.com/jekyll-mini-blog/jekyll-mini-blog.github.io.git
git push -u origin master
```

Figure 11-9. *The repository Quick setup page. The link at the top gives you the web address to clone. The lower half of this page contains the Git CLI instructions that allow us to manage the repository and push our changes.*

The first thing we need to do is to clone this empty repository. Copy that link at the top and use the `git clone` command to clone the repository.

```
$ git clone https://github.com/jekyll-mini-blog/jekyll-mini-blog.github.io.git
Cloning into 'jekyll-mini-blog.github.io'...
warning: You appear to have cloned an empty repository.
Checking connectivity... done.

$
```

This was within expectations. The code show in bold is actually the web address, and here Git tells us that we cloned an empty repository into the `jekyll-mini-blog.github.io` folder. Once this is done, we need to copy the contents of a Jekyll theme into the empty blog folder. For this project, we will be using the Clean Blog theme available at `http://jekyllthemes.org/themes/clean-blog/`. Download the zip release for the theme from GitHub, extract the file, and copy all of its contents to the new folder that Git created. Once the files have been copied over, they are ready to be added to the Git repository and then pushed as part of the initial commit. Remember the workflow that we just discussed: Add, commit, and push. Let's look at how these commands work and dissect the output produced by the terminal in depth. First is add.

```
$ git add -A :/

$
```

This produced no output; the silent return to prompt simply implies that the command included every file that we copied in Git. We can check this by using git status as follows:

```
$ git status
On branch master

Initial commit

Changes to be committed:
  (use "git rm --cached <file>..." to unstage)

        new file:   .gitignore
        new file:   Gruntfile.js
        new file:   LICENSE
        new file:   README.md
        new file:   _config.yml
        new file:   _includes/footer.html
        new file:   _includes/head.html
```

This command actually shows you every new file that we added; we showed only a part of the output here to analyze it. The first part in the Git output tells us that we are on the master branch and in the initial commit. After that, it lists the changes to be committed and tell us that a new file was created with each of the files added to the repository. Now it is time to commit these changes:

```
$ git commit -m "Initial commit - Adding the clean blog theme"
[master (root-commit) 0f3885a] Initial commit - Adding the clean blog theme
 52 files changed, 21639 insertions(+)

 create mode 100644 .gitignore
 create mode 100644 Gruntfile.js
 create mode 100644 LICENSE
 create mode 100644 README.md
 create mode 100644 _config.yml
 create mode 100644 _includes/footer.html
 create mode 100644 _includes/head.html
 create mode 100644 _includes/nav.html
```

Here, the git commit command is followed by the commit message and Git returns a lot of output. The first line that is shown in bold is actually a confirmation of the commit being made. It starts by telling us that we are on the master branch. This is the initial commit, followed by a commit ID and the commit message. The second line in the output actually tells us what happened: By copying the theme, we have 52 file changes and 21,639 additions to Git. These are the changes included in the first commit that will be pushed to GitHub. Now let's take care of the final step, which is a little more complicated. To push the changes, we need to make GitHub aware that our code is actually being stored locally, but we ultimately want to push our code to a remote location, a repository on GitHub. The boxed section in Figure 11-9 is what we will have to use to push our code initially; after that, simply using git push will work. The first line that GitHub tells us to use is git remote add origin https://github.com/jekyll-mini-blog/jekyll-mini-blog.github.io.git. This line will tell Git the location for our remote repository to push our code to.

```
$ git remote add origin https://github.com/jekyll-mini-blog/jekyll-mini-blog.github.io.git
fatal: remote origin already exists.

$
```

We actually got an error message this time, but that's perfectly fine. We got an error because Git has several configuration variables, and one of them is to define a remote repository. We used the same web address to clone the repository from GitHub so our Git instance already knows the remote repository exists. Let's push our code:

```
$ git push -u origin master
Counting objects: 63, done.
Delta compression using up to 4 threads.
Compressing objects: 100% (61/61), done.
Writing objects: 100% (63/63), 1.73 MiB | 70.00 KiB/s, done.
Total 63 (delta 5), reused 0 (delta 0)
To https://github.com/jekyll-mini-blog/jekyll-mini-blog.github.io.git
 * [new branch]      master -> master
Branch master set up to track remote branch master from origin.

$
```

The command itself was given to us by GitHub and it tells Git to push the local branch (the origin) online into the default branch (master) in our repository at GitHub. The output initially tells us the number of commit objects that Git computed, then it compresses the objects and finally uploads the objects to the remote repository. The upload statement ends with the word done, which signifies that the upload is complete. The remainder of the output confirms that our upload happened appropriately. In the next line, Git tells us that it uploaded the 63 objects to the remote location given in the following line. Finally, Git tells us that that our data was pushed into our repository on GitHub under the branch master, which is set up to sync from our local branch (the origin). This is the actual process of pushing or uploading our code in the form of commits from the local repository.

Recall that we used the HTTPS web address to clone the repository originally. This might have caused you to see two pop-ups after issuing the command to enter your user name and password. Unfortunately, even though HTTP cloning is faster and more efficient, it is very tedious to have to enter the user name and password each time. This can be changed to make the process automatic; you can always just re-enter the user name and password if you want for each commit but you can define the remote repository address in a way that Git will automatically know what to do for you. Let's look up what our remote address is currently, according to Git.

```
$ git config -l
```

remote.origin.url=https://github.com/jekyll-mini-blog/jekyll-mini-blog.github.io.git

The command git config -l lists the configuration of Git according to the current repository; however, what we really want is the line that defines the remote URL. Once we have it, the remote URL can be changed to accommodate both the user name and password. This is done by adding them to the URL itself so that Git can recognize them as part of the repository, therefore never prompting you to give your login credentials for GitHub. Your remote URL will be like this: `https://{USERNAME}@github.com/{USERNAME}/{REPONAME}.git`; what you actually need is something like this: `https://{USERNAME}:{PASSWORD}@github.com/{USERNAME}/{REPONAME}.git`.

This might seem more intimidating, but editing the remote URL is very straightforward. You do need to remember that your user name contains your e-mail address and the @ sign can't be present in the user name. To remove it, you have to use the %40 escape character. Let's see how the URL transforms.

```
https://github.com/jekyll-mini-blog/jekyll-mini-blog.github.io.git
https://vikram%40igknight.me:password@github.com/jekyll-mini-blog/jekyll-mini-blog.github.
io.git
```

To use this properly, we have to define the remote URL variable as follows:

```
$ git config remote.origin.url https://vikram%40igknight.me:password@github.com/jekyll-mini-
blog/jekyll-mini-blog.github.io.git
```

```
$
```

The git config command can allow you to override any variables that you might want to change; however, besides the remote URL, you are strongly advised to leave everything else as is. Now that we have the credentials set up, let's get started implementing all of the features. The first one up is KaTeX. To get started implementing it, we need to download the release first. The latest release is available at https://github.com/khan/katex/releases. After a little bit of scrolling, you will encounter the Downloads header. From there, download the zip file and extract it. We only need the katex.min.css and katex.min.js files to use KaTeX in Jekyll. Copy those files to a new folder called public. Place them inside the folder; once that's done, we just need to import them. To use KaTeX, we need to edit head.html in the _includes folder. Near the end of the file, before the <head> tag ends, add the following:

```
<!-- KaTeX -->
<link rel="stylesheet" href="/public/katex.min.css">
<script src="/public/katex.min.js"></script>
```

These lines provide the location of KaTeX CSS and JavaScript files to be imported into the theme.

Writing Equations

Now that the imports are done, we need to instantiate KaTeX so that any reference to it can render the equations properly. To do this, you have to place a bit of JavaScript in the posts layout. This is assuming we only use equations with posts. Create a new file called katex_render.html and place it in the _includes folder with the following content:

```
<script type="text/javascript">

    // grab all elements in DOM with the class 'equation'
    var tex = document.getElementsByClassName("equation");

    // for each element, render the expression attribute
    Array.prototype.forEach.call(tex, function(el) {
        katex.render(el.getAttribute("data-expr"), el);
    });

</script>
```

This snippet allows us to render anything with the div class equation into KaTeX. Save the katex_render.html file; now we need to include it within posts. To do so, go to the _layouts folder and then into the posts.html layout, and add the file as follows:

```
<div class="row">
    <div class="col-lg-8 col-lg-offset-2 col-md-10 col-md-offset-1">

                  {{ content }}

        {% include katex_render.html %}

    <hr>
```

This instantiates KaTeX for every post, so now we just need to make a reference and test this properly. Let's pick a random post and try this out. For the first post in the _posts directory, the 2014-06-10-dinosaurs.markdown file, let's edit it and add an equation. At the end of that blog post, add the following to display a simple equation:

```
{% raw %}
<!-- A simple addition equation -->
<div class="equation" data-expr="\displaystyle x=\frac{1+y}{1+2z^2}"></div>
{% endraw %}
```

The {% raw %} tag is actually an escape character for Liquid that keeps Liquid from parsing text between {% raw %} and {% endraw %} so that the equation can be presented to KaTeX for rendering. This should do the trick, so let's go ahead and start our Git magic again.

```
$ git add -A :/
warning: CRLF will be replaced by LF in _includes/katex_render.html.
The file will have its original line endings in your working directory.

$
```

You can ignore the warnings here. Basically these warnings come up because of how some line endings are structured. This will not edit your code in any manner; it's just a way that Git keeps track of objects. Now, let's commit these changes.

```
$ git commit -m "Adding KaTeX to the theme"
[master 67ce655] Adding KaTeX to the theme
warning: CRLF will be replaced by LF in _includes/katex_render.html.
The file will have its original line endings in your working directory.
 6 files changed, 30 insertions(+)
 create mode 100644 _includes/katex_render.html
 create mode 100644 public/katex.min.css
 create mode 100644 public/katex.min.js
```

This commits all of our changes so far to Git, and now we are ready to push the code. From this point on, all we need to do to push the code is use git push as shown here.

```
$ git push
warning: push.default is unset; its implicit value has changed in
Git 2.0 from 'matching' to 'simple'. To squelch this message
and maintain the traditional behavior, use:

  git config --global push.default matching

To squelch this message and adopt the new behavior now, use:

  git config --global push.default simple

When push.default is set to 'matching', git will push local branches
to the remote branches that already exist with the same name.

Since Git 2.0, Git defaults to the more conservative 'simple'
behavior, which only pushes the current branch to the corresponding
remote branch that 'git pull' uses to update the current branch.

See 'git help config' and search for 'push.default' for further information.
(the 'simple' mode was introduced in Git 1.7.11. Use the similar mode
'current' instead of 'simple' if you sometimes use older versions of Git)

Counting objects: 12, done.
Delta compression using up to 4 threads.
Compressing objects: 100% (12/12), done.
Writing objects: 100% (12/12), 33.73 KiB | 0 bytes/s, done.
Total 12 (delta 6), reused 0 (delta 0)
To https://vikram%40igknight.me:password@github.com/jekyll-mini-blog/jekyll-mini-blog.
github.io.git
   0f3885a..67ce655  master -> master

$
```

Even though the output here is very verbose, most of it is extraneous information that can be ignored. The first half of the output is just Git telling us that some configuration variables have not been set up. After that, the second half actually does the commit, starting with the Counting objects line. It tells us that all the data has been uploaded from the Writing objects line and finally, in the last line, a new SHA-1 ID is generated leading from the last commit. Git is telling us that the master branch locally with the given commit ID has been succeeded by the second commit ID down the line. If you actually view the web site after this, the results might be a bit disappointing because nothing is rendering properly. The reason is that we forgot to fix the baseurl and url variables in the _config.yml file.

```
baseurl: ""
url: "http://jekyll-mini-blog.github.io"
```

Now push this code and you should see the blog work perfectly. The commit is shown here.

```
$ git commit -m "Changing baseurl"
[master 9c65036] Changing baseurl
 1 file changed, 2 insertions(+), 2 deletions(-)
```

This renders the blog properly, and the post that we edited is on the second page. The equation renders perfectly on the page and the result is shown in Figure 11-10. This finishes the implementation of KaTeX. Recall the {% raw %} escape character that we used along with the <div class="equation"> tags that are used to instantiate KaTeX for each of the blog posts as necessary. The next tools is Plotly.js, and we implement the API within the blog, which is actually very simple to do.

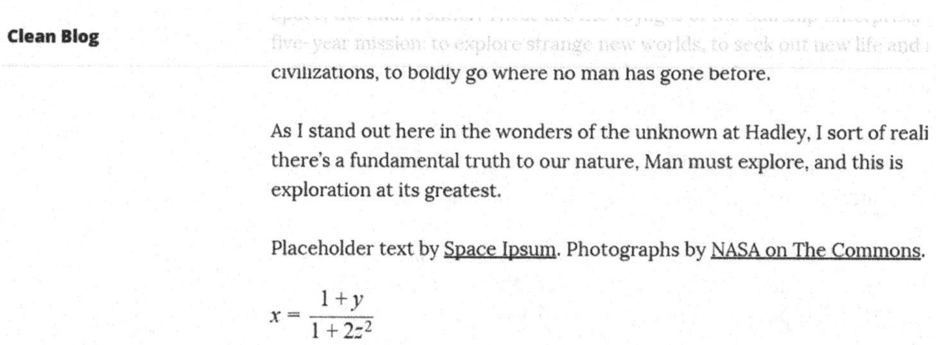

Clean Blog

five-year mission: to explore strange new worlds, to seek out new life and civilizations, to boldly go where no man has gone before.

As I stand out here in the wonders of the unknown at Hadley, I sort of reali there's a fundamental truth to our nature, Man must explore, and this is exploration at its greatest.

Placeholder text by Space Ipsum. Photographs by NASA on The Commons.

$$ x = \frac{1+y}{1+2z^2} $$

Figure 11-10. *Scrolling to the end of the blog post to see the sample equation we added renders perfectly*

Adding a Graph

To this same blog post, let's add a graph, this time using Plotly.js. The instructions for including the JavaScript API are available at https://plot.ly/javascript/. The only thing it requires us to do is an include. The method for doing that is very similar to how we have included font-awesome in the past. Go to the head.html file in the _includes folder and insert the following lines after the KaTeX includes.

```
<head>
    <script src="https://cdn.plot.ly/plotly-latest.min.js"></script>
</head>
```

This will allow us to access Plot.ly.js from any of the blog posts. Now to actually draw a graph, we need to create an instance that Plot.ly can use to draw. To do that, go back to the blog post and use the following <div> tag:

```
<div id="tester" style="width:600px;height:250px;"></div>
```

This tag creates an instance that Plot.ly can use to sketch the graph, so let's provide some data and create a sample graph. This has to be done as JavaScript.

```
<script>
        TESTER = document.getElementById('tester'); // Instance from the HTML canvas
        Plotly.plot( TESTER, [{                      // Creating the TESTER element
        x: [1, 2, 3, 4, 5],                          // The X and Y coordinates for the graph
        y: [1, 2, 4, 8, 16] }], {
        margin: { t: 0 } } );
</script>
```

This very simple example allows you to create a graph on the page. The best features of Plot.ly are that you can export the graph as a .png file, and even better, you can easily zoom in and see all the features right in front of you. The graph we made in the theme is shown in Figure 11-11. This finishes up our implementation of the Plotly.js API. Notice the similarities between implementing this tool and using font-awesome in the blog theme as we have done previously. They are almost exactly the same: font-awesome requires us to import the design files and then instantiate the icons using the <i> class tags each time.

Placeholder text by <u>Space Ipsum</u>. Photographs by <u>NASA on The Commons</u>.

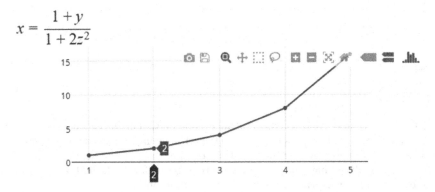

Figure 11-11. *Plot.ly.js graph rendered and embedded within the blog post*

Writing Bibliographies

The next two topics are focused on bibliographies. If you're a researcher who wants to blog about your work, it stands to reason that you would want to list out the work you've published or worked on. In some cases, if you want to point to a particular set of works as references, you would want to list the references with some ease. That's the goal here: to make it slightly easier for the researcher to list a bibliography or cite other papers. To do this, we have to interface with one of the most widely used tools, bibtex. Bibtex is a reference management tool that can help you format your references appropriately to be included in a paper or even your own blog as the work that you've done. Now interfacing bibtex with Jekyll is not at all easy, but there are two main ways to go about it.

- Use the jekyll-scholar plug-in. We haven't talked about plug-ins or local compiling yet, but we return to this method later in the book to see how sophisticated plug-ins can be.

- The other option is to parse the bibliography ourselves and then render it properly on the blog. This option is more time-consuming but fitting for this project, so let's try it.

In the second option, we have to use a JavaScript-based parser that can convert a bibtex file into HTML-based references that we can style. To do this, a project called bibtex-js was created by Henrik Muehe. We have created a port of that project on GitHub, available at `https://github.com/dhillonv10/bibtex-js` for your use. The GitHub page describes how to use this port, and it is similar to what we have been doing until now, involving just one more include. We also style the rendered bibliography with simple CSS. The bibliography will be presented on a new page, so we need to use the page layout for that. To create a new page, save a file called `bib.html` in the top level of the project. This file will contain all the magic that the bibtex-js parser needs.

```
---
layout: page
---

<!-- jquery import -->

<script type="text/javascript" src="http://ajax.googleapis.com/ajax/libs/jquery/1.4.2/
jquery.min.js"></script>

<!-- bibtex-js import -->

<script type="text/javascript" src="http://bibtex-js.googlecode.com/svn/trunk/src/bibtex_
js.js"></script>

{% include bib_info.html %}

<div id="bibtex_display"></div>
```

This file contains a wealth of information, and also the implementation present on the GitHub page for the fork of bibtex-js. It starts off declaring the layout for this file, and then the two imports, first for jquery and the second one for bibtex-js. After the imports, we have the actual bibliography that we modularized away to a file called `bib_info.html`, and finally we have the instantiating `<div>` tags to display the bibliography. Now let's look into the `bib_info.html` file, which actually contains the bibliography.

```
<textarea id="bibtex_input" style="display:none;">
@book{book1,
  author = "Donald Knuth",
  title = "Concrete Mathematics"
}

@book{ANTLR,
        author = {Terence Parr},
        edition = {First},
        interhash = {d9ef4ed82183b86b6a3004161de5ea44},
        intrahash = {1688029f4c14bd3b234933a48e902c03},
        publisher = {Pragmatic Bookshelf},
        series = {Pragmatic Programmers},
        title = {The Definitive ANTLR Reference: Building Domain-Specific Languages},
        url = {http://www.amazon.com/Definitive-ANTLR-Reference-Domain-Specific-Programmers/
        dp/0978739256%3FSubscriptionId%3D13CT5CVB80YFWJEPWSO2%26tag%3Dws%26linkCode%3Dxm2%26
        camp%3D2025%26creative%3D165953%26creativeASIN%3D0978739256},
        year = 2007,
        ean = {9780978739256},
        keywords = {Me:MastersThesis antlr compilers languages lexers parsers programming},
        asin = {0978739256},
        description = {Amazon.com: The Definitive ANTLR Reference: Building Domain-Specific
        Languages (Pragmatic Programmers): Terence Parr: Books},
        isbn = {0978739256},
        biburl = {http://www.bibsonomy.org/bibtex/21688029f4c14bd3b234933a48e902c03/gron},
        dewey = {005.45},
        month = May
}
</textarea>
```

In this code, the ⟨textarea⟩ tags actually contain the bibtex formatted bibliography. The way to read it is that each @ starts off a new entry in the database, and the brackets { } contain all the metadata associated with that entry. In this example, we have just two books listed with a lot of associated information. With the available information, the bibliography will render, but the main issue is how it will render. The result will be poor without any formatting and that's why in the GitHub page we have provided some styling tips. The main reason for doing this fork was to allow for easy styling.

```
<div class="bibtex_template">
    <ul>
        <li style="list-style: none"><span class="if author"></span></li>
        <li>
         <span class="if author"><span class="author" style="font-weight: bold;"></span>
         </span>

         <span class="if year">(<span class="year"></span>)</span>

         <span class="if publisher" style="font-weight: bold;"><span class="publisher"></
         span></span>

         <span class="if url" style="margin-left: 20px"><a class="url" style="color:black;
         font-size:10px">(view online)</a></span>

         <div style="margin-left: 10px; margin-bottom:5px;">
             <span class="title"></span>
         </div>

        </li>
    </ul>
</div>
```

This style class bibtex_template can be used to style the bibliography as necessary. We have included this simple scheme but you can create a more complex one. The resulting bibliography is shown in Figure 11-12.

- **Donald Knuth**
  Concrete Mathematics
- **Terence Parr** (2007) **Pragmatic Bookshelf** (view online)
  The Definitive ANTLR Reference: Building Domain-Specific Languages

Figure 11-12. *A sample bibliography rendered using the bibtex-js parser and styled with a simple div tag*

There is another way to hold global data variables aside from just this bibliography implementation that we did. This method is similar to Jekyll collections, but it is more limited to just data in YAML format. In Jekyll, there is another way to store data, using the _data folder. You can save a file in the _data folder and within the file, you can store text data that you want accessible to the entire blog. A perfect example could be the projects that you worked on. Create a folder in the top level for _data, and within the folder, create a file called projects.yml. Let's look at what this file has.

```
- name: Made a bridge
  description: Lorem ipsum

- name: Got a pusheen for my kitty
  description: CL

- name: Put on a screen protector
  description: Phone
```

This is some random data put together for the projects.yml file; now let's use it. The way to access this data is to programmatically access the file and then loop through each element. This can be done using the following syntax.

```
<ul>
{% for project in site.data.projects %}
  <li>
      {{ project.name }}
      <p> {{ project.description }} </p>
  </li>
{% endfor %}
</ul>
```

This is a simple for loop that will allow us to access the site data that we have created. The index variable can be anything, we're just calling it project here. To access the data, though, the file name inside the _data folder determines the reference, so we have index_variable in site.data.filename to access the site.data files. It is easy to imagine that a similar format can be created to parse and use bibtex files so that we wouldn't need to use a plug-in or a parser. The problem with using that approach is is that bibtex database entries are very intensive; they need a lot of preparation to be parsed and then represented properly. It makes more sense, therefore, to use a plug-in that is designed entirely for bibliographic purposes. The next tool for us is IPython.

Adding Notebooks

In pursuit of an open platform for data discovery and sharing, the use of IPython notebooks is a huge advantage. It allows for a very easy way to replicate the methods being used in a study and obtain the same results. The biggest advantage of the notebooks is the availability of input and output cells that let you do computational processing within the context of the problem being explained and a possible solution being derived. It is analogous to looking up a new word or an idea in reference books or on Google. The notebooks being in a portable format also helps tremendously in uploading them or transferring them. Notebooks in the past would have to be hosted and rendered through your own instance of Project Jupyter, but lately that has changed. The nbviewer is one example of this, where gists or other repositories can be used to store the notebooks, and they can be rendered automatically by server. There's some better news to make data sharing even easier using GitHub directly.

In May 2015, Project Jupyter announced a partnership with GitHub to make the IPython notebooks (.ipynb files) render as Markdown files, directly on GitHub, with no external third-party server or software needed. Several authors have taken advantage of this feature and actually published entire chapters, along with their code on GitHub, much like you would share blog posts using Jekyll. The only difference is that now the IPython notebooks being shared on GitHub actually render into the final form right away, instead of being processed and then rendered. You can read more about the announcement along with the specific examples of some authors who have posted their books at http://blog.jupyter.org/2015/05/07/ rendering-notebooks-on-github/.

Making Presentations

Finally, we are on the last of the tools to implement and perhaps also the most exciting one, reveal.js, which we use to make presentations. We discussed earlier that we will be adding reveal.js to the project as a submodule. The command to do that and the web address are given as follows:

```
$ git submodule add https://github.com/hakimel/reveal.js.git
Cloning into 'reveal.js'...
remote: Counting objects: 8488, done.
remote: Total 8488 (delta 0), reused 0 (deltRae ce0),i vipancgk -orbejuescetds :8
100488%48[8/84K8
Receiving objects: 100% (8488/8488), 6.50 MiB | 235.00 KiB/s, done.
Resolving deltas: 100% (4543/4543), done.
Checking connectivity... done.
```

The command git submodule <web_address> adds the repository present at the specified web address as a submodule. The rest of this output just tells us that Git copied the contents of that repository along with the history into a reveal.js folder. Using reveal.js is actually not that complicated, but the key is realizing that the files in the submodule that we just cloned need to be imported in the right places, and then reveal. js needs to be supplied all of the configuration. We also want to keep our writing consistent, so that we can make the presentations in the same manner that we write the blog posts. As we get started with our layout, remember that this layout has two main purposes: being able to import the reveal.js files and providing the YAML information from files to reveal.js. Here is the code for the new layout.

```
<!doctype html>
<html lang="en">
  <head>
    <meta charset="utf-8">

<!-- Showing the title of a page, if the title is present -->

    <title>
      {% if page.title %}
        {{ page.title }} | {{ site.title }}
      {% else %}
        {{ site.title }}
      {% endif %}
    </title>
```

```
    <!-- Site description -->

    {% if page.description %}
      <meta name="description" content="{{ page.description }}" />
    {% else %}
      <meta name="description" content="{{ site.description }}">
    {% endif %}
<!-- Just some standard meta tags -->

    <meta name="viewport" content="width=device-width, initial-scale=1.0, maximum-scale=1.0,
    user-scalable=no, minimal-ui">

<!-- Importing the core reveal.js files here -->

    <link rel="stylesheet" href="{{ "/reveal.js/css/reveal.css" | prepend: site.baseurl }}"/>
    {%if page.theme %}
      <link rel="stylesheet" href="{{ "/reveal.js/css/theme/" | prepend: site.baseurl |
      append: page.theme | append: '.css' }}" id="theme"/>
    {% else %}
      <link rel="stylesheet" href="{{ "/reveal.js/css/theme/black.css" | prepend: site.
      baseurl }}" id="theme"/>
    {% endif %}

<!-- Enabling code syntax highlighting -->

    <link rel="stylesheet" href="{{ "/reveal.js/lib/css/zenburn.css" | prepend:
    site.baseurl }}"/>

<!-- Printing and PDF export features -->

    <script>
      var link = document.createElement( 'link' );
      link.rel = 'stylesheet';
      link.type = 'text/css';
      link.href = window.location.search.match( /print-pdf/gi ) ? '{{ "/reveal.js/css/print/
      pdf.css" | prepend: site.baseurl }}' : '{{ "/reveal.js/css/print/paper.css" | prepend:
      site.baseurl }}';
      document.getElementsByTagName( 'head' )[0].appendChild( link );
    </script>

<!-- Favicon -->
    <link rel="apple-touch-icon" href="{{ "/apple-touch-icon.png" | prepend:
    site.baseurl }}" />

    <link rel="canonical" href="{{ page.url | replace:'index.html','' | prepend: site.
    baseurl | prepend: site.url }}">

  </head>

  <body>
```

```
<!-- Instantiating the reveal.js slides -->

    <div class="reveal">
      <div class="slides">
        {{ content }}
      </div>
    </div>

<!-- Importing more reveal.js scripts -->
    <script src="{{ "/reveal.js/lib/js/head.min.js" | prepend: site.baseurl }}"></script>
    <script src="{{ "/reveal.js/js/reveal.js" | prepend: site.baseurl }}"></script>

<!-- Default reveal.js configuration -->

    <script>
      // Full list of configuration options available at:
      // https://github.com/hakimel/reveal.js#configuration
      Reveal.initialize({
        controls: true,
        progress: true,
        history: true,
        center: true,
        {%if page.transition %}
          transition: '{{page.transition}}',
        {% else %}
          transition: 'slide', // Other options include: none/fade/slide/convex/concave/zoom
        {% endif %}

        // Optional reveal.js plug-ins

        dependencies: [
          { src: '{{ "/reveal.js/lib/js/classList.js" | prepend: site.baseurl }}',
          condition: function() { return !document.body.classList; } },
          { src: '{{ "/reveal.js/plugin/markdown/marked.js" | prepend: site.baseurl }}',
          condition: function() { return !!document.querySelector( '[data-markdown]' ); } },
          { src: '{{ "/reveal.js/plugin/markdown/markdown.js" | prepend: site.baseurl }}',
          condition: function() { return !!document.querySelector( '[data-markdown]' ); } },
          { src: '{{ "/reveal.js/plugin/highlight/highlight.js" | prepend: site.baseurl }}',
          async: true, condition: function() { return !!document.querySelector( 'pre code'
          ); }, callback: function() { hljs.initHighlightingOnLoad(); } },
          { src: '{{ "/reveal.js/plugin/zoom-js/zoom.js" | prepend: site.baseurl }}', async:
          true },
          { src: '{{ "/reveal.js/plugin/notes/notes.js" | prepend: site.baseurl }}', async:
          true }
        ]
      });

    </script>

  </body>
</html>
```

This code might look complicated, but this layout is designed in a manner that can be broken up into several pieces. The first piece is the title of the page and the site, followed by the description. Following the description are the core imports from the reveal.js project, and then importing a few other plug-ins, such as syntax highlighting, exporting the slides, and so on. This is followed by a `div` tag instantiating the reveal.js slides and then a few more imports from the project. After that, a script tag encloses the basic configuration for a reveal.js presentation and finally the optional features for the presentations. This layout renders an entire presentation using reveal.js and a simple blog post with the appropriate YAML formatting. The task might seem complicated, but it really is straightforward. In this example, we create a one-slide presentation, but the more important aspect here is the YAML. Save this file just as you would a blog post.

```
---
layout: slides
title: Ruby meetup
categories: presentation
theme: league
transition: slide
---


<section data-markdown>

## Overview

[reveal.js](https://github.com/hakimel/reveal.js/) enables you to create beautiful
interactive slide decks using HTML. This presentation will show you how to integrate it with
[Jekyll](http://jekyllrb.com/)

</section>
```

This is the beginning of a reveal.js presentation. The title is provided along with the theme and transition configuration variables. That's all that you need in YAML. The actual blog post or the presentation starts within the section tags, and each slide is contained within those tags. To write the slide itself, you can simply use Markdown. That's it! Now you can create presentations and list them as you would a regular blog post!

Summary

In this chapter, we designed an open platform to help researchers easily disseminate their own work and the methodologies used to achieve their results. The theme used in this project took a lot of modifications to showcase some tools used heavily in academia. All the changes to the blog were pushed by Git CLI this time, and we did an in-depth tutorial of how to use it and the most commonly used commands in Git. After the tutorial, we used the same workflow in Git throughout the chapter. We implemented KaTeX in a blog post, used a port of the bibtex-js to parse a bibliography, discussed the use of IPython, and finally created a new layout using reveal.js for a presentation. The tools themselves might not be used much by hobbyists, but the process of implementing each of the new tools was a valuable lesson to learn on its own.

Further Reading

1.   **Getting Started with Git:** https://git-scm.com/book/en/v2/Getting-
     Started-About-Version-Control

2.   **Storing Git credentials:** http://gitcredentialstore.codeplex.com/

3. **Git on Windows:** `http://guides.beanstalkapp.com/version-control/git-on-windows.html`

4. **Getting started with Plot.ly JS:** `https://plot.ly/javascript/getting-started/`

5. **Toyplot library:** `http://toyplot.readthedocs.org/en/stable/index.html`

6. **Interactive IPython notebooks:** `http://www.nature.com/news/interactive-notebooks-sharing-the-code-1.16261`

■ ■ ■

Open Health Care

Open should be the default, not the exception.

—Carl Malamund

Centralized discovery and rapid updates are two advantages provided by the Internet that are completely changing the way health care information is delivered to patients. Several advancements have been made to modes of delivery for health information. Here we build a platform around one such model. The main focus of this chapter is speed: from the time taken to deploy the platform, to the time a reader takes to access relevant information. This project optimizes on both sides, reducing the barriers to the deployment of such a platform and increasing the speed with which a reader can find the appropriate topic.

We begin by talking about a new kind of user interface (UI) to discover information easily. The content on this platform would have to be prepared in a manner that can take advantage of the UI. As such, we discuss some guidelines for writing content. We prototype the platform and start implementing features. The implementation is done within the browser using prose.io as an editor and file manager. We conclude by discussing the applications of this platform in the broader context of public health.

Overview

In this project, our goal is to create an information delivery platform (based on Jekyll) that can be packaged and deployed at short notice by, say, a public health organization. You might be wondering about the difference between an information delivery platform and a blog. They both serve the same purpose, so what's the difference? There are two main differences and they both have to do with the end objectives of the platform.

- The first difference is the format of the blog. We have followed a peculiar format for all the blogs in the projects that we created: Use a for loop and list every single post in the _post directory. This allows us to automatically list and update posts as they get added, and the listing format maybe with an excerpt allows the reader to browse through a typical blog. However, in this project, listing everything might become incredibly ineffective, so we need to be cautious about the format that we pick for the project.

- The second difference is the content itself. In a blog, you can talk about anything you want, and in any tone that you want. Your blog is your way of expressing your thoughts, so you can structure your ideas how you like. If our goal, however, is to minimize the time that readers need to reach the topic they want and absorb the information, we have to strictly control the format and structure of the content.

These two points allow us to paint a clear picture of what is required from our platform. This chapter is not so much project-oriented as it is goal-oriented, the difference being that in the past some features that we prototyped might be removed in the end, or new ones are added to the project. Here, the features that hinder our goals will be removed and only the features that optimize the project will be added. To understand the goals of this project, we need to understand the three parties participating in it. The first party is the developers, which includes you. Your goal is to create a modular project that is easy to maintain and that can be deployed easily on an open platform like GitHub by another party. The second party is the agency or party deploying the package. In the case of public health issues, this can be the Centers for Disease Control (CDC) or even local institutions. Their goals are to obtain a platform that they can use to send out information and update it regularly. An open source project becomes a huge preference because anyone can use the code and make changes to it that benefit all the parties using the code. The last participant, and perhaps the most important party, is the readers. They will consume the information made available by the public health organization. Their goals are simply to get access to relevant information faster and in an effective manner. The relationship among these three parties is displayed graphically in Figure 12-1.

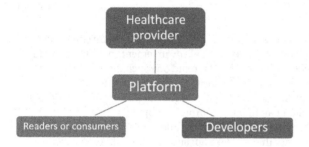

Figure 12-1. *The three parties involved in this platform*

Now that we have a better idea of the parties involved and their interests, it is easier to see what type of project we have to design. It must be one that can easily be deployed on GitHub, easy to read and obtain information from, and rapidly editable so that updates to the information presented can be done smoothly. Creating high-quality documentation requires a high level of control over the content of the project. To that end, we will be setting up some rules in the form of a content guide to make sure that the content is prepared in a manner that is easy to find and consume. In this chapter, we create an information platform that can be used by a health care provider to inform patients of their rights for data access and navigating through how to request specific data. Part of the motivation behind this idea is to support the Precision Medicine Initiative (PMI). This project was launched in 2015 and the initial steps include creating a volunteer program to collect biological samples from volunteers across the country. The creation of a biobank for sample collection also requires transparent policies about what will happen to the data collected and how the results of the testing will be shared. Along with the ethical obligation of the participating agencies, the volunteers also don't want to be turned away by confusing language that might not be accessible. The context of this project is yet another reason why we need content guides. There is yet another component required to make the process of editing the final platform easier: in-browser editing. So far, we have been using Git and doing the editing locally in Sublime. That won't work anymore, as downloading and installing additional tools requires more time spent on maintenance. We need to streamline this workflow, so in-browser editing seems to be the best solution. We use prose.io as the editor and a file manager to interface with the GitHub repository that contains our code. In that manner, Prose will allow us to add files and make changes, all within the browser. There are, however, some limitations and differences between using Prose and editing on GitHub itself.

- If you are using Github, you can actually create new files and then copy any text necessary. You can also edit or delete files if necessary. This allows for decent editing capabilities and file management; however, if you want to upload a picture, you will not be able to do so just using the web interface.

- Prose offers its own web interface for editing files online. You can edit the metadata and write in Markdown easily with pre-built shortcuts. In Prose, you can upload images and they will remain in your repository, then you can use them as normal in your posts.

- Despite the ability to upload pictures, even in Prose, you can't truly upload files. If the file contains text information, you have to simply copy and paste it in a new file that you created. This works in most of the cases and will definitely work for this project.

We discuss the distinguishing features of Prose at length in a later section. Now that we have a better idea of the overall picture, let's start looking into the details. The first major change in this platform and the other blogs we have built is the use of the cards interface for the web site. This is a fundamentally different architecture that is built for better accessibility of information.

Introduction to Cards

The special sauce in this project will be the cards UI. Cards are at the center of several modern web technologies. Today, they are becoming ubiquitous and a preferred source of updates to basic information such as weather. They are becoming the default option when it comes to balancing clear aesthetics with simple usability for obvious reasons. For organizing content with interactive media in one coherent structure such as an image with headline, a share button or link, cards have become the design of choice. Moreover, the emphasis on organization and clarity makes the use of cards ideal for mobile and responsive designs. Content from web sites is being broken down into individual components and reaggregated in new ways to interface better with the rise of mobile technologies. This is driving the users away from browsing multiple pages of content linked together and toward individual pieces of information and updates aggregated into one experience. Cards are far from a trend; they are becoming a practical method for designing applications where speed is a crucial factor.

The aggregation of information is allowing for the entire experience to become much more personalized. As a design framework, the aggregation depends on the following:

- The person consuming the content and their interests, preferences, and behavior.

- Their location and environmental context.

- Their social context including the interests, preferences, and behavior of their friends.

Cards are becoming very deeply rooted in social media. Pinterest was the first major web platform that relied heavily on cards, and later on integrated purchase buttons for e-commerce. Ever since Pinterest successfully implemented cards, Twitter and Facebook have replicated the UI on their own platforms. One of the best implementation of cards is Google Now, shown below Figure 12-2. It provides an interface for all sorts of information to be aggregated for the user to glance at and get updates. This implementation can be extended to provide text-based information as well. However, the template for each individual card and how it is represented on the canvas will ultimately determine how effective the layout becomes as a whole.

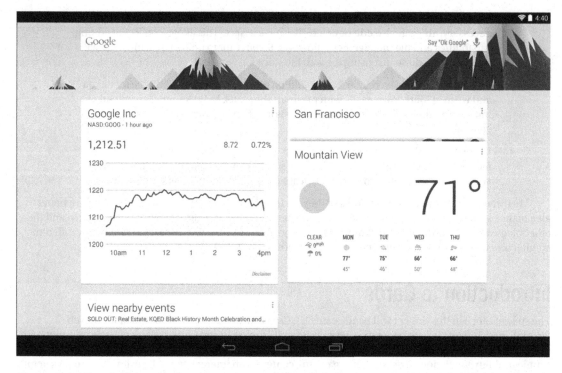

Figure 12-2. *Google Now cards showing stocks, weather, and nearby events. Cards are helpful in this situation because the information updates frequently and we just need a minimalistic, stylish container to render the information to the user.*

A card can essentially be thought of as an empty container with borders and a few rules that dictate the styles of content elements. Let's break down the general components of a card:

- **Title:** The first component that identifies a card. The title doesn't need to summarize the card but just introduce the updates it will provide.

- **Subheader:** The supporting information present in most cards to continue updating at the point where the title left off. Often this is a meeting address, schedule, or link for further information about the topic of the card.

- **Content:** The actual information provided by a specific card, given the preferences of the user. It provides a quick way of glancing at updates.

Creating Cards

Now that we have talked about the basic components of a card, let's play around with cards a bit more and explore what kind of cards we can create. The reason for experimenting with cards before we dive into editing a theme in Jekyll is to gain enough familiarity with the concept of cards and have a general idea of what is possible to do with cards. For this, we will be using a platform called CodePen, which allows us to write all the HTML, CSS, and JavaScript in one window and render the results live. It's an incredibly powerful tool for rapid prototyping and also to test new technologies. CodePen provides the most commonly used libraries and import features for external style files and libraries. We are using a design library called Semantic UI, which provides templates in user-friendly HTML to create cards with interactive content.

We do this entirely within the browser in CodePen, so let's get started. CodePen lets you create a new pen without having to sign up, which is perfect for us to experiment with Semantic UI. The home page is shown in Figure 12-3.

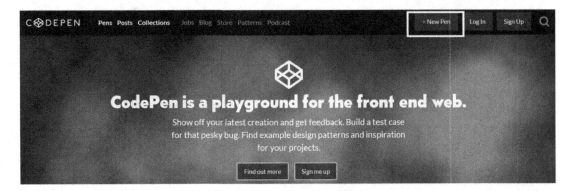

Figure 12-3. *CodePen home page. We use this tool to test out the Semantic UI. Clicking New Pen on the top right will get us started.*

Clicking New Pen takes us to a multicolumn layout with the left side displaying the canvas that will render the results and the right pane including three dividers for HTML, CSS, and JavaScript, respectively. We first need to import the styles required by Semantic UI into CodePen. To do this, click Settings on the top right to open the Pen Settings dialog box. Within this dialog box, click the CSS button near the top to access the CSS settings. Under CSS Settings, you will find a place for importing labeled Add External CSS. Here are the CSS files that we need to import.

```
//oss.maxcdn.com/semantic-ui/2.0.6/semantic.min.css
//oss.maxcdn.com/semantic-ui/2.0.6/components/card.min.css
//oss.maxcdn.com/semantic-ui/2.0.6/components/button.min.css
```

The final result after adding the style files is shown in Figure 12-4. These imports will now give us access to the cards interface, a few buttons and the overall semantic interface. The right side is where we will be doing most of our work. The panes can be collapsed or expanded by double-clicking the title of the pane. For the cards we will be making, there is no JavaScript needed, so let's close that panel. That leaves us with only the HTML and CSS panels to work with. The other option available is the small Tidy button that actually is used to format the code properly. The purpose behind the Tidy button is to automatically add the appropriate white space, brackets, and tabbing to your code and make it look clean.

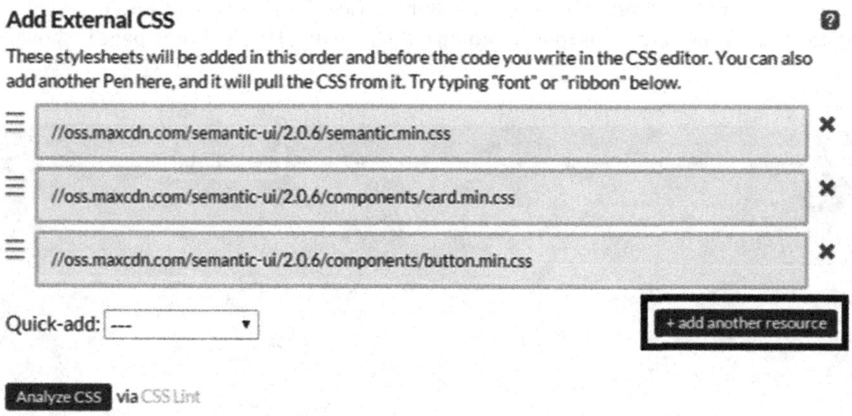

Add External CSS

These stylesheets will be added in this order and before the code you write in the CSS editor. You can also add another Pen here, and it will pull the CSS from it. Try typing "font" or "ribbon" below.

```
//oss.maxcdn.com/semantic-ui/2.0.6/semantic.min.css                          ✖

//oss.maxcdn.com/semantic-ui/2.0.6/components/card.min.css                   ✖

//oss.maxcdn.com/semantic-ui/2.0.6/components/button.min.css                 ✖
```

Quick-add: `---  ▼`   `+ add another resource`

`Analyze CSS` via CSS Lint

Figure 12-4. *Importing external CSS files into CodePen for Semantic UI*

Let's get started with the coding. First we add a bit of spacing to where the cards would render, with the only bit of CSS we use throughout this CodePen.

```css
body {
  padding: 20px 20px 20px 20px;
  font-family: 'Helvetica Neue', Arial, Helvetica, sans-serif;
}
```

The code for a simple card with an action button is actually very straightforward. Here is a look:

```html
<div class="ui cards">                  <!-- Declaring the beginning of a card for the CSS -->
  <div class="create-action card">      <!-- Action card -->
    <div class="content" style="opacity: 0.5;">          <!-- Style for content -->

<!-- Mail button -->
      <i class="right floated mail icon teal" style="font-size: 30px;"></i>
      <div class="header">            <!-- Action text -->
        Send to email
      </div>
    </div>

    <div class="ui attached bottom button" style="">              <!-- Action button -->
      Create this scan action
    </div>
  </div>
</div>
```

Using this snippet in CodePen will generate our first card, shown in Figure 12-5. This was a simple card with some text and an action button, but we can create more complex cards. The next card we create will be a profile card for a person that will give a short description of the person, including some minor details about them.

Figure 12-5a. *The resulting card drawn on the left pane which is the canvas*

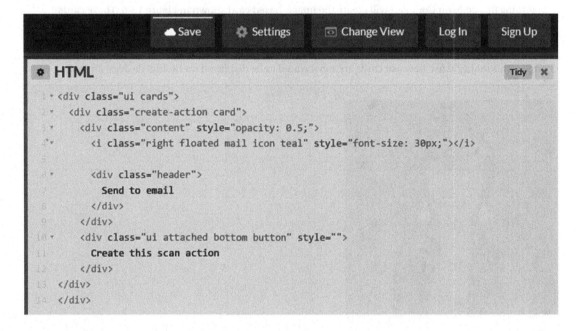

Figure 12-5b. *The HTML code ithe right pane*

The code that follows shows how to make the profile card. The code is very similar to the last block that we used, but there are minor differences in the classes being used. This code renders a block for showing the image, and underneath are two sections, the first one for a name, followed by supporting information and then a description. Finally under the description is a second block containing an extra content class.

```
<div class="ui card">        <!-- Render the card here -->
  <div class="image">        <!-- Display the image first -->
    <img src="http://semantic-ui.com/images/avatar2/large/molly.png">
  </div>

  <div class="content">      <!-- Information about the person -->
    <a class="header">Kristy</a>
    <div class="meta">
      <span class="date">Joined in 2013</span>        <!-- Name and basic details -->
    </div>
```

```
<div class="description">
    Kristy is an art director living in New York.
  </div>
</div>

<div class="extra content">          <!-- Social profile -->
  <a>
    <i class="user icon"></i>
    22 Friends
  </a>
</div>
</div>
```

Putting this code on CodePen will create the image-based card shown in Figure 12-6. These cards have a fluid property where the image being used automatically resizes itself to fit a certain card length. You do not need to be concerned about the image size, as it will automatically be resized to fit any screen responsively. All the elements in Semantic UI are responsive, meaning that they will resize if the window size changes. This makes sense because cards are most suited to be displayed on mobile devices, after all.

Figure 12-6. *A profile card displaying the picture, name, supporting information, description, a divider, and finally extra content. This card also has a responsive property if the window size is changed.*

Writing a Quote Card

The next card is a quote card, which will contain most of the same information as the previous card, however in the extra-content section, this card will have the quote source. The end result is shown in Figure 12-7.

Figure 12-7. *A normal card with an extra-content section that includes the author*

```
<div class="ui card">       <!-- Rendering a card, displaying title, subtitle and content -->
   <div class="content">
      <div class="header">Cute Dog</div>
      <div class="meta">             <!-- Subtitle is meta-data -->
        <span class="category">Animals</span>
      </div>
      <div class="description">
         Jenny is a student studying Media Management at the New School
      </div>
   </div>
   <div class="extra content">            <!-- Showing the quote author -->
      <div class="right floated author">
         <img class="ui avatar image" src="http://semantic-ui.com/images/avatar/small/matt.
         jpg"> Matt
      </div>
   </div>
</div>
```

The code is mostly the same, except for the extra-content class that takes on additional parameters to display the avatar. We're going to make one last card that extends an action card from Figure 12-5 and add tags or categories. This is incredibly helpful in organizing information, and once the tags are activated, they link to a page that contains a list of all the posts with that particular tag. In the following code, the parts shown in bold are what adds the tags.

```
<div class="ui cards">
<div class="card">
    <div class="content">
      <i class="right floated mail icon teal" style="font-size: 30px;"></i>

      <div class="header">
        Send to user email
      </div>
```

```
<div class="meta">
  <code>User email</code>
</div>
<div class="description">
  A description about send to user email.
</div>
</div>
<div class="extra content">        <!-- Adding the categories -->
  <div>
    <i class="users icon"></i> Staff, Students
  </div>
  <div>
    <i class="user icon"></i> Kaylee Fryee
  </div>
</div>
</div>
</div>
```

Most of the code remained the same, except for the last few lines that add the categories. So far, we made four different types of cards: The first one was an action card, the second one was a fluid profile card, the next one was a quote card with the avatar of an author, and the last one was a card that used categories. We use all of these features in one single card in the theme itself for the project. So let's go back to the information delivery platform. How would we go about concretely building it now that we have some experience with cards? The first thing we need to do is to lay out some rules. This is similar to an earlier chapter when we discussed a few rules for the debate platform. Those were the specifications that became the foundation for this project. Here, we have a content guide that dictates what kind of a platform would be built around it.

Content Guide

These recommendations are derived from a hybrid between a content guide written by 18F for government web sites and the Mallard documentation style. The guide provided by 18F provides insight into the way content should be written and Mallard provides guidelines for how the content should be wrapped by the title and supporting information. Combining them both here will allow us to reach our speed goals effectively, so let's get started.

- **Tone:** The tone of our writing should be conversational yet instructive. The patients are relying on this project to get information about their own data that is often hidden behind layers of organizational bureaucracy. We believe that being able to deploy an open health care platform to help patients is a privilege, and our voice needs to represent this.

- **Voice:** Our writing should be succinct and to the point. Using an active voice allows the reader to relate to the content more easily, and the content becomes more engaging as well. Avoid passive verb tenses whenever possible.

- **Plain language:** Readers prefer straightforward and clear English. The use of plain English might be obvious, but it is often ignored in projects where the goal is to break down complex information into easy-to-understand bits. It allows readers to go through information rapidly and arrive at what they need. Don't use formal language or long words when short, simple ones can work fine. For instance, use buy instead of purchase, help instead of assist, and about instead of approximately. This shouldn't be taken as a list of words to avoid, but rather a way of writing.

- **Address the users:** Address the users as "you" wherever possible. The content they are browsing is relevant to their personal health, so it should make a direct appeal to the readers. For example, "You can contact PMI at this e-mail address," or "Learn more about the way your data is stored by reading this quick summary."

- **Break up chunks:** Large chunks of text can overwhelm readers. Break down the content into small paragraphs and use bullet points where appropriate. You should craft sentences of 25 words or fewer when possible. The best case scenario is if a sentence has fewer than 14 words. Research shows that most readers understand 90 percent of content if a sentence is fewer than 14 words.

- **Acronyms:** Acronyms often confuse readers. If an acronym is necessary, spell out the full word and follow that with the acronym in parentheses on the first reference. Then you can use the acronym in the second instance. Avoid them whenever possible.

- **Organization:** Readers often scan text until they find the relevant information. Most readers will read only 25 percent of the content present in front of them. We can use this number to make sure that we structure our content in such a manner that the most important information gets read first. You can do this by putting the most important information in the first two paragraphs.

- **Titles:** The titles for each card must be topic-based. The title must contain a short description of the topic, maybe five or six words long. Each card must have two titles: One is an informal title displayed on the home page and the second one (that follows the Mallard specifications) should be topic-oriented.

- **Categories:** In Mallard, all content is organized as information related to individual topics under broad categories. The categories for each card must be listed in the expanded view, in two or three words. The topics become names of the cards (or blog posts) and the categories are simply an anchor to hold all the cards related to that category.

- **Authorship:** Each card must have a clearly defined author in the first line of the post. At the end of the post, a divider should be placed, and underneath the divider a short biography of the author must be provided. This will not only help establish credibility, but in combination with Google Analytics, this will also help determine which author is providing the best readable content.

- **Sources:** Each card should have clearly placed references or sources (where appropriate) at the end of the content.

- **Tags:** Each card should have a few tags listed near the end of the content, after the sources. The tags act as a marker for the audiences that are likely to be affected by the information present in this card.

■ **Note**   The content guide lists rules for content and the structure of the web site that contains the content. However, we are only be able to discuss the changes to the web site in detail.

Writing in Prose

Now that we have a definitive content guide, we can start talking about the tools we will be using in this project more concretely. The first of them is an in-browser editor and a file manager for Jekyll called Prose. The simple fact that Prose allows us to edit without having to download any additional tools also means that you can run Prose on any computer in a matter of minutes. The programming is no longer limited to a machine that runs Git and needs to be configured to clone the repository or push to it. The in-browser editing offers a lot of freedom for making quick changes, in addition to reduced maintenance of the downloaded tools. The way Prose works is straightforward: It interfaces directly with GitHub, and then you can pick the appropriate repository to work with through the web interface, just as you would select a folder to open and edit in a file manager. Besides being a file manager, there are some distinct advantages to using Prose that make it suitable for Jekyll.

- **Publish/unpublish workflow**: Once your post has been completed, you can publish it by simply clicking Published. The same function can be used when you clear the check box, to unpublish a blog post that's already live.

- **Drafts management**: Locally, you have to create a new folder for drafts. Within the folder, you can keep incomplete ideas. In Prose, you can save a post as a draft, and when you are done, your draft turns into an actual post with the click of a button.

- **Image uploading**: When editing Markdown documents, you can drag and drop images on the current page. Those images are then uploaded to a media directory you specify in your configuration or the current directory.

- **Mobile ready**: Prose is designed to be a mobile-ready editor so that any device can access your repository, and it is particularly well suited for the iPad.

- **Markdown ready**: The editor in Prose is designed just for Markdown with several common features such as headers, bold, and so on available in a toolbar and a live preview of the post.

- **Access control**: By modifying the configuration, you can provide access to maintainers so that they can create and edit content but not do much else on the blog or web site.

Many of these features are inspired by traditional CMS systems, however, Prose itself runs on Jekyll and Backbone.js. Let's briefly talk about our workflow locally, and then how Prose will change it. Usually, any blog post or theme edit starts with identification of the file that needs to be edited, then the actual editing is done in Sublime. After the edits have been made, the same cycle of using Git—add, commit, and push—makes all the local changes available online. In Prose, the workflow is much simpler: You find the specific file that needs to be changed, make the change within the browser, and just click Save. In that last step, you can add what would be equivalent to a commit message and your changes are instantly available on GitHub. This process involves fewer steps and the best part is that you don't have to download any tools to use offline. The real advantage of in-browser editing and why it's important is that the entire process can be standardized. This is an important design consideration because when a platform such as this one gets packaged and an organization wants to use it, they have to train their employees on a new platform. The easier it is to use, the less training they need to do. In that sense, keeping the process simple by just editing the theme in a browser, completely eliminating the use of Git, could be very desirable and incredibly helpful.

So how exactly does Prose get access to your repository? The mechanism of access is called OAuth, which stands for Open Authentication, used very broadly across the Internet. This is a way for users to log into third-party web sites using their Microsoft, Google, Facebook, or Twitter accounts to gain a third-party access token. This access token makes it possible for them to create an account without exposing their password. It's a convenient way of using new services, and each of the access tokens essentially becomes an application that runs under one of your existing accounts.

Prosing Through

Now that we have an idea of how Prose works and how it will change our workflow, let's do a thorough walkthrough of setting it up with a repository, editing files, and committing the final changes. We begin by visiting `http://prose.io/`. The home page of the web site asks us to start the OAuth process with GitHub, so that you can access your repositories. This is shown in Figure 12-8.

Figure 12-8. *Prose.io home page requesting OAuth initiation for your GitHub account*

The authentication starts with the dialog box in Figure 12-8, but the user must also know what exactly is edited and what this application can do once it gains an access token from GitHub. The next screen shown after clicking Authorize on GitHub is shown in Figure 12-9. Once the authentication has been completed, the Prose editor opens and displays all the repositories that are available for editing. We only have one for this project and the repository name is displayed, as shown in Figure 12-10. The editor gives a View Project option, which is the equivalent of opening a folder to see the contents and then editing as needed. At this point, a good knowledge of the Jekyll tree and what each folder represents is necessary because that can save time needed to search through the files. Going back to the point about standardizing the process of editing, the process of looking through a file structure to quickly determine where the target files are can be easily standardized. These small optimizations might not matter much in the context of making this project, but they become incredibly important when a project is deployed in production and there are people working on it in real time.

Authorize application

Prose by @prose would like permission to access your account

Figure 12-9. *Completing the authentication by Prose. On this page, you can clearly see what Prose can access, what the permissions for this application are, and a description of the app on the right.*

Figure 12-10. *After authenticating to Prose, the repository browser mode displays all the repositories you have. You can also search through repositories using the top navigation bar if you have several repositories.*

■ **Note** Once authenticated, Prose can work with your GitHub repository and allow you to edit in-browser on any computer. The access token relies on your GitHub account, not the computer you are on. For instance, to use Prose on a public library computer, you just have to log in to your GitHub account and then visit `prose.io`. Your repository will be available just as shown in Figure 12-10.

After clicking View Project button, we see the file browser in Prose, as shown in Figure 12-11.

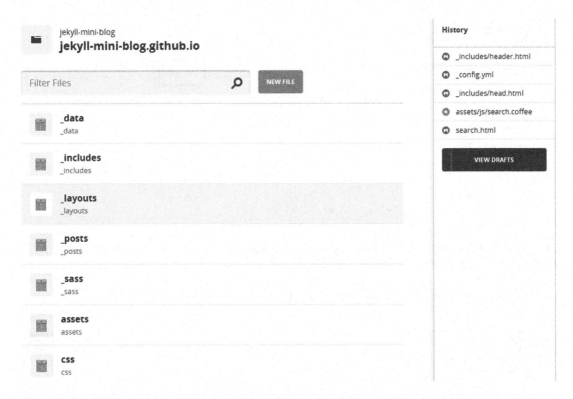

Figure 12-11. *File browsing mode for a repository. This is a central feature of Prose, providing access to most of the operations such as search, history, and drafts. We discuss the individual components in text.*

This file browsing mode starts on top with naming the repository that you are currently browsing. This is followed by a search bar to find files within the folders included, and a button to create a new file. Note that a similar button is also available on GitHub, but there are significant differences between this code editor and GitHub's editor. The mode that Prose is currently in (e.g., file-browsing mode, editing mode, etc.) is denoted by a small icon, present in the top left corner. In Figure 12-11, the icon displays a folder and Prose is in file-browsing mode. Below the search bar is a listing of all the files and folders present in this repository. On the right side is the history pane, which contains a list of the most recently edited files along with a button to view the current draft posts. We talk at length about the code-editor mode and the history shortly, but think of the history being displayed here as similar to the Git log that we used in the terminal. Deleting files is also hassle-free. If you find a file that is no longer necessary in the project, just click the garbage can button next to the file name (shown in Figure 12-12) and the file is gone. You don't even have to commit these changes, as the delete operation for files gets pushed automatically to the GitHub repository.

Figure 12-12. *File-browser mode, scrolling down the same page to view individual files. The two options for editing and deleting are available for easy operations.*

Let's look at the code-editor mode next in Figure 12-13.

Figure 12-13. *In code-editor mode, the top left icon changes to represent the new mode. The next feature to the right of the icon is the path of the file being edited below. On the top right is the shortcut toolbar that contains editing features such as file preview, YAML edits, settings, and commiting changes. Finally, on the left is the actual code that has been syntax highlighted for HTML. Currently, the status of this page is shown as published.*

The Markdown editing features available for the blog posts are very convenient if you want to make some quick changes without manually inputting the markup for them. This is another additional feature that becomes useful for training newcomers to Markdown. The formatting toolbar is shown in Figure 12-14.

jekyll-mini-blog / jekyll-mini-blog.github.io

Welcome to Jekyll!

| h2 | h3 | ↻ | 🖾 | B | *i* | 66 | ≔ | ≣ | ❓ | | Published ✅ |

You'll find this post in your `_posts` directory. Go ahead and edit it and re-build the site to see your changes. You can rebuild the site in many different ways, but the most common way is to run `jekyll serve`, which launches a web server and auto-regenerates your site when a file is updated.

Figure 12-14. *The formatting toolbar contains all the Markdown basics such as header formats, bold typeface, hyperlinking, quotes, and bullet points*

One of the features from the code-editor mode that regularly comes in handy is the YAML-edits button to make metadata changes for files and blog posts. We use the YAML edits feature in the code-editor mode, shown in Figure 12-15.

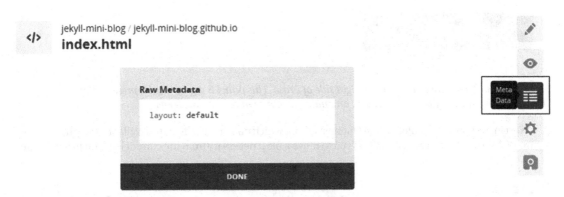

Figure 12-15. *Clicking the YAML edits button displays the raw metadata associated with the file that is currently being edited. This allows us to insert metadata as needed. Clicking Done applies the new metadata to the file.*

This setting allows us to edit metadata for the files and add new information as necessary, and the newly edited data automatically gets saved. Let's take a look at the history panel, shown in Figure 12-16. This panel contains a list of recent files that were edited and the panel also tells us what type of change occurred. The use of M in the icons denotes a modification, the use of a down arrow icon indicates a new file has been created, and the use of a red button with a file icon on it denotes that a file has been deleted.

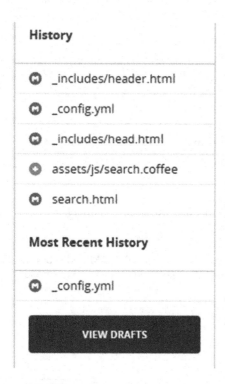

Figure 12-16. *The history panel on the right side of Prose. This panel is a graphical representation of all the changes being made to files in the project, an analogue of the Git commit message.*

Next in the shortcuts toolbar is the Options button, which only has two features available, shown in Figure 12-17. The file path actually allows you to move a file if necessary from the current location to a new one.

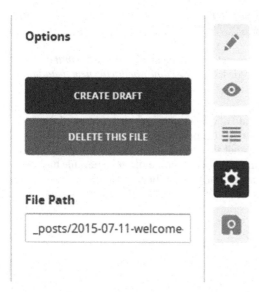

Figure 12-17. *The Options button provides the feature of turning the current post into a draft, if you want to come back and work on the idea later and the ability to delete the current file*

Finally we are on the last button of the shortcut toolbar, and this button is the equivalent of adding all the changes, committing them, and pushing the resulting commit to GitHub. This button streamlines the workflow from three commands to one button. The commit message is shown along with the Save button in Figure 12-18.

Figure 12-18. *The Save button with commit changes. The sidebar to the left of the Save button takes the commit message and pushes the changes to GitHub.*

This concludes our walkthrough of Prose, as we have touched on most of the important features that you will be using throughout this project. Now let's start implementing features from the content guide to a theme.

Material Design

There are a few requirements that we need to keep in mind while searching for a suitable theme. The first one is that we need to use cards within the theme and the second is that we don't want to pick a theme that has a grid system in use. Removing a grid system and replacing it with something else is very time consuming and difficult to accomplish. Choosing the cards UI makes the search for Jekyll themes very narrow, and a simple search revealed an excellent theme for our use called Jekyll Material Design Lite. This theme lists blog posts as cards, and follows the material design specification (which is used perfectly within the theme). The theme is available on Jekyll Themes at `http://jekyllthemes.org/themes/jekyll-mdl/`, created by the Google Developers Group Managua.

The edits we are going to make to this theme are broken down into four broad categories.

- The first one is the edits to the top bar.

- The second category is the edits to the way cards are displayed.

- The third is the edits to the cards layout when expanded.

- The last one is the sidebar edits.

Let's get started with the first set of edits. Note that this theme is built using material design specifications and styles, so we can look to the material design library for inspiration, in terms of site colors and themes to use. The README file for this blog tells us how to customize the theme. For custom theme options, we need to visit http://www.getmdl.io/customize/index.html, so let's start there. This web site provides a color selector to help us pick different colors and then import them into the theme. You can pick any two custom colors to use, and instead of downloading the associated CSS files, we will just use the hosted CDN links to import the CSS. This saves us the hassle of including the files in the commit as well, when we can simply just add the import as another line of code. Here's the CSS import line from the theme builder:

```
<link rel="stylesheet" href="https://storage.googleapis.com/code.getmdl.io/1.0.6/material.
blue_grey-orange.min.css" />
```

This line needs to be placed in the _includes/head.html file, near the end of the file:

```
<link rel="stylesheet" href="https://storage.googleapis.com/code.getmdl.io/1.0.6/material.
blue_grey-orange.min.css" />
</head>
```

After the styles have been imported, we need to edit some basic information and metadata for this platform. To do so, let's look at _config.yml and start making changes. The following are some sample changes.

```
# Site settings
title: Open Health Care
email: your-email@domain.com
description: A platform for the delivery of patient-care information and patient-data
requests to patients in a intuitive manner.
baseurl: "" # Leave this as is
url: "http://jekyll-mini-blog.github.io" # The site address given in the format username.
github.io
```

This set of edits allows us to change the metadata and reuse this theme for our Open Health Care platform. After the metadata edits have been made, we can leave the rest of the configuration for this file alone. We can revisit this file for changes later on. Now the top bar displays the title of the web site, but there is a lot more work to be done. For our platform, this top bar will act as a shortcut bar where the users can quickly access the most important components of the platform. Therefore, this top bar will contain a home button, a link to live updates, and syndication through a mailing list and RSS. Syndication is crucial for this platform: Once the users start reading from our platform, any changes made to the information provided must be reported to the users. The two most effective ways to do this are using a mailing list, which can be created and managed through MailChimp, and RSS, which is an old-school but incredibly reliable way of receiving site updates. First, let's import font-awesome before we start implementing any icons. The import for font-awesome also needs to be placed below the CSS import from earlier in the _includes/head.html file.

```
<link rel="stylesheet" href="https://maxcdn.bootstrapcdn.com/font-awesome/4.5.0/css/font-
awesome.min.css">

</head>
```

Now that we have access to font-awesome, let's start creating the icons for the top bar that we need. The relevant code that we need to start editing is present in `header.html`. First we need to remove the `more_vert` button and the for loop associated with it. Now we can start adding the icons.

- **Home:** `<i class="fa fa-home"></i>`

- **Live updates:** `<i class="fa fa-gratipay"></i>`

- **Mailing list:** `<i class="fa fa-envelope-o"></i>`

- **RSS:** `<i class="fa fa-rss"></i>`

These buttons need to be added responsively because the search button causes the search bar to expand. If the buttons are added without any regard for proper placement, when the search bar expands, the buttons will all be distorted. Luckily, there is a responsive space available within the `header.html` file that we can use: `<div class="mdl-layout-spacer"></div>`

After all the edits have been made, here's what the `<header>` tag looks like:

```
<!-- Beginning of header -->
<header class="mdl-layout__header">

  <div class="mdl-layout__header-row">

    <!-- Title -->
    <span class="mdl-layout-title">{{ site.title }}</span>

    <!-- Add spacer, to align navigation to the right -->
    <div class="mdl-layout-spacer"></div>

    <!-- Font-awesome icons -->
    <a href=""><i class="fa fa-home fa-2x"></i></a>       <div class="mdl-layout-spacer">
    </div>
    <a href=""><i class="fa fa-gratipay fa-2x"></i></a>  <div class="mdl-layout-spacer">
    </div>
    <a href=""><i class="fa fa-envelope-o fa-2x"></i></a><div class="mdl-layout-spacer">
    </div>
    <a href=""><i class="fa fa-rss fa-2x"></i></a>       <div class="mdl-layout-spacer">
    </div>

    <!-- Search box -->
    <div class="mdl-textfield mdl-js-textfield mdl-textfield--expandable is-upgraded">
      <label class="mdl-button mdl-js-button mdl-button--icon" for="js-search__input">
        <i class="material-icons">search</i>
      </label>

      <!-- Search input and expand -->
      <div class="mdl-textfield__expandable-holder" >
        <input class="mdl-textfield__input super-search__input" type="text" id="js-
        search__input" />
      </div>
    </div>

  </div>
</header>
```

This code has mostly remained unchanged, except for the font-awesome icons that we added to the file. The use of the `mdl-layout-spacer` tag after each icon makes the icons responsive so they are repositioned when the search bar expands completely. The remainder of this file describes the sidebar (or drawer) and the `for` loop that will add elements to the sidebar as new pages are added to the project. This will come handy later on when we want to make sure that any links to further reading or resources are made available to patients so that they can get an overview of the platform as a whole. Now that we have the header fixed, let's move to the actual cards. This is the second set of changes where we need to fix the layout of the cards themselves.

So what exactly do we need to change? Here's a short list: Remove the background image on cards, add share buttons, make the title more noticeable, make the Read More button more appealing, and so on. Let's get started first with how the cards are being rendered through `index.html`. If you open that file, you will notice that it has a huge amount of HTML code, mostly the same code repeated with different conditions and Liquid control loops. We want to create a fairly simple layout, so we will take the last of the `{% else %}` options from the index file and bring it out. The new index file looks more like this.

```
---
layout: default
---

<!-- Beginning of the index.html code, first creating a grid to render for cards -->
<div class="page-content">
  <div class="mdl-grid">

<!-- Loop through all the posts -->
    {% for post in site.posts %}

<!-- Style class for an individual card -->
    <div class="mdl-card mdl-shadow--2dp mdl-cell mdl-cell--4-col mdl-cell--4-col-desktop
    mdl-cell--4-col-tablet  mdl-cell--12-col-phone">

<!-- Simple colored heading for each card, with a font-awesome icon in front of the title -->
      <h4 align="center" style="color:rgb(108, 122, 137)">
      <i class="fa fa-caret-square-o-right"></i> {{ post.title }} </h4>

<!-- Bold date, excerpt follows the date -->
      <div class="mdl-card__supporting-text">
        <strong> <span>{{ post.date | date: "%b %-d, %Y" }}</span></strong>

<!-- Include for social buttons -->
        {% include social.html %}
        <p>{{ post.excerpt }}</p>
      </div>

<!-- Read More button, with a pointing arrow font-awesome icon -->
      <div class="mdl-card__actions mdl-card--border">

        <div class="mdl-layout-spacer"></div>
        <a class="mdl-button mdl-button--colored mdl-js-button mdl-js-ripple-effect"
        href="{{ post.url | prepend: site.url }}"> Read More
```

```
<!-- Font-awesome icon for Read More button -->
            <i class="fa fa-chevron-circle-right"></i>
            </a>

            </div>

        </div>
        {% endfor %}
    </div>

</div>
```

The index file might look complicated, but individually, all the components are very straightforward. The rationale of the code is to first create a grid where the rest of the code can render cards. This grid is important because it will allow the web site to be responsive and wrap the cards if necessary on the screen. After creating the grid, the for loop goes through each of the posts and displays them. Next is a div tag calling the CSS styles for an individual card. We have changed this distinctly from the original version in the theme. In our version, the title is a header tag with color and a font-awesome icon. The title is followed by date and an include for the social icons (which we haven't created yet). Finally, we have the Read More button, which now has a font-awesome icon next to it.

Let's get started with the social buttons for the cards. We want to give the reader an ability to share the card from the home page. We will go with a very simple social buttons setup by AddToAny that offers a toolbar including the major social-media sites. To get started, visit https://www.addtoany.com/buttons/for/website and pick the second button set. Then after selecting it, click Get Button Code and see Figure 12-19.

Get the button code for any site

Figure 12-19. *Select the second button set and then click Get Button Code, which opens a small text area underneath that contains the embed code that you need to copy and paste in a new file named* _includes/ social.html.

Take the embed code provided by AddToThis and paste it in a new file named social.html, which provides the social buttons for each of the cards. Note that we discussed the code for index.html first and then the social icons. If the changes are made in this order, GitHub will throw an error saying that an include file that was referenced in index.html is not present in the _includes folder. In any case, if you create the social.html file next and push the changes afterward, that will fix the error automatically and the social icons will render normally. Another optional feature would be to add the categories right here for the cards. Originally, the categories would have been added to the top of the post, but they can also be added next to the Read More button with the snippet shown here in bold.

```
        <div class="mdl-card__actions mdl-card--border">

            <div class="mdl-layout-spacer"></div>
            <a class="mdl-button mdl-button--colored mdl-js-button mdl-js-ripple-effect"
href="{{ post.url | prepend: site.url }}" >Read More <i class="fa fa-chevron-circle-
right"></i></a> <small> Category: {% for cat in post.categories %} {{ cat }} {% endfor %}
</small>


        </div>
```

Most of the code remains the same actually; the only difference in this snippet is the `<small>` style and the addition of `{{ post.categories }}` to the card. This allows each card to display the category to which it belongs. In this project, the categories are not the traditional tags that show related posts. Instead, they follow the Mallard specification of being short phrases (two or three words long) that serve as a heading to organize all of the cards associated with that category.

The next set of edits is for the cards expanded; that is, the view the users reach after clicking the Read More button. This set of edits is also divided into four sections: Above the post, the title, post-end info, and the biography. Let's start with the edits above the post. According to our content guide, we need to start with the name of the author, followed by the date and clearly defined category. The first edit we make is for the author name, and we use a built-in data structure to do this. In the previous chapters, we have used Jekyll collections and briefly touched on `site.data` variables. To store the author information that we need to use again in the biography, let's take advantage of centralized data storage through `site.data` here. First, we need to create the data files. Create a folder _data and within the folder, a file `authors.yml`. The contents of this file are shown here.

```
# Author details
robert_rawlins:
    name: Robert Rawlins
    img_path: http://welcomehomerealty.ca/wp-content/uploads/2015/07/thumbnail-face-study.
    jpg
    bio: Testing a biography
robin_geall:
    name: Robin Geall
    img_path: https://greensealblog.files.wordpress.com/2013/07/face-thumbnail.jpg
    bio: New biography
```

In this data file, we have stored some basic information about each of the authors and provided a reference name that can be called in the posts. Now we need to show this information in the posts. All the code to make the required edits is present in _layouts/post.html and the snippet in bold here shows the code that needs to be added:

```
<div class="post-section mdl-color--white mdl-shadow--4dp content mdl-color-text--grey-800
mdl-cell mdl-cell--8-col">

<!-- Assigning the author variable to the author defined by a post in its front matter. This
tells Jekyll to pull the info associated with that particular author from authors.yml file -->

    {% assign author = site.data.authors[page.author] %}

<!--Now that we have access to info about that particular author, display his name-->
    <span>
```

```
<!-- Personal Info -->
<i class="fa fa-pencil-square-o"></i> Written by {{ author.name }}
</span>
```

This only does part of the job. After adding this code, we allow each post to have access to the data file, but now we actually need to call one of the authors defined in the authors.yml file from the YAML front matter of a post. Here's what the front matter looks like when we want to reference an author.

```
---
layout: post
title:   "Jekyll Material Design Lite"
date:    2015-08-11 09:34:20
categories: mdl
author: robert_rawlins
---
```

That last line is the reference call. With this, the post will display the name of the author on top. The next element to be changed is the date, and this is also the location where we state the category of the card. We just need to edit the Liquid tags that are already present in the <div> to make it simpler, as follows:

```
<div class="mdl-color-text--grey-500">
{{ page.date | date: "%b %-d, %Y" }}
<i class="fa fa-commenting-o"></i>
<strong>{% for cat in page.categories %} {{ cat }} {% endfor %} </strong>
</div>
```

Those are all the tags we need, as there is no need for the remainder of the if tags and so on. Now to properly state the category, we need to edit it as well. Here's the edited version.

```
---
layout: post
title:   "Jekyll Material Design Lite"
date:    2015-08-11 09:34:20
categories: "Informed consent"
author: robert_rawlins
---
```

The quotation marks actually preserve the formatting of the category, and this is what we would need to keep the space between the words "informed" and "consent." The change show in bold allows the category to show after the date on the top of the blog post. The next edit is for the titles. According to our content guide, the cards should have Mallard-style titles, but the cards also cannot display lengthy titles due to limited space. One way to tackle this problem is to create two titles: one that would show on the home page and the second that would be displayed in the expanded view. To do this, we use a custom YAML variable help_title, which will represent the shortened title to be displayed on the home page. The implementation is actually very straightforward: We use a control loop on index.html as shown here.

```
<h4 align="center" style="color:rgb(108, 122, 137)"> <i class="fa fa-caret-square-o-
right"></i>
{% if post.help_title %}
    {{ post.help_title }}
{% else %}
```

```
    {{ post.title }}
{% endif %}
</h4>
```

This if loop ensures that as long as a post has a help_title, the card will display that on the home page; if it doesn't, the card will display the original title in YAML. So how does it look when implemented for a post? See the front matter shown here.

```
---
layout: post
title:  "Jekyll Material Design Lite"
help_title: "Not Mallard"
date:    2015-08-11 09:34:20
categories: "Informed consent"
author: robert_rawlins
---
```

From each of the cards, we also need to remove the comments feature. The content for these cards is supposed to be written by experts, so gathering comments from readers might add confusion to the content being discussed earlier. We discuss another way to gather feedback later on in this chapter. Here's what the post layout file (post.html) looks like after the author name edits and the removal of comments.

```
        <!-- Personal Info -->
        <i class="fa fa-pencil-square-o"></i> Written by {{ author.name }}
    </span>

    <div class="mdl-color-text--grey-500">
    {{ page.date | date: "%b %-d, %Y" }}
    <i class="fa fa-commenting-o"></i>
    <strong>{% for cat in page.categories %} {{ cat }} {% endfor %} </strong>
    </div>

    <h3> <i class="fa fa-bookmark"></i> {{ page.title }} </h3>

    <article class="post-content">
      <p>{{ content }}</p>
    </article>

    </div>
  </div>
</main>
```

With this, the comments have been removed from the post layout. The next set of edits are at the end of the post, after the {{ content }} and before the end of the article. There are two elements we need to add: reference(s) related to this card and the author biography. Let's get started with the posts layout where we need to add more files.

```
<p>{{ content }}</p>
{% include further_info.html %}
{% include author_bio.html %}
</article>
```

The further_info.html file contains the source or references for the information presented in the card along with the tags that link to similar information. Let's start with the source of the card, which can be added as a custom variable to the front matter.

```
---
layout: post
title:  "Jekyll Material Design Lite"
help_title: "Not Mallard"
date:    2015-08-11 09:34:20
categories: "Informed consent"
author: robert_rawlins
source: http://taylordavidson.com/2014/cards
tags: patient
---
```

Now to use this source variable in the post itself, we can put the code into the further_info.html file as follows:

```
<i class="fa fa-hashtag"></i> Source of this card: <a href="{{ page.source }}">Link</a> <br>
```

That single line can put the source from YAML at the end of the card. Let's move on to tags. We need to create a simple mechanism to list the cards associated with a tag on an archive page. Let's say your task is to count all the windows each building in the local downtown area has. How would you approach this? One way to solve this problem is to first make a list of all the buildings in the local downtown area. You could then go through each building in the list and count the windows it has. What did you really do there? Programmatically, you used a for loop that makes a list of all the buildings and then another for loop to count the windows in each individual building. The inner for loop ensures that you can count all the windows for each building, and the outer loop ensures you count all the buildings. That's the concept of a nested loop that we need to use for the tags page.

The rationale in this code is to create a for loop to list all the tags, then set a variable equal to the first tag, loop through all the posts to find the posts associated with that tag, and list those posts along with that first tag. After that, the for loop repeats, moving to the next tag, and now this new tag is set to the same variable as before. We loop through all the posts associated with that tag, and then list out those posts and this second tag. This same nested loop repeats through all of the tags, first listing the tag and then listing the associated posts with that tag. Create a new file, tag.md, and let's see this logic in action.

```
---
layout: page
title: Card Archive
permalink: /tag/
---
```

```
The posts associated with each tag are shown below:
```

```
<!-- The outer for-loop, this one loops through all the available tags -->
{% for tag in site.tags %}
```

```
<!-- The first tag in the whole series of tags is assigned to the variable t and the tag
assigned to it changes each time the for loop goes through to the next one. -->
```

```
{% assign t = tag | first %}
{% assign posts = tag | last %}
```

`<i class="fa fa-tags"></i> <strong> {{ t }} </strong>` **`<!-- Display the current tag -->`**

`<ul>`

`<!-- Time to loop through all the posts to see if they contain the current tag -->`

`{% for post in posts %}`

`<!-- List the posts if they contain the tag currently defined by the variable t. After looping, a new tag will be assigned to the variable t and then we will list the posts associated with that new tag -->`

```
  {% if post.tags contains t %}
  <li>
    <a href="{{ post.url }}">{{ post.title }}</a>
    <span class="date">{{ post.date | date: "%B %-d, %Y" }}</span>
  </li>
  {% endif %}
```

`{% endfor %}`

`</ul>`

`{% endfor %}`

Now that the tags file has been built, let's go to the `further_info.html` and finish it up. The completed file looks like this.

`<i class="fa fa-hashtag"></i> Source of this card: <a href="{{ page.source }}">Link</a> <br>`

`<i class="fa fa-tag"></i> Related tags:`

```
{% for tag in page.tags %}
<a href='/tag/'>{{tag}}</a>
{% endfor %}
```

This lists out all the tags associated with the card, and this snippet is present in the `further_info.html` file, which renders the source and the tags after the content has been displayed. This file and the tag's nested loop takes care of the external sources and the tags for similar cards. To use multiple tags in one card, type the tags space separated shown here.

`tags: Patient Testing`

The next feature to implement is the biography. Recall that earlier in this chapter, we created a data file called `authors.yml` that has metadata about the authors saved as YAML entries. One of those elements is a short line biography and an image that goes along with it. We use the `site.data` technique again to draw that information out and display it at the bottom of the page through the `author_bio.html` file. The code to do this is actually very straightforward and similar to the last time we used `site.data`, however, the only difference here is that we are using a table tag to contain the biography.

```
<hr /> <!-- Start with a horizontal rule to separate this from the rest of the card -->

<table>
      {% assign author = site.data.authors[page.author] %}

<!-- Each entry in the table is a row with the tr tag -->
    <tr>
        <td valign="top" style="padding-right: 1em;">
        <img src="{{ author.img_path }}" /></td> <!-- Display the image first -->
        <td valign="middle"> <strong> {{ author.name }}:</strong></td> <!-- The author name
-->
        <td valign="middle"> {{ author.bio }} </td> <!-- Finally, a short biography -->
    </tr>
</table>
```

This code should be copied into a new file and saved as _includes/author_bio.html, and this file allows Jekyll to pull a picture and the biography associated with the author from the data file. This concludes another set of edits; so far, we have edited how the cards are displayed on the home page, the theme coloring itself, and finally how the card appears in the expanded view according to our guidelines. The last set of edits remaining deal with live updates on topics relevant to patients, collecting feedback, and finally a few minor sidebar edits.

Providing live updates on issues is crucial for a patient-care information platform. To allow for easy live updates, we will be using a third-party tool called Storify. Essentially, Storify allows you to drag and drop events, news, tweets, and much more directly from social media using their search function; add formatting within the story editor; and create a story. This story you just created contains elements pulled directly from sources across the Web and social platforms, all without the need for any coding or formatting knowledge. In the end, the story that you created can be shared or embedded within a blog, and this is what we will be using for live updates.

Once a story has been published, you can always keep adding new updates from information-rich sources such as Twitter or news media social channels. This is a very powerful feature, as there is no coding knowledge required and most of the process is just searching for accurate information to drag and drop onto the story editor. After that, you can publish your story that contains the history of the issue at hand and the current status. You can keep updating that story as you discover new information. Before we start using Storify, though, we have to prepare this web site to organize that information properly. This will allow us to do updates periodically without worrying about old stories getting lost and new ones not being shown appropriately. We use the site.data storage to save the links to stories. Let's start by creating a _data/previous.yml file, the contents of which are shown here.

```
- name: Snowstorm
  link: http://welcomehomerealty.ca/wp-content/uploads/2015/07/thumbnail-face-study.jpg

- name: Forest fire
  link: http://welcomehomerealty.ca/wp-content/uploads/2015/07/thumbnail-face-study.jpg

- name: Tsunami
  link: http://welcomehomerealty.ca/wp-content/uploads/2015/07/thumbnail-face-study.jpg

- name: Lava
  link: http://welcomehomerealty.ca/wp-content/uploads/2015/07/thumbnail-face-study.jpg
```

All the data here is also recorded in YAML format, which makes it easier for Jekyll to access the information. We can separate the current reporting from the past stories by using a global variable to denote the current crisis and move all the previous working information as an entry into the previous.yml file. This will neatly separate the two stories and streamline the organization. Let's define the current variable as current_crisis; to use it, we need to add it to the _config.yml file as follows:

```
# Live story feed
current_crisis: Finishing chapter 12
```

Now that we have this global variable, we can use it along with site.data to render the current reporting events. We have to display the live updates on a new page. Create a file named updates.md; the contents of this file are explained here.

```
---
layout: page
Title: Live Updates
---

<!-- First, link to the current updates from the global variable -->
### **Current Updates** - {{ site.current_crisis }} - [Live reporting](http://jekyll-mini-blog.github.io/)

--- <!-- Horizontal rule to separate the current from previous -->

### **Previous updates:**

<!-- List the previous updates using a for-loop, taking information from previous.yml -->

<ul>
{% for disease in site.data.previous %}
  <li>
    {{ disease.name }} - {{ disease.link }}
    </a>
  </li>
{% endfor %}
</ul>
```

▨ **Note** Rendering the elements from the previous.yml file can be done in several ways. Inside the for loop, any type of formatting can be applied to how the final elements are rendered on the site. These elements can be edited either using Markdown or plain HTML. The link property can be hyperlinked to reach the story quickly, or the title can be displayed in bold to place emphasis on the name, if necessary.

The code here isn't much different from the past times we have used site.data based storage. First, we report on the current crisis, followed by a list of the previous updates. We obtain the data for the previous updates from the _data/previous.yml file and list it out using the for loop. Let's finally look at the tool that we will be using for making the stories. Storify is straightforward to use. After creating an account and logging in, click New Story and we will do a short walkthrough of how to use it. Storify has an incredible story editor where you can search for rich media across the Internet to drag and drop into your story, shown in

Figure 12-20. The editor is made from two panes: the story pane, which dictates the overall flow of the story and the search pane that allows you to search for new media across the Internet. You can even place custom embeds within the story if you want. For most other events, you can simply search for media to be used straight from the source.

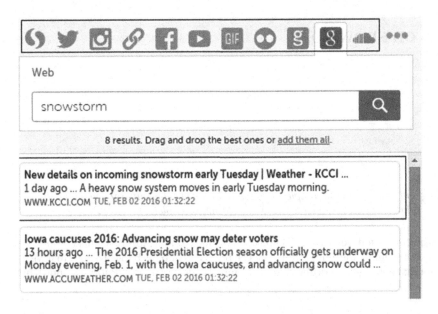

Figure 12-20. *Search pane from Storify's story edior. The top bar allows you to select which social media you want to search, and then you can simply drag and drop any of the results onto the story pane to the left.*

The story pane is shown in Figure 12-21.

Figure 12-21. *The story pane in Storify. The headline and description provide you with some organization to start reporting on the current events. Even within the story, you can include text boxes that will fill up or comment on any included media. This allows you to include rich media and add your own organization scheme to the reporting.*

This story pane contains the pieces of the story from the search pane. The end result is shown in Figure 12-22.

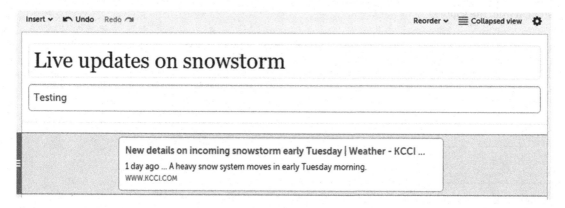

Figure 12-22. *The heading and description are completed, followed by a news element dropped on the story pane from a Google search. Addition of more elements in a similar fashion completes the story.*

Once the story has been completed, you can click Publish on the top bar and Storify will make your story publicly available. Here, we obtain the embed code that can be pasted into the body of a page that will serve as the live updates for that particular reporting story. The embed code and finalized story are shown in Figure 12-23.

Live updates on snowstorm

Testing

by 👤 Vikram Dhillon   a few seconds ago

Figure 12-23. *Finalized version of a story on Storify. The toolbar on the top provides some shortcuts and one of them is the Embed button, which provides us with the embed code. The Edit button also comes in handy, particularly if we need to update the reporting frequently.*

In the last stretch of edits, the only feature left to implement is a way of gathering feedback from users. We use a form to gather feedback from users, which is a classic method of collecting feedback. For this, we do not make a form on Jekyll, but instead use a third-party service called Typeform. In Typeform, you can create beautiful forms that can be served as an entire page of their own.

To use the service, you can create an account at http://www.typeform.com/ and get started. Click Create a new typeform to start making your own form, as shown in Figure 12-24. This takes you through a wizard with a few steps that help you Build ➤ Design ➤ Configure ➤ Distribute. In brief, you first pick the type of form to build, and you are given several options as templates to be used. You also write all the questions you want to ask here in this step. In the next step, you design the form with different styles or colors as needed. You can also import themes from ThemeKit if you want, and then your form is almost ready to be deployed. We won't do a full walkthrough, but instead cover the key features.

Figure 12-24. *Creating a new typeform. This allows you to start the process of building and designing the form.*

The distribute phase is shown in Figure 12-25. It gives you a few options, but only the last one is important.

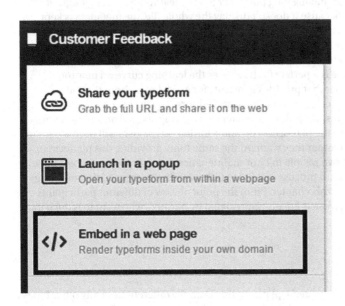

Figure 12-25. *Obtaining the embed code from Typeform. This option gives us two further choices: Embed in a web page or Deploy as a separate page. This option allows us to keep feedback collection separate from everything else.*

After clicking Embed in a web page, we have two choices: Embed within a page or deploy as a single-page application. We use the second option in this project. After clicking the option, you will see the screen shown in Figure 12-26. Click Get the code and paste the result in a new file, `survey.html`, which will deploy the survey as a single-page application.

Full page code

Make this typeform a page on your website. Make it your whole website, even.

 On all screens

Your typeform gets loaded in an iframe, taking up the entire window area. (Basically, the same as it looks on your domain.typeform.com.)

Figure 12-26. Full page embed code from Typeform. This allows us to deploy the survey as a single-page application.

Before we conclude this chapter, a word is in order about where Prose fits in this platform and how to best use it in the context of deploying this platform. In the end, for developers, what matters greatly is the ability to fix bugs and build features fast. For quick edits when you are away from a computer that has Git on it, Prose would undoubtedly work better than GitHub's native editor. Additionally, you can even switch entirely to Prose for creating new content and making blog posts. For adding features and fixing bugs, Prose might not be the most effective way; simply because it doesn't display the whole file, the metadata is kept away from the file. It is still accessible, however, and at this point it is up to the preference of the developer.

On the other hand, if you focus on the content creators, this entire point of view shifts away. For content creators, the main focus is the ability to prepare the information that will be shared through this platform in a distraction-free manner. To do that, Prose is a perfect fit: It reduces the learning curve on new tools to be used, and it even has a formatting toolbar that provides shortcuts for Markdown. From that side of development, Prose is a perfect fit for content creators, reviewers, and editors. The user access control options allow you to fine-tune the roles and responsibilities even more. Thinking about who will be using this platform, let's return to Figure 12-1. Once the platform is up and running, developers will have access to it through GitHub and they can edit in any manner they want. At the same time, providing this platform to an organization that might only have one or two people in IT or maintenance, using Prose would be a huge benefit. It would allow them to create a standard process and help guides within the organization on using Prose, much like the walkthrough provided in this chapter. From the point of view of different participants in this project, Prose is only an add-on, but its use is greatly appreciated by partners who want to reduce the technical learning curve and maintenance.

Summary

We covered a lot of ground in this chapter and created a platform that is totally different from any other blogs that we have worked on thus far. We started by getting familiar with the idea of cards and how the cards UI is suitable for quick glance information and perfect for mobile. We used Semantic UI and played with a few different types of cards that we later implemented in the theme. After discussing cards, we started to talk about why we need to control the type of content that goes in this blog. The content guide allows us to set some rules that will make the way our platform delivers information much more effective. We went through a set of rules made from Mallard and a guide from 18-F. Once we had the content guide prepared, we did a thorough walk-through of `prose.io` and talked about why using it would make sense in such a platform.

After going through Prose, we started editing the theme to confine it to the standards described in our earlier content guide. We went through editing how the cards appear on the home page, how they look in the expanded view, and finally collecting feedback and providing live updates. Open Health Care is only just getting started. Platforms like this one will become mature and eventually be deployed as small packages or blogs to provide fast, free, and factual information. Exciting times are ahead, aren't they?

Further Reading

1. **Google Cards UI:** https://www.google.com/design/spec/components/cards.html

2. **Patterns of Cards UI design:** https://speakerdeck.com/christse/patterns-of-card-ui-design

3. **Using cards in web design:** http://www.sitepoint.com/card-tricks-using-cards-in-web-design-layouts/

4. **Getting started with Google Material Design:** http://www.getmdl.io/started/

5. **Introduction to Mallard:** https://en.flossmanuals.net/_booki/introduction-to-mallard/introduction-to-mallard.pdf

6. **About Prose:** http://prose.io/#about

7. **Typeform help guides:** http://helpcenter.typeform.com/hc/en-us

8. **Digital storytelling with Storify:** https://storify.com/craignewman/tips-for-using-storify-in-you-reporting

CHAPTER 13

■ ■ ■

Open Jekyll?

We shall not cease from exploration and the end of all our exploring will be to arrive where we started and know the place for the first time.

—T. S. Eliot

Interchangeable parts were, in a sense, the beginning of the modern machine era. The idea that one part can replace another one while preserving the overall structure is very powerful, and thoroughly embodied in Jekyll. Our projects so far have substituted the default components of a theme with new parts, and more precisely, web technologies that served as perfect replacements. One interchangeable part freely replaced another, without any fundamental changes to Jekyll, and we obtained a new functionality or feature. What happens, though, when you open the hood and look inside? In this chapter, we are going to open Jekyll, look inside, and extend the functionalities that it offers. We will be customizing the feature set that Jekyll offers by adding plug-ins. We start by discussing the role Ruby plays in the making of Jekyll and how to install Ruby offline for your own use. We play with it briefly and use it to create a skeleton Jekyll project. In this chapter, we use a different code-hosting platform called Bitbucket to host the code and show that the implementation of Git across various platforms remains the same. We also go through the workflow of continuous integration and compiling Jekyll in the cloud to include the plug-ins. After the compilation, we discuss the concept of secure keys and how to automate the build process using Codeship to push the code to Bitbucket and Rake, which is a build tool for Ruby. We are not only opening Jekyll to look inside, but also opening a design studio using a Jekyll theme and the plug-ins as add-ons for the various tasks a design studio needs to accomplish.

We have integrated a lot of technologies with Jekyll thus far in the book, but to look deeper, we have to start classifying the integrations into different types. Broadly speaking, there are general two categories: The first one is the overlay assets layer. This layer is defined by integrations that are overlaid on an existing Jekyll skeleton. Most of these web technologies are imported into the theme and served on top of an already existing page, so they only load up when the user reaches the appropriate location on the web site. They are also mostly compatible with GitHub Pages. It is important to remember that the components of this layer add functionality to an existing Jekyll theme, or by replacing an existing feature with a better one. This layer contains all the integrations that we have implemented in previous projects. One distinguishing characteristic of the integrations belonging to this layer is that all of them have been included in the projects using the {% include integration.html %} snippet.

The second layer is what we discuss in this chapter: the shared features layer. This layer is very different from the last one, as it is more fundamental and almost invisible. We only hear from this layer when we run into trouble and get an error message from GitHub. This layer is defined by core functionality that Jekyll provides us, features such as a defined folder structure, conventions for folder and file naming, configuration files, custom data source, and layouts. We can use these features right out of the box (without importing

© Vikram Dhillon 2016

V. Dhillon, *Creating Blogs with Jekyll*, DOI 10.1007/978-1-4842-1464-0_13

third-party tools) and most of the work that we have done either edits or adds to the features offered by this layer. A graphical representation of these two layers is provided in Figure 13-1. This intrinsic layer remains hidden for several reasons.

- **Simplicity:** To focus on learning the basis of Jekyll, we have the integrations limited to the assets layer. These integrations are overlaid on a page after it gets compiled by Jekyll, when a user accesses it.

- **Limited editing:** We limited editing the configuration files to `config.yml` and the `_include` directory. As a result, we never had a need to look any deeper.

- **Better tools:** More often than not, building a plug-in or an add-on that we can then use as an asset within the theme would not be as functional as a third-party tool customized for a particular job with the appropriate features.

- **GitHub Pages:** Hosting on GitHub also limited our opportunities. We had to make sure that all the integrations were compatible with Jekyll. As a result, we never looked into the advanced features available within Jekyll.

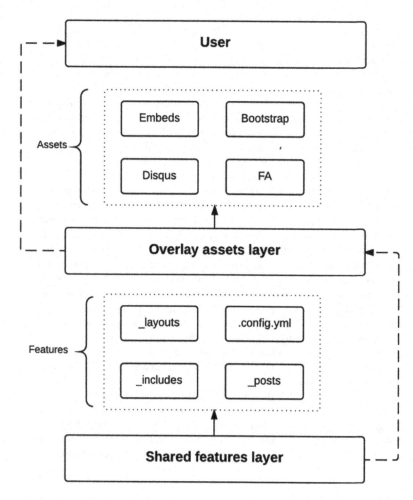

Figure 13-1. *This flowchart shows the connection between the layers and the components that each of them contain*

Our main focus from the shared assets layer is the use of plug-ins to provide additional functionality. We will talk about that in depth shortly, but first, let's focus on the last point just mentioned: Why can't we use custom plug-ins freely with GitHub? The main reason is in how Jekyll is used on the GitHub Pages server. Recall that all Jekyll-based sites are compiled by GitHub Pages, which in turn is powered by Jekyll and uses the command `jekyll build` to compile your blog and layouts into a static web site that can be served over the Internet.

However, all Pages sites are generated using the `--safe` option to disable custom plug-ins for security reasons. Unfortunately, this means your plug-ins won't be working on the sites compiled by GitHub Pages. This is mostly a security concern: A malicious user can make a plug-in to attack the GitHub server and cause problems. To avoid this problem altogether, no plug-ins are allowed on GitHub Pages. To bypass this limitation, you have to compile your blog locally, and then use GitHub Pages only as a web server to serve your static pages to users. In such a scenario, you would have to push your compiled static files to the GitHub repository, instead of your Jekyll source files. In an earlier chapter, we discussed the file structure of Jekyll, and there is one folder that has not received much attention because it had been mostly invisible: the `_site` folder. This folder is the location where your site will be saved after it has been locally compiled. So far, we have just relied on GitHub Pages to compile and present the site, but in this chapter, we actually do the compilation locally and go through how to install Jekyll on Windows.

GitHub actually does support a few simple plug-ins that can be enabled in `_config.yml` by listing them as Ruby gems, using `gem ['jekyll-feed']`. These add-ons offer functionality that extends core Jekyll features to comply with web standards or just for fun. The following is a list of the plug-ins supported by GitHub Pages.

- **Jemoji:** Provides support for emojis to be used within Jekyll posts and pages.

- **Jekyll-mentions:** Provides support for hyperlinking @ mentions within Jekyll posts and pages.

- **Jekyll-redirect-from:** Provides support for redirecting visitors to an updated URL when post or page file names change.

- **Jekyll-sitemap:** Provides a standards-compliant site map to your GitHub Pages site.

- **Jekyll-feed:** Provides an Atom Feed to your GitHub Pages site.

There is a lot of information in Figure 13-1, but let's look go through it carefully. The order of complexity starts from the top down as we move away from what the user sees and toward what the developer sees. In the end, the user browses the compiled site. Underneath the site are all the assets that we included; these are the third-party tools that we included in our Jekyll projects. This comprises the overlay asset layer. This layer is powered by Jekyll; after all, without Jekyll's include feature, there wouldn't be anything to include and display. Now we are going at the lowest level, the developer layer. The shared features layer contains the features that Jekyll offers that are accessible to any theme built on top of it. This layer contains all the accessible configuration that we can edit, such as the config file and the layouts that we can build to organize information. Looking at the flowchart from the bottom up, we can see that the shared features power the assets that power the web site that gets served to the user.

Now Open: Jekyll Design Studio

This project is different from the ones we have done in another way: The blog here is not central to the studio. It is only a small component, provided with the design studio to help build a brand. The web site will serve as a showcase of the web development capabilities (specializing in Jekyll) that our studio has, and it will also have a portal where users can purchase specific web design services. Being a design studio, the web site will have a number of requirements to be completely functional and promote the materials or services that we are creating. We would also need a method of providing the clients with the finished product or web sites.

Let's go over the features that we implement in this design studio. Not all of them will make sense right away, but their purpose will become clear as we move along.

- A parallel advertising platform like **Fiverr** where you can sell basic design services, in addition to your own web site. This will not only help you with initial advertisement, but also in lead generation and converting more customers to long-term users.

- A shopping cart like **Snipcart** to buy services straight from your studio. This will be larger or more comprehensive services as compared to Fiverr. Having the cart on your own web site also allows you to hire personnel for a fee who have expertise in a particular area. For example, you can charge $100 to make an expert available who can optimize SEO.

- Optimizing your customer channels such as mailing lists for sales through **Gumroad**, which allows you to accept preorders for a product before it is released, and create subscriptions if you have a stream of content (i.e., a book being released chapter-by-chapter).

- Creating video content for digital marketing and hosting it on **YouTube** and **Wistia**, where you can use annotations and cards to drive customer call-for-action. You can provide some educational resources to help your clients understand the unique web technologies that you offer and how they take advantage of Jekyll. These instructional videos can help you convert more visitors into customers by providing the content in a freemium model.

- Building on the last feature, you can take a very similar approach to raise donations and create a fundraiser for a nonprofit or a community project. **YouTube** offers a very simple and easy-to-use card for donations that can be added to your videos with just a few clicks.

- Product prototyping and functional demos through **InVision**, which allows designers to create mockups with advanced animations and walkthroughs. Most modern design studios have to adopt InVision because there simply isn't a better alternative to create and share prototypes.

- Creating live embeds by using **embed.ly** for InVision and sharing the live previews on social platforms like Twitter. Additionally, embed the live previews for demos on your own web site.

- Provide customer support through live chat with **HipChat**, an absolutely amazing tool for workspace collaboration, where you can give guest access with a link to your clients so that they can come to the chat room for live customer support or presales chat.

- Creating password-protected live demos of web sites or web components that customers might want, powered by Jekyll. This will be done through a basic auth plug-in provided by **Aerobatic,** the first implementation of an add-on for our design studio.

- Implementing the ability to create and add custom plug-ins, some of which might help the web site, whereas others will help showcase unique features that only our design studio has created and customers can license.

- Creating a workflow to compile Jekyll if your customers want a custom implementation and automate this process so that the customer doesn't have to touch the back end. The more technical and back-end components that your design studio takes away, the higher your sales will be, because most of your customers are not developers, nor have they read this book. In general, customers only want to deal with the front end and web site development, so they want solutions that make the back end painless, which is a huge advantage of Jekyll.

- Creating a deployment pipeline that relies on continuous integration through **Codeship**, compiling your design studio web site each time a new change is made to ensure that any new changes to the overall web site incorporate all the plug-ins. This is not just limited to the design studio, but can also be used for any custom web sites that you make for your client. Automating the compilation of Jekyll can become one step of the pipeline that eventually deploys the web site to a remote location.

■ **Tip** What do plug-ins and all this talk about continuous integration have in common? What is continuous integration to begin with? To enable plug-ins, you have to compile Jekyll using the command `jekyll build`, and this is assumed to be done locally. However, in this chapter, we want to focus on doing this in the cloud using something called build tools that are designed to compile code when it has specific supporting files that the build tool can recognize. In doing so, the build tool can be directed to take information from a particular source, compile it, and then place the result back in the same location. We want to automate this process for every commit that is made such that anytime we make a change, the whole web site is up-to-date with it. Where will something like this matter? Imagine adding an archive plug-in. If you make a new post on your blog, you want the commit that pushes the new post to also rebuild the archive. This process of rebuilding automatically and then placing your code in the right location securely is called continuous integration. As the name implies, it allows us to continuously integrate new features in the production web sites.

We return to the design studio shortly after setting up the background and all the necessary components for it. As seen earlier, there is a long list of them, but we start locally with a bare-bones project to help break down the advanced concepts into simpler applicable tasks. To that end, we begin with installations, Ruby first and Jekyll later on. After Ruby has been installed, we briefly explore the language and provide some simple examples to play with. Then, we slowly ease into advanced concepts such as package management, gems, and how to go about installing Jekyll on Windows and other platforms (for Linux and OS X, the installation is far easier). Finally, we play with Jekyll 3.0 and create a skeleton project that we can use to learn advanced concepts such as compilation in the cloud.

A Ruby from Japan

In the mid-1990s, Yukihiro Matsumoto released a programming language that would later become the foundation for a revolution in the Internet era. Although his initial intentions were very down to earth, Matsumoto (also known as Matz) set out to design a language that emphasized human needs over those of the computer, which is why Ruby is so easy to pick up. He wanted to spend his time creating Ruby such that it would encourage programmer productivity and fun.

Ruby is a dynamically typed, object-oriented programming language. The first property implies that in Ruby, variables don't need to be defined by types; the compiler can figure out what those types are, depending on how the variables have been assigned. The second property is unique to Ruby, as every value in Ruby is an object. These two properties are found in many modern programming languages, but their application to the language as a whole and extension to frameworks built on top of the language makes Ruby very powerful. Following a few stable releases of Ruby, David Heinemeier Hansson created a framework called Ruby on Rails, which became the backbone for GitHub and many other modern web companies. Let's start installing Ruby. On OS X, Ruby is included by default. Many people on OS X use Homebrew as a package manager. It is really easy to get a newer version of Ruby using Homebrew.

```
$ brew install ruby
```

On Linux, you can install Ruby by going to your package manager and finding the appropriate packages. On Ubuntu, this can be done with:

```
$ sudo apt-get install ruby-full
```

This installs an older but stable version of Ruby available from the sources. On Windows, the situation becomes a little more complicated. There is no package management and the installers don't always work reliably. To make Ruby easy to install, we first install a package management system for Windows called Chocolatey. The install process is easy: Open an administrative `cmd.exe` command prompt and type the following command:

```
@powershell -NoProfile -ExecutionPolicy Bypass -Command "iex ((new-object net.webclient).
DownloadString('https://chocolatey.org/install.ps1'))" && SET PATH=%PATH%;%ALLUSERSPROFILE%\
chocolatey\bin
```

This installation command has been made available from Chocolatey home page (`https://chocolatey.org/`) and it essentially calls for powershell to download an installer and then install the package manager. After typing that command, you should start to see output similar to this:

```
C:\WINDOWS\system32>@powershell -NoProfile -ExecutionPolicy Bypass -Command
"iex ((new-object net.webclient).DownloadString('https://chocolatey.org/install.ps1'))" &&
SET PATH=%PATH%;%ALLUSERSPROFILE%\chocolatey\bin


Mode            LastWriteTime         Length Name
----            -------------         ------ ----
d-----          2/18/2016   2:33 AM   chocInstall
Downloading https://packages.chocolatey.org/chocolatey.0.9.9.11.nupkg to
```

... [snipped output] ...

```
7-Zip (A) 9.20  Copyright (c) 1999-2010 Igor Pavlov  2010-11-18

Processing archive: C:\Users\Vikram\AppData\Local\Temp\chocolatey\chocInstall\chocolatey.zip
```

A visual of the output shown after the command executes is provided in Figure 13-2.

```
Administrator: Command Prompt
Microsoft Windows [Version 10.0.10586]
(c) 2015 Microsoft Corporation. All rights reserved.

C:\WINDOWS\system32>@powershell -NoProfile -ExecutionPolicy Bypass -Command "iex ((new-object net.webclient).DownloadString('https://chocolatey.org/insta
ET PATH=%PATH%;%ALLUSERSPROFILE%\chocolatey\bin

Mode            LastWriteTime         Length Name
----            -------------         ------ ----
d-----     2/18/2016   2:33 AM               chocInstall
Downloading https://packages.chocolatey.org/chocolatey.0.9.9.11.nupkg to C:\Users\Vikram\AppData\Local\Temp\chocolatey\chocInstall\chocolatey.zip
Download 7Zip commandline tool
Downloading https://chocolatey.org/7za.exe to C:\Users\Vikram\AppData\Local\Temp\chocolatey\chocInstall\7za.exe
Extracting C:\Users\Vikram\AppData\Local\Temp\chocolatey\chocInstall\chocolatey.zip to C:\Users\Vikram\AppData\Local\Temp\chocolatey\chocInstall...

7-Zip (A) 9.20 Copyright (c) 1999-2010 Igor Pavlov  2010-11-18

Processing archive: C:\Users\Vikram\AppData\Local\Temp\chocolatey\chocInstall\chocolatey.zip

Extracting  _rels\.rels
Extracting  chocolatey.nuspec
Extracting  tools\chocolateyInstall.ps1
Extracting  tools\chocolateysetup.psm1
Extracting  tools\init.ps1
Extracting  tools\chocolateyInstall\choco.exe
```

Figure 13-2. The command we provided first downloads the appropriate package manager binary file. It then seems to extract it using 7-zip and finally after all the files are extracted, they get copied to an executable location and added to the PATH variable so that they are accessible again through an administrative command prompt.

The one problem with Chocolatey after installing it is that to access the package manager and install new packages, you have to close the command prompt window and then open another administrative command prompt, a simple, but slightly inconvenient task. After opening a second command prompt, your package manager should be ready and this can be observed as follows:

```
C:\WINDOWS\system32>choco -v
0.9.9.11
```

This command prompts Chocolatey to display the version currently installed. Now let's move on to installing Ruby. The idea here is simple: A package manager will go grab the binary for a package that you specify and install it on your computer. This process is entirely automated and very painless.

```
C:\WINDOWS\system32>choco install ruby -y
Installing the following packages:
ruby
By installing you accept licenses for the packages.
ruby v2.2.3
 Get-BinRoot is going to be deprecated by v1. Many packages no longer require it since the
folders no longer have versions on them.
 Downloading ruby 64 bit
    from 'http://dl.bintray.com/oneclick/rubyinstaller/rubyinstaller-2.2.3-x64.exe?direct'
 Installing ruby...
 ruby has been installed.
 Adding 'C:\tools\ruby22\bin' to the local path
The install of ruby was successful.

Chocolatey installed 1/1 package(s). 0 package(s) failed.
 See the log for details (C:\ProgramData\chocolatey\logs\chocolatey.log).
```

Notice how simple that was? Package managers are absolutely amazing and they make life easier, another reason why they are a part of every major Linux distribution. Let's check if we can access Ruby right now.

```
C:\WINDOWS\system32>ruby -v
ruby 2.2.3p173 (2015-08-18 revision 51636) [x64-mingw32]
```

The same command as before verifies that a 64-bit version of Ruby has been installed with the mingw environment for Windows. To access Ruby, you can go to the Start menu and in the list of programs, you should see a new folder for Ruby. For our install, this folder is called `Ruby 2.2.3p173-x64`, shown in Figure 13-3.

Figure 13-3. The Ruby folder present in the Start menu following successful installation by Chocolatey. Notice the Ruby-enabled command prompt and the additional option to use Interactive Ruby.

The installation process was fairly painless, but we won't be using this console for Ruby just yet. This is not a limited programming environment and it doesn't make for a convenient playground to test Ruby. Instead, we use an online interpreter called repl.it that has a very clean environment to run code and obtain output. The web interface is available at `https://repl.it/languages/ruby`.

The interface is split into two components: The left pane is for writing the code that will get executed and the right side displays the output. The right pane is like an in-browser console, as it displays output and also acts as the input interface if your program asks the user for input. A natural question arises at this point: Why are we covering Ruby? There are entire books written on the fundamental principles, design, and programming concepts in Ruby. Our overview only spans the next few pages, so we can cover only a few essential concepts. The idea here is that most programming languages have an inherent structure that we can use to learn them systematically. Our overview illustrates how to learn Ruby in a particular format and make it easier for readers to jump into learning Ruby, should they decide to do it on their own. There are six main components to the system that we talked about.

- **Variables and assignment:** Learn about assigning variables and the primitives available in the language.

- **Hello world:** Learn about the standard input and output syntax along with the structure of a simple program in the language.

- **Control flow:** Learn how to control the way a user interacts with the program and how the program can respond to inputs by the user. Involves the use of if–then–else type statements.

- **Iteration:** Learn about the next level of control flow for programmatic logic using iterators. This involves the use of `for` and `while` loops in conjunction with if–then–else logic.

- **Data structures:** Learn about the composite data structures that are available in the language built on the primitives. This involves the use of arrays, hashes, and so on.

- **Advanced concepts:** Finally, the last stretch of learning a new programming language is the advanced concepts that cover objected-oriented development. After all, in Ruby, everything is an object, so this last component is probably as extensive as the other five combined. Beyond object orientation, there are advanced features available in Ruby such as package management that we discuss later in this chapter.

Playing with Ruby

Let's go through some of the components that we mentioned earlier. We will be running all this code online in the repl.it editor mentioned previously. Running the code is as simple as clicking Run, as shown in Figure 13-4.

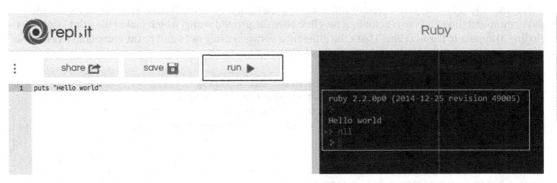

Figure 13-4. *The left side is the code editor and clicking Run makes the code execute. The right side is the interpreter that shows the result of the code that was just executed.*

In Ruby, there are three primitives, meaning that there are three different types of variables that you can use: integers, which are numbers; booleans, which are true or false statements; and strings, which are made from a collection of letters. Recall that we said Ruby is dynamically typed and now we'll see that property in use.

```
# This is how you can write a comment

my_num = 25      # my_num is an integer

my_boolean = true    # my_boolean is a boolean statement

my_string = "Ruby"    # my_string is a string
```

Here, we can see that assigning variables to the appropriate data type is sufficient to tell Ruby what the type of that variable should be. In programming languages that are not dynamically typed, you would have to specify the variable type as follows:

```
int my_num = 25
```

Next, let's take a look at how to print out simple strings. In Ruby, you have two options. The `print` command just takes whatever you give it and prints it to the screen. The other option is using the `puts` command (for put string), which is slightly different: It adds a new (blank) line after the thing you want it to print. Let's look at how this difference appears in the output.

```
print "Hello world" #1
puts "Hello world"  #2
print "This is on a new line"  #3
```

The output from the right pane is shown here.

```
Hello worldHello world
This is on a new line
```

Tracing the preceding code, the first statement prints out the string but no new line is added afterward. This makes the output from the second statement appear right after the first statement. When we use the `puts` command (line 2) there is actually a new line after the printed string, which makes the print statement (in line 3) appear in the next line. That's the difference between using `puts` and `print` commands. Let's look at input and output in Ruby through our Hello World program.

```
puts "Hello world!"                     # Print out a string
puts "What would you like me to say?"   # Prompt the user a question
phrase = gets.chomp                     # Read in the string that the user typed
puts "You said: " + phrase              # Repeat the string they typed
```

The output is shown here.

```
ruby 2.2.0p0 (2014-12-25 revision 49005)
Hello world!
What would you like me to say?
Ruby is great.
You said: Ruby is great.
```

The code shown in bold is the input. Notice that in Ruby you can add symbols such as the question mark in the `puts` command without the need for an escape character. This simple program shows you the input and output routines in Ruby. We already covered the `print` command, but to record the input entered by the user, we have to use the `gets` command. The `gets.chomp` method retrieves the string entered and in the preceding code, we assigned that input to a variable called `phrase`. Finally, the last `puts` command actually prints a statement along with the variable phrase that contained the recorded input. In this manner, Ruby can take input from a user and display it right back on the screen.

We also mentioned that Ruby is an object-oriented language, but actually in Ruby everything is an object. Let us review the model of an object as we discussed earlier in the book. Often an object in a computer program tries to model a real-world entity. Let's take the example of a car. This car could be modeled in a computer by providing information about the size, number of doors, engine, and color. These features uniquely identify a car that we want to model. In addition, there would be little pieces of associated code called methods that manipulate the car; for example, `start_car()` would simulate turning the engine on, `break()` would simulate slowing the car down, and `change_color()` would simulate painting the car with a new color. These methods, combined with the features about the car, make up an object.

In Ruby, everything is an object. This might be hard to grasp conceptually, but functionally this implies that we can manipulate variables that we define very easily, as in this example.

```
"This is the best book on Jekyll ever!".length

ruby 2.2.0p0 (2014-12-25 revision 49005)
=> 37
```

Notice that all we did was write out a string on quotes. Ruby recognized that it was a string and this string being an object, we could access the `.length` property, which gave us the number of characters in that string. This is how powerful object-orientation is in Ruby. We discuss more concepts later, but let's play with a few more methods or properties.

```
"This is the best book on Jekyll ever!".upcase

ruby 2.2.0p0 (2014-12-25 revision 49005)
=> "THIS IS THE BEST BOOK ON JEKYLL EVER!"
```

This is a very simple example showing the string being converted to uppercase using the `.upcase` method directly on the string. Because this string is an object, we can call any of the methods associated with it. If the string weren't being stored as an object, the string would reject any operations on it. This is just one of the few interesting design features in Ruby to keep in mind.

Another interesting property of Ruby is that multiple methods can be called on one object and they are evaluated one at a time. This technique is called method chaining; more than one method gets called on the same object. Let's see it in action.

```
print "What's your name: "          # Ask for input from user
last_name = gets.chomp.capitalize!  # Process the input provided, and then capitalize it

ruby 2.2.0p0 (2014-12-25 revision 49005)

What's your name: vikram
=> "Vikram"
```

In this example, we applied two new techniques in the second line. The first one is method chaining, where we used the `.chomp` and `.capitalize` methods in succession. We had to use the variable `last_name` to store the input that was provided by the user, but method chaining can be done directly on an object as well. The second technique involves the `!` character present at the end of the second line after `.capitalize`. This character tells Ruby to perform the capitalize operation and then store the value in `last_name`. At first, `last_name` stores the input string provided by the user, but that string gets overwritten with the result from `.capitalize` because `.capitalize!` was used.

The next topic we want to touch on concerns how variables change. So far, the variables we have used are not flexible at all. They perform a very simple purpose: Take the user input, although they always produce the same result regardless of what the input actually is; that is, they don't change their behavior in reaction to the environment. Control flow gives us the flexibility we're looking for. We can select different outcomes depending on the information the user provides us. Let's start by looking at the `if` statement for control flow, which we have used several times in the past for Jekyll code directly.

```
if 1 < 2
  print "I'm getting printed because one is less than two!"
end
```

This is the essence of control flow: Depending on the user behavior, we can guide the flow for the rest of the program. This idea is not only relevant to the preceding snippet, but also to full-scale applications like the Jekyll blogs that we have made where we needed to change behavior on web pages depending on the user input. There are a few variations of this that we can rely on, involving the use of else and elsif statements, as shown here.

```ruby
if x < y
  puts "x is less than y!"
elsif x > y
  puts "x is greater than y!"
else
  puts "x equals y!"
end
```

The values of x and y determine which of the three statements they fit and then the corresponding puts command gets triggered. If x is indeed less than y, then the first print statement is triggered. If that condition is not satisfied, then the else if choice gets triggered. After exhausting the else if choices, the last resort is the else command, which now gets triggered. This combination of if, else-if, and else is the foundation of control flow.

In this example, we rely on the < or > operators to evaluate x and y. A quicker way of evaluating statements in Ruby uses the ? operator. Let's work through an example (with strings) where we need to check whether the user input contains a specific character.

```ruby
print "Input: "                                    # Ask for input
user_input = gets.chomp                            # Store input
if user_input.include? "s"                         # Check if input contains character "s"
    puts "Your string is valid"                    # First puts statement
else                                               # Else segment
    puts "Your string is not valid: " + user_input # Second puts statement
end
```

```
ruby 2.2.0p0 (2014-12-25 revision 49005)

Input:  This book is awesome
Your string is valid
```

The bold if statement is crucial to this program. We use the .include method on user_input to search for the character "s" and, if present, it will trigger the associated puts statement. Otherwise, the second puts statement in the else segment gets executed. The .include? method evaluates to true if it finds what it is looking for and false otherwise. In general, all Ruby methods that end with a ? character evaluate to boolean values true or false.

Control flow is not just limited to if statements; more broadly, loops are also an essential component. A loop is a sequence of statements that is specified once but can be executed several times in succession. The code inside the loop is executed a specified number of times, until some condition(s) are satisfied. Let's go over loop-based control flow, and two loops in particular, beginning with the unless statement. The unless statement is somewhat similar to the if-else statements, but often inverted. Often, given a certain condition, we can invert it and still verify the opposite. In this case, the if and else results swap places but this reversal becomes more practical if you have a very large data set that must conform to a specific threshold.

```
if i < 10
   puts "Student failed"
else
   puts "Student passed"
end
```

The unless construct inverts this.

```
unless i >= 10
   puts "Student failed"
else
   puts "Student passed"
end
```

Sometimes, you want to repeat an action in Ruby while a certain condition is true, but you don't know how many times you'll have to repeat that action. A good example would be prompting users for a certain type of input: If they insist on giving you an invalid response, you might have to ask them several times before you get the kind of input that you're looking for. The complement to a while loop is the until loop. It can be thought of as a backward while loop. Here is an example.

```
counter = 1          # Counter is the condition that the loop needs to satisfy

until counter > 10   # Beginning of the loop - Only repeat until counter is less than 10
   puts counter      # Print the counter
   counter += 1      # Update counter, then go back to check if the condition is satisfied
end                  # After counter hits 10, end the loop
```

In the preceding code, the variable counter sets the initial conditions for the until loop to get started, and that loop will keep going until a new condition is satisfied, that is, the counter reaches 10. The counter updating within the body of the loop is what allows for the while loop to eventually end. We are using a shorthand assignment operator to update the counter, instead of writing out the whole statement. You already know one assignment operator, =, which defines a variable. This operator has a few variations, one of which is +=, which expands to counter = counter + 1 and this statement updates the counter for each succession of the until loop.

The next loop is the for loop. We have used it several times in past projects, but it is worth mentioning because the syntax of Liquid and Ruby are very different. A for loop is a count-controlled execution of code contained within the body of the loop and it can easily model most situations where we need to repeat a particular task. The counter used in the loop is specified as a condition to be met in the beginning of the loop. Let's look at an example of a for loop that prints out numbers from 1 to 20.

```
for num in 1..20       # Print numbers from 1-20, all numbers inclusive
   puts num
end
```

There are a few new things in this for loop. The output from this snippet is to print out numbers from 1 to 20, but the two dots determine how many numbers get printed in the end. The two dots tell Ruby to include the highest number in the range and print it out as well. If we had used three dots, Ruby would exclude the final number in the count, so the output would go from 1 to 19. Essentially, the following code produces a different output from the preceding segment. Try it out on your own in repl.it.

```
for num in 1...20          # Print numbers from 1-20, excluding the highest number in the set
   puts num
end
```

This simple convention allows us to change the upper and lower bounds on the for loop. So far, we have seen that loops go on a set number of times or until certain conditions are satisfied. Loops don't always have to follow through and complete their duration. In some cases where the upper or lower bounds are not well defined, we could risk creating an infinite loop, but a break statement can avoid that situation. Let's use it to fix a loop. In this example, the loop will be printing out a very large number of integers, mimicking an infinite loop that prints out numbers. Our job will be to stop it after the first few numbers.

```
counter = 1                        # Initial counter

until counter > 100000000000       # A very large loop
   puts counter                    # Printing numbers

   counter += 1                    # Incrementing counter to print the next number
   break if counter > 6            # Breaking the if-loop after 6

end

ruby 2.2.0p0 (2014-12-25 revision 49005)

1
2
3
4
5
6
```

In this snippet, the large loop continues to print numbers until it is broken by the if statement. This allows us to control the flow of the loop and exit as needed. In practical applications, the break statement often takes on a different form entirely. The core ideas are still the same: Breaking the control flow with higher level logic is used to stop a program if its behavior becomes unpredictable. At this point, the program throws an exception and exists because it encountered unknown behavior instead of following through with it and compromising the entire application. This security mechanism not only protects the application itself, but also lets the developers know the type of input that can be provided to the app so that they can direct it appropriately.

Next, we begin looking at data structures, and there are two in particular on which we want to focus. In Ruby, we can pack multiple values into a single variable using an array. An array is just a list of items between square brackets, defined like so: [1, 2, 3, 4]. The items don't have to be in any particular order, so you can just as easily have an array that looks like [10, 31, 19, 400]. Each element in the array can be identified and referenced by what's called an index, shown here.

```
        +---+---+---+---+---+
array   | 5 | 7 | 9 | 2 | 0 |
        +---+---+---+---+---+
index     0   1   2   3   4
```

The index of an array often becomes the loop counter (the number of times a loop needs to run) because the upper bound on the index is the length of the array. It's a convenient way of looping through every element in the array. Let's look at some methods that can be applied to arrays, beginning with an example that prints all the elements of an array.

```
numbers = [1, 2, 3, 4, 5]              # Define the array

numbers.each do |item|                 # Another way to loop through each item
  puts item                            # Print each item
end
```

In this snippet, we first define the array and then use a loop to go through each element and print it out. The logic looks very similar to a for loop and the loop counter is defined by putting it in |here|. Just as with a for loop, you can use the counter to manipulate the items in the array as you go through it.

```
numbers = [1, 2, 3, 4, 5]

numbers.each do |item|                 # Read each item from numbers
  puts (item*4)/2                      # Print each item, after multiplying and dividing it
end
```

This snippet multiplies each of the numbers by four and then cuts it in half. The end result is that the numbers are doubled. The roundabout operations in the code were just there to show that you can perform arithmetic on each item as you read it in the loop. This also prevents the value of each item in numbers from being changed permanently. The next data structure that we will cover is hashes.

Each element in an array has an index that is an integer. Arrays have this limitation where each index refers to an object, but the index itself can only be a number. What if you want to create an array of superhero secret identities, where a string (their name) points to another string (their identity)? You would have to use a hash. Hashes are similar to arrays in that they are a collection of indexes that have references to objects. However, whereas arrays are indexed using integers, hashes can be indexed using any types of objects, such as strings. A hash is essentially a collection of key-value pairs. Each key corresponds to a value using the => sign, and the keys or values can be any type of object. A generic example of the hash syntax is provided here.

```
hash = {
  key1 => value1,
  key2 => value2,
  key3 => value3
}
```

Now let's see how using a hash can be more powerful than an array. We'll create a hash that holds secret identities of superheroes and then prints them out, each key corresponding to its value.

```
secret_identities = {                          # Defining the hash
  "The Batman" => "Bruce Wayne",
  "Superman" => "Clark Kent",
  "Wonder Woman" => "Diana Prince",
  "Freakazoid" => "Dexter Douglas"
}

secret_identities.each do |x, y|               # Same as before, but now we need 2 counters
  puts x + ": " + y                            # One counter for key, another for symbol
end
```

In this example, a string "The Batman" is the index that points to "Bruce Wayne". To refer to "Bruce Wayne", we would have to refer to its index. In this snippet, we defined a hash with a few keys and values in strings and put them in quotation marks. To loop through the hash, we have modified the previous each-do loop where we only used one loop counter. Here we need two counters: one that counts for keys and another that counts for values. The next line in that loop simply prints out the value that the x and y index refer to. The output of this hash doesn't look any different from the input, but the main difference is that now we can manipulate this hash. Let's start by adding new elements to it.

```ruby
secret_identities = {
  "The Batman" => "Bruce Wayne",
  "Superman" => "Clark Kent",
  "Wonder Woman" => "Diana Prince",
  "Freakazoid" => "Dexter Douglas"
}

secret_identities.each do |x, y|
    puts x + ": " + y
end
```

```ruby
secret_identities["CL"] = "Kitty Cat"        # Adding new key-value pair

puts                                          # Adding a blank line
puts "Identities updated:"                    # Print statement to differentiate output

secret_identities.each do |x, y|              # Printing the hash again
    puts x + ": " + y
end
```

Adding a new key-hash pair is very similar to adding a new item in an array; you simply refer to the key and assign it a value, and that adds a new entry in the hash. Data structures like hashes often become important for storing structured data to interpret and manipulate it further. The concept behind hashes also becomes relevant when designing data mappings, where an object or properties of known objects are compared against a collection with an unknown amount of objects to find matches that are close to each other. Let's look at one more example using hashes before moving on to advanced concepts. In this example, we search for a value in the hash.

```ruby
movie_ratings = {                # Creating the hash
  inception: 3,
  primer: 3.5,
  x-men_origins: 4,
  her: 2,
  avatar_airbender: 1,
  the_matrix: 5,
  lion_king: 3.5
}
```

```ruby
good_movies = movie_ratings.select { |name, rating| rating > 3 }
```

In this example, we first created a hash for movie ratings and instead of the has-rocket symbol, we just used a colon. Both are equally valid, but this notation is more compact. The bold line at the end uses the .select method to choose all the values from the hash and then searches for ratings greater than 3 from all the values. In this statement, the keys are ignored completely because Ruby understands that the first variable name refers to keys and the search criteria only uses the second variable, which refers to the values.

Finally, the last topic to discuss in Ruby is the advanced concepts involving methods, objects, and creating a very simple class. Let's start with methods. We have used several of them in this chapter but so far, all of those methods were available to us. Methods are defined by using the keyword def, short for define. Most methods can be broken down into three parts.

- **Header:** It includes the def keyword, the name of the method, and any arguments the method takes. These arguments can be any object type.

- **Body:** It is a block of code that contains the instructions or procedures that the method must execute. The code present in the body often uses the arguments provided by the header for computation and prints the result.

- **Ending:** The method ends with the end keyword.

Here's an example of a simple function that prints out Hello World!.

```
def hello                 # Header
  puts "Hello World!"     # Body
end                       # Ending
```

Methods become useful only when they are called; often you can call a method just by typing its name. Let's call the hello method we just defined.

```
def hello
  puts "Hello World!"
end
```

```
hello                     # Calling the method
ruby 2.2.0p0 (2014-12-25 revision 49005)
```

```
Hello World!
```

A method can also take an argument when you call it. An argument is the piece of code you put between the method's parentheses when you call it. Now that we have an idea of what a method is, we can create one of our own. Let's start with a method that can square any number (value) passed to it.

```
def square(num)           # Square method defined with a parameter num
  puts num ** 2           # Operation performed on the parameter
end
```

```
square(12)                # Calling the method, passing an argument 12
```

```
ruby 2.2.0p0 (2014-12-25 revision 49005)
```

```
144
```

This method takes in a number num (also called a parameter) and raises that num to the power of 2, thus squaring it. A parameter is the name you put between the method's parentheses when you define it. Notice the difference between an argument and a parameter: An argument is passed to a method when it is called and a parameter is passed to a method when it is defined. For instance, when we defined square earlier, we gave it the parameter num (for number), but passed it the argument 12 when we called it. A function can have any number of arguments, but those arguments must be specified when the function is called or Ruby will throw an error; for example, wrong number of arguments (1 for 2) in the case of a function having two parameters but only one is given when the method is called.

A method can have more than one argument, but what if the number of arguments is unknown? The solution is to use splat arguments. Splat arguments are arguments preceded by a *, which signals to Ruby that an unknown number of arguments can be given to the method at runtime. Let's look at an example of this.

```ruby
def what_up(greeting, *bros)              # Defining the method
  bros.each do |bro|                      # Looping through each bro argument provided
      puts "#{greeting}, #{bro}!"         # Printing out the greeting for each bro
  end
end

what_up("What up", "Vikram", "Ben", "Mark")     # Listing the bros

ruby 2.2.0p0 (2014-12-25 revision 49005)

What up, Vikram!
What up, Ben!
What up, Mark!
```

The define statement lists two arguments: a string greeting, followed by any number of bros arguments that will receive the greeting. Then, we loop through each bro out of all the bros given as arguments, and print the greeting for each one of them. The notation #{greeting} is simply a placeholder for the greeting provided from the argument and similarly, #{bro} is a placeholder for each of the bros passed in as arguments. When we call the function, the first string is passed as the greeting argument and that's it. Ruby knows that greeting is not a splat argument, so the remaining arguments must be passed as bros to the method. This method is analogous to running a for loop and printing out the greeting for each of the bros passed as arguments, but the method makes it more precise and it can be run many times with entirely new arguments.

What if we want to use a method to evaluate statements? We can use a method to evaluate statements and return a true or false based on the result of the computation we just performed. Let's create a method that determines if a number is even.

```ruby
def is_even? (num)          # Defining a method, taking an argument num
    if num % 2 == 0         # Performing a modulus operation and checking
        return true         # Return true if modulus gives 0
else
    return false            # Return false otherwise
end                         # Ending if-loop
end                         # Ending method

if is_even(9) == false
    puts "Not even"
end

ruby 2.2.0p0 (2014-12-25 revision 49005)

Not even
```

Being able to return a boolean answer and then using that result in further evaluations is what makes the return command very powerful. By using a return statement, you can modularize a method, pass an argument to it, and let it do the computation. After the computation has been completed, you can simply use the result that was provided by the method and returned to further into your program. Why are methods important? The plug-ins that we will implement and use in Jekyll for our design studio contain numerous methods that, when combined, perform the task of that plug-in.

The notion of an object that we discussed earlier is not complete. In reality, an object only models a small portion of the bigger picture. An object contains data that describes a component along with instructions on how to manipulate that data in a limited and specific manner. This bigger picture is a collection of many objects and methods that add little bits to complete the description. The full picture (or description) is called a class. Perhaps an analogy will help make the concepts clear. Suppose we have a class called Animal. All animals have bodies and brains and these could be the shared attributes of our Animal class. The attributes shared by all animals can be put together into one single animal object, which constructs the most basic description of all animals in the Animal class. We can also add some methods that describe other properties that animals have, like movement and growth. This is the idea of a class. Essentially, we can say that whereas a class is a general concept (like an animal), an object is a very specific embodiment of that class, with a limited life span (like a lion, cat, or a zebra). Let's look at an example to apply what we just learned, creating a Person class.

```ruby
class Person                        # Defining a class

  def initialize(name, age)         # First method, constructing a simple object
    @name = name                    # Internal variables referring to arguments
    @age = age
  end

  def about                         # Using the internal variables to print a statement
    puts "I'm #{@name} and I'm #{@age} years old!"
  end

  def bank_account_number           # Another method using an internally defined
                                    # variable
    @account_number = 12345
    puts "My bank account number is #{@account_number}."
  end

end

eric = Person.new("Eric", 26)    # Constructing a person object with name and age arguments
eric.about                       # Using the name and age previously defined in statements
eric.bank_account_number         # Using another internal variable
```

There is a lot going on in this class, but let's break it down method by method. The first method in this class is initialize, which is also known as the constructor because it creates an object. Whenever Ruby creates a new object, it looks for a method named initialize and executes it. One simple thing we can do is use an initialize method and construct an object by setting the instance variables equal to the arguments. An instance variable is a variable defined within a method but accessible anywhere within that class. In Ruby, instance variables are always prefaced with an @ symbol. In this case, @name and @age are the instance variables and the constructor method initialize sets them equal to the arguments of that method. The about method is next, and this method prints out both instance variables that we created using initialize along with a short statement. The last method prints out the bank account number defined within the method by another instance variable, @account_number.

The fun begins when we call the methods. As mentioned previously, methods by themselves are not of much use; they become functional only when called. The first line (after the methods) is particularly important because it supplies the information needed to create an object. Each of these statements has three parts.

- **Declaration:** The left side of the statement (before the = operator) is declaring the name of an object that will soon be constructed using the right side.

- **Instantiation:** The new keyword tells Ruby that a new object needs to be created. In this case, `Person.new` tells Ruby that the object is an instance of the `Person` class.

- **Initialization:** The new operator is followed by arguments supplied to a constructor that uses those arguments as properties of the new object.

The name of this object is `eric` and he is being created as an instance of the class `Person` (that makes more sense in plain English: Eric is an instance of a person). The arguments supplied to the constructor are the name of the `Person` along with his or her age and the instance variables are set to those arguments. That makes sense because after defining the `Person`, we need to have their `@name` and `@age` accessible throughout the class if we want to make more methods defining `eric` more completely. The next two lines simply call on the methods we defined in the class. After we have constructed the object `eric`, just like anything else in Ruby, we can call methods on it: `eric.about` uses the about method with instance variables provided by the constructor and `eric.bank_account_number` uses the last method to print out the account number defined within the method. The concept of a class is very powerful in object-oriented programming, especially when you start including multiple classes in a full-scale application.

This concludes our overview of Ruby. Although we couldn't even come close to capturing the beauty of this language, the goal here was to provide a conceptual framework to help readers approach Ruby should they be interested in pursuing this further. Next, we focus on the web application side of Ruby and talk about features such as package management and how Jekyll fits in with Ruby.

Gems of Ruby

In the last section, we talked about classes being a cornerstone of object-oriented programming. Often in large applications, developers implement a collection of classes that are interdependent on each other. These classes can share resources among each other, such as methods and any stored data. Such a collection is called a library. In Ruby, there are libraries of all sizes, from complete web applications to small tools containing only a few classes. To distribute these libraries and install them with ease, Ruby has created a self-sufficient distribution system using packages. The packages easily integrate into projects when new functionality is needed and Ruby has a default package manager called RubyGems that makes it easier to manage adding new libraries. The libraries themselves are better known as gems in Ruby, and we spend the remainder of this section talking about how to play with gems and use them in your own projects.

RubyGems has an online interface that acts as a community network to find new gems and install them in your own projects. The web site at `https://rubygems.org/` is shown in Figure 13-5.

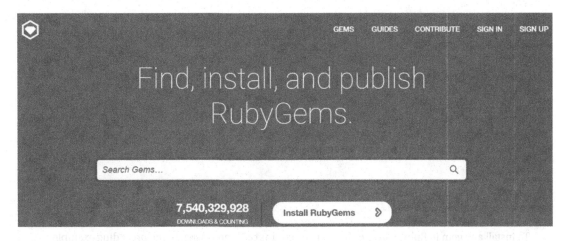

Figure 13-5. *The RubyGems web site is a centralized community network containing most of the gems available in Ruby. The search bar leads you to the appropriate gem along with a command that you can use to install that gem.*

You can imagine gems to be similar to plug-ins or add-ons that you install in your browser, as each gem allows for new functionality to be added to your application. Essentially you end up an application that can take advantage of features and methods across multiple libraries. From the command line, the gem command allows you to interact with RubyGems. We use it here to install a hello world gem, but before we do that, let's take a look at what the gem profile page looks like in Figure 13-6.

hello-world *1.2.0*

longer description of your gem

VERSIONS:

1.2.0 - January 13, 2010 (6 KB)
1.1.0 - January 13, 2010 (6 KB)
1.0.0 - January 13, 2010 (6 KB)
0.1.0 - December 31, 2009 (6 KB)

AUTHORS:

TOTAL DOWNLOADS
8,977

FOR THIS VERSION
3,135

GEMFILE:

```
gem 'hello-world',
```

INSTALL:

```
gem install hello-w
```

Figure 13-6. *The profile page for a gem. This page contains a lot of information, such as the description of the gem, how many versions have been released, who the authors are, information about the home page of the gem, and if it has any other related documentation. Under the Install label from the boxed content is the command that you can use to install this gem on your machine.*

To install this gem, fire up your command prompt with Ruby that we saw in Figure 13-3. We use this Ruby command prompt to install gems and play with them. To install this gem, just copy the command provided in the profile page.

```
C:\Users\Vikram>gem install hello-world
Fetching: hello-world-1.2.0.gem (100%)
Successfully installed hello-world-1.2.0
Parsing documentation for hello-world-1.2.0
Installing ri documentation for hello-world-1.2.0
Done installing documentation for hello-world after 1 seconds
1 gem installed
```

```
C:\Users\Vikram>hello-world
this is executable hello-world
```

To install any gem in Ruby, you can simply use gem install gem_name. In the preceding example, we installed the hello-world gem and you can see how Ruby's package manager went about it. It first downloaded the gem, then installed it and updated the ri (Ruby Index), which is Ruby's help documentation. The messages end with Ruby verifying that the installation was successful. Finally, to run the gem, we just call it by its name, the same approach we would take to call a method. This gem just displays hello world in the output, but other gems are much more powerful. Jekyll is actually a gem in Ruby, too, but before we get into installing larger gems like Jekyll, we need to get a better understanding of dependencies and what a Gemfile is.

Recall that we would always import font-awesome to use the icons in our Jekyll blogs. Similarly, your project might import other components to build itself; then to deploy your project, those components or packages are necessary. Otherwise, your project will not build appropriately. The components that your blog needs that are external to it are called dependencies because your project depends on them. Font-awesome is one such example, but at the level of gems, you can add more gems to your project and they become a dependency for it. A Gemfile is a Ruby file that defines the dependencies (all the other gems) required by your project. The Gemfile is like a recipe and the dependencies are the ingredients that we need to cook up your dish, which is your project. Let's look at an example Gemfile.

```
source 'https://rubygems.org'

gem 'cocoapods'
gem "cocoapods-keys"
gem 'xcpretty'
gem 'fastlane'
```

This file lists the gems that are needed for a project. The Gemfile tells Ruby that it needs to find those gems from the database and install them to make sure the project compiles and runs smoothly. Jekyll can be installed as a gem, but it has several dependencies. Let's see how this works.

```
C:\Users\Vikram>gem install jekyll
Fetching: colorator-0.1.gem (100%)
Successfully installed colorator-0.1
Fetching: sass-3.4.21.gem (100%)
Successfully installed sass-3.4.21
Fetching: jekyll-sass-converter-1.4.0.gem (100%)
Successfully installed jekyll-sass-converter-1.4.0
Fetching: rb-fsevent-0.9.7.gem (100%)
```

```
Successfully installed rb-fsevent-0.9.7
Fetching: ffi-1.9.10-x64-mingw32.gem (100%)
Successfully installed ffi-1.9.10-x64-mingw32
Fetching: rb-inotify-0.9.6.gem (100%)
... [ snip ] ...
Fetching: jekyll-3.1.1.gem (100%)
Successfully installed jekyll-3.1.1
Installing ri documentation for jekyll-3.1.1
... [ snip ] ...
Done installing documentation for colorator, sass, jekyll-sass-converter, rb-fsevent, ffi,
rb-inotify, listen, jekyll-watch, kramdown, liquid, mercenary, rouge, safe_yaml, jekyll
after 42 seconds
14 gems installed
```

The process of installing Jekyll locally is not much different from any other gem, except that there are numerous dependencies that come along with Jekyll and have to be installed. In the output, we see a lot of packages being fetched (downloaded) and installed locally. Several portions of the output have been removed (snipped) to only show the relevant pieces. Finally, a summary of the gems installed along with confirmation of their entry into the help documentation is provided. That's how simple it is to install entire applications like Jekyll in Ruby. Now that the gem has been installed, we can access it anywhere within the console. Let's verify that Jekyll has been installed.

```
C:\Users\Vikram>jekyll -v
jekyll 3.1.2
```

Now that Jekyll is up and running, let's play with it and use the command line to get a boilerplate Jekyll site up and running.

```
C:\Users\Vikram\Documents\sample_site>jekyll new myblog
New jekyll site installed in C:/Users/Vikram/Documents/sample_site/myblog.
```

The command jekyll new myblog created a skeletal Jekyll site in the folder myblog. Let's take a look at what Jekyll created for us in this boilerplate template.

```
C:\Users\Vikram\Documents\sample_site>cd myblog && dir

 Directory of C:\Users\Vikram\Documents\sample_site\myblog

02/25/2016  02:26 PM    <DIR>          .
02/25/2016  02:26 PM    <DIR>          ..
02/25/2016  02:26 PM                35 .gitignore
02/25/2016  02:26 PM               536 about.md
02/25/2016  02:26 PM    <DIR>          css
02/25/2016  02:26 PM             1,291 feed.xml
02/25/2016  02:26 PM               506 index.html
02/25/2016  02:26 PM               891 _config.yml
02/25/2016  02:26 PM    <DIR>          _includes
02/25/2016  02:26 PM    <DIR>          _layouts
02/25/2016  02:26 PM    <DIR>          _posts
02/25/2016  02:26 PM    <DIR>          _sass
               5 File(s)          3,259 bytes
               7 Dir(s)  322,978,512,896 bytes free
```

The folder structure of this Jekyll app looks typical, like what we saw earlier when creating the news brief site. Even though the app is minimal, it contains all the necessary components that a simple blog site would have. It's enough for us to play with and learn the basics of command-line Jekyll operations. Here are the most useful Jekyll commands:

- `jekyll build`: The Jekyll site will be compiled and the result will be generated into `_site`.

- `jekyll build --watch`: The Jekyll site will be generated into `./_site`, watched for changes, and regenerated automatically on updating.

- `jekyll serve`: The Jekyll site will be compiled and a development server will run at `http://localhost:4000/` with the watch feature enabled; that is, the site will be generated after changes.

- `jekyll clean`: The generated Jekyll site is cleaned from the `_site` folder, getting it ready for another compile.

Let's put these commands into action. To compile the source files into Jekyll processed HTML, we use the `build` command first.

```
C:\Users\Vikram\Documents\sample_site\myblog>jekyll build
Configuration file: C:/Users/Vikram/Documents/sample_site/myblog/_config.yml
            Source: C:/Users/Vikram/Documents/sample_site/myblog
       Destination: C:/Users/Vikram/Documents/sample_site/myblog/_site
 Incremental build: disabled. Enable with --incremental
        Generating...
                    done in 3.83 seconds.
 Auto-regeneration: disabled. Use --watch to enable.
```

This output also contains a lot of information. First it locates the configuration file, which in this case is `_config.yml`, and then it uses that to compile the site. The source files are located under the myblog folder and the destination for the compiled files is the `_site` folder. It took Jekyll close to four seconds to generate the site and it tells us that autoregeneration is disabled, meaning that if we updated the site now, we would have to run `jekyll build` again to see the effects. But what if we want to see how the compiled site looks? For this, we have to tell Jekyll to serve the site.

```
C:\Users\Vikram\Documents\sample_site\myblog>jekyll serve
Configuration file: C:/Users/Vikram/Documents/sample_site/myblog/_config.yml
            Source: C:/Users/Vikram/Documents/sample_site/myblog
       Destination: C:/Users/Vikram/Documents/sample_site/myblog/_site
 Incremental build: disabled. Enable with --incremental
        Generating...
                    done in 0.447 seconds.
  Please add the following to your Gemfile to avoid polling for changes:
    gem 'wdm', '>= 0.1.0' if Gem.win_platform?
 Auto-regeneration: enabled for 'C:/Users/Vikram/Documents/sample_site/myblog'
Configuration file: C:/Users/Vikram/Documents/sample_site/myblog/_config.yml
     Server address: http://127.0.0.1:4000/
  Server running... press ctrl-c to stop.
```

This output is similar to what we saw when building the site and generating the compiled files. Here the difference is that after generating the site, Jekyll uses a local web server to serve the pages that it just compiled. This is a foreground running process, meaning that if you made changes to the site while jekyll serve was running, the changes would trigger a rebuild and Jekyll would compile again to update the site. This is also shown by the fact that autoregeneration is enabled for the compile. In the last two lines of the configuration, we can see the local server information. Jekyll is serving the site that it just compiled on the web address http://127.0.0.1:4000/ and this server is running continuously. The site available at that web address is shown in Figure 13-7.

■ **Note**   The warning regarding adding wdm gem to the Gemfile can be safely ignored. That particular gem is specific to Windows and it might become necessary if we did all of our development offline. However, for the purposes of learning how to use Jekyll offline and the command-line operations, we can continue without worrying about the wdm gem.

Similar to the serve command, we can also ask Jekyll to watch the code for changes and simply rebuild the site in case of changes. To do this, we use the --watch switch with the build command shown here.

```
C:\Users\Vikram\Documents\sample_site\myblog>jekyll build --watch
Configuration file: C:/Users/Vikram/Documents/sample_site/myblog/_config.yml
          Source: C:/Users/Vikram/Documents/sample_site/myblog
     Destination: C:/Users/Vikram/Documents/sample_site/myblog/_site
 Incremental build: disabled. Enable with --incremental
       Generating...
                  done in 0.767 seconds.
Auto-regeneration: enabled for 'C:/Users/Vikram/Documents/sample_site/myblog'
```

This output is pretty much the same as what we got from running jekyll build, except that the process runs in the foreground, and looks for any possible changes to the site, compiling it again if necessary. This time, the autoregeneration option has been enabled for the blog site. After making edits to the site and saving the file, you should start to see the following in the output where the jekyll build -- watch process is running.

```
Auto-regeneration: enabled for 'C:/Users/Vikram/Documents/sample_site/myblog'
     Regenerating: 1 file(s) changed at 2016-02-25 16:16:26 ...done in 0.115596 seconds.
```

This line shows that a recompilation was performed on the site after edits were recorded. The --watch feature can be used with both serve and build commands and it adds an autoupdate ability to both. In the first case, the browser refreshes to show the newly compiled web site any time a change is made, and the build command simply recompiles the source files if it records any new edits to the source files.

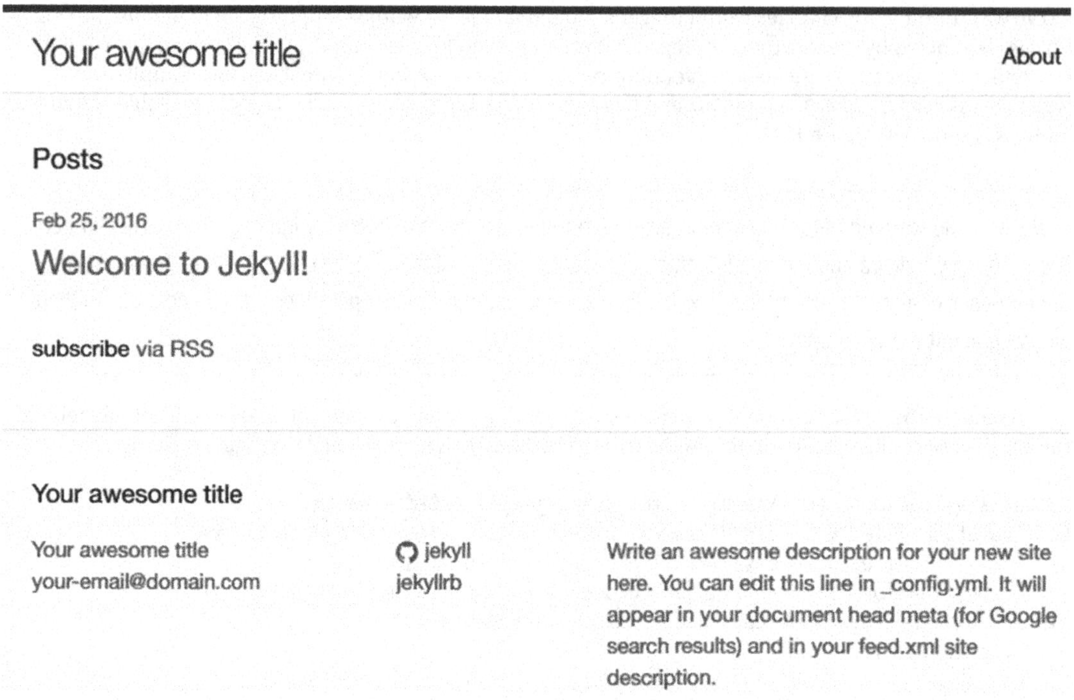

Your awesome title   About

Posts

Feb 25, 2016

Welcome to Jekyll!

subscribe via RSS

Your awesome title

Your awesome title   ○ jekyll   Write an awesome description for your new site
your-email@domain.com   jekyllrb   here. You can edit this line in _config.yml. It will
                                                         appear in your document head meta (for Google
                                                         search results) and in your feed.xml site
                                                         description.

Figure 13-7. *Jekyll barebones template served locally in the browser. The contents displayed here are being pulled directly from the* `_site` *directory that contains the Jekyll-compiled web site.*

A Bucket of Gems

So far in this book, we have used Git to put our code under version control and then pushed the code to GitHub, a code-sharing and hosting platform. On GitHub, if we had named the central repository in a particular format, then GitHub Pages would compile the source into a static web site that can be hosted on GitHub alone. Our interaction and dependence on GitHub might have given the impression that it can be very difficult to host and manage Jekyll web sites on any other platforms. Actually quite the opposite is true: Jekyll web sites can be hosted and served with ease. To show that, in this chapter we use a different code hosting platform, Bitbucket.

The main focus of this book has been the interaction between Jekyll and Git. GitHub is the easiest to use platform, so we eased into it and took advantage of all the features offered by the platform. Git can interface with many platforms, though, and Bitbucket is one of those major platforms. In this section, we do a walkthrough of Bitbucket to get you familiar with it and use it to host this project. One distinguishing feature of Bitbucket on the free plan is that you can get a private repository, which is only available as a paid feature on GitHub. Let's get started by creating an account on Bitbucket. After confirming your e-mail, you are presented with the Dashboard, shown in Figure 13-8.

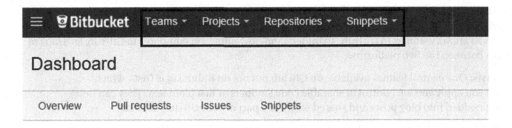

Figure 13-8a. Top navigation bars for the Bitbucket Dashboard. Bitbucket has a traditional project-management feel to it, but this Dashboard offers a tremendous amount of information available at your fingertips. The boxed drop-down menus give you access to the repositories or projects that you have in your account along with the team to which you belong. Underneath, for every repository that you have, you can obtain at-a-glance information about the repository.

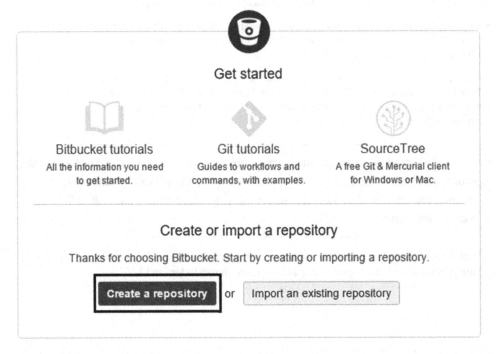

Figure 13-8b. Bitbucket's Dashboard without any repositories. The dashboard here offers links to several resources to help get a user started with Bitbucket. Along with the resources is the link to downloading SourceTree, which is analogous to using GitHub Desktop. Finally, underneath the resources is the button to create a new repository.

Let's go through the process of creating a repository in Bitbucket and then we will look at all the settings available for the repository. We also briefly talk about how to import code into this repository and how the protocols to do so are very similar to GitHub. To understand how Bitbucket compares to GitHub, let's look at the differences between the two platforms.

- **Gists:** One central feature available on GitHub but not on Bitbucket is Gists, which let you apply version control to sharable code snippets or just plain text. They can be embedded into blog posts and shared easily as a part of your GitHub account.

- **Static pages:** A nice feature both services share is creating static sites out of the repositories. This feature is pretty much the same on both services. You can create a repository named `username.bitbucket.com` and get your own nifty URL with the project site hosted on it.

- **Community support:** A quick look at the newest questions on Stackoverflow will reveal that GitHub is asked about every couple of minutes, whereas Bitbucket questions take about an hour or two to resurface. In general, GitHub has better support than Bitbucket, but you will find an answer to either question you might have.

- **Switching:** Bitbucket makes it pretty straightforward to import your repositories from GitHub. The same is not true for GitHub, but in the end Git works the same for both platforms.

- **Other version control:** Although not the focus of our discussion, Bitbucket was originally conceived as a tool for using Mercurial (another version control system) and Git support was added later on. On the other hand, GitHub was all about Git from the beginning.

■ **Tip**   It might seem like a good idea to import an existing GitHub repository in Bitbucket and make it private, but doing so is actually harmful. Keeping your code open allows others to propose edits or feature fixes in the case of broken commits. This principle should be followed even for large-scale projects and making them open source will only increase adoption rates.

Next, let's look at how the the process of creating a repository works in Bitbucket. After clicking Create a repository, you are presented with the repository options screen, shown in Figure 13-9.

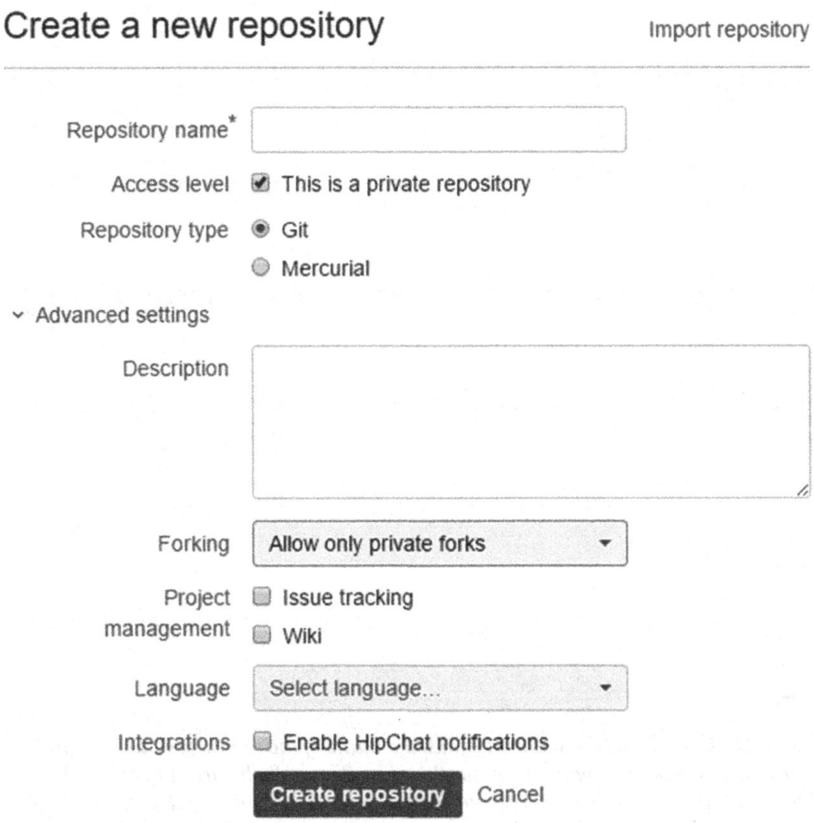

Create a new repository

Import repository

Repository name* [   ]

Access level ☑ This is a private repository

Repository type ◉ Git
○ Mercurial

˅ Advanced settings

Description [   ]

Forking [Allow only private forks   ▼]

Project management ☐ Issue tracking
☐ Wiki

Language [Select language...   ▼]

Integrations ☐ Enable HipChat notifications

[Create repository] Cancel

Figure 13-9. Creating a repository and the advanced settings available. This is yet another subtle difference between Bitbucket and GitHub: There are more options available when creating a repository in Bitbucket. It is far easier to create a repository in GitHub and most of the settings offered here are available later on in the Settings view for a repository. After naming the repository, you are given the choice of picking a version control system. After that, you can add a description and then have fine-grained control over who can fork your code. You can also choose to add an issue tracker (similar to Issues on GitHub) and a wiki, which are enabled by default in GitHub. Finally, you can pick the language that you will be using throughout the repository and enable notifications in HipChat, which is a team collaboration tool.

We already covered all the features available during repository creation in Figure 13-9, so let's get started: First, minimize the advanced settings and let's use the defaults to create a repository named Testing. After creating a repository, you are brought to the repository dashboard, which currently shows that we have no activity. This repository dashboard view will become the starting point, and this view is very similar to GitHub, where we saw the Git commands to get started pushing code to the repository. The dashboard is shown in Figure 13-10.

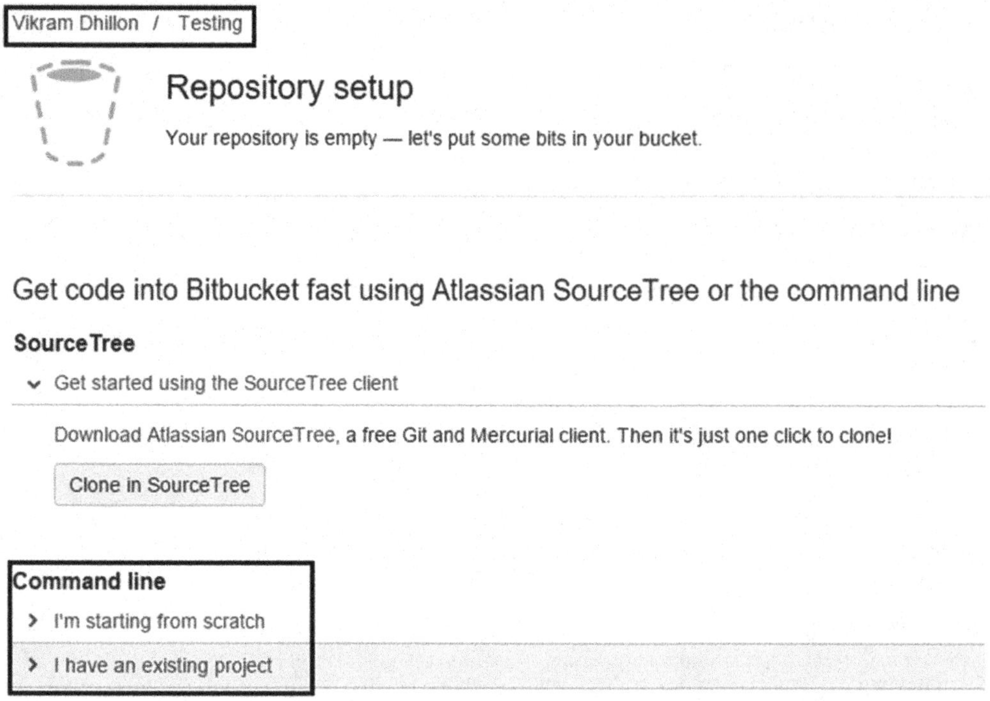

Vikram Dhillon / Testing

Repository setup

Your repository is empty — let's put some bits in your bucket.

Get code into Bitbucket fast using Atlassian SourceTree or the command line

SourceTree

ᵛ Get started using the SourceTree client

Download Atlassian SourceTree, a free Git and Mercurial client. Then it's just one click to clone!

Clone in SourceTree

Command line

› I'm starting from scratch

› I have an existing project

Figure 13-10. The repository dashboard. The top boxed part shows the name of the repository along with the owner's name. Underneath, there is information available about this repository, which currently has nothing in it. To get started with Bitbucket, we do not use SourceTree, but instead rely on the command line, which as been our friend in past chapters. Just like Bitbucket, we will have easy-to-follow instructions to get our code online.

We will push our barebones Jekyll project to this repository after finishing this walkthrough. Let's move on and look at the sidebar on the left. This sidebar is split into two pieces, as shown in Figure 13-11. The top half contains the repository actions and the bottom half includes navigation functions to look around within the repository. The repository actions allow for basic operations such as cloning the code, forking the code, and even making branches using the web interface rather than the command-line way of doing it with the git checking new_branch_name command. Even advanced features such as creating pull requests or comparing repositories are available. Under the repository actions are the navigation links that allow you to move within the repository easily. By default, we are on the repository dashboard which is the first option, Overview. The Source option takes you to browsing the source code present within the repository. Currently there is nothing present in this repository, as seen in Figure 13-12. Unlike GitHub, where the latest commit is shown on top of the code in the repository view, Bitbucket lets you browse the commits separately with the Commit option. Here, you can see all the commits made, along with the branch history. After some commits have been made, a small information box appears on the right side in the repository overview to provide at-a-glance information about the latest commits. Finally in the navigation options, there is the ability to download the repository as a zip file and view any pull requests that have been made for the repository. Underneath the navigation actions is the Settings option, which takes you to the settings page for the repository for even more options to manage the repository.

Figure 13-11a. *The repository actions available in the sidebar. These links represent some of the most commonly used operations for a repository and we create a branch using this web interface shortly.*

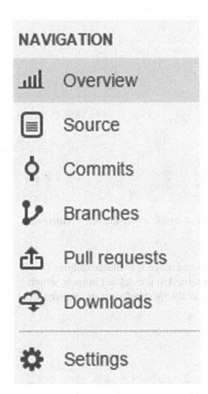

Figure 13-11b. *The navigation options for the repository. It is interesting to note that Bitbucket separates the commits, source, and branches, whereas on GitHub, this information is available on a single page.*

Vikram Dhillon / Testing

Source

The source directory is empty.

Get started with your first commit.

Figure 13-12. *The Source view from the navigation bar. Currently, this repository doesn't have any code, so the Source view is recommending making a commit to get started.*

Let's take a look at some of the operations available through this web interface, particularly creating a branch, because we return to it later in the chapter. Moreover, so far, we have only created branches with the command line. This time around, though, we use the web interface. It must be noted that branches can also be created using GitHub's web interface, but we preferred to use the command line to do so. In any case, clicking the Create branch option opens up the dialog box shown in Figure 13-13.

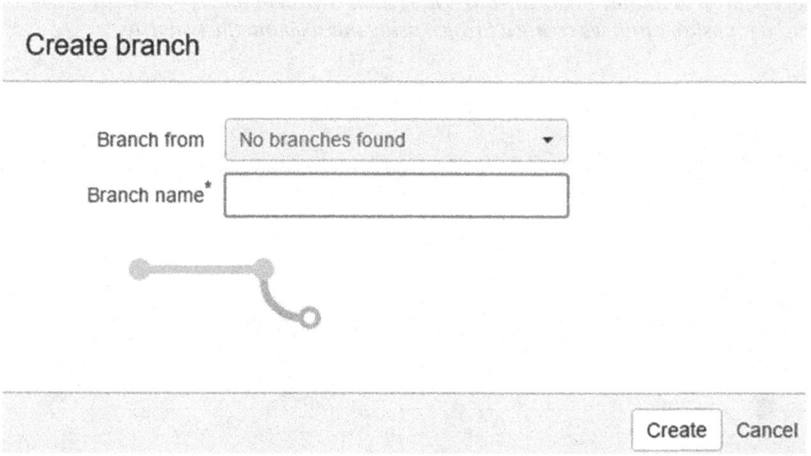

Create branch

Branch from   No branches found   ▼

Branch name*   [   ]

                             | Create | Cancel

Figure 13-13. *The Create branch dialog box. Currently this box won't let us create a new branch because no previous code is available to branch from.*

The option to create a branch won't work until we push some code and make it available online. This is because branching can only be carried out based on previous code contained in the default branch, which serves as a source from which to branch. We need the master branch available first before trying to create a new branch because without a master, there is nothing to branch from.

The next stop in our walkthrough is the repository settings, shown in Figure 13-14. The settings are similar to what we saw on GitHub in the past, but there are a few interesting options available here. The first is that you can change the access control and make your repository private at any time necessary. You can also change the page that you see when you visit the repository; for instance, you can change from the Overview mode to seeing the source code directly by picking the Source landing page. Additionally, you can make a different branch the master branch if necessary through this web interface. The sidebar in Figure 13-14 also shows additional user management features to provide fine-controlled access to branches and the code base. These features are more relevant to larger teams where not everyone has access to modify the entire code base; rather, they add features by creating patches against the code already present. Those patches get reviewed and then finally incorporated into the main project. By configuring user management, a developer can provide read-only or clone-only access to their repository using features like deployment keys.

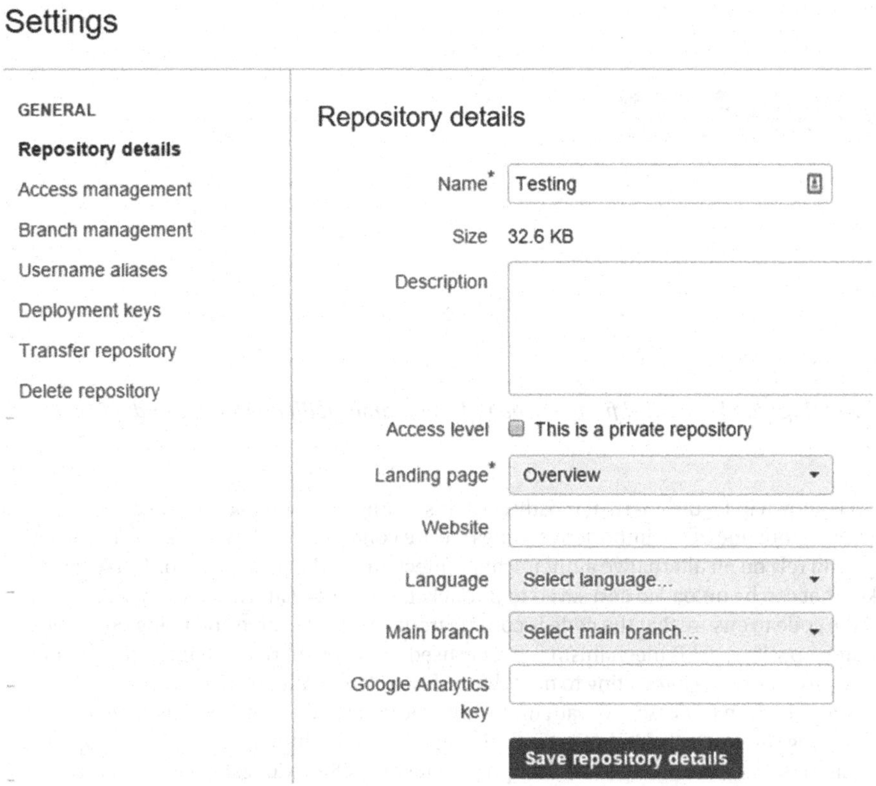

Settings

GENERAL	Repository details
Repository details	
Access management	Name* Testing
Branch management	Size 32.6 KB
Username aliases	Description
Deployment keys	
Transfer repository	
Delete repository	
	Access level ☐ This is a private repository
	Landing page* Overview ▾
	Website
	Language Select language... ▾
	Main branch Select main branch... ▾
	Google Analytics key
	Save repository details

Figure 13-14. The repository settings. Most of the access control features available in Bitbucket mimic the ones in GitHub, and they are only optimal for large teams, not individuals.

Now that we have looked through the repository settings, let's examine a few account settings in Bitbucket. These settings are important to discuss because we revisit them later in this chapter in our design studio. The settings themselves are not so important, per se, but rather what those settings mean, because we will be using them shortly. The settings can be reached from the top right, as shown in Figure 13-15.

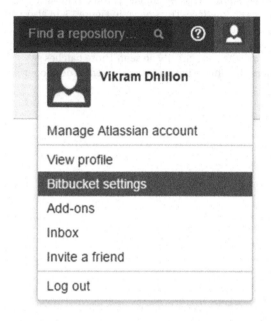

Figure 13-15. *Account settings can be reached from the top right side, along with user profile and add-on settings*

The Settings panel is shown in Figure 13-16. It mostly contains routine account maintenance and edits and billing preferences, but one of the important settings we are concerned with is SSH keys. The idea behind using SSH keys is to rely on an alternative authentication mechanism that isn't passwords. We use a device to generate a key that can be uploaded and saved to Bitbucket. After that, Git will check the SSH key of the system pushing the code to ensure that the code is coming from a trusted source and being pushed or synced to the appropriate repository. This mechanism is widely used to establish trust and identities in open source communities such as Linux. It is interesting to note that SSH and Open Auth work based on similar principles to provide write access. In our case, we want to compile the code in the cloud and then push it to Bitbucket so that the resulting site can be hosted. We use Codeship to do the compilation and it uses Open Auth to access the repositories. Once we have picked the appropriate repository, Codeship can read the code present and then using the instructions we give it, compile the source. What happens with the result, though? We need to push that compiled result back to the repository. There are a few clever ways of doing this actually. One of them is to create an API token that will allow write access to push code back to the repository. However, if we just keep committing and pushing the resulting code back to the branch, this will result in a mismatch between how the tags are being synced from the source (Codeship) to the destination (the branch on Bitbucket). That solution is not viable without some complex scripting, but we can allow Codeship to write back to the repository using the SSH keys associated with that account. With the SSH key, Codeship will have full access to that repository, and it can sync to it as if we were locally pushing the code online.

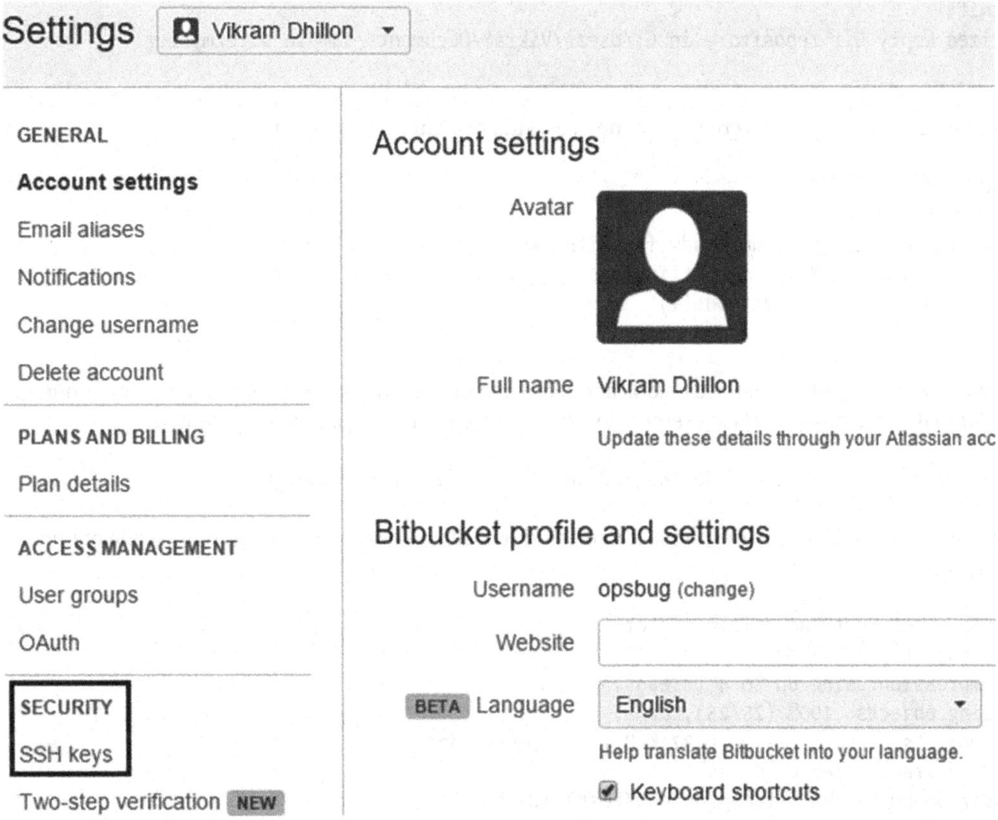

Settings 👤 Vikram Dhillon ▾

GENERAL

Account settings

Email aliases

Notifications

Change username

Delete account

PLANS AND BILLING

Plan details

ACCESS MANAGEMENT

User groups

OAuth

SECURITY

SSH keys

Two-step verification NEW

Account settings

Avatar

Full name   Vikram Dhillon

Update these details through your Atlassian acc

Bitbucket profile and settings

Username   opsbug (change)

Website

BETA Language   English ▾

Help translate Bitbucket into your language.

☑ Keyboard shortcuts

Figure 13-16. *Account settings for Bitbucket. In the left sidebar, the top section is Account settings, followed by billing and access management options. The OAuth option allows us to manage any applications authenticated with Bitbucket or create new API tokens.*

Let's briefly talk about SSH keys and how they function. A device generates a public–private key pair, and the public key is distributed to other services that the user wants to access. SSH verifies whether the same person offering the public key also owns the matching private key and a secure connection is established that allows us read and write access. Recall that GitHub also gave us an option to clone repositories using SSH, and Bitbucket has one, too, but generating SSH keys on Windows requires additional software and configuration. For that reason, we simply choose to clone repositories using HTTP and then modify Git settings to store the password.

Now let's push the sample Jekyll project we created in the last section to Bitbucket. The process is actually very simple because the instructions are provided to us on the repository overview page. In this case, like in the past projects, we use HTTP to transfer data. The instructions are present in the I have an existing project drop-down list, but we won't be using those exact commands. In either case, the logic behind those commands is this: Add the code to version control by initializing a new Git repository, add and commit the present code to that repository, tell Git about the remote location, and push code to that location. Go to the location of the site that was created using Jekyll—ours was present at: `C:/Users/Vikram/Documents/sample_site/myblog/`—and let's get started.

```
$ git init
Initialized empty Git repository in C:/Users/Vikram/Documents/sample_site/myblog
/.git/
```

After the repository has been created, we need to add and commit these changes.

```
$ git add -A :/
```

```
$ git commit -m "Getting code ready for Bitbucket"
[master (root-commit) 8175dbc] Getting code ready for Bitbucket
 20 files changed, 819 insertions(+)
[ ... ]
```

To push the code online, you have to look at the instructions for an existing project that we mentioned earlier. Within those instructions is the remote location, and the one for this project account is

```
$ git remote add origin https://opsbug@bitbucket.org/opsbug/testing.git
```

You will find a similar one with your user name and repository address. Finally, push the code online using this syntax.

```
$ git push --set-upstream origin master
Counting objects: 27, done.
Delta compression using up to 4 threads.
Compressing objects: 100% (25/25), done.
Writing objects: 100% (27/27), 9.37 KiB | 0 bytes/s, done.
Total 27 (delta 1), reused 0 (delta 0)
To https://opsbug@bitbucket.org/opsbug/testing.git
 * [new branch]      master -> master
Branch master set up to track remote branch master from origin.
```

The repository view (shown in Figure 13-17) looks a lot different after being updated with information about the code we just added.

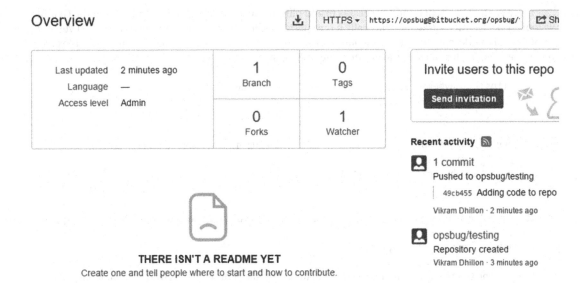

Figure 13-17. *The new repository overview. The Recent activity section on the right also shows the progression of our repository.*

Build Tools

Our design studio will be relying on plug-ins and also offer custom compilation and builds. The plug-ins that we will be using are essentially gems and to incorporate them into our projects, we use a tool called bundler. Before we get into integrating plug-ins, we have to first talk about the process of compiling Jekyll and what is required on both ends.

- What dependencies (or gems) does the cloud compiler need to download for Jekyll?

- How should the cloud compiler access the repository that incorporates the downloaded dependencies and recompiles the Jekyll-based site?

- Both sides require a solution, and ultimately we will be using two tools, Rake and bundler.

Bundler is like a dependency manager for Ruby projects. A dependency manager is similar in function to a package manager like RubyGems, but bundler automatically finds the appropriate versions of the gems that we specify or updates old gems that are being used in the project. The best feature of bundler is that additional gems can be added to the project with minimal edits. We don't have to find the plug-ins and then add the plug-in files to the _plugins folder. Only two files need to be changed; even then, the additions are one line each. This keeps the project clean and the clutter minimal. Essentially that means that even though additional plug-ins are being added to the project, bundler only fetches them during compilation. Then, Jekyll can access them to compile the web site and create the final product. The source code itself remains spared from any additional Ruby (in the plug-ins) and the plug-ins mostly remain invisible. You only have to work with your usual Jekyll source code, and this familiarity makes the process of adding plug-ins much easier. We can rely on a similar workflow that we have used in the past: In a way, the plug-ins become imports like font-awesome. To use font-awesome, all you need to do is find the icon and then the grab the corresponding `<i>` tag. The `import` statement along with the `<i>` tag automatically displays the appropriate icon, similar to how bundler adds the gems to the project and we just see the final result.

There are two files that bundler accesses to add plug-ins or gems, the _config.yml file and the Gemfile. We looked at a Gemfile earlier and basically it is a specification of where to find the gems and what version to obtain. This works out nicely because bundler uses the Gemfile as a phone directory and finds us exactly what we are looking for. Let's look at another one with versions.

```
source 'https://rubygems.org'                # Source of gems

gem 'jekyll', '~> 2.5'                       # Version of the gem (Jekyll)

group :jekyll_plugins do                     # Plug-ins associated with Jekyll
        gem "jekyll-less"
        gem 'therubyracer', '~> 0.12.2'
end                                          # A loop of plug-ins associated with Jekyll
```

This Gemfile can now be used by bundler. Let's look at the edits that need to be made to _config.yml.

```
gems: ['jekyll-less', 'therubyracer']
```

That's it. The Gemfile tells bundler to download those specific gems with the given version. What can it do after downloading them? The handover of those gems from bundler to Jekyll is accomplished through the config file and with that line of code shown above. The _config.yml file tells Jekyll to actually use those plug-ins, and during the compile process and if the source code calls on those gems, they are incorporated in the proper places. These two edits are all we need to use plug-ins in Jekyll, a practical demonstration of how bundler keeps the project clean, looking for gems and then incorporating them into projects. What about the actual compilation and then pushing the code back to the appropriate repository? That's where Rake enters the picture.

Rake (Ruby make) is a build tool (or task manager) in Ruby that can execute tasks provided to it in a certain order. It is similar to the build tool make, which is often used in C/C++ languages. Usually, make needs instructions to compile and those instructions are found in a makefile. The makefile directs make how to compile a program and produce the integrated final product that can be executed. Rake is built on similar principles; the main idea is that you would use Rake to automate running multiple commands in series. Think about the Git add-commit-push workflow and what if that all could be done automatically each time with a single command. That's what Rake basically allows you to do. By the end of this section, we talk about how to remove even that single command from the whole compile process. In our design studio, we use Rake primarily in the following manner:

- Access Bitbucket and find the repository that we want to compile.

- Download the code from that remote repository into a temporary location.

- Compile the code and generate the result in the _site directory.

- Push the code from the _site directory back to the remote location, keeping Git tags in sync.

In this project, our application of Rake is in the context of system commands and less focused on Ruby itself. We use it for system commands, like the ones you have been typing in the terminal so far. The point of using Rake and a cloud compiler is to automate the whole compile process. Codeship can rely on Rake to tell it exactly how to get our data and publish back the results. To do so, we have to instruct Rake to issue commands to the terminal one at a time. Let's look at a Rakefile (similar to a makefile) that accomplishes the steps we just outlined.

```
desc "Generate jekyll site"              # Description of the task
task :generate do                        # What to execute when Rake is asked to
generate
  puts "## Generating Site with Jekyll"
  system "jekyll build"                  # Rake generate will build the Jekyll site
end

desc "Push code to Bitbucket"            # Second task
task :publish do                         # What to execute when Rake is asked to
publish
    system "git add ."                   # Rake goes through add-commit-push workflow
    system "git commit -am 'Codeship Update'"
    system "git push -u origin master"
  end
end
```

This was just an example to illustrate how tasks in Rake work. The previously mentioned Rake file will not compile or actually work because we need to add more information. However, we can use this to build on and create the Rakefile that will ultimately be used in the design studio and also that you can use for custom builds. The Rakefile is divided into tasks that Rake can then execute, and essentially, the tasks are step-by-step instructions telling Rake what to do. The first task is generate, and the syntax tells Rake to execute it (rebuilding the Jekyll site) if we were to type rake generate in a terminal. The second task is publish, and it can be executed by issuing the rake publish command. The syntax here tells Rake to publish the resulting Jekyll site from the first task back to the remote location (in this case, the Bitbucket repository). Rake satisfies the second requirement that we originally talked about; the cloud compiler can rely on the Rakefile to tell it where to get the code and where to put it after finishing up. Now that we have talked about the build tools, let's start playing with Codeship.

Continuous Integration

Codeship is a continuous integration service that we will be using in this project. Codeship provides free builds for open source projects, which is great for us because the code will be hosted on Bitbucket. Continuous integration (CI) is a development practice that requires developers to check in their code into a shared repository as soon as a feature is ready. Each check-in is then verified by automated build tools, allowing a team to detect problems early and fix them as a project moves along. Essentially, a CI service rebuilds a project any time a new feature is added, so that the source code is always remains compile-ready and error free. We are taking advantage of this principle to recompile Jekyll with each commit to the repository, so that our plug-ins properly integrated within the site. Codeship will provide the infrastructure where both bundler and Rake can be used and the resulting code will be pushed back to the same repository as a new commit. Then, our web site will be updated automatically based on this new commit.

How does Codeship know to rebuild the site each time a new commit is made? Codeship is using commit hooks. Git has a way to trigger custom scripts when some known actions are registered. A commit hook listens for specific events; when they are registered, it performs a specific action in return. Codeship uses server-side hooks that look for network operations such as receiving pushed commits. Once a commit happens, the hook is triggered and then it passes on the control to a deployment pipeline, which in turn uses Rake and Bundler to rebuild the code and push it back to the appropriate location. This is the continuous integration mechanism that we use in this chapter. To get started with Codeship, visit https://codeship.com/ and click Login to start setting up a deployment pipeline.

You should then see a screen that lets you create an account. We just log in with our Bitbucket account using OAuth, as shown in Figure 13-18. After logging in, the dashboard, shown in Figure 13-19, looks fairly empty because we haven't done anything yet.

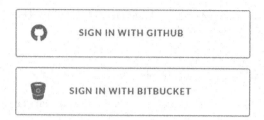

Sign in with GitHub or Bitbucket

Figure 13-18. *Instead of creating an account, we log in directly with our Bitbucket repository*

Figure 13-19a. *Top bar on Codeship home page. This bar has a few navigation features to select and browse among the various projects that you can manage on Codeship.*

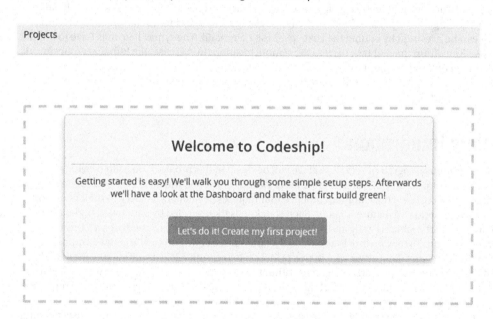

Figure 13-19b. *The dashboard below the navigation bar. This is where the build status of your projects would show up and eventually the build process itself would appear.*

Let's start with the walkthrough. There are three distinct steps to connecting Codeship to Bitbucket. The first one is to link the source code manager (GitHub or Bitbucket) to Codeship. After that, pick the appropriate repository. Then, select the build environment and configure any tests if you want to run them. In the first step, we link our Bitbucket repository. Click Connect with Bitbucket repository as shown in Figure 13-20a. After that, you are required to pick the repository, shown in Figure 13-20b. At this time, we only have one option available, but you can imagine a user having multiple repositories. Once you have configured the source repository, you can start configuring the cloud environment. The first step here is to let Codeship know that we need a Ruby environment. This can be seen by selecting Ruby from the Select your technology to populate basic commands drop-down list, shown in Figure 13-21. After selecting Ruby, you will see that the setup commands are calling bundler. This call essentially prepares the cloud environment to eventually compile Jekyll in it. The idea here is to retrieve the Gemfile that will then instruct bundler on what gems to install into this new cloud environment.

Figure 13-20a. *Selecting the choice to connect Bitbucket SCM because it contains our repository*

Figure 13-20b. *The search bar allows you to narrow down the repositories and find the right one*

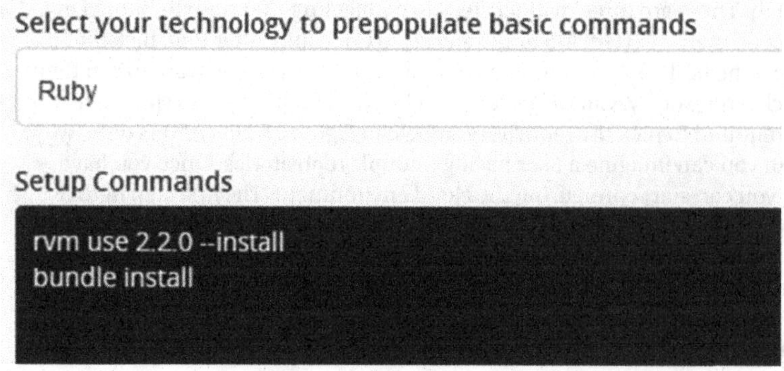

Select your technology to prepopulate basic commands

Ruby

Setup Commands

```
rvm use 2.2.0 --install
bundle install
```

Figure 13-21. *The cloud environment that will eventually receive our Jekyll site needs to be prepared for it. To manage what gets installed, we rely on bundler and the Gemfile that we created. Here, we just tell the cloud environment to use bundler and let it do what we instructed. With this process, all our dependencies will get installed.*

Once the installation is complete, bundler is ready to hand over the control flow to the deployment pipeline, which will retrieve the source code from the repository, compile it, and then push the the result back into the same repository. Codeship also allows you to write tests for your repository that can be triggered when a commit is made. The test pipeline can be seen in Figure 13-22, but we leave the test pipeline blank.

Configure Test Pipelines (1 / 1 Used)

Test Commands   + Add Pipeline

Did you know you can split up test commands and let them run in pa
Activate ParallelCI Trial

‹ Back   Save and go to dashboard   Cancel

Figure 13-22. *Second half of the setup commands page. The test pipeline can be configured here with the appropriate commands but we leave this blank. Delete the contents of that box and then click Save.*

After saving the initial setup configuration, the project dashboard takes on a new look, as shown in Figure 13-23. This screen signifies that Codeship is ready for our repository to start receiving code and rebuilding it. A few more steps are necessary in this process, though. Remember that bundler will only install the dependencies, so we will need Rake to be ready when bundler passes control flow of the project to it. Rake will be configured directly with the deployment pipeline. On the right side, click Project Settings and select Deployment as shown in Figure 13-24.

Push to your repository to trigger your first build

What to push?

Figure 13-23. *After clicking Save and go to dashboard on the setup page, you return to this page. This is a confirmation that the cloud environment is ready for the repository transfer between Codeship and Bitbucket.*

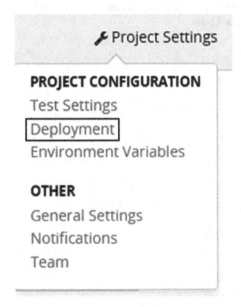

Figure 13-24. *Under Project Settings, select Deployment to start editing the deployment pipeline*

The first step is setting up a commit hook, and we need to tell Codeship which branch to listen and register commits, as depicted in Figure 13-25.

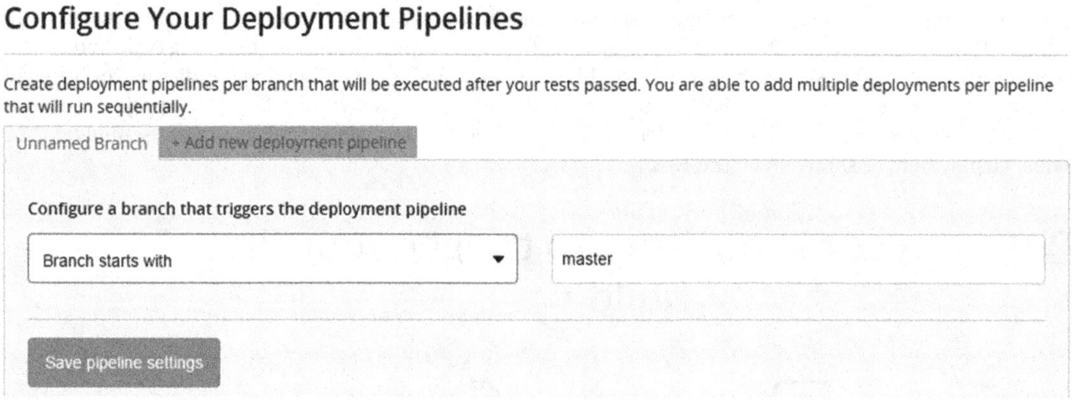

Configure Your Deployment Pipelines

Create deployment pipelines per branch that will be executed after your tests passed. You are able to add multiple deployments per pipeline that will run sequentially.

Unnamed Branch   + Add new deployment pipeline

Configure a branch that triggers the deployment pipeline

Branch starts with ▼   master

Save pipeline settings

Figure 13-25. *Configuring deployment pipelines. First we need to tell Codeship to look for a branch that starts with master to listen for commits. After entering the configuration as shown earlier, click Save pipeline settings to start defining the commit hook.*

After entering the branch that triggers the deployment process, you are presented with a host of options on how exactly to trigger the pipeline. In our project, we just want the control flow to be passed on to Rake, which will then take care of managing the code and putting it back in the repository. To tell Codeship that we are using Rake, select the Custom Script option as shown in Figure 13-26.

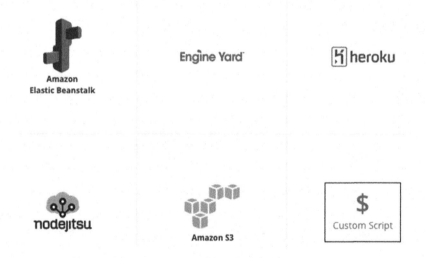

Figure 13-26. *Selecting the deployment pipeline trigger. We use two commands that use Rake tasks*

After clicking Custom Scripts, you will be presented with the custom scripts deployment box shown in Figure 13-27, where you can enter the commands that will be executed after the commit. Essentially, we want to invoke Rake so that it can compile the site and push it back to the proper location according to the instructions in the Rakefile. To do that, we use the rake generate and rake publish tasks. Once those commands have been entered, click Create Deployment and that will create our deployment pipeline. At this point, Codeship is ready to register commits to our Bitbucket repository and recompile Jekyll as we instruct Rake to do. Let's take a moment to discuss one more design choice: Why did we use bundler and Rake, which rely on makefiles? Going back to the original point about avoiding clutter, a significant advantage of using those two tools is that the only change to the project's source code is the makefiles. Once the deployment pipeline is in place, we don't have to touch it again. The same holds true if the design studio wants to deploy custom builds for customers. When the pipeline is working, you can reduce your focus to just the source code in the repository. Any changes from that point on can be made to the makefiles and they will work just the same through the pipeline that you have deployed.

Custom script

Enter your custom deployment script line by line. Disable them by putting # at the beginning of a line

Deployment Commands:

```
rake generate
rake publish
```

Each line is like a command that you execute in a local shell from within the project path.

Create Deployment

Figure 13-27. *Here, we enter deployment commands that will be triggered after bundler, and the deployment pipeline takes over. Executing these two commands will run corresponding tasks defined in the Rakefile.*

The last step in this walkthrough is to get the SSH keys from Codeship and then add them to Bitbucket. Click Project Settings again and then select General Settings from the drop-down menu. The General Project Settings page is shown in Figure 13-28.

⚙ PROJECT SETTINGS

Test
Deployment
Environment
Notification
Team members
Repository
General

General Project Settings

Bitbucket Connection

Codeship is properly connected with "opsbug/testing" on Bitbucket.

Codeship is currently using **Vikram Dhillon's** authentication when connecting to the project repository on **Bitbucket.**

Figure 13-28. *General Project Settings page. Scrolling down further on this page brings you to the SSH public key that you need to add to Bitbucket*

Scroll down a little more and you will find the public SSH key, which might look similar to the following:

```
ssh-rsa AAAAB3NzaC1yc2EAAAADAQABAAAABAQDDnIjKwRBDDOp+1mX88dyiaztqbeyf8cgEghw1ejBlchHaxONNB
yXUtXymXtWeBv5S3wOIiCQem4E6gL1zG/iw3VRQP7k2YOPSaJDvhBf9f5A4z/O6scSnngBlqvPfEohVp7GRcR3VR
NOy2v/Hq/YznOQWzstUau1TgOFt7i9oIgjvm+hr450hs+rYXWdjdgpPOWa3WgVO3v4O1ua69Q9yoKSAKGjacnJGEOg
5EKBRTBlZX8xOBLAh7eo/Bzo/fc6xgxslOfcD25L2VjmOd8tOMdlP6pbODO/Wl/P63ObJhKMpwIbNOobcm
fpOOVjIMIdI+h63RbKXzlVO4cCqVYwN Codeship/opsbug/testing
```

Copy this key and then head back to Bitbucket. On the right side, go to the Bitbucket Settings. In the left sidebar, one of the navigation topics is Security; underneath that you will find a link to SSH Keys. Click that to open the SSH keys page, which currently shows nothing. You have to add the key that you just copied from Codeship. Click Add Key to open a dialogue box similar to the one shown in Figure 13-29.

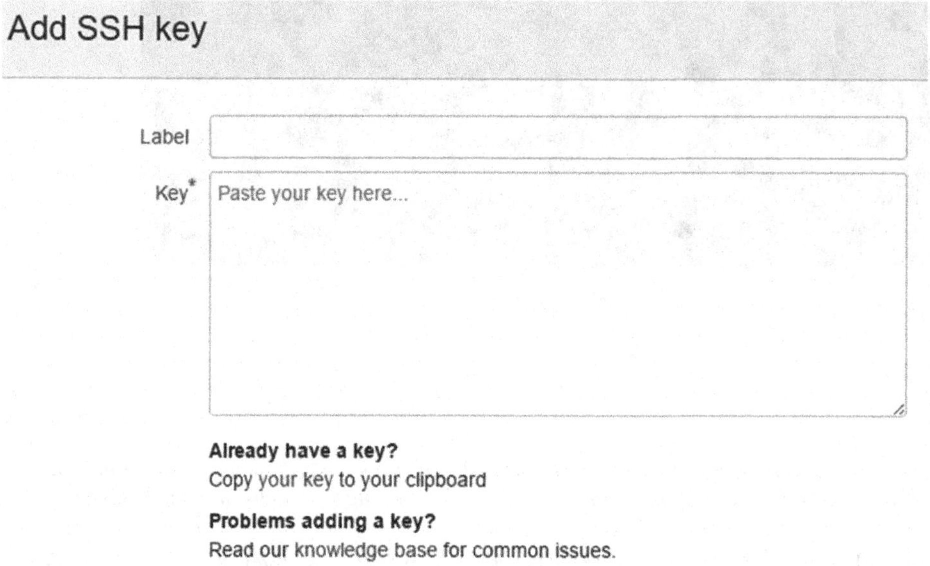

Add SSH key

Label

Key*   Paste your key here...

Already have a key?
Copy your key to your clipboard

Problems adding a key?
Read our knowledge base for common issues.

Figure 13-29. Adding an SSH key to Bitbucket. You can use anything as a label, maybe Codeship. The key should be pasted directly from Codeship, then click Add Key to finalize the process.

Once the key has been added, Codeship can now actually push data back to the Bitbucket repository. The next task for us is to manage the control flow of the project once the code has been pushed to the repository. What steps do we need to take so that the compiled result can be served to users? There's a plug-in that can be added to Bitbucket to make this process smooth and also allow for additional functionality, called Aerobatic.

Essentially, Aerobatic is an advanced version of GitHub Pages with additional features. Aerobatic makes it easier to deploy a static site from your Bitbucket repository, and it offers features such as basic authentication and automatic deployment of the newer version of a site, once it comes back from being processed in Codeship. Aerobatic is in Figure 13-30, and can be found at https://www.aerobatic.com/.

Features   Documentation   Pricing   Blog

Git push and your web site is live

The *easiest* way to deploy and manage your static HTML website straight from Bitbucket

Install Bitbucket Add-On

Figure 13-30. *Site manager for Bitbucket Aerobatic. This plug-in installs on the Bitbucket account after being authenticated. Use this plug-in to access advanced features like authentication and site updates.*

Installing Aerobatic to your Bitbucket repository is very straightforward. Click Install Bitbucket Add-On on Aerobatic's web site as shown in Figure 13-30. After that, you should be presented with the OAuth screen shown in Figure 13-31.

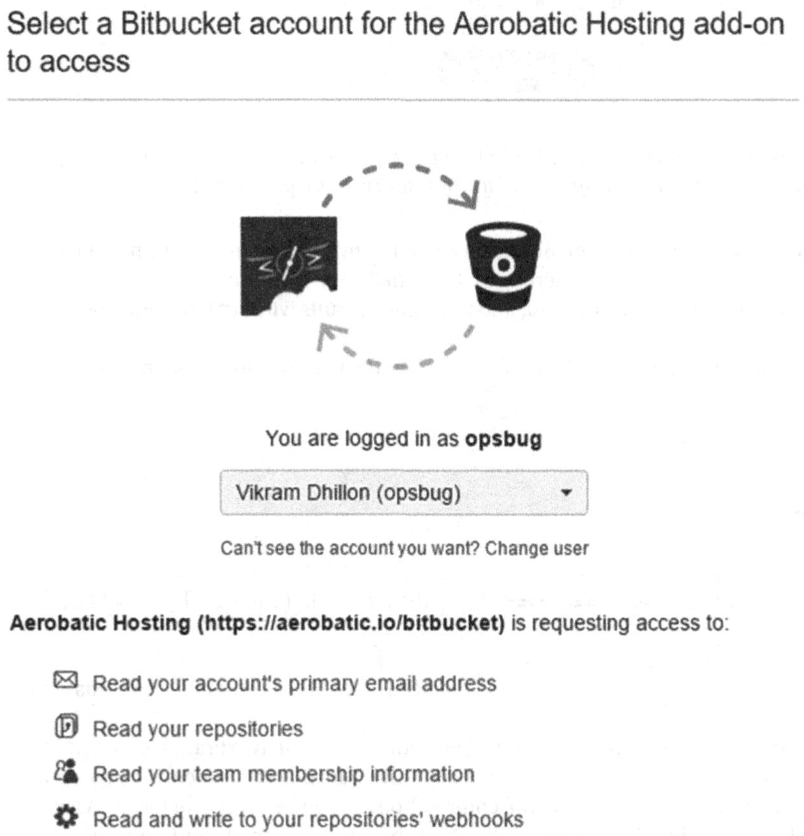

Select a Bitbucket account for the Aerobatic Hosting add-on to access

You are logged in as **opsbug**

Vikram Dhillon (opsbug)   ▾

Can't see the account you want? Change user

Aerobatic Hosting (https://aerobatic.io/bitbucket) is requesting access to:

✉ Read your account's primary email address

🗇 Read your repositories

👥 Read your team membership information

⚙ Read and write to your repositories' webhooks

Figure 13-31. *OAuth for Aerobatic plug-in. Click the "Grant access" button on this screen (not shown in the image) to get Aerobatic on your account.*

Aerobatic actually lets us do more than what we previously described and also what we would get from GitHub Pages. Note that GitHub Pages is fundamentally a platform designed to run sites built with Jekyll, whereas Bitbucket doesn't have a similar architecture. It is actually built in Python, but in any case, Bitbucket and Aerobatic are more focused on hosting static sites that might not only be Jekyll-built. Just like Bitbucket, Aerobatic is more general; it will host any sort of static pages that aren't even organized as a site or project with a parser. After installation, you will see in your account dashboard a new tab for Aerobatic. Clicking it reveals the settings, as shown in Figure 13-32. The beauty of Aerobatic is that it strives to be a fully featured theme manager, so it comes with a few basic HTML5 themes that can be installed and hosted in a repository with a single click. This one-click installation, followed by hosting within a repository, makes Aerobatic a very powerful companion even for small projects. We use it to assist in hosting our design studio's main site and simplify the workflow for adding new plug-ins or rebuilding easily after new features get added. To understand how this new plug-in will help us, we first need to create a new workflow involving a repository that is hosted and managed by Aerobatic.

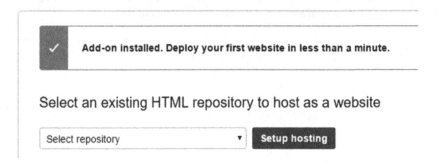

Figure 13-32. *Confirmation that Aerobatic was installed in Bitbucket. Below the confirmation message are the settings available to Aerobatic. To get started, specify which repository to use for hosting*

At this point, we have installed Aerobatic to the Bitbucket account and now we need to think about the deployment pipeline and how it will integrate with Aerobatic. Essentially, the idea is that we want to simplify our workflow so that the cloud compiler can access data and push back results without interfering with our hosting process.

The workflow using Aerobatic with the Bitbucket account for hosting is shown in this schematic.

Schematic

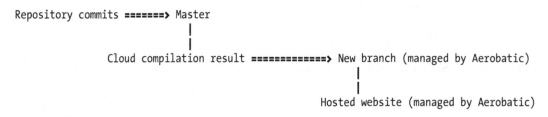

Let's go through it to understand it properly. For our design studio, we create two branches: a master branch and an aerobatic branch. The workflow begins with a commit to the master branch. This commit triggers Codeship to recompile Jekyll because we have the commit hook set up in a way that it listens for commits to the master. Recall that we did this in Figure 13-25. After the commit is made and Codeship is done, the resulting site needs to be pushed back, and Rake takes care of that. The resulting site will be pushed back to a new branch; we can call it aerobatic, but the point here is that we are trying to keep the source code free from the hosting production code. When the compilation is done, Rake will push the result to the new branch and we will configure Aerobatic to host the contents of this branch. In this manner, the source code is kept in a different branch and the result is kept in a different branch that will continuously get updated from each update. The end result is still the same: Make edits to master and those edits will eventually make their way into the site from the new branch. This concludes our walkthrough of Codeship and installing Aerobatic on Bitbucket. Now we can finally get started creating the design studio. As we go through implementing the features for the design studio, we have to divide them into categories: advertisement, deployment, plug-ins, shopping cart, prototyping, cards, and finally customer support. For each of these categories, we talk about the tools best suited to do the job and provide a brief overview regarding how these tools can make you more efficient.

Solid Studio

The theme that we will be using for the design studio is called Solid. It can be found on the Jekyll Themes web site at https://github.com/st4ple/solid-jekyll. This theme is designed for agencies or freelancers. The theme is almost a perfect match for us in terms of compatibility and required features. It has a minimalistic and elegant layout, with the relevant information about a studio on the home page. Aside from the content, this theme is usable out of the box; because of that we won't be spending time editing the theme. Instead, we focus entirely on implementing the features we discussed earlier. So far, we have had the luxury of being able to push our code and see the results instantly on a site generated by GitHub Pages. In this case, you won't be seeing the compiled web site until after Aerobatic has finished hosting it. If you want to see if your newly downloaded Solid theme works, just run jekyll build in the extracted zip folder. Here's the output you should obtain from Jekyll locally.

```
C:\Users\Vikram\Desktop\solid-jekyll-master\>jekyll build
Configuration file: C:/Users/Vikram/Desktop/solid-jekyll-master/_config.yml
            Source: C:/Users/Vikram/Desktop/solid-jekyll-master/
       Destination: C:/Users/Vikram/Desktop/solid-jekyll-master/_site
 Incremental build: disabled. Enable with --incremental
        Generating...
     Build Warning: Layout 'none' requested in feed.xml does not exist.
                    done in 3.064 seconds.
 Auto-regeneration: disabled. Use --watch to enable.
```

Fiverr and Gumroad

The first feature we want to build is the ability to advertise our services on other platforms and make a credible name for our design studio. Users will only buy services or web themes from a trusted source and using a different platform to get started will only give us another avenue to convert users into paid customers. Fiverr is an online marketplace where freelancers offer services (or gigs as they are called) to customers. The name of the web site came from a large number of gigs worth only $5. If you browse Fiverr or search for design or web-related gigs, there are thousands available. A sample design gig is shown in Figure 13-33. For a design studio, individuals can create Fiverr profiles and set up low-priced gigs that are unique to their own specialty. In a sense, this is how a design studio operates in the early stages: You have to get customers paying for services; through their referral, you can get more clients. Fiverr makes that process incredibly easy and also puts your design studio in front of thousands of potential clients.

Figure 13-33. *An example of a logo design gig sold on Fiverr. In this case, clicking on the gig takes us to the purchase page where we see that the basic gig is $5 and this premium gig is worth $30.*

Aside from gigs, there are some very interesting features available on the platform. One of the most useful and powerful features is the availability of pricing packages. This is very handy in two ways. First, the seller (or freelancer) can provide multiple levels of a gig, such as a simple version for $5 and premium versions that include additional services. You can split up a web service that you would offer on your own web site into several simple gigs and then create packages that will offer more features accordingly. The second advantage of using packages is to combine several gigs into one collection and charge for the whole package. This second option is seemingly close to a web design package that you would want to offer from your own studio. The importance of testing the pricing and composition of packages before you start selling them from your own web site can't be overstated. A sample of some collections currently being sold on Fiverr are shown in Figure 13-34.

TRENDING COLLECTIONS
Choose from our most popular services

BOOST YOUR RANKING
6 ways to improve your site's ranking

ENGAGE YOUR AUDIENCE
Explainer videos that sell!

Figure 13-34. *Two of the trending collections available on Fiverr. Notice that both of these collections deal with web design: One talks about SEO and page views, and the second is about video marketing. In a similar manner, you could make a collection from your gigs and sell your package of web services to test the waters.*

Whereas Fiverr is a marketplace for small gigs and services, Gumroad is a marketplace for digital products to be sold with a variety of payment structures, including subscription. Gumroad comes into play when you have customers interested in a few of your most popular gigs, and you want to target them and sell guides or ebooks that those customers can use to take their own projects a step further. You can even use your MailChimp subscribers to generate leads for sales. One really interesting feature in Gumroad is subscription-based pricing of products that you can use to do presales, sell Jekyll themes as zip files, or continually sell request-based guides and ebooks. Let's go over how subscriptions work, sign up for an account on Gumroad, and perform a very brief walkthrough. Start by clicking on the top navigation bar notifications to add a product, as shown in Figure 13-35.

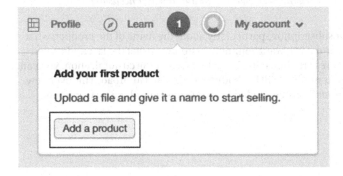

Figure 13-35. *Getting started with adding a new product from the Gumroad dashboard*

When you click Add a product, you are presented with options for what type of products can be added, as shown in Figure 13-36a; in this case, select Digital product. This will further show options like adding a product sale, a subscription for a product, and collecting preorders. Select Subscription and provide a name, as shown in Figure 13-36b. After giving a name to the subscription, you have the option of customizing it.

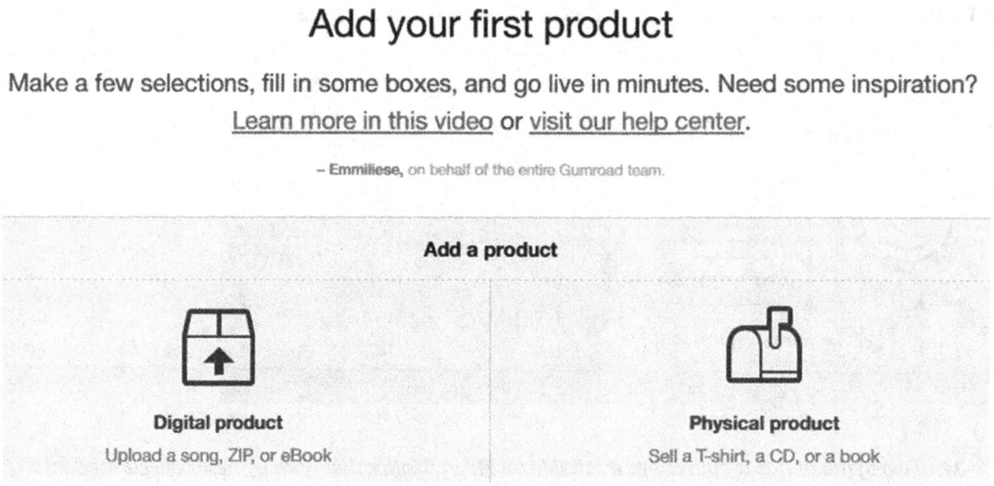

Add your first product

Make a few selections, fill in some boxes, and go live in minutes. Need some inspiration?
Learn more in this video or visit our help center.

– Emmiliese, on behalf of the entire Gumroad team.

Add a product

Digital product	**Physical product**
Upload a song, ZIP, or eBook	Sell a T-shirt, a CD, or a book

Figure 13-36a. Selecting the type of product to add in Gumroad. We will go with a digital product.

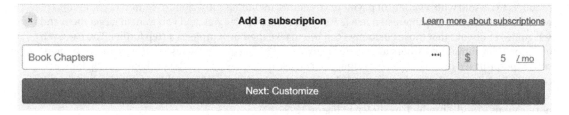

Add a subscription   Learn more about subscriptions

Book Chapters   •••| $ 5   / mo

Next: Customize

Figure 13-36b. Naming the subscription and setting the price per month that the user needs to pay

Now we need to add more details to our subscription, particularly about the name of the product, what exactly are we selling, what the price will be, and if you want your new customers to get the last update you sent to your product. The customization features are shown in Figure 13-37. After the customization, you can save the changes from top of the page and your product will be ready to be sold on Gumroad. This overview is not comprehensive, but it does cover the basic features needed to start using and selling on Gumroad.

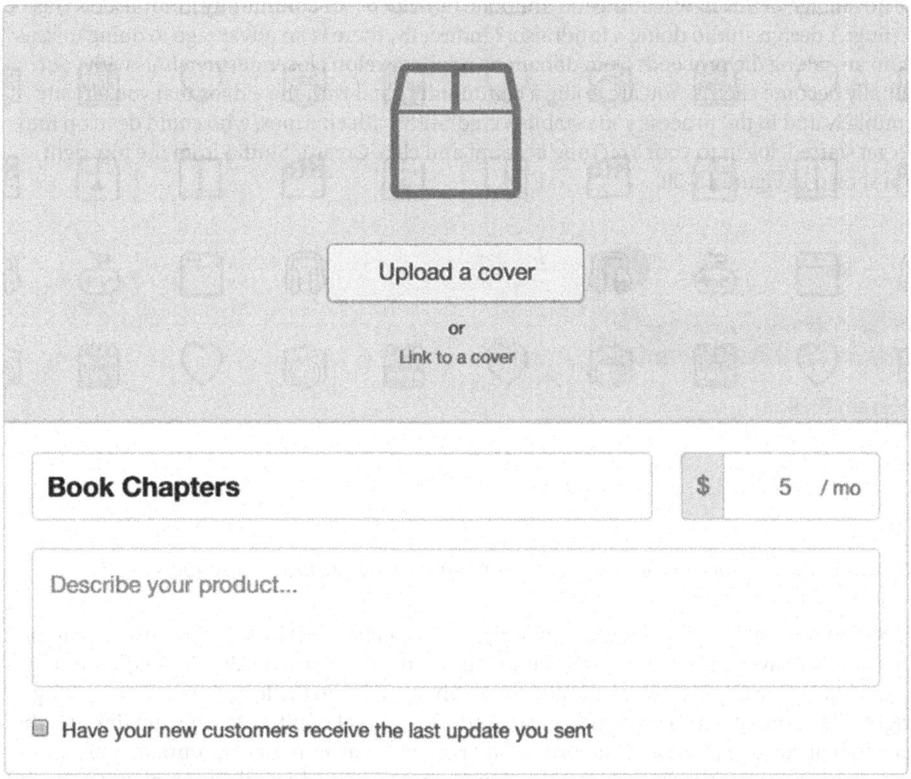

Figure 13-37. *Customizing the subscription sale page. The page contains options for adding a cover photo, name of the product, description, and price.*

Updates are sent as e-mails with file attachments that go out to your subscribers. Once you have subscribers, you can send them updates about how the product is coming along in the case of presales or upcoming features and updates to the content of their current subscription. There are many possibilities involving what you can send through these updates: You can send your subscribers new book chapters, videos, or other digital content, which can be downloaded directly from the update e-mail.

YouTube and Wistia

Video marketing is new, but very lucrative, simply because people like videos more than they would enjoy reading text that describes features and updates. A person explaining why you would want to use something, how it could help you, and a touching story of how a product helped a user is far more persuasive than reading testimonials and white papers prepared by product managers. Videos on YouTube about products and people reviewing those products have become a common way of reaching mass audiences. Uploading to YouTube has become as easy as having a mobile device, and the new platform even offers several editing features in the browser so you don't have to do offline editing. This has made the process incredibly fast, and it has become easier to create high-quality videos. Recently, YouTube introduced cards along with annotations that can be overlaid on videos at specific times throughout the video. The addition of cards also comes with a unique feature of collecting donations for a charity or nonprofit of your choice.

We can take advantage of this new feature and annotate our videos for community fundraisers. This might seem puzzling: A design studio doing a fundraiser? Indirectly, there is an advantage to doing this, as the nonprofits who are taking the proceeds from donations might develop closer partnerships with your studio and eventually become clients. You are doing a community good with the videos that you already made available publicly and in the process you establish credibility with charities, who could develop into future clients. To get started, log in to your YouTube account and click Creator Studio from the top-right drop-down menu shown in Figure 13-38.

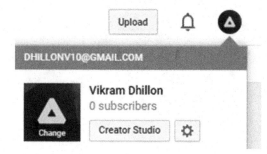

Figure 13-38. *Reaching the Creator Studio from the account options. Ignore the 0 subscribers*

The Creator Studio provides in-browser video editing and annotation services. In the Creator Studio, you will see the videos you have uploaded; an example video is shown in Figure 13-39. Click Edit button to reveal the options, including Cards. Edit mode launches with the video in the left pane and the editing options on the right side of the screen. The video is displayed with several pointers for the timeline and these are all put in place so that you can place annotations or other features easily at the appropriate time, and you can even control the duration for which the annotation appears. Click Add card option on the right and select Donation, which brings you to a search bar and lets you pick to which charity you want to donate. It might be a good idea to reach out to a local chapter of that nonprofit so that they know you are sending them some traffic and donations. Edit mode is shown in Figure 13-40.

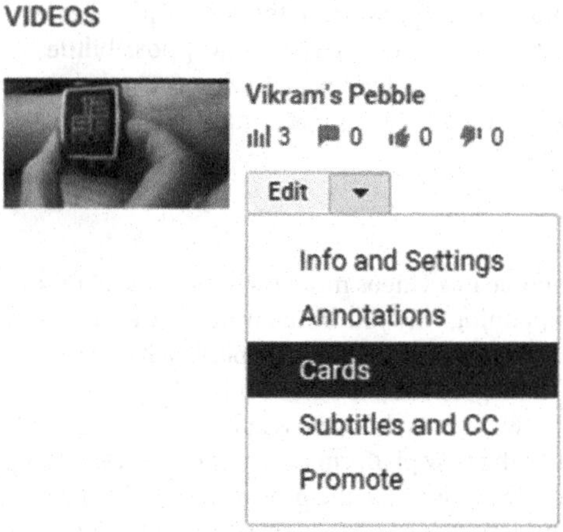

VIDEOS

Vikram's Pebble

ılıl 3   ⚐ 0   👍 0   👎 0

Edit ▼

Info and Settings

Annotations

Cards

Subtitles and CC

Promote

Figure 13-39. *Creator Studio mode lists the videos uploaded by the account, and clicking Edit reveals the cards*

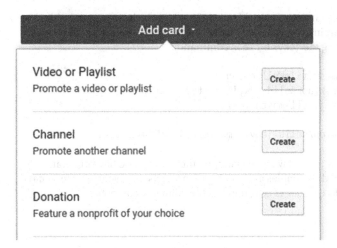

Figure 13-40. *Edit mode with the Add card feature displayed. Click Create next to Donation to add a donation card at a certain time during the video.*

Wistia was founded in 2006 as a video hosting and analytics company. You can think of Wistia as a more serious cousin of YouTube, designed for video marketers who want in-depth analytics and data on how their videos are performing. Here are some of the most interesting features that Wistia offers that a design studio might be able to take advantage of.

- **Heatmaps:** In Wistia, every video view generates a heatmap, which shows exactly which parts of the video were watched, skipped, and rewatched. These trends become very valuable data that can be tracked over time that might influence your overall video marketing strategy.

- **Better quality:** The streaming server for Wistia automatically determines each viewer's connection speed and delivers the best quality video within those parameters to avoid buffering.

- **Calls to action:** Just like YouTube, Wistia offers a version of cards and annotations, but these annotations can be animated and have other valuable features. If you have a video that shows how to add a new feature to a particular theme, wouldn't it be helpful if you could add a call to action toward the viewer to download that theme and make those edits, too? This can allow you to turn passive viewers into active members or even paid customers.

- **E-mail lists:** At some point during the video, you can ask the user to subscribe using a call to action for the viewer entering an e-mail address. You are offering free content that's valuable to the viewer; in return, they could easily become a lead for sales down the line.

- **Customization:** The video player and controls of that player can have a custom theme or colors to ensure that the video fits in with the design of your web site.

Shopping Cart

We started by talking about using other platforms to advertise your products and services, but eventually you will have to start selling packages and services from your own design studio as well. We need to add a shopping cart to our design studio, and to do so we use Snipcart. It integrates very nicely with many other static site generators and therefore it is a good choice to use with Jekyll. In addition, the process of adding it along with new items to the web site is something you have seen and done repeatedly in the past. Let's first clean out our old build in the local folder using the jekyll clean command.

```
C:\Users\Vikram\Desktop\solid-jekyll-master>jekyll clean
Configuration file: C:/Users/Vikram/Desktop/solid-jekyll-master/_config.yml
Cleaning C:/Users/Vikram/Desktop/solid-jekyll-master/_site...
                    done.
Nothing to do for C:/Users/Vikram/Desktop/solid-jekyll-master/.jekyll-metadata.
```

That should clean up the _site folder for us, and we will recompile the site after we have integrated Snipcart. This shopping cart relies on site.data variables as a catalog of products to be sold. Create a _data folder in the theme and add a file in that called products.yml that has the following contents.

```
- name: Change by Design
  price: 29.99
  slug: change-by-design
  sku: CBD
  image: http://d.gr-assets.com/books/1348453734l/6671664.jpg

- name: Creative Confidence
  price: 16.90
  slug: creative-confidence
  sku: CC
  image: http://d.gr-assets.com/books/1375677702l/17288649.jpg

- name: The Art of Innovation
  price: 16.34
  slug: art-of-innovation
  sku: AOI
  image: http://d.gr-assets.com/books/1429647369l/40958.jpg
```

As you can see, this is the metadata for the three books we want to sell on the page, and all of it is stored inside the _data folder so it can be accessed using site.data variables. All we need now is to create a new page called books.html to render this data along with the images.

```
---
layout: default
title: Books
---

<div class="home">
  <h1 class="page-heading">Books</h1>           # Header of the page

  <ul class="products-list">                    # List of books from products.yml file
    {% for product in site.data.products %}     # For loop going through each book

    <li>                                        # Display the image first
      <img src="{{ product.image }}" alt="{{ product.name }}" class="thumbnail"/>

      {{ product.name }}                        # Followed by the product name
```

```
      <button class="snipcart-add-item"       # Finally, add the purchase button
        data-item-name="{{product.name}}"
        data-item-id="{{product.sku}}"
        data-item-image="{{product.image}}"
        data-item-url="{{site.baseurl}}"
        data-item-price="{{product.price}}">
        Buy it for {{product.price}} $        # data-item variables provide info to
                                                 Snipcart

      </button>
    </li>

  {% endfor %}                                 # Closing the for-loop
  </ul>
</div>
```

This will create a very rudimentary page that contains the images of the book followed by the price and a buy button. All the data item variables provide the information that Snipcart needs to process the items and make it through checkout. To see how it looks, you can generate the web site locally and see the cart, and you can browse to localhost:4000/books.html and see it in action. A sample books page is shown in Figure 13-41. Note that you will not be able to do a complete checkout when you are viewing the site locally. Snipcart will not be able to validate prices, but once it is deployed to production, the cart will work. Snipcart is only one way to integrate a shopping cart into the web site; you could also use payment providers such as Stripe directly to pay for services. Those services have excellent guides on how to integrate the payment APIs. Another very easy-to-use payment platform is Helium. It allows customers to pay using a simple form that slides in over your web site. Without being taken to another page, visitors can pay on the spot using any major credit card. They don't even need to create an account. Although Helium integrates very easily into web sites, you don't necessarily have to have one. The product page can be hosted on Helium itself, so all you need to do is e-mail, tweet, or post that link for customers to pay. This concludes our discussion of adding a shopping cart. Next we discuss about InVision and prototyping.

Figure 13-41. *Snipcart in action, after being deployed locally*

Prototyping in InVision

For a design studio, getting clients and providing them with initial prototypes is almost two thirds of the way to closing the deal. Most designers presently use InVision for rapid prototyping and, more important, to give live and interactive demos. This might be the most important tool in your tool set that we have discussed so far, as almost any modern design studio must learn how to use and navigate through InVision. The reason for using InVision is very simple: Static demos of product features are not as tangible as a live, interactive demo that the user can navigate through and feel as an almost real version. InVision provides the ability to create clickable demos from static Photoshop UI elements. It's great for taking images and making clickable image prototypes that go from screen to screen, and you can see how a feature is actually supposed look.

The closer your clients feel to seeing the polished or finished product, the more satisfied they will be with your work. Even more important, InVision's demos help the client see even small interactions like how one click takes the user from one screen to another. They can pinpoint any issues that they encounter, saving both you and them some valuable time. Essentially, InVision is design-driven project management. This is important to realize because the same type of thinking involved in creating Jekyll-based web sites can be carried over to designing wireframes or prototypes. Most of the work involved in designing these clickable demos originates in the static mockups that designers create using Photoshop and UI kits. They can often take common elements such as sliders or menu bars from design kits and use them in their own projects. InVision takes this process a step further by allowing the drop-down menu to actually appear when clicking a menu bar item. It makes that menu bar navigation item come to life by assigning properties to it in a new fashion. Some of the most impressive add-ons that come from InVision are the UI or mobile design kits created by them and offered for free. These kits are perfect for creating mockups that can be used later in the web interface for converting them into demos. Here are the UI kits offered by InVision currently.

- **TETHR:** iOS mobile applications design kit, available at `http://www.invisionapp.com/tethr`

- **DO:** Clean, minimal, colorful, and Retina-ready for all kinds of iOS apps, available at `http://www.invisionapp.com/do`

- **NOW:** Cross-platform design UI kit, available at `http://www.invisionapp.com/now`

- **Craft:** When prototyping applications, we often leave items such as drop-down lists empty, but Craft automatically populates text-based objects with names, e-mail addresses, countries, cities, and ZIP codes from a preset database. The idea is to provide contextually relevant content to make your demo and UI flow smoother. You can also do the same with photos using Craft: Either upload them from your computer or a web source. This is available as a feature within InVision.

These kits should turn out to be immensely useful for designers looking to have standard elements that they can use to create mockups. Each of these kits is general enough to have elements that both mobile and web applications need. Although we can't go over using InVision in our brief discussion, there are plenty of examples both in the web interface and guides available through their Help Center. For us, though, sharing a prototype is just as important as building one in the first place. By default, an InVision app offers a link that you can give to your clients so that they can look through the demo themselves and play with it on their phone. However, there are a few other ways that we want to discuss in the remainder of this section.

Embedding an InVision prototype is a very powerful feature because you could use it directly in a blog post or your portfolio. Additionally, one of the recent new features is to share a prototype directly to Twitter. You can grab the InVision link for a project, paste it in a tweet, and automatically, the link will be expanded into a clickable prototype. Basically, a GIF containing the live mockup will be attached to the tweet. Another incredible tool to help embed InVision prototypes is called embed.ly, and this tool also works in an incredibly simple fashion: Just grab your project link and paste it in the Embed bar to generate an embed code that will have your live mockup. The Embed bar is shown in Figure 13-42.

Figure 13-42. Embed bar for InVision live and clickable demos

Even though there is some learning curve to getting familiar with InVision and using the web interface, it is one of the most important design tools available to a design studio. There are plenty of guides available online that show step-by-step how to design a basic prototype in Photoshop and then how to make it come to life in the web interface. Let's move on to integrating live chat now.

Customer Support

Bitbucket is part of the Atlassian product development and management suite. This suite contains another project management and collaboration tool called HipChat that we can use to provide customer support. Although initially intended to be used simply for sharing files and collaboration, it can play the role of a customer support chat room with guest access enabled. You can use the same account as Bitbucket to log in to HipChat at `https://hipchat.com/`. After logging in, you will be asked to create a new team, as shown below in Figure 13-43.

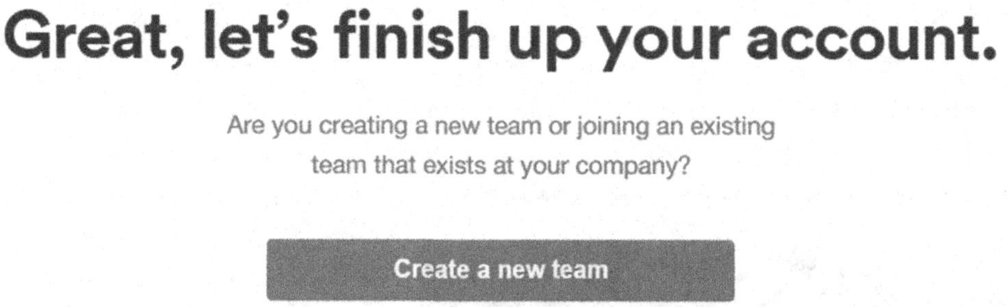

Great, let's finish up your account.

Are you creating a new team or joining an existing
team that exists at your company?

Create a new team

Figure 13-43. You can use your Bitbucket account to access HipChat. Once you log in with your Atlassian account, you will be required to create a new team and an associated team URL that other members can access

Clicking Create a new team takes you to the next screen, which asks for a team URL. You can assign any URL that hasn't been taken, and this becomes the link that your team will need to use to access the HipChat room. After that, click Create team URL, as shown in Figure 13-44, which finalizes the process and brings you to the chat room. At first, there is a lot going on in the chat room, but let's break it down piece by piece. At the top is the navigation bar, which contains a New Chat button that allows us to navigate between rooms or message other users directly. The left side displays the room navigation bar, where you can see the chat rooms that exist and an option to create new ones. The middle portion of the screen is actually the chat room itself; here you can use the text bar at the bottom to chat with other users in the room and share files with them. You can create a new room for customer support that your clients can access. At the top right is a button to access room options that opens a drop-down menu, as shown in Figure 13-45. Clicking the drop-down menu shows an Enable Guest Access option; clicking that allows you to get a link that you can share with your clients in case they need live support. Now you can provide access to the chat room by simply taking the URL mentioned in Figure 13-45 and hyperlinking it with a button from the design studio. The link will open the chat room and your client can be talking to a designer to resolve his or her issue. The more frictionless this process, the higher customer satisfaction will be.

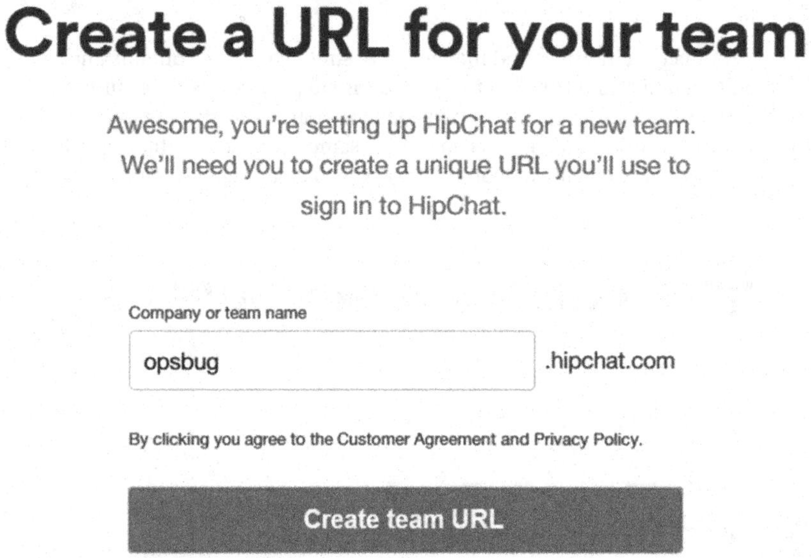

Create a URL for your team

Awesome, you're setting up HipChat for a new team.
We'll need you to create a unique URL you'll use to
sign in to HipChat.

Company or team name

| opsbug | .hipchat.com |

By clicking you agree to the Customer Agreement and Privacy Policy.

Create team URL

Figure 13-44. Creating a team and then a unique team URL to access HipChat

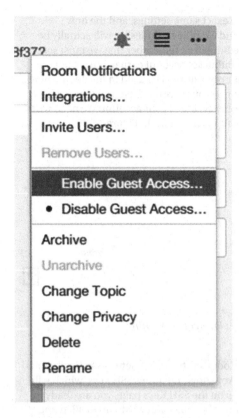

Figure 13-45. *Enabling guest access for the room. Once guest access is turned on, you'll see the room URL in the People sidebar. Copy the URL and send it to your guests. Guests can use this URL to access the room in their browser until guest access is turned off.*

Deployment and Custom Builds

We have already talked at length about deployment and what this process should look like, let's briefly review it: Push code to Bitbucket, link Codeship to Bitbucket, configure the deployment pipeline, and then push the Rakefile and Gemfile. The last commit will be to the _config.yml file, which will trigger Codeship to recompile Jekyll and push back the results into another branch that we can then host using Aerobatic. First let's clean the previous build from the local Solid theme folder, create a new Bitbucket repository called design-studio, and then push the code to it.

```
$ git push --set-upstream origin master
Counting objects: 157, done.
Delta compression using up to 4 threads.
Compressing objects: 100% (151/151), done.
Writing objects: 100% (157/157), 3.13 MiB | 68.00 KiB/s, done.
Total 157 (delta 22), reused 0 (delta 0)
To https://opsbug@bitbucket.org/opsbug/design-studio.git
 * [new branch]      master -> master
Branch master set up to track remote branch master from origin.
```

Next, set up Codeship as shown previously. We are using the exact same settings, and the only difference this time is that our commit will contain the Rakefile and Gemfile so Codeship will actually be able to compile the project. Before we can allow Codeship to use Bitbucket, remember that we must set up the SSH keys. Recall that we discussed how to add SSH keys to a Bitbucket account earlier, but we left out one nuance. When you register with Codeship and configure your repository to be used in the deployment pipeline, Codeship automatically adds the SSH key corresponding to your account. The problem is that this key is added as a deployment key, meaning that it has read-only access to your account. We need write access as well, and to do that, we must first remove the deployment key as shown in Figure 13-46.

Figure 13-46. Removing the existing deployment keys from the Deployment keys settings screen

After removing the deployment key, you have to go back to Codeship ➤ Project Settings ➤ Settings and then add the public SSH key to the Bitbucket account so that the key shows up under SSH keys, which will give Codeship write access to this account. Once the keys show up on the SSH Keys page, you are ready to start the deployment pipeline. There are three more things that must be done, and we do them all in one commit: add a Gemfile, add a Rakefile, and make the necessary changes to the _config.yml file so that plug-ins can work. Once we push that commit, Codeship will start the deployment pipeline. You get to sit back and watch the magic happen. Let's look at contents of the Gemfile (this file must be named Gemfile to work properly).

```
source 'https://rubygems.org'        # Source of gems

gem 'jekyll', '~> 2.5'               # First gem to install is Jekyll

group :jekyll_plugins do             # Next is a group of jekyll plug-ins
      gem "jekyll-less"              # Jekyll-less plug-ins
      gem 'therubyracer', '~> 0.12.2' # A dependency for jekyll-less plug-in
end
```

We are testing here whether Codeship can compile Jekyll successfully, and one of the ways we will see it function is that the plug-ins will be integrated in the site. We chose a very simple plug-in, a Jekyll LESS converter that simply converts files that have LESS syntax into the corresponding CSS. In the Gemfile, we install the gem by calling it from the collection of plug-ins that will be associated with Jekyll. This file is all we need for bundler to do the job. Now that the gems can be installed, we need to take care of obtaining the source and then pushing it back to Bitbucket. The Rakefile is a bit more involved, so let's break it down line by line.

```
require 'tmpdir'                        # Create a temporary directory

desc "Generate jekyll site"            # First task, generate the Jekyll site
task :generate do
  puts "## Generating Site with Jekyll"
  system "jekyll build"                # System command to build Jekyll
end

desc "Generate and publish blog to Bitbucket"
task :publish do                       # Publish Jekyll site to Bitbucket
  Dir.mktmpdir do |tmp|                # Creating a temporary dir to move contents of _site
    system "mv _site/* #{tmp}"         # Moving contents of _site
    system "git checkout -b aerobatic" # A new branch to push result back to
    system "rm -rf *"                  # Cleaning up
    system "mv #{tmp}/* ."
    system 'git config --global user.email "dhillonv10@knights.ucf.edu"'
    system 'git config --global user.name "opsbug"'
    system "git add ."                 # Authenticating and pushing the code back
    system "git commit -am 'Codeship Update'"
    system "git remote add bb git@bitbucket.org:opsbug/design-studio.git"
    system "git push -f bb aerobatic"
  end
end
```

There's a lot of new code here, but it still draws from the same ideas discussed earlier in our generic Rakefile. The file starts with a system call to use tmpdir, which is a command to create a temporary space where files can be stored for a short period. After that is the first task and its description provided by the desc variable. What follows is a loop named :generate that contains the task that Rake needs to perform. Here, we just instruct Rake to issue the jekyll build command, and using system in front of it lets us issue terminal commands. This task was simple; the next one is more complex because we push code.

The next task is named :publish and there is a loop nested within the task loop. The purpose of the second loop is to create a temporary directory where our files can be saved. The rest of this loop does two things. The first part of the loop copies the contents of the _site directory (where the compiled site is saved) and saves them in the temporary directory that was created. The second part defines the user credentials, then it adds the changes to a commit and writes a commit message. Now it's time to push the code. To do so, we add the SSH address of the remote repository (which is Bitbucket) and then Git can force-push to a new branch of that repository. The publish task does most of the heavy lifting, but the logic is fairly straightforward.

1. Create temporary directory.

2. Save the contents of _site, which contains the compiled repository to the temporary location.

3. Define the user who will access Bitbucket and provide their credentials.

4. Given that the Codeship SSH key has already been added to the Bitbucket account, you just need to provide the user name and e-mail.

5. Add the remote location's SSH URL and push the code to a new branch.

With the Rakefile added to the repository, let's test our plug-in. The main purpose of this plug-in is to convert LESS code to CSS, and we can test it by making a file called test.less with the following contents:

```
@base: #f938ab;

.box-shadow(@style, @c) when (iscolor(@c)) {
  -webkit-box-shadow: @style @c;
  box-shadow:         @style @c;
}
.box-shadow(@style, @alpha: 50%) when (isnumber(@alpha)) {
  .box-shadow(@style, rgba(0, 0, 0, @alpha));
}
.box {
  color: saturate(@base, 5%);
  border-color: lighten(@base, 30%);
  div { .box-shadow(0 0 5px, 30%) }
}
```

This is the LESS source code that we hope gets compiled to CSS. Next, we need to make sure that the _config.yml file knows that our plug-ins exist. To do that, add the following line at the end of the file:

```
gems: ['jekyll-less', 'therubyracer']
```

Now let's make sure everything is in order before committing these changes and then pushing the code to Bitbucket.

- The deployment key has been deleted. SSH keys from Codeship have been added to Bitbucket.

- The Rakefile and Gemfile are present and _config.yml has been edited to include the gems.

- The test for your plug-in test.less is present in the repository.

After adding these changes, commit them to the repository and then push the solid theme to Bitbucket. As soon as you push these changes, the deployment pipeline will fire up and compile the site. The result of the build can be seen in Figure 13-47.

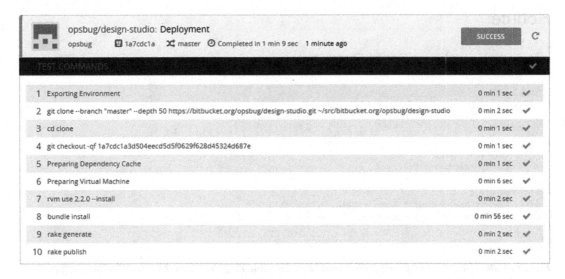

Figure 13-47. *Codeship giving us the green light: The build was successfully compiled. Notice the 10 steps it took to compile the site, and how similar they are to what we instructed Rake to do.*

Finally, we want to check if our plug-in worked. If it did, the file that we pushed to Bitbucket (test.less) should have been compiled to test.css and its contents updated to the following CSS:

```
.box {
  color: #fe33ac;
  border-color: #fdcdea;
}
.box div {
  -webkit-box-shadow: 0 0 5px rgba(0, 0, 0, 0.3);
  box-shadow: 0 0 5px rgba(0, 0, 0, 0.3);
}
```

Let's take a look at the web interface, and recall that the resulting compiled code should be present in the aerobatic branch, as shown in Figure 13-48. The code was successfully translated to CSS, which means our plug-in worked!

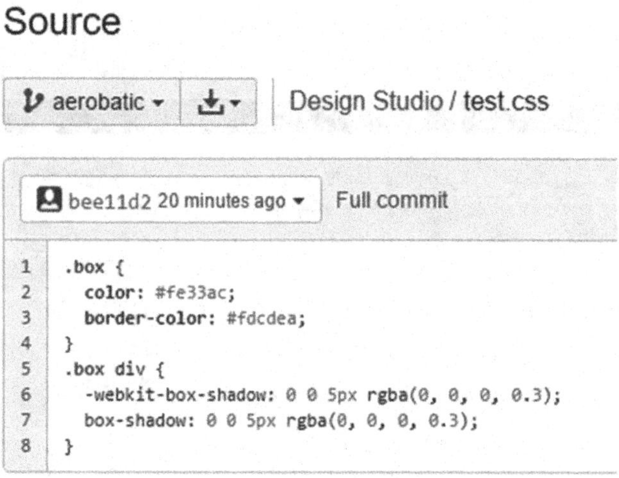

Figure 13-48. *The `test.css` file compiled from `test.less` showing that Codeship compiled our plug-in successfully*

There are two steps remaining at this point. The first is to host the web site using Aerobatic and the last one is to use Aerobatic to create password-protected pages. After pushing updates to the repository that allow Codeship to work, go back to the repository overview page. In the left sidebar, under Navigation, you should see an Aerobatic Hosting option. Click that option to open the Aerobatic hosting options page shown in Figure 13-49. These options are essentially similar to what GitHub Pages does for us if we define our repository a certain way. Give your web site a name so that you can pick a URL. You can even use a custom domain, as the free plan on Aerobatic allows for two CNAMES. Select the `aerobatic` branch to deploy so the production web site always contains the latest code compiled by Codeship, a very straightforward implementation of CI. Finally, click Create Website and Aerobatic should host the web site, providing you a link for it. The hosting view is shown in Figure 13-50, and this page also contains the URL of the final web site. Notice a green label for Production on the right side, which denotes the current status of the web site. Each time that Codeship pushes to the `aerobatic` branch, this hosting tool takes over and updates the web site with the latest code so you will see an increment of version for each commit.

Create website

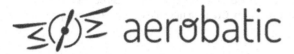

Aerobatic lets you host your Bitbucket repo as a static HTML website. Edit your code, push your changes, and your website is live — automatically.

Website name	design-studio	⑦
	https://your-app-name.aerobatic.io	
Custom domain	No registered domains ▾	⑦
	Register a new domain	
Deploy branch	aerobatic ▾	⑦
Deploy directory	/	⑦
	Leave blank to deploy the entire branch contents.	
Deploy Now?	⦿ Yes, deploy my site now!	
	○ No, I'll push to this repo when I'm ready	

Create website

Figure 13-49. *Aerobatic hosting plug-in. This page provides the configuration that you can edit to deploy your web site.*

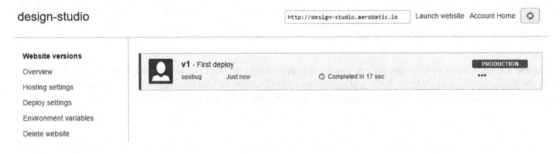

Figure 13-50. *The hosting settings in Aerobatic. This page appears after the web site has been deployed, and the box at the top provides the link for the web site. First deploy corresponds to the first version of the web site, but Aerobatic stores the older versions as well in case you need to check a feature in an older version. On the left side are the hosting settings; we will be using Environment variables to add basic authentication to the web site.*

In Aerobatic, passwords can be enabled in the settings as environmental variables (shown in Figure 13-51) for the deployed site. Remember the books.html page we made? Let's put that page under basic authentication. To do so, create a folder called books and put the books.html file inside that folder. Now rename that file index.html so that books come up if we browse the sitename.com/books/ address. First, we need to tell Aerobatic to add password authentication. Create a new file called package.json; its contents are shown here.

```
{
  "_aerobatic": {
    "router": [
      {
        "module": "basic-auth",
        "path": "/books",
        "options": {
          "username": "$BASIC_AUTH_USERNAME",
          "password": "$BASIC_AUTH_PASSWORD"
        }
      },
      {
        "module": "webpage"
      }
    ]
  }
}
```

Environment variables

Environment variables are used to store sensitive values used by plugins. By default a variable value is applicable to both production and all staging branches, however you can also provide deploy branch specific overrides. The production and staging branches are configured in the Deploy settings.

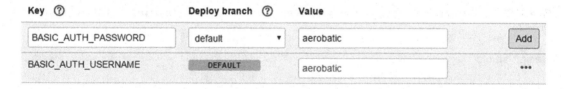

Figure 13-51. *The answer to life, the universe, and everything else. Add the two environment variables defined in the package.json file, BASIC_AUTH_USERNAME and BASIC_AUTH_PASSWORD, with a value assigned to them here. This should enable password authentication for the contents of the books folder.*

Further Reading

1. **Prototyping tools:** https://www.enolalabs.com/blog/archives/best-app-prototyping-tool-proto.io-vs.-invision-vs.-marvel

2. **MailChimp + Gumroad integration:** https://connect.mailchimp.com/integrations/gumroad-integration

3. **Video data and analytics:** http://wistia.com/blog/incorporating-video-data

4. **HipChat documentation:** https://confluence.atlassian.com/hipchat/hipchat-documentation-740262341.html

5. **Launching a business on Fiverr:** http://blog.fiverr.com/diy-guide-launching-successful-fiverr-business/

6. **Product subscriptions:** https://help.gumroad.com/11163-Products-and-Customizations/subscriptions

Appendix

The projects in this book are powered by Jekyll and hosted on GitHub. Our projects rely on a root repository that gets compiled by GitHub Pages, but it has a defined web address. In this appendix, we talk about how to get a custom domain name for the projects hosted on GitHub. This will be applied to both root repositories and project pages associated with repositories present within a GitHub account.

Let's begin this appendix by discussing the two different types of web sites that GitHub Pages can compile and host. The first type of web site is created from source code present in a root repository. This web site is available at the web address `username.github.io`. The second type of web site is often a single-page template that acts as a landing page for a repository. These single-page templates are often called project pages. The project pages associated with a repository are stored within a branch of that repository. Let's begin our discussion of custom domains starting with a root repository.

Custom Domain for a Root Repository

A web site in the root repository is compiled and made available at `username.github.io`. This web address format is the default domain name provided to every root repository by GitHub. To get a custom domain for a root repository, we need to add a file to our repository and make some changes to the domain registrar. There are three main steps to setting up a custom domain for your root repository:

1. Select a custom domain and register it with a domain registrar like GoDaddy.

2. Set up your repository by creating and adding a CNAME file that contains your custom domain.

3. Set up your custom domain with the domain registrar.

We handle each step separately, starting with the root repository. After obtaining a domain from a registrar like GoDaddy, we have to prepare GitHub to recognize that our root repository will use this custom domain. To do that, you have to create a file named `CNAME` and commit it to the repository. The file must be named exactly as displayed, and in this file, add a single line that specifies the bare custom domain without `https://` or `http://`. For instance, simply use `example.com`, not `https://www.example.com`. Commit this file and push the code to GitHub. It must be noted that there can only be one domain in the `CNAME` file. To confirm that your custom domain is ready on GitHub, click Settings in your repository. You will reach the repository settings and under GitHub Pages, you should see the custom domain that you entered in the `CNAME` file.

This takes care of GitHub, and now this root repository points to the custom domain. Now we have to adjust the domain register to redirect to GitHub. To do this, we need to edit the A records. You have to create two A records on GoDaddy that point your custom domain to the following IP addresses:

```
192.30.252.153
192.30.252.154
```

The end result should look like Figure A-1.

RECORDS

TYPE	NAME	VALUE	TTL
A	@	192.30.252.153	1/2 Hour
A	@	192.30.252.154	1/2 Hour

Figure A-1. *Adding the two A records that point to GitHub's IP addresses*

Once the A records have been set up, if you type your custom domain name in the browser, it should take you to your root repository web site. Similarly, now when you type your root repository address (`username.github.io`), you should reach the custom domain that you just set up.

■ **Note**   Let's talk about the three most common errors that users encounter while trying to set up a custom domain or a GitHub repository site. The most common one is not setting up the custom domain properly in the CNAME file. You can only have one domain in that file and it needs to be written exactly as just specified. Another common problem is the `_config.yml` file where you need to adjust the `url` and `baseurl` parameters. If a theme is pushed to Github without changing the parameters, it could cause the web site to render in a broken manner. Finally, the third type of error is referring to a file (in Liquid by using the `{% include filename.html %}` tag) that doesn't exist under the `_includes` folder.

Custom Domain for a Project Page?

Project pages are generally single-page web sites or landing pages associated with a repository. A project page can be created using the Automatic Page Generator on GitHub. The generator will automatically assign the project page a URL in the form of `username.github.io/REPO-NAME`. So if a repository was named `testing`, it would have a web address of `username.github.io/testing`. Once a custom domain name has been assigned to a root repository, all the project pages are redirected to be under the custom domain. Using our example of the testing repository, its new address will be `custom-domain.com/testing`. In a case where the project page repository is renamed, all the links will be updated to the new URL.

Project pages can also be created manually. Much like a root repository that stores the source code for a Jekyll web site, a project page is stored in a `gh-pages` branch that contains the code for the single-page template. Often, the templates that power project pages are simple HTML pages, but the `gh-pages` branch can compile Jekyll code if it is present. In this case, there is no automatic page generator; we simply push a Jekyll theme to the `gh-pages` branch of a repository. The process of manually creating project pages is very simple.

1.   Create a regular repository as shown in Figure A-2.

2.   Clone this repository locally following the instructions on GitHub.

3.   Commit Jekyll code to this repository.

4.   Create a `gh-pages` branch, make edits to the code, and push it online.

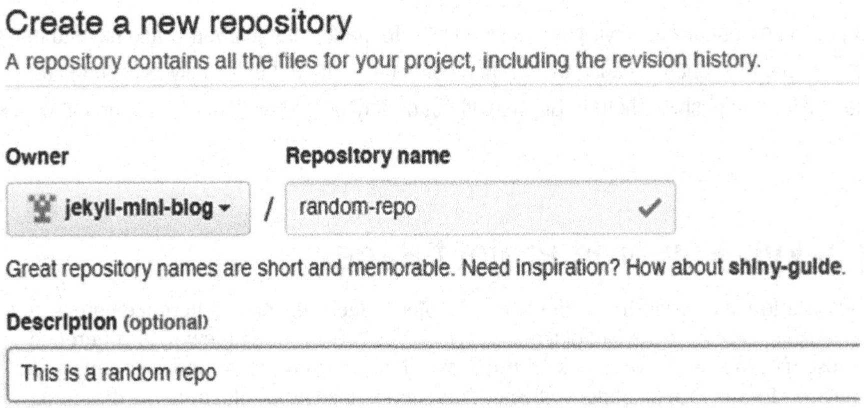

Create a new repository
A repository contains all the files for your project, including the revision history.

Owner   **Repository name**

  🐙 **jekyll-mini-blog ▾** / random-repo   ✓

Great repository names are short and memorable. Need inspiration? How about **shiny-guide**.

Description (optional)

This is a random repo

Figure A-2. *Creating a project-page repository on GitHub*

Let's take a look at the last step. To create a new branch, you need to use the git branch command:

```
$ git branch gh-pages
$ git checkout gh-pages
$ git branch
* gh-pages
  master
```

Once you are on the gh-pages branch, you can start making edits to the theme as if you were editing any other Jekyll-based project. The reason for making the edits only to this branch is because the source code present in this branch will get compiled and made available online as a project page. Now pushing code to the gh-pages branch also requires special consideration for the first time. You can't use git push and expect it to work because Git does not know what to do with this new branch. To push the code to GitHub, we have to tell Git to set up a branch in the remote location called gh-pages that will be synced to this local gh-pages branch that we just created. In this manner, all the local changes to the gh-pages branch get pushed online and consequently to the project page.

```
$ git push --set-upstream origin gh-pages
```

```
To https://github.com/jekyll-mini-blog/random-repo.git
 * [new branch]      gh-pages -> gh-pages
Branch gh-pages set up to track remote branch gh-pages from origin.
```

The bold line shows that a new branch was set up in the remote location to be synced with our local branch. This is exactly what we need because any changes we make to the gh-pages branch get compiled and carried over to the project pages web site. After this first time, you can push your changes by simply using git push because now Git knows exactly where to push the changes.

■ **Note** This project page is essentially a Jekyll-powered web site. To make changes, you would have to make sure that you are on the `gh-pages` branch because that branch holds the code that eventually gets compiled. Making changes to the master and pushing them to GitHub will not do anything at all. Use `git branch` to check your current status.

Configuring Jekyll-Powered Project Pages

Essentially, all the configuration of a Jekyll site carries over to project pages. The only difference here is that all the code lives in the `gh-pages` branch instead of a master. However, there is one noteworthy difference in project pages. For most of our projects, we have kept the `baseurl` variable empty, but now we can use it very effectively to route links for the project pages web site. This section also helps illustrate the difference between `site.baseurl` and `site.url` more practically. For a project pages web site, the `url` assigned to it is the custom domain that has been configured for the root repository. The `baseurl` is the URL assigned to the project pages web site. Let's look at an example for the `random repository` that we created. That repository was given the web address `jekyll-mini-blog.github.io/random-repo` and this is the complete URL. To configure the link routing for this web site, in the `_config.yml` file, we would have to use

```
baseurl: '/random-repo'
url: "http://custom-domain.com"
```

In this example, it is easy to see why we need to define `baseurl`. The project pages web site is under the root address (`username.github.io`). If we were to use `site.url` to create navigation links, we would end up with links that point to locations that do not exist. For example, imagine a page with a permalink about and if we used `site.url` to navigate, we would have a final URL that looks like `username.github.io/about`. That page does not exist, and we need to use the `baseurl` assigned to the project pages site for this link to function properly. We need to configure our navigation to use the `baseurl` variable that contains the project pages address as well, so the links don't point to the root repository. Going back to our example, if we used `site.baseurl` instead, the final URL would look like `username.github.io/random-repo/`**about**, which is exactly what we need.

Domain Directory

A URL of the type `username.github.io/`**random-repo** contains an attachment often called a domain directory. In a hosting environment, the `random repository` portion of the URL represents a folder named `random-repo` and browsing to that address will show you the contents of that folder. In this case, we are using GitHub as our host and we have a somewhat restricted hosting environment. As mentioned before, GitHub is not a hosting platform, but it works very well for almost everything that we need. One of the shortcomings that results from using GitHub as the host is that project pages cannot be assigned custom domains. When a custom domain is assigned to a root repository, all the project pages are redirected to be under that domain, but a project pages web site can't have a custom domain name for itself.

The same holds true for subdomains. A subdomain can be created from a domain, in the form of `random-repo.custom-domain.com`, but when using GitHub, there are a lot of modifications that need to be made at the domain registrar. Some of these changes could result in unexpected behavior for routing or linking, and therefore it is not practical to create subdomains. On GitHub, we are only limiting ourselves to creating domain directories, not subdomains. Even if we were to create a subdomain, it would point to the domain directory URL, but the process of creating it at the registrar has been known to cause issues. Overall, GitHub provides a very simple and effective means to host a web site or any of the project created throughout this book, but advanced features require a shared web hosting service.

Index

Get the eBook for only $5!

Why limit yourself?

Now you can take the weightless companion with you wherever you go and access your content on your PC, phone, tablet, or reader.

Since you've purchased this print book, we're happy to offer you the eBook in all 3 formats for just $5.

Convenient and fully searchable, the PDF version enables you to easily find and copy code—or perform examples by quickly toggling between instructions and applications. The MOBI format is ideal for your Kindle, while the ePUB can be utilized on a variety of mobile devices.

To learn more, go to www.apress.com/companion or contact support@apress.com.